THE COLOR OF THEATER

THE COLOR OF THEATER

Race, Culture, and Contemporary Performance

Edited by

ROBERTA UNO with
LUCY MAE SAN PABLO BURNS

continuum
LONDON • NEW YORK

Continuum

The Tower Building, 11 York Road, London, SE1 7NX

370 Lexington Avenue, New York, NY 10017–6503

First published 2002

British Library Cataloguing-in-Publication Data
A catalogue record for this book is available from the British Library.

ISBN 0-8264-7881-6

Library of Congress Cataloging-in-Publication Data
The color of theater: race, culture, and contemporary performance / edited by Roberta Uno with Lucy Mae San Pablo Burns.
    p. cm.
Papers presented at a conference and play festival held Oct. 8–11, 1998 in Amherst, Mass.
Includes bibliographical references and index.
ISBN 0-8264-5638-3 — ISBN 0-8264-5639-1 (pbk.)
    1. Hispanic American theater—Congresses.   2. African American theater—Congresses.   3. Ethnic theater—United States—Congresses.   I. Uno, Roberta, 1956– II. Burns, Lucy Mae San Pablo, 1971–

PN2270.H57 C65 2002
792′.086′930973—dc21   2001047042

Typeset by BookEns Ltd, Royston, Herts.
Printed in Great Britain by
MPG Books Ltd, Bodmin, Cornwall

Contents

Notes on contributors

Awam Amkpa is Assistant Professor of Drama at the New York University's Tisch School of the Arts, Department of Drama. He was a former Senior Lecturer of Drama and Television at King Alfred's University College, Winchester, England and Assistant Professor of Theatre Arts at Mount Holyoke College, Massachusetts. His forthcoming books include *Overpowered But Not Tamed: Theatre of Colonial Conditions and Postcolonial Desires* and *Homes and Border Crossings: Cinemas of the Black Atlantic.*

Alberto Antonio Araiza is a native of Los Angeles. He first ventured into theater in the late 1960s when he wrote, directed, and performed with two Latino activist 'Street Theater' companies. He is a founding member of Plaza De La Raza players, former Executive Director of Teatro !VIVA!, and was an Associate Artistic Director of Alice B. Theater. His works encompasses both traditional and experimental theater works.

Marlon M. Bailey is a third year Ph.D. student in African Diaspora Studies at the University of California, Berkeley. Currently, he is working on an ethnographic project examining Black queer performance and kinship. He is a former Assistant Professor of Africana Studies at the University of Michigan, Flint, where he was founder of the Axe: Performance Collective. He was also an Assistant Professor of Theatre at the University of Kentucky and Knight Foundation Fellow in Dramatic Art and Dance at Macalester College. In 1998, he served as a Guest Artist in Residence at the National Theatre of Ghana in West Africa, where he directed a new play called *Desert Dreams*, as well as teaching acting techniques to the resident company. He has performed and directed at professional theaters in Minneapolis, Detroit, DC, Louisville, Lexington, and San Francisco. He has earned an MFA in Acting from West Virginia University, an MA in African American Studies from the University of California, Berkeley, and a BA in Theatre/Speech Education from Olivet College, Michigan.

Rustom Bharucha is an independent writer, director, and dramaturg based in Calcutta. He is the author of several books including *Rehearsals of Revolution*, *Theatre and the World: Performance and the Politics of Culture*, *In the Name of the Secular: Contemporary Cultural Activism in India*, and *The Politics of Cultural Practice: Thinking through Theatre in an Age of Globalization*. He has lectured extensively in cultural and activist forums in different parts of the world, and is currently engaged in the task of bringing theater workers and cultural activists into creative dialogue, across the borders and disciplines.

Paul Bonin-Rodriguez is a writer, performer, and dancer who teaches and creates multidisciplinary theater. Currently, he is a Ford Fellow at the University of Texas in Austin, where he is completing a doctorate in Performance as a Public Practice program. Twice he has been named a Tennessee Williams Fellow at the University of the South, where he worked with 25 students to make *Common Sources*, a multidisciplinary play about student drinking. In addition to *Quinceañera*, works include his solo trilogy, *The Texas Trinity*, *Memory's Caretaker*, a solo piece about his family's journey towards cultural assimilation, as well as other plays. Based in San Antonio, he is a member of Jump-Start Performance Co.

Lucy Mae San Pablo Burns is a doctoral candidate in the American Studies Program in the English Department at the University of Massachusetts at Amherst. Her dissertation focuses on Pilipino American theater. She has also served as the Literary Manager at the New WORLD Theater. Her dramaturgy projects include *Quinceañera*, *The Good Guys: An American Tragedy*, and *When the Mississippi Meets the Amazon* (workshop). Her more recent project was a community-based theater piece entitled *Native Immigrant*, directed by Leilani Chan and premièred at the Japanese American Community Cultural Center in Los Angeles. Her writings have appeared in *Asian Pacific American Journal*, *Journal of Asian American Studies*, *Pilipinas*, and the *North American Review*, and forthcoming, in *Asian American Playwrights: A Bio-bibliography Source*, edited by Miles Lin.

Una Chaudhuri is Professor of English at New York University. She is the author of *No Man's Stage: A Semiotic Study of Jean Genet's Plays* and *Staging Place: The Geography of Modern Drama*. She is the editor of *Rachel's Brain and Other Storms: The Performance Scripts of Rachel Rosenthal*, and co-editor, with Elinor Fuchs, of the forthcoming collection *Land/Scape/Theater*.

Roselyn Costantino is an Associate Professor of Spanish and Women's Studies at the Pennsylvania State University, where she coordinates the Spanish program at the Altoona College. She teaches courses in Latin American and Latina narrative, performance and theater, film, and in cultural and women's studies. Her publications include essays on women's writing in Mexico and Mexican theater, in particular the theater and performance of Astrid Hadad, Maris Bustamante, and Jesusa Rodríguez. She is presently completing a book-length manuscript on contemporary Mexican women's theater and performance, *The Body in Play: Contemporary Women's Performance in Mexico*. She is co-editor, with Diana Taylor, of *Holy Terrors: Latin American Women Perform*.

Jaye T. Darby is an Assistant Professor in the College of Education at San Diego State University, with research interests in transformative scholarship in multiethnic theater and literature. She is a founding co-director with Hanay Geiogamah of Project HOOP (Honoring Our Origins and People through Native Theater, Education, and Community Development). With Hanay Geiogamah, Dr. Darby co-edited *Stories of Our Way: An Anthology of American Indian Plays* and *American Indian Theater in Performance: A Reader*. She is also the co-editor with Stephanie Fitzgerald of the forthcoming anthology *Keepers of the Morning Star: An Anthology of Native American Women's Theater* (UCLA American Indian Studies Center).

Thulani Davis is a published poet, playwright, librettist, and novelist. Her play *Everybody's Ruby* had an extended run at New York's Public Theater. Her work also includes the libretto for Anthony Davis's *X: The Life and Times of Malcolm X*, for which she won a Grammy. She has written and edited a number of works including *Playing the Changes* and *All the Renegade Ghost Rise*, and the accompanying text for *Malcolm X: The Great Photographs*. Her first novel, *1959*, was nominated for the Los Angeles Times Book Award. Her latest book project is *Into the Light*, a collection of essays and African American family photographs. She teaches writing at Princeton University and Barnard College, and is an ordained Buddhist priest.

Harry J. Elam, Jr. is the Robert and Ruth Halperin Undergraduate Fellow, Professor of Drama, Director of Graduate Studies in Drama, and Director of the Committee on Black Performing Arts at Stanford University. He is the author of *Taking It to the Streets: The Social Protest Theater of Luis Valdez and Amiri Baraka*, and co-editor of *Colored Contradictions: An Anthology of Contemporary African American Plays* and *African American Performance and Theatre History, A Critical Reader*. He is co-editor, with Robert Alexander, of *The Fire This Time! African American Plays for the New Millennium*, and has just finished a book entitled *(W)Righting History: The Past as Present in the Drama of August Wilson*. He has published articles in *Theatre Journal*, *Text and Performance Quarterly* and *American Drama* as well as having contributed to several critical anthologies.

Alvin Eng, a playwright/performer, lyricist, journalist, and educator, is the editor of the anthology/oral history *Tokens? The NYC Asian American Experience on Stage* (which includes his play *The Last Hand Laundry in Chinatown*). Excerpts from his memoire monologue, *The Flushing Cycle*, were published in *Performing Arts Journal*, and in the *Floating World* and *Second Word Thursdays Anthology*. Other writings have appeared in *Aloud: Voices from the Nuyorican Poets Cafe* and *Action: The Nuyorican Poets Café Theater Festival*.

Harley Erdman is an Associate Professor of Theater and Dramaturgy at the University of Massachusetts at Amherst. Harley's areas of interest include dramaturgy, translations, playwriting, and theater history. His research focus is the performance of ethnicity, especially in Jewish–American theater. Other research interests include Spanish and Latin American theater, musical theater, and community-based theater. Harley is currently the editor of *Theater Topics*, the national scholarly journal published by the Association for Theatre in Higher Education (ATHE). Publications include his book *Staging the Jew*. He is the co-creator of a new work, *Archipelago of Delight*, an original puppet musical produced in 2001 at the University of Massachusetts at Amherst.

Guillermo Goméz-Peña has created and performed in videos, performances, and installations in over 200 venues in the U.S., Canada, Mexico, Europe, Australia, the Soviet Union, Colombia, Puerto Rico, and Cuba. He is the author of numerous pieces of critical writing and poetry. His books include *Dangerous Border Crossers, Mexican Beasts and Living Santos, The New World Border* (American Book Award), and *Warrior for Gringostroika*. He was a founding member of the binational arts collective Border Arts Workshop/Taller de Arte Fronterizo. Among his fellowships and prizes are *Prix de la Parole*, the New York Bessie Award, and the Los Angeles Music Center's Viva Los Artistas Awards. He was the first Chicano/Mexicano artist to receive a MacArthur Fellowship. In 1995 he was included in *The Utne Reader*'s 'List of 100 Visionaries.'

Ann Haugo is an Instructional Assistant Professor in the School of Theatre and the Women's Studies Program at Illinois State University. Her publications have appeared in *American Indian Theatre: A Reader, The Journal of Dramatic Theory and Criticism, Women & Performance: A Journal of Feminist Theory*, and the *Native Playwrights' Newsletter*.

Velina Hasu Houston is the author of internationally produced plays including *Tea, Kokoro, Ikebana, Shedding the Tiger*, and *Waiting for Tadashi*. Among the producers are Pittsburgh Public Theatre, The Globe Theatre, Manhattan Theatre Club, Sacramento Theatre Company, Syracuse Stage, George Street Playhouse, Whole Theatre, Japan Society, Nippon Hoso Kai,

Negro Ensemble Company. She has written film and television screenplays for Columbia Pictures, Sidney Poitier, PBS, and others. Plays, critical essays and poetry appear in several anthologies. Her honors include Japan Foundation Fellow, Rockefeller Foundation Fellow, James Zumberge Fellow, Remy Martin Screenwriting Award, National Japanese American Historical Society Woman of Merit, and others. She is an Associate Professor/resident playwright at the University of Southern California School of Theatre.

Joni L. Jones is an Associate Professor in the Department of Theatre and Dance, and the Associate Director of the Center for African and African American Studies at the University of Texas in Austin. Her print scholarship has appeared in *Text and Performance Quarterly*, *TDR*, *Black Theatre Network News*, and *Theatre Journal*. Her performance scholarship has been presented at Northwestern University, Amherst College, University of Rhode Island, and Black Women in the Academy Conference II.

Josh D. Kun is Assistant Professor of English at the University of California, Riverside. He is an arts columnist for the *SF Bay Guardian* and the *Boston Phoenix*, and his writings have appeared in *SPIN*, *Rolling Stone*, *LA Weekly*, and the *Village Voice*.

lê thi diem thúy is a writer and solo performance artist. Her performance works *Red Fiery Summer* (*Mua He Do Lua*) and *the bodies between us* have been presented at the Whitney Museum of American Art at Philip Morris, the International Women Playwrights' Festival in Galway, Ireland, and the Third New Immigrants' Play Festival at the Vineyard Theater in New York City. Her writings have appeared in *Massachusetts Review* and *Harper's Magazine*, and anthologized in *Best American Essays 1997*, *The Very Inside*, *Half and Half*, *Bold Words*, and other collections. A book of stories, *The Gangster We Are All Looking For*, is about to be published.

Michael Marinez is a visual artist based in San Antonio, Texas. His work has been exhibited in numerous venues including La Peña Arts Center in Austin, Texas. He is an active board member of the Esperanza Center in San Antonio. The play *Quinceañera* was inspired by Marinez's exhibit with the same title, celebrating Latino communities' survival from AIDS and remembering those who have died from the epidemic.

Cherríe Moraga is the co-editor of *This Bridge Called My Back: Writings by Radical Women of Color*. She is the author of numerous plays including *Shadow of a Man* and *Watsonville: Some Place Not Here* (both Fund for New American Plays Award), and *Heroes and Saints* (Pen West Drama Award). Ms. Moraga is also a recipient of the National Endowment for the Arts' Theatre Playwrights'

Fellowship and is the Artist-in-Residence in the Department of Drama at Stanford University.

David Román is Associate Professor of English and American Studies at the University of Southern California. He is the author of *Acts of Intervention: Performance, Gay Culture, and AIDS*, which received the Outstanding Book Award from the Association for Theatre in Higher Education, the professional organization of theater and performance scholars. He is also the co-editor with Holly Hughes of *O Solo Homo: The New Queer Performance*, which received the Lambda Literary Award in Drama. He is also the editor of *Theatre Journal*.

Joe Salvatore is a Brooklyn-based theater artist and educator, currently working as the Education and Humanities Manager at the Brooklyn Academy of Music, and as the Artistic/Education Director for Learning Stages. Recent directing projects have been seen at the Lincoln Center Directors Lab, LAByrinth Theater Company, and the Brooklyn Arts Exchange. He has also worked as a dramaturg for various companies including the Ko International Festival and the Culture Project. His original writing includes *fag/hag* and *At Wit's End: You Are Here* (both with Kate Nugent), *full of grace* ... (James Baldwin Playwriting Award), and *mindlynes*, a theater piece inspired by the life and photographs of George Platt Lynes. He also teaches in the Department of Communication Studies, Performance Studies, and Theatre at Long Island University.

Alberto Sandoval-Sánchez is Professor of Spanish and U.S. Latino Literature at Mount Holyoke College. He is both a creative writer and a cultural critic. His theatrical piece *Side Effects*, based on his personal experiences with AIDS. He has edited a special issue of *Ollantay Theater Magazine* on U.S. Latino theatre and AIDS, was produced at Mount Holyoke College in Hadley, Massachusetts. He has edited a special issue of *Ollantay Theater Magazine* on U.S. Latino theatre and AIDS. He has published numerous articles on U.S. Latino theater, Latin American colonial theater and colonial identity formation, Spanish baroque theater, Puerto Rican migration. His books include *José Can You See?: Latinos on and off Broadway, Puro Teatro: A Latina Anthology*, and *Stages of Life: Transcultural Performance and Identity in Latina Theater* in collaboration with Nancy S. Sternbach from Smith College). He has just finished a new book on Latina theater and performance: *Stages of Life: Transcultural Performance and Identity Formation in Latina Theater* (also in collaboration with Sternbach).

Roberto Sifuentes is an interdisciplinary artist whose work examines popular perception of Chicano and Mexican cultures. He has performed with Guillermo Goméz-Peña, with whom he created an interactive television special *El*

Naftazteca: Cyber-Aztec TV for 2000 AD, and the performance art pieces *Borderama* and *Dangerous Border Games*. His works incorporate digital media, interactive technologies, and the Internet into live performances.

Sekou Sundiata is a poet who writes for both print and performance as well as music and theater. He has recorded and performed with a wide variety of artists, including Craig Harris, David Murray, Nona Hendryx, and Vernon Reid. He co-produced a series of concerts at the American Center in Paris. Sekou wrote and performed in the highly acclaimed performance theater work *The Circle Unbroken Is a Hard Bop*, and his music theater work, *The Mystery of Love*, was commissioned and produced by New Voices/New Visions at Aaron Davis Hall and the American Music Theater Festival. He was a Sundance Institute Screenwriting Fellow, a Columbia University Revson Fellow, and the first Writer-in-Residence at the New School University. Sekou was featured in the Bill Moyers PBS series on poetry, *The Language of Life*, and his work appears in the anthology based on the series. As a recording artist, Sekou has released the CD *The Blue Oneness of Dreams*.

Diana Taylor is Professor and Chair of Performance Studies at New York University. She is the author of *Theatre of Crisis: Drama and Politics in Latin America* (Best Book Award given by New England Council on Latin American Studies and Honorable Mention in the Joe E. Callaway Prize for the Best Book on Drama) and *Disappearing Acts: Spectacles of Gender and Nationalism in Argentina's 'Dirty Wars.'* She co-edited *Negotiating Performance in Latin/o America: Gender, Sexuality and Theatricality* and *The Politics of Motherhood: Activists from Left to Right*. She has edited three volumes of critical essays on Latin American, Latino, and Spanish playwrights. Her articles on Latin American and Latino performance have appeared in *The Drama Review, Theatre Journal, Performing Arts Journal, Latin American Theatre Review, Estreno, Gestos, MLQ*, and other scholarly journals. She is Director of the Hemispheric Institute of Performance and Politics, funded by the Ford Foundation and the Rockefeller Foundation.

Roberta Uno is the Artistic Director of the New WORLD Theater, in residence at the Fine Arts Center at the University of Massachusetts in Amherst, and Professor in the University's Department of Theater. Her directing credits include *Clothes* by Chitra Divakaruni, *Unmerciful Good Fortune* by Edwin Sanchez, *Flyin' West* by Pearl Cleage, *Sheila's Day* by Duma Ndlovu, *WALLS* by Jeannie Barroga, *R.A.W. ('Cause I'm a Woman)* by Diana Son, *Tea* by Velina Hasu Houston, *Dance and the Railroad* by David Henry Hwang, *Sneaky* by William Yellow Robe, *Do Lord Remember Me* by James De Jongh, and *Blues for Mr. Charlie* by James Baldwin. She is the editor of *Unbroken*

Thread: An Anthology of Plays by Asian American Women and *Monologues for Actors of Color: Men* and *Monologues for Actors of Color: Women*, and co-editor with Kathy Perkins of *Contemporary Plays by Women of Color*, which received the Oustanding Book Award from the Association for Theatre in High Education.

Talvin Wilks is a playwright, director, and dramaturg based in New York City. His plays include *Tod, the Boy Tod, The Trial of Uncle S&M, Bread of Heaven*, and *An American Triptych*. Recent directorial projects include the world première production of *Udu by Sekou Sundiata at 651 Arts/Harvey Theatre, No Black Male Show* by Carl Hancock Rux at Joe's Pub/The Public Theatre, *Legends* by Leslie Lee at the St Louis Black Repertory Co., *Three Willies* by Homer Jackson and Leroy Jenkins at The Kitchen and the Obie/AUDELCO award-winning *The Shaneequa Chronicles* by Stephanie Berry at Ensemble Studio Theatre. Recent writings and dramaturgical collaborations include Ping Chong's *Secret Histories/Charleston* at the Spoleto Festival, *Undesirable Elements/Atlanta* at Seven Stages, and the Bessie award-winning *Verge* with the Bebe Miller Company at 651 Arts/Harvey Theatre.

Lisa Wolford teaches American Culture Studies and Theatre at Bowling Green State University and is a dramaturg for Theatre Labyrinth. She has collaborated with Pocha Nostra periodically since 1997, and is currently authoring a book with Guillermo Goméz-Peña tentatively titled *Mexterminator: Ethno-Techno Art*. Her writings on Goméz-Peña have appeared in numerous journals and collected volumes including *Theatre Forum, Essays in Theatre*, and *Art Papers*. She has also edited and contributed material to Goméz-Peña's *Dangerous Border Crossers*, and served as dramaturg for stagings of Pocha Nostra's *Mexterminator Project* and an early version of *The Museum of Fetishized Identities*, as well as *BORDERscape 2000*.

Danny Bolero Zaldivar, a Los Angeles native, has performed in theatrical productions from regional theaters throughout the United States to major Broadway shows, for the past twenty years. He is the recipient of two Los Angeles Dramalogue awards and has appeared in several television projects. His work as an activist/organizer includes numerous benefit performances for Equity Fight AIDS, a national organization dedicated to assisting people living with HIV and AIDS.

Acknowledgments

We are deeply indebted to the staff of New WORLD Theater, especially Yvonne Mendez, for their creativity, leadership, and dedication in support of New WORLD Theater, this book, and the *Intersection* project. We would also like to acknowledge other New WORLD Theater current and former staff who made the *Intersection* project possible: Cathy Schlund-Vials, Elaine Qualter, Marion Wright, Dennis Conway, Jen Werner, Javiera Benavente, Mary Muratore, Wesley Montgomery, Irma Mayorga, Uday Joshi, Dawn L. Martin, Charles Barley, Jose Tolson, Lisa Hori-Garcia, Karima Atiya Robinson, Angelica Castro, and Richard Pleasant; as well as current and former students and interns who dedicated countless hours to the project: Megan Smith, Angel Hardy, Aaron Brandes, Onyinyechi Ihedigbo, Priscilla Page, Andrea Reece, Michael Yap, Tavar Davis, Shaunacy Peabody, Marta Carlson, Steven Ginsburg, Joe Salvatore, Abe Henderson, Jesus MacLean, and Thao Pho. Special thanks are due to Sam Miller of the New England Foundation for the Arts and Joan Shigekawa of the Rockefeller Foundation for deeply understanding and supporting our work. We would like to express our heartfelt appreciation of Dean Lee Edwards, Dr. Frederick Tillis, Vice Chancellor Fred Byron, Marie Hess, and Dean William Field of the University of Massachusetts at Amherst for their commitment to New WORLD Theater over the years. Thank you to the staff of the Fine Arts Center for collegial and generous support of our projects and mission and to Richard Trousdell and the University of Massachusetts Department of Theater faculty and staff for collaborating with New WORLD Theater on multiple projects. We also appreciate assistance we received from Shelby Jiggetts-Tivony, Brenda Cotto-Escalera, Jaye Darby, Quang Bao, Elizabeth Theobald, Beth Nathanson, Glenn Siegel, Robert Antil, Abe Rybeck, Jim Gemmell, Felice Yeskel and the Stonewall Center, Terry Jenoure and the Augusta Savage Gallery, Barbara Aldridge, Lew Louraine, Fritz Farrington, Gerry Stockman, Brenda Cortina, Steven Coombs, Richard Ballon, Shawn Farley, Sonia Kudla, Carol Symanski,

Connie Whigham, Cheryl Symister-Masterson, Christine Texiera, Carlos Bermuda, Dr. Willie Hill, Greg Prince, Suzanne Dougan, Peter Lobdell, Gilbert McCauley, Harley Erdman, Denise Wagner, Mark Dean, Cecilia Precciozzi, Vanessa James, Leandro Soto, Ellen Donkin, San San Wong, Karen Baxter, Sidonio Ferrera, Rebecca Blunk, Tony Tapia, Laura Greer, Mark Baszak, Kathy Perkins, Joyce Devlin, Len Berkman, Andrea Hairston, Caron Atlas, Lorna Peterson, Murray Schwartz, and Miriam Laughlin.

We are grateful to our colleagues for advice as we evolved this manuscript, especially Rustom Bharucha and Alberto Sandoval-Sánchez who generously shared ideas, information, and insights. We thank Cathy Schlund-Vials, Charity Henson, Elaine Qualter, and Patty Jang for support with research and manuscript preparation. And we thank the editorial staff at Continuum, Janet Joyce, Tristan Palmer, Valerie Hall, and Neil Dowden, for their infinite patience and subtle guidance.

We wish to thank our families for their love and unwavering encouragement: Chinua and Mikiko Thelwell, Andrew Condron, Kiku Uno, Riki, James, Jacob, and Ellen Hing, Josie Camacho and Victor Uno, Amado Camacho Uno, Roger and Teresa Uno, Njeri Thelwell, Desiree and Craig Josias, Mariko Miho, Stan and Tulani Kinard, Akemi Kochiyama-Ladson, Elinor Bowles, Emma Kaplan, William Burns, Purificacion San Pablo Burns, Ana Liza Burns-Johnson and Terence Johnson, Anjali Arondekar, Metta Dael, Juliana de Zavalia, Mary Grace Glenn, Brooke and Logann Burns, and Tavis Mahal Johnson.

We honor Yvette C. Mendez and the spirit of our ancestors as we walk forward in their light.

Roberta Uno
Lucy Mae San Pablo Burns

For Andrew

Part I

Introduction

The color of theater

Roberta Uno

the bodies between us

'I want to hear something from the person who is on the ground with the rifle up their ass,' an African American woman theater artist demands of thúy lê, the Vietnamese American writer and performer of *the bodies between us.* 'I need to know did you see your teeth flying out of your mouth?' A Chicana playwright had prompted this line of interrogation from the audience when she implored lê to focus on the culturally specific. 'I honor the sister, I found the writing exquisite, so rich in fact, I had to close my eyes ... As a Chicana writer with no images on the stage, I'm looking at your work like a sister and I'm saying, what do we see? I want it to be culturally specific.'

It is the tensest moment in what has been a remarkable four days of performance, dialogue, and exchange during an unprecedented gathering of artists, scholars, and activists examining new ways of seeing and making theater by artists of color.[1] A heated exchange breaks out as certain audience members assert their expectations of the solo work which, in its meditative performance, poetic language, and unyielding refusal to engage media images of the Vietnam War, has frustrated some and captivated others. lê, a slight young woman, faces her peers, carefully answering each passionate statement with her intentions for the piece. She says: 'The way this culture looks at Vietnam is very spectacular, it's very big – "We lost our innocence," "We lost our boys" ... the Vietnamese presence too is very en masse, nothing specific. This is about the specific body, not the words.' Her comments engender even stronger positions from the audience. A Caucasian woman audience member says, 'Don't condescend to us ... I don't believe you don't care about the words. Your language is so beautiful, why does it even need to be performed?' The African American woman artist continues, 'You have very good use of your language and the way you use it. You need to claim that.'

From the stage, the scholar commentator, Una Chaudhuri, and artist commentator, Robbie McCauley, wear twin expressions of shock, as they reel to respond to a situation that appears to have gotten seriously out of hand. Ironically, it was Robbie's very thoughtful statement, intended to create a respectful space for the artist, that appears to have released a critical melee. McCauley stated that we must recognize that the audience brings its own expectations to a narrative (in this case, the Vietnam War) and that those may be very different from what an artist brings to the same narrative.

lê, addressing the question of language and performance, asserts:

> I'm not concerned with the beauty of the language and the eloquence of it, I'm concerned with what it's not saying, the ruptures of language and that's why it's on the stage and not just on the page ... Because you have to see me say it, hear me ... it's about the body ... I'm trying to bring you the bones ... I embody what the word doesn't say ... When people say, 'You speak English well.' What is prized by my ability to speak English well? What is covered? Yes, I know I'm speaking perfect English, but speaking beautifully doesn't mean you are telling your truth. Just because you are understandable, doesn't mean you are revealing truth. I wasn't performing the 'authenticity' of a specific ethnicity. I was performing the difference between my written language and the time it takes for someone to say all those beautiful words in real time, in breath, for the body to speak to the lie.

Several people vie to respond, as the organizers attempt to end the session, which has run overtime. Latino cultural critic Alberto Sandoval-Sánchez interjects a final comment from the floor:

> I feel very uncomfortable about the way we're talking here to the person who created the work. I cannot believe that Gomez-Peña [whose work was discussed in an earlier session] walked away as an authority ... and everybody within an academic discourse just worshipped his work. And I've seen this turn into such a verbal position, mediated by emotion, and forcing her to justify her work. There's a powerful correlation between what it means to have a man there [at the center of a critical discussion], and to have an Asian American young woman.

In many ways, the intense interaction described catalyzes and encapsulates this volume. It was an extraordinarily raw, complicated, honest, and revealing session that spoke to issues of race, gender, culture, generation, ethnicity, identity, expectation, perception, media representation, artistic approach, cultural authenticity, and critical authority. Later lê would wryly comment, 'Why did she say, "I honor the sister," if she couldn't watch me? And these are my "sisters"?' lê's *the bodies between us* is not the traditional Vietnam War saga from either on the ground or in the air. It is a complex and nuanced performance about the fragments of body memory between violently fractured political geographies: the endless hallucinatory state of floating, adrift at sea; the waking nightmare of the refugee camp; and the efforts to resurrect the fading images of a half-remembered mother. The response session the piece generated, unexpected and painful as it was, pointed out how rare such forums are. Where artists, intellectuals, and community members interact; where race, gender, and generation are neither tokenized nor represented, but are fully present, unmediated and uncensored; where the discourse is *between* us, not *about* us. And between us are bodies, separated by category and position, of knowledge, perspective, and experience that have yet to be fully brought into conversation.

FIRST VOICE/PRIMARY PERSPECTIVE

The Color of Theater is an effort to create the primary perspective of a discourse and resource on race and performance emanating from artistic practice. It is a dialogue of artistic method and vision, with scholarship and intellectual insight. It is an attempt to place artistic work at the core of critical reflection and to foster a dialogue that crosses discipline and geographic borders. Existing publications in the field of performance and contemporary theater have tended to engage the issues of race and ethnicity primarily in one of two distinct approaches. Race and ethnicity are either peripherally included within a more generalized study (or as they are related to larger themes) or they are contained within the territory of an ethnically specific project. In the first example, race and ethnicity are frequently defined in terms of difference or otherness, providing a site of examination of the dichotomy between dominant and minority cultures. Theater by artists of color in this instance is defined in terms of response to or reaction against a dominant norm. For example, in *Staging Difference: Cultural Pluralism in American Theatre and Drama*, Marc Maufort characterizes innovative theater work by artists of color by its relationship to dominant culture: '... this new vision often coincides with a radical departure from conventional stage realism, resulting in the creation of new dramatic forms. These new shapes serve to express the minorities' ambivalence towards cultural assimilation into mainstream America.'[2] In contrast, ethnically specific studies, while engaging the impact and influence of dominant culture, have asserted a trajectory and provenance of cultural, political, and aesthetic continuum. Jaye T. Darby states, in the co-edited critical collection *American Indian Theater in Performance: A Reader*: 'While there has been some scholarly debate about the advent of Native theater, whether it occurred before or after the Red Power movement during the 1960s and 1970s, it is somewhat limiting to see it as an either–or situation. Drama in an array of forms, from the highly spontaneous to the carefully planned, has always been an integral part of Native peoples' lives throughout history ...'[3] In another ethnic realm, Annemarie Bean, in *A Sourcebook of African-American Performance*, echoes Darby's position, and ties contemporary African American theater to the aesthetic challenge articulated by Larry Neal during the 1960s Black Arts Movement, asserting that African American performance has a history based in continuum.[4] Other publications including *Tokens: The NYC Asian American Experience on Stage, Stages of Life: Transcultural Performance in Latina Theatre*, and *Out of the Fringe: Contemporary Latina/o Theatre and Performance* also provide excellent examples of recent scholarship which amplify issues of race, ethnicity, and aesthetics within a specific cultural and ethnic perspective.

The Color of Theater places the discussion of race and ethnicity within a third context, compelled by how the nature of theater has changed and how the world is changing. It explores the spaces between the ethnically specific, beyond the limitations of cultural nationalism. It seeks new language and points of entry to explore the complex interrelationship within and across national boundaries. It was conceived and constructed as an artist-driven dialogue, emanating from the place of creation; the myriad locations where performance is being made in traditional and community settings. Its materials are critical and artistic essays, artist-to-artist and scholar-to-artist interviews and conversations, and performance texts contextualized by introductions and commentaries. At the center are four performance texts: *Quinceañera* by Alberto Antonio Araiza, Paul Bonin-Rodriguez, Michael Marinez, and Danny Bolero Zaldivar; *the bodies between us* by thúy lê; *BORDERscape 2000* by Guillermo Goméz-Peña and Roberto Sifuentes; and *Elijah* written by Sekou Sundiata, with music composed by Craig Harris. These texts provide evidence of diverse approaches to performance and theater making. *Quinceañera* was collectively devised, catalyzed by a visual arts installation, and created through collaborative community workshops. *the bodies between us* is a solo performance work that intercut auditory texts with the author's writing, using visual design as its point of departure for performance. *BORDERscape 2000* is a multi-collaborator visual and auditory, performed spectacle. *Elijah* is a synthesis of poetry and narrative interpreted through a musical score. These texts are presented as a literary point of reference to the performed work; the missing bodies lê insists must complete the language are suggested through photographs and introductions by Joe Salvatore, Lucy Mae San Pablo Burns, Lisa Wolford, and Talvin Wilks. Their comments reveal artistic process and intention. Alberto Sandoval-Sánchez, Una Chaudhuri, Josh D. Kun, and Joni

Jones provide responses that offer thematic insight and place the work within larger discussions.

The four productions from which these performance texts were derived were developed at New WORLD Theater, the site where several of the discussions included also originally occurred. This volume evolves intimately from this location, a theater dedicated to the work of artists of color, based in an area of the United States, New England, which has been at the periphery of discussions of race and the theater. I founded the New WORLD Theater in 1979, at the University of Massachusetts at Amherst, as a student-organizing project, when students of color numbered a marginal 6 percent at the University[5] and were minimally reflected in campus life or the curriculum.[5] The founding vision was to create a theatrical space that would offer a contemporary program of works by Black, Latino, Asian, and Native Americans, a repertory that was completely invisible within the existing arts environment of the region. The theater was founded while apartheid was still the rule in South Africa, and it drew parallels between supporting the anti-apartheid movement and combating racial and cultural de facto segregation in America.[6] It was an anti-racist, multiracial project that, in addition to producing theater, recognized New England's geographic isolation and included visiting touring productions in its season. It was in many ways a desegregation project, as opposed to an integration effort. By this I mean it was not an effort to bring 'color' to the existing theater production paradigm through multiracial or ethnically transposed productions of the European or Euro-American canon. It was an effort to desegregate a public institution by gaining the means of production to offer a completely autonomous and self-defined artistic program.

Over the years the theater has evolved organically from its original mission. While implicitly feminist (the majority of the founding and current staff members were/are women, as are the majority of lead artists in the artistic work), it grappled with homophobia within communities of color and racism in the gay community. In 1994 it embraced queer theater, not as a segregated laboratory, but woven through all aspects of the artistic program: presenting, producing, commissioning, and play development. In 1995, a deeper commitment to youth communities was made, particularly in recent immigrant and refugee communities, through the Looking In/To the Future (LIFe) program which worked with various Southeast Asian, Latino, and Black youth living in geographically segregated areas of Western Massachusetts. LIFe established independent projects that enabled each cultural and ethnic enclave to establish a primary or first voice. Subsequently these groups were brought into situations of cross-cultural interaction.[7] This idea of primary voice was also extended to documentation and publication projects in the early 1990s with the establishment of an archive of plays by Asian American women in cooperation with the University of Massachusetts W. E. B. DuBois Special Collections and various publication projects intended to widen the dramatic literary canon.[8] The interview of Nobuko Miyamoto by Lucy Mae San Pablo Burns included here is an example of first voice documentation; it is an effort by a younger Asian American artist and scholar to restore, to the historical record, the five-decade career of an iconoclast artist and political activist.

In 1996 a performance development initiative was launched, entitled 'New Works for a New World.' Its focus, through commissioning and laboratory play development, was to create a responsive new site of production that would recognize the innovative ways artists of color are working in the theater, beyond the single-author well-made play. These methods include solo performance, performance art, interdisciplinary and collaborative work (music, visual art, dance and theater), and community-devised works. An extension of this initiative is 'Intersections,' a national and international convening intended to widen the circle of participation to practitioners, scholars, and community members domestically and worldwide.

The above brief history of New WORLD Theater illustrates the thematic terrain, ideological platform, and artistic practices traversed in this collection. At the epicenter is color, literally race, the initial and continued alteration of the environment that New WORLD Theater's presence affects. The aftershocks, divides, and shifts of this intervention are compounded by ethnicity, gender, sexuality, class, generation, and cultural aesthetic. In the practical work, as in this collection, the domestic and global have existed simultaneously. The conversation between theater activists Awam Amkpa, a Nigerian based in the United States, and Chuck Mike, an American based in Nigeria, is an example of artistic and political interconnection, and new definitions of identity and agency within national and international boundaries. International work has never been included as part of an exotic menu, nor featured as preserved, performed authenticity; nor added on in response to a funder's initiative. International work, within the New WORLD Theater context, has always been engaged from a political, social, and cultural imperative, the ramifications of which have points of domestic intersection and relation.

TO BE OR NOT TO BE MULTICULTI

As an Asian American, specifically *sansei* (third-generation Japanese American), I have located my work within the context of other artists of color, first because of the invisibility I felt upon my arrival in Western Massachusetts in the 1970s, encountering a bleak, culturally homogenous world. Also, I was born in Hawaii and raised in Los Angeles; the multiethnic, with its implicit tensions and blessings, was expected and normal. When I founded New WORLD Theater in 1979, I wasn't aware of the term multicultural. I became uneasily familiar with the term, as a hegemonic, discursive site to which I was assigned, by funders, scholars, journalists, and some members of the public. Often the expectation of us, as a multicultural organization, was of an art that minimizes difference, that celebrates common human experience, and that provides representation in often rigidly defined slots (something appropriate for Black History Month, Asian Heritage Week, Gay Pride Day, A Multicultural Minute, etc.). The term attributed different meanings to our work than what we intended: from commemorative and representative to exclusionary and reductive. For example, it might be assumed that our theater work should only show a particular community in its best possible light. This expectation came from audience members of color entering a space where they were self-conscious of the double gaze of the white audience member; of 'them' watching images on stage and shifting that gaze to extrapolate meaning to those seated nearby. We received pressure to sanitize the work, to not expose our 'dirty linen;' in fact, to censor it. As Thulani Davis observes in the opening essay: 'Sometimes the last people to get ready for what we are doing are the very people for whom we may hope to create – our communities.' At the opposite extreme was the assertion that multicultural implied that whites were excluded, simply because they were not the central focus of address. We have refused to cater our work to either position and, in so doing, have gained an audience with the highest degree of cultural literacy. In this volume, essays by Thulani Davis, Harry J. Elam, Jr., Rustom Bharucha, Cherríe Moraga, and Velina Houston further contest multiculturalism, offering new critical and theoretical frameworks, and providing an expanded vocabulary for an evolving, complex, interculturality of geography, economy, biology, and cultural expression.

In another context, the term multicultural has been used between communities of color to delineate the boundaries of the racially specific. In the included Alvin Eng conversation with La Mama ETC founder, Ellen Stewart, an African American woman, she describes how her pioneering, tenacious grasp on the concept of a multiethnic world theater provoked her censorship and condemnation by African American cultural nationalists of the 1960s. This position appears to continue to define the parameters of certain racialized projects. In 1998, during the planning of an historic convening, the National Black Theatre Summit, I received a call from playwright Paul Carter Harrison, one of the summit's organizers and an authority on Black theater.[9] In describing the upcoming summit and its participants he informed me that 'while New WORLD Theater works with many Black theater artists, not all of the work they do is necessarily Black theater.' Asked for clarification, he added:

'Those Black artists whose first focus is on gender or sexuality, in either women's projects or gay theater, are not making Black theater, they are making multicultural theater.'[10] Pressed further he elaborated on theater made by gay and lesbian artists whose sexuality is the subject of their artistic work: 'They don't represent what Black people are concerned about. Their work is not particularly enlightening for Black America. It is not within the interests of Black theater − it just is too narrow a concern for the larger interests of Black theater.'[11] The interview of Brian Freeman by Marlon Bailey gives an individual artist's account of this exclusion, when his now disbanded troupe, the Pomo Afro Homos, was barred from the National Black Theater Festival in Winston Salem, NC. This double marginalization, from the mainstream because of race and from the ethnically specific because of sexuality, has been redefined by many artists as a location where existing traditions and structures can be re-appropriated, subverted, and transculturated, as in the performance text *Quinceañera*. Thulani Davis, in coining the term 'intersection artists,' subverts the marginalizing and reductive effect of the multiculturalism nomenclature, suggesting numerous possibilities of approaches, materials, and perspectives. Like the term 'doubles' that has emerged in discussions of race, countering denigrating historical terms referring to multiraciality (e.g. half-breed, mongrel, mulatto, mixed, part, half), the term asserts an enhanced position: the capacity to inhabit a complex physical space, to see from multiple perspectives, and to cross imposed boundaries and borders.

TOWARD 2050

It is projected that by the year 2050, Caucasians will become a minority in the United States, outnumbered by people of color, a monolithic category that, while affirming unity, obscures the complexity of difference. In their essays, both Jaye Darby and Diana Taylor, in discussing different arenas of indigenous contemporary performance, speak to the naming and misnaming of Indians, underscoring the power of terminology to obscure and even obliterate. According to Taylor, 'the naming of the "people called Indians" both conjured up and disappeared a people' conflating the Incas, Mexica, Mayas, and other autonomous groups. Having organized New WORLD Theater around the principles of racial visibility, access, and autonomy, within the context of coalition and community building, how will the terminology, 'people of color' move forward into this projected near future of 2050? In this prediction, social scientists question the diminishing relevance or new meanings of traditional assignations of race as categories increasingly blur due to racial, cultural and ethnic hybridity. Others predict an increase in the balkanization and ethnic strife that has been forecasted globally in the internecine horrors of Rwanda and Bosnia, and domestically in the 1992 Los Angeles Uprising (referred to as the first multicultural riots) as people become more protective of their essential identities and political territory. Alternatively, and equally dire, *BORDERscape 2000*, Roselyn Costantino's interview with Jesusa Rodríguez, and Rustom Bharucha's essay all vividly explicate the rapidly growing reality of a globalized homogenous culture imposed on the South by the Northern hemisphere.

This demographic shift has already occurred in major US urban centers, although mainstream theater institutions have yet to reflect this change. In David Román's interview with Chay Yew, multiple entrepreneurial production strategies for working with historically intransigent mainstream institutions are described. These tactics, including commissioning, development, and co-production, pragmatically and creatively recognize that main stage production cannot be the only contested arena, as it is the least likely to be won.[12] Conversely, Ann Haugo's interview with Spiderwoman Theater's Muriel Miguel posits that autonomy from the mainstream, at least in the case of Native theater, is the only viable path to artistic control.

In the case of New WORLD Theater, we are located in a region approaching the 2050 demographic shift. Like most of the rest of the country, the state is still predominantly Caucasian, but has experienced an accelerated growth in communities of color. In Western Massachusetts, between the 1990 and 2000 censuses, each category of Black, Latino, Asian Pacific, Native American, and Other increased; only the Caucasian population declined.[13] But these racial demographic changes do not speak to the attendant issues of class and social divides. For example, in Western Massachusetts, the greatest growth has occurred in the economically depressed cities of Holyoke and Springfield. The 1990 census revealed that Holyoke, MA, a city of 43,700 inhabitants, had a Latino (predominantly Puerto Rican) population of 31 percent. Over 60 percent of that population lives under the poverty level; the majority of the population is also under 24. Latinos in Holyoke have among the highest high school dropout, teen pregnancy, and HIV infection levels statewide.[14] A former mill town that saw its heyday at the end of the nineteenth century, Holyoke never had a transportation system connecting it to neighboring affluent towns, including Amherst, where New WORLD Theater is located. Consequently, the strategies we have developed to connect to communities within our region include collaborations with community-based organizations, participatory intergenerational and youth play creation projects, workshops at community-based sites, touring performances, and the production of community-developed theater work with professional artists, within our regular season.

Diana Taylor further amplifies this concern for developing relationships with communities, through production and artistic strategies, in her discussion of the political theater ensemble Yuyachkani's work within the multilingual, multiethnic society of Peru. She examines borders of nation, race, class, and culture by questioning why many theater artists in Latin America find themselves linguistically and culturally closer to the theater of Europe and the US than to indigenous cultures within their own country. She observes: 'Class, racial, and linguistic affinities often supersede bonds that grow out of geographical and national interconnectedness.' In the U.S., I've repeatedly heard white theater directors and students talk about how they are reluctant to direct (or white professors to teach) a contemporary work by a playwright of color because they have no point of entry into the world of the play (as opposed, say, to the unquestioned accessibility of a Chekhov play written from the location of another country, language, and century). Yuyachkani's evolution as an urban, white/mestizo, middle-class theater troupe engaging rural, indigenous populations confronts, head-on, issues of elitism, cultural appropriation, and the role of the arts in creating an inclusive national identity. From the opposite location, Harley Erdman's interview with Petrona de la Cruz and Isabel Juárez Espinosa (of the Mayan women's theater collective La FOMMA in Chiapas) shows the efforts of indigenous theater artists to bring the perspective of women and children into a traditionally non-indigenous male-dominated performance arena. Erdman points out that theirs is not the commodified Chiapas of export, although they have come to be known in the international sphere as the first indigenous women playwrights of Mexico. Their dramaturgy, in Spanish, Tzotzil, and Tzeltal, speaks to the communities and cultures they mediate. La FOMMA and Yuyachkani exemplify theaters of transformation and engagement, from positions in society that conventionally are perceived as immutable.

HEADING FOR DEEP WATER

Ultimately, the contributions to *The Color of Theater* find their collective meaning in the deliberate and inadvertent talking across social, geographical, and cultural position, and the subsequent refractions, collisions, and interjections that occur throughout the collection. For example, Rustom Bharucha eloquently critiques an intercultural dynamic of North/South, where the First World is tourist/voyeur/infiltrator in the Third World; he points out that most intercultural international collaborative projects originate with a mediating funder in the Northern Hemisphere, and that the artist's primary motive is a curiosity of other cultures, a desire for the exotic other. He proposes not only an examination of rejection by the other, but emphasizes the need to make possible a South/South intercultural encounter. In reading across this collection, his critique of voluntary interculturalism is further complicated and expanded by other intercultural scenarios, not randomly voluntary, but driven by a desire for transformation, a politic of affinity, or an artistic acknowledgement of cultural collision. Thus La FOMMA and Yuyachkani speak to intercultural examples of gender/generation within a perceived homogenous indigenous culture; and white/mestizo and indigenous inter-cultural negotiations within a socially striated society. The intercultural territory they have sought is in itself transformative. It transcends the realm of artistic product and creates new loci of agency within a society. In *Quinceañera*, the intercultural collaboration is between the HIV-positive and the HIV-negative gay communities, a painful confrontation of guilt and blame that transforms HIV status from a victim politic to a rite of passage to be survived. In *Elijah*, the intercultural is what Sekou Sundiata calls 'riding the mighty hyphen' of the term 'African-American' where he and Craig Harris sought Africa to fully understand the contemporary condition of Black America through its historical trauma. These are voluntary intercultural explorations, but ones in which the artists have a deep personal connection and investment; the risk they take to seek the unknown is enormous.

Returning to my opening discussion of *the bodies between us*, and the metaphor it provides, this book is not only about the obstacles, issues, and experiences standing between us that must be fully examined for genuine exchange and apprehension to occur. It is about being willing to enter an immense space, the unrecognized; the territory of where and how this artistic work is occurring and being made. It is not about the fixed and familiar landmarks of here and there, what theater was then and what it has become now. This work is about the wider sea of what and how the work is becoming. And, as James Baldwin told us in *Sonny's Blues*, we have to leave the shoreline and strike out for deep water, knowing that deep water and drowning are not the same thing.

NOTES

1. 'New Works for a New World: An Intersection of Performance, Practice, and Ideas,' a conference and play festival, was convened by the New WORLD Theater, in Amherst, MA, October 8–11, 1998. It was made possible by the Rockefeller Foundation, with additional assistance from the New England Foundation for the Arts, the LEF Foundation, the National Endowment for the Arts, Nathan Cummings Foundation, Lila Wallace Reader's Digest Arts Partner Program, the Massachusetts

Cultural Council, the Surdna Foundation, the National Performance Network, the Ford Foundation, the UMass Arts Council, the Vice Chancellor of Economic Development and Research, the Dean of Humanities and Fine Arts, and the Fine Arts Center at the University of Massachusetts at Amherst. The Department of Theater of the University of Massachusetts at Amherst was a primary co-producer of the festival productions, which are included as performance texts in this book. The incident described in this introduction was derived from a video recording of the critical response session to thúy lê's *the bodies between us* on October 11, 1998. Special thanks to Jean Shigekawa of the Rockefeller Foundation, Dr. Fred Tillis, Vice Chancellor Fred Byron, Dean Lee Edwards, and Professor Richard Trousdell for their support of *Intersections*.

2. Marc Maufort, *Staging Difference: Cultural Pluralism in American Theatre and Drama* (New York: Peter Lang P, 1995, p. 1).

3. Hanay Geiogamah and Jaye T. Darby (eds), *American Indian Theater in Performance: A Reader* (Los Angeles: UCLA American Indian Studies Center, 2000, p. v).

4. Annemarie Bean (ed.), *A Sourcebook of African-American Performance: Plays, People, Movements* (London: Routledge, 1999).

5. Special thanks to Rustom Bharucha who urged me to frame the introduction of this collection within the context of my work at New WORLD Theater. An independent writer based in Calcutta, Bharucha commented to me that despite his experience of having spent several years in New Haven, a city with a sizeable Black population, while studying at Yale and being an invitee to a number of U. S. convenings, coming to New WORLD Theater was the first time he became fully aware of 'the Third World in the First World.'

6. South African productions and collaborations have been part of New WORLD Theater's artistic program since our first season in 1979 which featured Selaelo Maredi's and Steve Friedman's *Homeland*, a Modern Times Theater production (1979). Other South African works presented include *Sizwe Banzi is Dead* by Athol Fugard, John Kani, and Winston Nshoha, an Afro-American Studio Theater production (1980); *Asinamali!* by Mbongeni Ngema, a Committed Artists of South Africa production (1986); *Born in the RSA* by Barney Simon and the cast of the Market Theatre of Johannesburg, SA (1986); *You Strike the Woman You Strike the Rock* by The Vusiszwe Players (1988); *Woza Albert!* by Mbongeni Ngema, a Crossroads Theater Company production (1989); *Sarafina!* by Mbongeni Ngema, a Roadworks Productions, Inc. production (co-sponsored by the Fine Arts Center Performing Arts Series) (1990). Original New WORLD Theater South African productions include *Bird of My Luck* by Bheki Langa (1980), *Homeland* by Steve Friedman and Selaelo Maredi (1979), and *Sheila's Day* by Duma Ndlovu and cast (1994).

7. The current youth work is entitled *Project 2050*, based on the projected demographic shift when Caucasians will become a minority in the U.S. It brings together youth, professional artists, and scholars in a series of discussions, creative collaborations, and professional commissions imagining the near future.

8. The play anthologies I have edited – *Unbroken Thread: An Anthology of Plays by Asian American Women* (Amherst: University of Massachusetts Press, 1993), *Contemporary Plays by Women of Color*, with Kathy Perkins (London: Routledge, 1996), and *Monologues for Actors of Color: Men* and *Monologues for Actors of Color: Women* (New York: Routledge, 1999) – originated from production work at New WORLD Theater. The Uno Asian American Women Playwrights' Script Collection 1924–present in Special Collections at the W. E. B. Dubois Library at the University of Massachusetts at Amherst contains over 200 plays by Asian American women writers, along with selected audio and video interviews, playbills, photographs, and production histories. These are all efforts to create documentation and scholarship emanating from artistic practice.

9. In addition to being a playwright, Paul Carter Harrison is a theorist whose *Drama of Nommo: Black Theatre in the African Continuum* (New York: Grove Press, 1972) defines a Black theater aesthetic rooted in African culture and cosmology.

10. New WORLD Theater has produced the following plays by Black artists (in addition to the South African works already cited): *Prisms* by Mascheri Chapelle and Jerome Robinson (1979); *Lucky Strikes Legacy* by Freida Jones (1980); *The Healing of Sugar* by Carlos Anderson (1980); *Black Girl* by J. E. Franklin (1980); *The Mighty Gents* by Richard Wesley (1981); *Dance Bongo* by Errol Hill (1982); *Day of Absence* by Douglas Turner Ward (1982); *Do Lord Remember Me* by James deJongh (1983); *Gullah* by Alice Childress (1984); *Blues for Mister Charlie* by James Baldwin (1984); *Moon on a Rainbow Shawl* by Errol Hill (1985); *Loners* by Joan California Cooper (1985); *To Be Young, Gifted and Black* by Lorraine Hansberry (1986); *Be Still and Know* by Stephen Newby (1986); *The Lion and the Jewel** by Wole Soyinka (1987); *Nzinga's Children* by Veona Thomas (1988); *Unfinished Women Cry in No Man's Land While a Bird Dies in a Gilded Cage** by Aishah Rahman (1989); *Twenty-First Century Groove* by Alonzo D. Lamont (1990); *Miss Ida B. Wells* by Endesha Ida Mae Holland (1992); *Flyin' West*** by Pearl Cleage (1995); *The Return of Elijah, The African** by Sekou Sundiata (1996); *Combination Skin**** by Lisa Jones (1996); *Clay Angels** by Daniel Alexander Jones and Todd Christopher Jones (1997); *Evening of One-Acts by Early Black Women Playwrights**: Plumes* by Georgia Douglas Johnson, *The Purple Flower* by Marita Bonner, and *'Tis Morning* by Shirley Graham Dubois (1997); *The Doll Plays** by Alva Rogers (1998); *Sanango** by azande (1999); *Anybody Seen Marie Laveau?* by Aisha Rahman (1999); and *Shakin' the Mess Outta Misery*** by Shay Youngblood (1999). *Co-produced with the Department of Theater, University of Massachusetts at Amherst; **co-produced with the Mt. Holyoke College Department of Theatre Arts; ***co-produced with the Smith College Theatre Department.

In addition, we have presented the following touring works: *Sister, Sister* by Vinie Burrows (1981); *'Ol' Sis Goose*, New African Company (1981); *An Evening with Ossie Davis and Rubie Dee* (1982); *Home* by Samm-Art Williams, Daedelus Incorporated (1982); *Stepping into Tomorrow* by Yolanda King and Attalah Shabazz, Nucleus Theater (1983); *Proud* by C. Bernard Jackson, Innercity Theater

(1984); *Love to All, Lorraine* by Elizabeth Van Dyke, the National Black Touring Company (1984); *A Soldier's Play* by Charles Fuller, the Negro Ensemble Company (1985); *Voices in the Rain,* Jomandi Productions (1985); *Ceremonies in Dark Old Men* by Lonne Elder III, the Negro Ensemble Company (1986); *Williams and Walker* by Vincent D. Smith, National Black Touring Circuit (1987); *Wine in the Wilderness* by Alice Childress, First World Images (1987); *Muffet Inna All a We,* Sistern Theater Collective (1988); *Dark Cowgirls and Prairie Queens,* Carpetbag Theater (1988); *Ma Rainey's Black Bottom* by August Wilson, Amaryllis Productions (1988); *Don't Start Me Talking or I'll Tell Everything I Know (From the Life and Writing of Junebug Jabbo Jones)* by John O'Neal for Roadside Productions, co-sponsored with the Fine Arts Center Performing Arts Series (1989); *Robeson!* by Dan Oliver (1990); *Praise House,* Urban Bush Women (1991); *Sisters* by Marsha Jackson (1991); *Camp Logan* by Celeste Bedford Walker, performed by Mountain Top Productions (1991); *Tragedy of Macbeth,* the Committed Artists of Great Britain, co-sponsored by the Fine Arts Center Performing Arts Series (1992); *Fierce Love,* Pomo Afro Homos (1993); *Dark Fruit,* Pomo Afro Homos (1993); *Cric? Crac!,* Carpetbag Theater (1993); *From the Mississippi Delta* by Endesha Ida Mae Holland, Daedalus Productions (1994); *A Revival of Black Women's Stories: One Deaf Experience,* Onyx Theater (1994); *Sing: Silence Is Never Golden, An Exploration of the Complexities of African American Lesbian Lives,* Women's Theater Project (1994); *Frederick Douglass Now* by Roger Guenevere Smith (1995); *Maija of Chaggaland* by Sheela Langeberg (1995); *Ndito and Masia Girls* by Sheela Langeberg (1995); *Voices in the Rain* by Michael Keck (1998); *Of Urban Intimacies,* Marlies Yearby's Movin Spirits Dance Theater (1998); *Things Fall Apart* by Chinua Achebe, play adaptation by Biyi Bandele, Performance Studio of Nigeria (1999); *Junebug/Jack,* Junebug Productions and Roadside Theater (1999); *Universes: 'U' Fresh out of the Box* (1999); *Civil Sex* by Brian Freeman, Berkeley Repertory Theatre (2000).

11. Author's interview by telephone with Paul Carter Harrison, January 7, 1998. I thank him for his permission to reproduce our conversation.

12. Chay Yew, in addition to being an accomplished playwright, is the director of the Asian American Theater Laboratory of the Mark Taper Forum. The Taper, Los Angeles' primary resident professional theater, has long been criticized for not adequately representing the city's diverse population on stage. For example, over a span of 23 years, only two main stage productions by Asian American playwrights have been produced (*Sansei,* created by Hiroshima, 1988–9 season, and *The Wash* by Philip Kan Gotanda, 1990–1 season) in a city where Asian Americans number 10.77 percent of the total population of 9,884,300. A June 7, 2000 article in the *Los Angeles Times* named Yew as one of the Taper's corps of play developers 'who work on projects that usually are not ready or aesthetically appropriate for the Taper main stage.' It announced 'a modest festival of fully staged productions at the 99-seat Actor's Gang in Hollywood.' The article asserted that 'the developmental troops were growing restless' waiting for the Taper to develop its own alternative space. Fellow play developer and writer Luis

Alfaro said: 'Not being produced gets more and more frustrating. If we had not produced this season, it would have been time to go.'

13. Fred Bayles, 'Minorities Account for Population Growth', *USA Today*, March 3, 2001.
14. This data was originally collected and processed by the Pioneer Valley Planning Commission. The data was taken from the 1990 U.S. census, and the percentages were subsequently presented in public form in 1994 by the University of Massachusetts Arts Extension Service in 1994.

Part II
Essays

1

Theater beyond borders: reconfiguring the artist's relationship to community in the twenty-first century – moving beyond *bantustans*

Thulani Davis

I come to this place by a very special path. My first theater experience was getting measles before the school play. My second theater experience was to play Pocahontas. In my school there were two of us with long braids and I got the part. My third experience was integrating the Washington Theater Club when I was 13. The first piece I worked on was by Shalom Aleichem. So I have been crossing borders for a long time.

Recently I went to a temple in Japan, which holds a huge gold Buddha, given by the Emperor of Korea 900 years ago. You have to see the Buddha in your mind because it was put away 700 years ago to protect it and a replacement was made. The replacement was itself covered up 500 years ago and so now there is a black space, and below the stage built for it, the Womb of Buddha.

The Womb of Buddha is basically a very, very, very dark tunnel under the altar, winding around the huge pillars that support this massive temple. You are told to remove your shoes and belongings, bag them, and go down the stairs. My teacher, who was our translator, heard the instructions and said, 'We go down the steps and then I don't know what happens.' Someone else said we should run our hands along the wall and search for a key, which would bring us happiness.

It was so black down there that I was sure I could not breathe. I followed the wall with my right hand. It was glass smooth from the hundreds of thousands of visitors who had caressed it in their searches for happiness over 900 years. You are to hold onto the person in front of you with your left hand, but I lost touch of my teacher immediately and kept calling, 'Are you there?' Someone had peed on the floor. I thought I wouldn't make it, couldn't make it, didn't have the stuff to make it. And yet, eventually, there was a tiny light ahead. As I came out, I burst out laughing. I was so relieved to be out of there that I was in a great mood for three days.

I thought, I didn't find the key but I am so damn happy anyway that I can't imagine what the key could do for me. And I thought, wow, that is what my daily life is like – being just about ready to pee from fear that I can't make it work. Working in the dark. Calling out for support: 'Are you there?'

My teacher told me that his teacher had explained the Womb of Buddha as a metaphor for life – our travel through ignorance and suffering towards the light. The light is true understanding. Later I saw that it was also a metaphor for what artists do, for our struggle. There are many institutions, of course, that do not want to risk going down the stairs and not knowing what's going to happen. But we do.

If you are following what's going on in Washington or on Wall Street, you know the people who run the world do not know what's going on, and don't want to know. What's going on is what Buddhists call 'the interdependence of all beings.' Some of them are pretending that as markets fall around the world, we can sit here and be safe. We know better. The people here work at the intersections of this global interdependence.

I am talking to people who already do what I am going to talk about, to those I would refer to as intersection artists. Intersection artists and writers have given direction to work that a few years ago had certain critics declaring the end of the American hegemony. It is work that has revealed tales from the hidden histories of this society, that confronts stereotyping, and has catalyzed art now emerging from communities invisible, even to us, until recently. We work in a great variety of tongues. As Fats Waller often used to say, 'What key are you strugglin' in?'

Artists at the intersection continue a long tradition of innovation. They do not simply replicate and preserve, as is the priority when people are first cut off from homelands, but we follow another tradition, which uses and reshapes the traditional materials, the found texts, or classical forms to make new kinds of work. With luck, these new kinds of work will speak truthfully and powerfully of our evolving realities.

A master drummer I heard speak last year said that whenever African American drummers come to Africa to learn traditional drumming he could see them thinking, even as they learned, how to change and use it to create something else. 'In a way,' he said, 'creation is part of modernity.' Is not then our culture, in which transformation is a value, the quintessence of modernity? Or as composer Anthony Davis once said of jazz, 'It is my understanding of the tradition that I honor Thelonious Monk by finding my own voice.'

We serve our communities, defy our communities, lead and are taught by our communities. Sometimes the last people to get ready for what we are doing are the very people for whom we may hope to create – our communities. Fats Waller said, 'They stopped me from swinging in the church, so I had to swing outside.' This is what Greg Tate calls a 'dialectic between orthodoxy and heresy.' We have always had, and maintain, an important role as heretics and as griots, or 'rememberers' and have consciously used the griots' crafts to create works of collective memory.

Many who are frustrated by an apparent decline of 'consciousness' and support for the arts are looking backward. Some say that young people need the kinds of social movements that shaped my generation. But those people do not know where they are and what time it is. We cannot shape a reality for youth without listening to them and letting them help to define what we're doing. And the past is full of *bantustans*, artificial homelands built for us by others on barren land.

The challenge is to make theater a public space where many private worlds can be seen and heard; to make a public space where the fictional boundaries of the past can be our metaphors, rather than our prisons. American theater is the natural public space for a society no longer able to keep its fictional fences standing. It is a space of creative energy that is a shelter where people try to understand a world in which we are all materially, spiritually, elbow-to-elbow, interdependent.

People living at the periphery of society are the translators, the boundary crossers, moving back and forth from main to margin, making autonomy in the shadows. The work always affects the mainstream of the culture, and artists always start at the margins, and often return. The cultural mainstream is not there to nourish – it is a marketplace. The borders are fluid places and their fluidity nourishes us.

We are building communities and ideas instead of monuments. And I hope that we can continue that with a vengeance. We need to resist turning our communities and our cultures into static monoliths that cannot nourish. Monoliths that imitate the mainstream. And we need to resist turning our community institutions into replicas of our past – even our past struggles. There was a time in the African American past when we struggled to build institutions that would last. Many of these were begun during the prosperity brought on by a war people were protesting at the time. Many institutions died during the following decades. What lasts are the minds reached by the work, not the buildings.

Ralph Ellison said: 'The true artist destroys the accepted world by way of revealing the unseen, and creating that which is new and uniquely his own. ... The work of art is ... an act of faith in our ability to communicate symbolically.' Often works of identity come first in an artist's journey. What comes after that? The encounter with invisibility and with survival. We struggle to keep our work visible and reaching out. I believe we will prevail by keeping the survival tools developed by hardship. Being able to move, change, and create community are tools that will suit the nomadic nature of the twenty-first century.

African American artists offer good examples of the patterns of the past. At the beginning of every entrance of African American work into the mainstream is someone who learned how to get their work out without producers, publishers, and publicists, who these days are often celebrities in their own right. As work moves back and forth across the road from margin to mainstream, from the shoulder to the dividing line, we have to look at how control of the work is a gift of the margin. We have to look at how losing control (or losing popularity) sometimes sends the artist back to independent producing.

Blacks were run out of Broadway theaters at the beginning of the century, just as they were trying to develop what would become the Broadway musical and stand-up comedy, and more important, trying to develop work that spoke of our experience after slavery — stories of the buffalo soldiers or the Spanish American war, of love and struggle. The humor was aimed at life, not race. The white press moaned over the death of the good ol' darkey show. The artists went uptown to the Lafayette Theater in Harlem — back to the margin, or the bantustan. And Black theater prospered. Throughout World War I they made shows and Flo Zeigfeld and other Broadway producers came uptown and bought all the songs, took them to midtown, gave them to white performers and Fanny Brice and Al Jolson were in the lights. And there were many others. This, you could say, was the deal between the margin and the mainstream.

And when Broadway or near-Broadway opened up after the war, they went back downtown — to make all the money, not just the money for tunes but the producers', directors', and writers' share of their own work and 'Blackbirds' were in the lights. And theater uptown was moribund until the Harlem Renaissancers decided to bring it back home, literally and politically. The history of jazz and rap are hardly different from this model. The tension between work that resists and nurtures and work that lands in the mainstream and can support the artist is enormous. And this tension, this back and forth, is a continuous thread in American history. The past is the present.

Nearly all the debates of the past are still contemporary. Alain Locke believed in the conscious artist, who could reinterpret, maybe refine the material made by the folk. Alberta Hunter said, 'The musicians that didn't know music could play the best blues. I know that I don't want no musicians who know all about music playin' for me.' Zora Hurston believed in folk art, knew that if we didn't collect it there could be no argument about whether to save it, ignore it or use it. Some have said all art should be political, and others have said art need only be true. Some say these two ideas are the same thing. W. E. B. DuBois said both things at different times.

Ornette Coleman said: 'We live in a world where someone can ask who the richest man in the world is and be given a name. But you can't name the poorest man in the world. They come in millions. I decided, if I'm going to be poor and black and all, the least thing I'm going to do is try and find out who I am. I created everything about me.'

DuBois said: 'Negro art is today plowing a difficult row. We want everything that is said about us to tell of the best and highest and noblest in us. We insist that our Art and Propaganda be one. We fear that evil in us will be called racial, while in others it is viewed as individual.'

This is a dialogue we can have at the intersection, on the periphery, any day of the week. Our work raises these questions. It is easier done where we work than in a Flo Zeigfeld show. Our ancestors gave us that – taught us the difference between home and the marketplace. The connections are all still there.

Taking African American examples again, I can talk about material from communal experience, individual experience – literally what was seen, heard, read, and taught. I can talk about the amazing connections from generation to generation: Katherine Dunham, Ishmael Reed, and Edwidge Danticat looking at Haitian culture. George Clinton looking at Ishmael Reed. Savion Glover looking at the Katherine Dunham dancers in the movies rerun on TV in Newark, NJ. Alice Walker looking at Zora Neale Hurston; George C. Wolfe looking at Hurston, and Glover looking at Wolfe. Gregory Hines looking at Michael Jackson and seeing what I could not see – Michael revamping a famous solo of Fred Astaire from a movie rerun on TV. Fred Astaire looking at Vernon and Irene Castle doing a dance taught them by James Reese Europe, who got it from W. C. Handy. Maybe Michael Jackson is dancing W. C. Handy.

The work travels from juke joints to Broadway and back to the projects in Newark. In Newark, something is made new again. But now the intersections are literally everywhere. It is about spotting the periphery within your view: seeing new work that can be made wherever we work. It does not mean going back to the past. It does not mean building institutions where one group pretends it does not see any others. It does not mean building institutions that only revive works of the past, that will not risk works of the present. Our work is the incubus of the future, the nest, the nurturer of people's sanity. Our work is a shelter for people who see but cannot speak. Some think the key to overcoming our isolation in the past is to turn to a time in which we ruled the lands. They are building barricades for the battles that reached their parents and friends, not for remaking a world where a stone wall does not keep anyone away from anyone else.

Most of us artists remain outsiders throughout our lives. Some artists have in later years become so angered by their isolation and the hardships of their struggle that they feel too invisible to try to reach out and tell their stories. Many are particularly sensitive about the lack of acknowledgment when their ideas have been appropriated without proper credit or mainstreamed without benefit. I think of Baldwin telling Quincy Troupe in his last interview: 'There's no point in saying this again. It's all been said, and it's been said, and it's been said. It's been heard and not heard.' But he was heard, and we continue to try to get it said, get it said right, and put it where people can hear, so the children of the twenty-first century will know it.

Over the past few years, as arts funding has been contested and dwindling, I've been asked many times to speak about what relevance our work holds for the rest of society. I am often asked to discuss my work inside of a dichotomy like art-for-art's sake vs. art that 'appeals to certain communities, and may need quality control.' (It was put to me this way last summer at an opera meeting.) I always find this funny because I come from a tradition that is ill-supported and has never needed to explain itself in that way. I try to tell these folk what I do is as important for them to see as for my community.

Sometimes I tell these folk about my mother, who was a photographer even when she was supposed to be cooking dinner, or even when she taught young men and women how to play basketball on a playground she cleared from a stand of trees in my home town. She built the playground because of racism and segregation; she taught basketball and dance because they enhanced the spirit of the youth and gave them a discipline and a vehicle for expression. She took pictures of it all – for herself.

And though she sometimes shot the ball players to practice getting a clear image in stop-action, or to capture a bit of their choreography as dance, everyone invented their own use for her work. The kids stopped and looked at the photos and laughed at this one's bullet-head, and another fumbling a pass, laughed in recognition of their own beauty. And she never showed her work in a gallery. And other people should have seen it, to see us as we saw ourselves then; to enjoy our beauty; to take in my mother's ideas, which were often ahead of her time. Still, even without that kind of regard, she was considered an artist and a valuable member of her society. So, when I am asked how to explain the importance to society of people like you, artists at the intersection, I laugh. I laugh and I say, how important is your mother?

2

Interculturalism and multiculturalism in an age of globalization: discriminations, discontents, and dialogue

Rustom Bharucha

I would like to begin by retrieving an image that set me thinking about interculturalism more than twenty years ago in my home city of Calcutta. The image relates to a performance of one of our folk dance-theater traditions in India called Chhau from the eastern state of Orissa, which I was seeing for the first time. Chhau, however, was merely the backdrop for another performance that was going on simultaneously in front of the stage. This was a performance being enacted rather unconsciously by a group of interculturalists from Europe and America, who were totally absorbed in clicking their cameras throughout the Chhau dance. I remember seeing the backs of the interculturalists, and a very glittering array of cameras, zoom lenses, videos, and projectors, which at that point in time signified for me, at a very visceral level, an image of Western technology and power: the power of capital. When I look back on this image, I realize that my first exposure to interculturalism was already refracted, in so far as I was seeing at least two things at the same time: the Chhau dance on a makeshift stage, cut by the bodies and technology of the interculturalists.

At a personal level, I remember asking myself: who are these people? What are they seeing? And why are they so oblivious to the hundreds and thousands of people sitting behind them? These questions suggest a context of exclusion on my part, but also by implication, a relatively uninterrogated sense of cultural belongingness and territoriality that is being assumed, even as it is in the process of being disturbed.

In a more reflexive mode, therefore, I would turn the critical gaze on to myself and ask: was I overreacting to what I saw? Were we being made into voyeurs of our own culture as we saw Chhau through the screen of alien bodies? To what extent can we regard Chhau as 'our' culture? What goes into the construction of this possessive adjective 'our' — our culture, our language, our nation?

In a more polemical mode, I would focus on a different set of details relating to the photographs, images, and recordings that were taken during the performance. Where have they been circulated? To whom have they been circulated? And with whose permission? Does access to technology ensure the rights of ownership, representation, and distribution? I'm aware that I am opening a can of worms here relating to 'intellectual property rights' that have yet to be addressed adequately in the context of the globalization of cultures in our times.

It is well known that Third World countries like India are often accused of abusing these rights by pharmaceutical companies and multinational corporations, the consciences of the First World. But is it possible to reverse these charges, as indeed environmentalists have succeeded in doing, by exposing the violent hypocrisies of those industries that have presumed to patent indigenous plants like *neem*, the bark of which is used by millions of Indians as a toothbrush and for medicinal purposes? How do we counter similar instances of 'cultural piracy' that have yet to be acknowledged? To what extent is it viable to speak of 'cultural property rights' relating to the diversities of indigenous people, tribal communities, and those unacknowledged citizens of the Fourth World, whose allegiance to pre-modern rituals and practices does not always get represented in global forums on 'intellectual property?'

These forums still tend to be constrained by anachronistic and Eurocentrist notions of individual authorship, originality, and invention, at the expense of taking into account collaborative and communitarian modes of production, inherited legacies of oral and folk wisdom. It is important to keep in mind that these legacies are not *owned* by any individual party: they *belong* to the entire community and are ready to be shared with the entire world. Unfortunately, it is this very universality upheld in good faith that gets ruthlessly appropriated, so that the 'common heritage of mankind' as embodied and celebrated in so many holistic disciplines, rituals, and ceremonies can with a few strategic adjustments become the *properties* of particular agencies and corporations. How, in such exploitative and demeaning circumstances, can the 'cultural commons' of indigenous cultures be democratically recognized and shared in the 'public domain,' without being ripped off by the speculators of the culture industry?

There is a loaded political context in this question that looks, perhaps, too harshly into the future. But since the future in a sense is already in the process of being patented, a pre-emptive attitude to the exploitative potential of intellectual property cannot be sufficiently emphasized, particularly in an age of globalization. By globalization I mean specifically that expansion of global capitalism and markets through multinational and transnational corporations that are supposed to be liberalizing the world economy through an apparent dissolution of national sovereignties and borders. Interculturalism is unavoidably affected by this process of globalization. However, the first discrimination that needs to be made is that the intercultural – the exchange of cultures across nations – is not necessarily global. Not every cultural exchange needs to subscribe to the global agenda determined by the market economy, the satellite media culture, the McDonaldization of commodities. Unfortunately, the 'intercultural' and the 'global' are often used synonymously and even harmoniously, particularly in First World economies, where globalization is not just taken for granted but actively promoted.

In India, the situation is somewhat different insofar as there is a tremendous resistance at ground levels to the homogenizing, commoditizing, and anti-democratic tendencies of globalization, whether this involves the construction of a dam in Narmada or the proposed installation of the power plant of Cogentrix in Dakshina Kannada. Both projects violate biodiversity and displace tribal communities. The resistance to globalization has also extended more arbitrarily to its cultural ancillaries, which would include the Miss World Beauty Pageant in Bangalore, which was attacked by sections of feminists who specifically linked the commodification of beauty to the consumerist propaganda of the global market. In this opposition, they received unprecedented support from the farmers' movement, which had earlier opposed the introduction of Kentucky Fried Chicken into the Indian market. It is worth keeping in mind that while KFC is a thoroughly domesticated global icon in developed societies, so much so that it would be regarded as 'indigenous' if not disparagingly associated with the kind of junk food that the poorer sections of society eat, this very KFC becomes a status symbol in countries like India. In other words, the cultural signs of this commodity are totally different in Third World economies, thereby challenging one of the most illusory norms of globalization that it is capable of leveling differences across borders.

I would claim the privilege as a resident in the Third World to resist globalization within the framework of a contested national culture, a privilege that may not be available to my colleagues from more globalized economies. They may have no other choice but to live with KFC, which has been normalized in their cultures. It has not yet been normalized in mine, so I have the relative freedom to oppose such global icons. I would like to use this freedom as strategically and responsibly as possible, extending it to my own practice and thinking of interculturalism, in order to subvert its affiliations to global capitalism from within its privileged ranks. In other words, I am not restricting my opposition to globalization to Third World contexts, even though it would appear to make more sense in such contexts than in First World locations, where globalization has been normalized both in the financial and cultural sectors. To oppose globalization in one political context, and to conform to its agenda in another, is the surest way of subscribing to cultural schizophrenia.

The interculturalist, I would like to believe, is not a schizoid opportunist who shifts his/her position out of convenience. Nor is the interculturalist a free-floating signifier oscillating in a seemingly permanent state of liminality and in-betweenness. The interculturalist is more of an infiltrator in specific domains of cultural capital, which could exist in First and Third World contexts as well. The ubiquity of global capitalism compels the interculturalist to negotiate different systems of power in order to sustain the exchange of cultures at democratic and equitable levels.

Back in 1977, I was not thinking about globalization. The new economic policies of the Indian government under the dictates of the World Bank and the IMF had not yet been determined. Nor could one have anticipated the imminence of the satellite media invasion, for the simple reason that television had yet to enter our homes. In 1977, I found myself implicated within an increasingly uncomfortable awareness of what Frantz Fanon has described as the 'pitfalls of national consciousness,' where the necessary task of decolonization continues to elude us in India at many critical levels. I remember thinking to myself: if the interculturalists at the Chhau performance were there, it's because they had been invited to be there. They were not intruders, but the honored guests of the local impresarios of the organization and state cultural officials, who sought some kind of 'foreign' endorsement for their display of indigenous culture at home. Such endorsements in the intercultural scenario are invariably made possible through a series of complicities not just at economic, political, and professional levels, but more acutely, through the ideological bases and biases of different cultural institutions across systems of power that would like to believe in the *autonomy* of their interactions.

Interculturalism is not autonomous. Nor is it fair play, insofar as its practice is made possible through fundamental inequities of exchange. To this day, interculturalism continues to be theorized, rhetoricized, conceptualized, framed, mapped, and funded, almost entirely in First World locations. Intercultural decision-makers would like to believe that they function with a certain map of the world that counters the official maps and borders. But one finds that even on these seemingly altruistic, humanitarian, border-less/border-free maps, the routes of cultural exchange have already been charted, the zones of cultural interaction have already been fixed. And some zones may not exist at all, which means that one could be reduced to an absence. For instance, one could be slotted in the category of 'Asia,' where 'South Asia' may be entirely eclipsed by the predominance of 'ASEAN' countries. So there can be discriminations within discriminations, exclusions within exclusions.

If one wanted to shift these zones – break the dichotomies of the North and South, East and West – or if one desired to reroute the map – bring the cultures of the South closer together – the possibilities of doing so are extremely remote in the absence of alternative routes, structures of representation, and infrastructures of support. If I wanted to establish a bilateral South–South intercultural exchange with Burma, for instance, this encounter would in all probability be made possible through the mediation of some organization and funding agency based in the North. As a matter of fact, I did encounter 'Burma' for the first time in my life as part of a Ford-funded intercultural jamboree organized at UCLA, which was significantly entitled 'Inroads/Asia.' Apart from the obvious undirectionality of 'inroads,' as opposed to 'crossroads,' there is an underlying aggression written into the word ('you make inroads into something'), which in this context was somewhat ironic insofar as it is the U.S. that has made inroads into the cultures of the South and not the other way around (or at least, not to the same degree). Such South–South cultural 'exchanges' are no exchanges because they are mediated, circumvented, and ultimately hijacked by agencies in the North. And while it could be argued that these mediations are well-intentioned and not intrinsically undemocratic, I would acknowledge that they are extremely constraining because they work against the basic premises of voluntarism on which interculturalism is based as a theory and practice.

Voluntarism as a critical principle is unavoidably linked to the larger framework of liberalism which assumes a freedom of choice, that may not, in reality, exist for all its assumed beneficiaries. At an ideational level, however, it is a useful term insofar as it enables us to discriminate interculturalism from the larger, more emphatic, if not overdetermined narratives of multiculturalism, which does not function on a voluntarist basis. For all its constraints, interculturalism is not thrust on us: it is a process of exchange that artists seek out for any number of reasons – curiosity of other cultures, and a desire to interact and collaborate with them; a need for spiritual rejuvenation or exotic, sensual diversion; or, perhaps, to travel at someone else's expense and thereby deflect (or reinforce) the agendas of cultural tourism. There are any number of reasons that contribute to the voluntarist dynamics of intercultural encounters. Multiculturalism, on the other hand, is increasingly identified with the official policies of the State. Keep in mind that while Western democracies like Australia, Canada, and Britain have multicultural policies, none of them can presume to have an intercultural policy – the 'inter' will always lie outside of the direct control of the State, even though it may be circumscribed by the agencies of the State and the Market. Multiculturalism, however, has been hegemonized by the State in countries such as Britain, for instance, with the influx of labor from ex-colonial countries like India from the late 1950s onwards. It is only after these immigrants sought their rights as citizens in these ostensibly democratic societies that the monocultural, monolingual monoreligious premises of these democracies became explicit. In fact, it is now widely accepted that multiculturalism, for all its good intentions, has merely succeeded in dividing entire communities – against each other, within themselves. In its worst manifestations, it has become another mode of promoting sectarianism, thereby perpetuating the policy of 'divide and rule' in former colonies, but camouflaged within the multicultural aura of respecting a plurality of cultural identities and differences.

It goes without saying that our context of multiculturalism in countries like India is very different. For a start, we don't have any official policy of multiculturalism, which is taken for granted, assumed as a 'natural' inheritance that has come down to us through generations of legacies, ethnic histories, and 'living traditions,' which have been consolidated in a vast spectrum of cultural diversities. And yet, we cannot afford to be euphoric about this *intrinsic* multiculturalism not only because it is increasingly under attack by sectarian and fundamentalist forces, but because even in its most ideal manifestations, our diversities cannot be assumed to constitute a plurality. This is a fundamental point that is not often taken into account by cultural analysts who assume that our diversities are intrinsically pluralist, when in actuality, they are marked, sealed, bordered, hierarchized, and, above all, regionalized.

If we wish to develop a more genuinely pluralist multicultural society in India, therefore, we will need to develop new infrastructures for the interaction, translation, and exchange of cultural diversities on an ongoing basis. Above all, we will need to develop a more critical respect for differences that tend to be elided in the valorization of diversities – differences relating in particular to the disparities and injustices of caste, which produce diversities in their own right, even though they may not be acknowledged. Obviously this is a very different context of problems and considerations that is best theorized, to my mind, within the larger demands and struggle for secularism in India, which requires another narrative.

To return to the Western theories of multiculturalism, I think there is much for us to learn from them not because they need to be emulated or rejected, but because despite the discontents surrounding the subject, one is obliged to defend the democratic possibilities of multiculturalism against the recent backlash of conservative opinion that would like to reduce its agenda to a caricature of affirmative action for essentially underserving minorities. It is in this context that I would now like to present a series of schematic positions (and provocations) on multiculturalism that I would like to interrogate – and interrupt – with some emergent lessons drawn from intercultural practices. I will be bringing the 'inter' and the 'multi' into some kind of collision. Simultaneously, I will be attempting a dialogue between the languages of political philosophy and cultural practice, which may result in some theoretical awkwardness – a problem that may be unavoidable in dealing with the intercontextuality of a layered and polyphonic phenomenon like multi-culturalism.

I begin my critique of multiculturalism by turning to one of the most subversive readings provided by the Slovenian critic Slavoj Žižek, who gets to the point when he says:

> Multiculturalism is a disavowed, inverted, self-referential form of racism, a 'racism with a distance' – it respects the Other's identity, conceiving the Other as a self-enclosed 'authentic' community towards which he, the multiculturalist, maintains a distance rendered possible by his privileged universal position. ... [T]he multiculturalist respect for the Other's specificity is the very form of asserting one's own superiority.[1]

This is a strong statement with disturbing echoes of my own critique of universality in intercultural practice which I had situated within the context of ethnocentricity rather than racism. It would be interesting to speculate why it had been difficult for me to name 'racism' in the intercultural context: Was this some kind of self-censorship, marked as I have been as a dissenting 'Third World' voice in the predominantly White, liberal field of interculturalism? Was it too strong a word? Does it have something to do with the fact that we don't use the word 'racism' in India, which is subsumed within the dominant political category of the 'communal' (which does not mean 'communitarian' but 'sectarian')?

If racism remained unnamed in my critique of interculturalism, it is because interculturalism functions with an abundance of good faith and an aura of beneficence. Unlike the multiculturalist who 'distances' himself from the Other through a privileged universality, in Žižek's formulation, the interculturalist, at least in his/her most idealized manifestations, erases all distinctions through an assumption of a shared universality. In the empty space of the intercultural meeting ground, which assumes the 'point zero' of an authentic 'first contact' between 'essential human beings' – a 'first contact' that is often ritualized through the exchange of bodies and pre-expressive energies – there is a total erasure of the participants' ethnicities in favor of their universal human identities, creativities, and potentialities. The interculturalist is above ethnicity;

s/he is always already human. And, therefore, it becomes possible to propose a universality for all, cast in an invariably White, paternal, heterosexist image.

Through Žižek, I am now beginning to unread my earlier position, which had assumed somewhat too naively that the interculturalist's universality is a kind of mask that disguises his/her 'real' ethnocentricity. Perhaps, it is this ethnocentricity that is the 'phantasmatic screen,' in Žižek's words, which 'conceals the fact that the subject is already thoroughly "rootless," that his true position is the void of universality.' This 'void,' however, can be *filled* with a thoroughly 'rooted' Eurocentricity, if not racism, that does not attempt to screen its arrogance. Racism does not always work with screens; it can be most respectably enunciated through the most cultivated opinions.

Consider, for example, the following notorious statement allegedly made by the American novelist Saul Bellow: 'When the Zulus produce a Tolstoy, we will read him [the Zulu Tolstoy].' The explicit cultural superiority of this statement can be read as racist (not least by the Zulus themselves), who must be thoroughly fed up of being metaphorized as the nadir of primitivism. As Charles Taylor,[2] one of the more reflective interlocutors in the debate around multiculturalism, has pointed out, it obviously assumes that:

1. The Zulus have to produce a *Tolstoy* in order to prove themselves. Nothing within their own cultural heritage can serve as an appropriate point of reference. The standards of excellence have already been determined in Europe, and the Zulus have to live up to them.

2. The Zulus *have yet* to produce a Tolstoy ('When the Zulus ...'). This indicates some kind of feigned familiarity with the existing oeuvre of Zulu literature, with which Mr. Bellow might be quite unfamiliar, not unlike our very own Salman Rushdie (and here I am consciously shifting the context in order to emphasize that cultural superiority is not the prerogative of European and American authors alone). In response to our 'fifty years of independence,' Rushdie has recently had the audacity to affirm an Indian pantheon of literature that has the dubious distinction of excluding all contemporary Indian writers writing in Indian languages, apart from English – languages that Rushdie might not have read, even in translation. This 'privileged voice of the diaspora,' to appropriate a phrase used by Geeta Kapur in another context, is legitimized not through the invocation of a legacy (as in Bellow's invocation of Tolstoy) but by the sanction of the Market and the liberal endorsement of *The New Yorker* – a lucrative combination.

3. Back to the Zulus and Tolstoy, I would add a third reservation: perhaps the Zulus are not interested in producing a Tolstoy. He would, in all probability, bore them to death. Not reading Tolstoy could be a 'cultural

choice' that should not be denied to them. Rejecting Tolstoy, however, without having read him, could pose a liberal dilemma.

4. Taylor, however, adds a more provocative complication into the argument: 'The possibility that the Zulus, while having the same potential for culture formation as anyone else, might nevertheless have come up with a culture that is less valuable than others is ruled out from the start. Even to entertain this possibility is to deny human equality.' Taylor suggests that we do entertain this possibility for our own good.

We are obviously entering troubled waters here through Taylor's insistence on seeking adequate criteria in order to evaluate the relative worth of other cultures, instead of assuming their equality without knowing anything about them, which amounts, in his view, to another kind of patronization. While Taylor's reasoning is eminently sound, it can be read as another 'screen' that barely conceals his vehement rejection of those subjectivist, half-baked, 'neo-Nietzschean' positions which assume that all judgments of worth are based on standards that are intrinsically hegemonistic and power-ridden. Put in simpler language, this could be translated in the following terms: because we are so marginal, and no one understands us anyway, we alone have the right to determine our own standards and critical criteria. This attitude can easily degenerate into self-mystification, if not an intolerance of other positions, which Taylor would castigate for its undermining of the human capacity to discriminate and make reasoned choices.

On the other hand, one could argue that Taylor is so locked within the philosophical rigor of his own continental tradition (Rousseau, Herder, Hegel) that he theorizes multiculturalism from above without taking into account the humiliation and rejection of a wide spectrum of multicultural artists from the Third World, who may have no other option but to create their own 'neo-Nietzschean' criteria for their self-respect, if not survival.

Totally distanced from the subversive ways in which artists have negotiated difference and sameness as two sides of the same coin – you can be rejected for being 'too different/not different enough?/just like us' – Taylor settles for a middle ground by opting for a 'fusion of horizons,' a thoroughly regressive, if not utopic postponement of any real interaction with ongoing cultural differences. Do we need a fusion in order to meet through differences? Surely an intersection or collision or ellipsis of horizons is more likely to resist the risks of cultural homogenization.

Likewise, while one can agree with Taylor that human identities are created dialogically through an encounter with significant others, one is nonetheless compelled to ask, what about the existing – and emergent – cultures of *insignificant* others? Why does the narrative of multiculturalism need to perpetuate a post-enlightenment notion of 'enrichment' through the 'significance' derived from the 'rich human languages' of other cultures? Besides, multiculturalism is enriched not through accretion and absorption alone, but through a surrender, if not dismantling of predetermined legacies and genealogies. In order to gain something, we may have to give something up. Taylor does not begin to grasp the pertinence of this axiom which assumes, in my view, the multicultural necessity of *betraying* one's culture of origins. This betrayal is not merely the burden of the immigrant who is displaced from his or her homeland: those who assume a citizenship that is being granted to others may need to re-think their own norms. The challenge is not merely, as Taylor puts it, 'to deal with *their* sense of marginalization without compromising *our* basic political principles.' Taylor, I would suggest, needs to accept the dialogic possibility of *his* marginalization as well. Why should minorities always be 'othered' for the enrichment of their assumed benefactors?

If Taylor suffers from an excess of caution, which almost legitimizes his not entering into any messy or indeterminate relationship with other cultures, as much as he advocates it, most inter/multicultural artists whom I have encountered would seem to function with an excess of desire for the Other. Clearly, their preoccupation is not with the worth of 'other cultures,' but with the mystique of their difference ('I'd love to work with the Zulus' would be their enthusiastic response). While much work has been done on the politics of othering, otherness, being othered, relatively little work has been explored not in the politics of desiring the Other, but of being rejected by the Other. In this context, I would acknowledge from my own inter/intracultural experience that the desire for the Other need not always be reciprocated for very strong social, historical, and political reasons. And one needs to respect – and inscribe – this resistance to, if not absence of, reciprocity in our search for collaborations.

Keeping this in mind, I would acknowledge my resistance to the neo-liberal euphoria that celebrates the pursuit of 'cultures of choice' (Richard Schechner) from within the comforts of a metropolis, where cultures can be readily consumed along with their cuisines. It would be necessary to question whether these cultures want to be consumed in the first place. Secondly, one needs to resist the fatuous belief that ethnicities are so fluid that they can be 'bartered' and 'swapped'; they can 'hybridize' and enter into all kinds of 'promiscuous' relationships – regulated or otherwise. The individuals who can afford to barter and swap their ethnicities have obviously no difficulty in affirming their multiple selves. But if you happen to belong to an under-privileged community like the *dalits* (low castes) in India, whose ethnicities have been stamped on, demeaned, and inferiorized for centuries, then the task of upholding one's identity as a *dalit* is part of a long and hard-earned struggle, that involves a disidentification from earlier, hallowed, patronizing descriptions of untouchables as *harijans* ('children of God'). In this contradictory struggle, where identity is politicized in a consciously affirmative mode, a *dalit* cultural worker or activist is not likely to let go of his or her ethnicity, because this could be the only lever for self-respect through social and political mobilization.

At this point, the counter-argument could be that interculturalism is not dealing with the *dalits* of this world, the wretched of the earth. Who then are the appropriate candidates for intercultural exchange? Are we – and I include myself here – part of an exclusive club of frequent flyers, the privileged diaspora, the global intelligentsia, the enlightened exiles? If that, indeed, is the case, could we then account for our exclusions? Or can we perhaps extend the privilege of interculturalism not merely to 'one of us' but to cultural and community workers as well, who have as much right as we do to crossing borders? This extension of privilege, however, is only possible through an implosion of its values by its most self-confident beneficiaries. A crisis of faith is needed – yet another betrayal, if not infiltration of global capitalism from within its cultural enclaves – before the resources that make interculturalism possible can be redistributed at more subversive, yet democratic levels.

While multiculturalism works within the 'cultural logic of multinational capitalism,' as Žižek puts it, I would like to believe – and perhaps this is the utopic thrust in my own discourse – that interculturalism has the potential to work against this logic. But for this to happen, its practitioners will have to dispense with many proliferating myths of globalization – its invincibility, inevitability, non-negotiability, accompanied by the hoax of a liberalized world economy that has emerged through the apparent dissolution of national sovereignties and borders. Along with the 'myth of the powerless state' (Linda Weiss), one needs to undermine the bogey of the essentially demonic, anachronistic state, which underlies some of the fantasies of Third World intellectuals in First World academe, who have been largely responsible for the invention of post-coloniality and, more recently, postnationalism (Arjun Appadurai) – constructs that dispense with conventional notions of place, community, and belonging, which could be more tenacious than we imagine, in favor of emergent cultural identities in 'diasporic public spheres.'

I would like to emphasize that 'emergent identities' are not the prerogatives of the diaspora alone, and that they are very much in the making along with new subject-formations within the fractious and contradictory domain of political society in India, positioned tensely within *and against* the parameters of the nation-state, which is not yet dead. In so far as artists and cultural workers wish to participate in this democratization of political society, it becomes imperative for us to re-align our own increasingly atomized constituencies to these cultures of struggle, which do not merely exist in

India but which are emergent in almost every part of the world in different forms and with different degrees of visibility.

Should I end, therefore, by saying 'Cultural workers of the world unite'? This slogan may seem too unreal and utopic in an age of globalization when workers and unions across national borders are more divided than ever before. Perhaps, it is more cogent to say, 'Cultural workers, open yourselves to each other's struggles,' which are not going to be represented in the world information order; indeed, they are even erased in much postmodern, post-colonial theory, where cultural differences are celebrated at the expense of acknowledging – or inscribing – the economic inequalities and social disparities of migrant communities. It is by making a conscious attempt to open ourselves to these cultures of struggle that we will be able to find the most concrete commonalities that bind us together through the increased poverty and unemployment of artists almost anywhere in the world; the increased apathy of governments to the arts (which seems to be increasing in direct proportion to the rhetoric of multiculturalism); the systematic destruction of the ecological bases of world cultures and of indigenous communities in particular; and finally, the glib (and violent) displacement of the human in favor of what can be commodified, marketed, and patented. It is out of a recognition of these realities that I do believe we can restore our faith in what Slavoj Žižek describes as 'the true Universality to come,' which should not be assumed to exist in our inequitous practices, but which needs to be worked on, struggled for, and strategized through a more sustainable, reflexive, and dialogic intercultural praxis.

NOTES

1. Slavoj Žižek, 'Multiculturalism, or, the Cultural Logic of Multinational Capitalism', *New Left Review*, 225, Sept./Oct. 1997.
2. Charles Taylor, 'The Politics of Recognition', in Amy Gutman (ed.), *Multi-culturalism* (Princeton: Princeton University Press, 1994, p. 71).

3

Staging social memory: Yuyachkani

Diana Taylor

In her trance, an Andean peasant woman, Coya, sees two forces colliding, destroying everything. As a traumatized Coya speaks of what she sees, she transmits her anguish to her sister, Huaco, and their father, Papai. In her vision, an army tramples the population. The devastation is complete. The corpses have 'disappeared' but, then, so has life itself: 'Ningún cuerpo quedaba sobre la tierra, y ustedes ya no estaban más conmigo.' (There were no bodies left on earth, and you two were no longer near me.) Her father reminds the women that they need to seek the seeds of life. The task seems both terrifying and ludicrous: 'I've witnessed so much death,' states Huaco, 'and you're asking me to go look for the seeds of life?'

Masked dancers from pre- and post-Hispanic performative traditions appear onstage and fight ferociously for influence over the peasants – dancing devils and spiteful archangels with trumpets like muskets, transformed into crazed figures of power. The archangels fight for ownership of the peasants' souls in the 'danza de la diablada' or Devil dance from the Fiesta de la Candelaria in Puno. These dances, performed annually for hundreds of years, tell a story as old as the Conquest, as recent as the criminal violence associated with *Sendero luminoso*, the 'shining path.' The peasants die, but not before they have found the seeds of life. They throw some into the ground, and entrust the rest into the hands of the patient Equeco, the good-luck figure from Andean folklore who ends the play as s/he began: 'these seeds were given to me by a woman, who told me a story . . .'

The play, *Contraelviento* (Against the Wind), was created by Peru's leading theater collective, Yuyachkani, in 1989, at the height of the country's most recent civil conflict. It recounts the testimony of an indigenous survivor of the 1986 massacre at Soccos, in Ayacucho.

'In Quechua, the expressions "I am thinking," "I am remembering," "I am your thought" are translated by just one word: Yuyachkani,' the noted Peruvian commentator Hugo Salazar del Alcazar wrote in one of his many pieces on the Yuyachkani theater group.[1] The term 'Yuyachkani' signals embodied knowledge and memory, and blurs the line between thinking subjects and the subjects of thought. The reciprocity and mutual constructedness that links the 'I' and the 'you' is not a shared or negotiated identity politics – 'I' am not 'you,' nor claiming to *be* you or act *for* you. 'I' and 'you' are a product of each other's experiences and memories, of historical trauma, of enacted space, of socio-political crisis. But what is 'embodied' knowledge/memory, and how is it transmitted? And how does it differ from the 'archival,' usually thought of as a permanent and tangible resource of materials available over time for revision and reinterpretation? What is at stake in differentiating between these systems of organized thought?

The transitive notion of embodied memory encapsulated in 'Yuyachkani' – the 'I am remembering/I am your thought' – entails a relational, non-individualistic understanding of subjectivity. Coya, the indigenous survivor, recounts a vision of annihilation that is and is not her own. The 'I' who remembers is simultaneously active and passive (thinking subject/subject of thought). Yuyachkani, a collective theatre group, sees itself implicated – both as product and as producer – in various modes of cultural transmission in an ethnically mixed and complex country. For the past twenty-five years, the group has participated in at least three interconnected survival struggles – that of Peru, plagued by centuries of civil conflict; that of the diverse performance practices that have been obscured (and at times 'disappeared') in a racially divided, though multiethnic, Peruvian culture; and that of Yuyachkani itself, made up of nine artists who for decades have worked together in the face of political, personal, and economic crisis. In adopting the Quechua name, the predominantly 'white' Spanish-speaking group signals its cultural engagement with indigenous and mestizo populations and with complex, transcultured (Andean-Spanish) ways of knowing, thinking, remembering. Yuyachkani attempts to make visible a multilingual, multiethnic praxis and epistemology in a country that pits nationality against ethnicity, literacy against orality, the archive against the repertoire of embodied knowledge. In Peru, the urban turns its back on the rural, and languages (Spanish, Quechua, and Ayamara) serve more to differentiate between groups and silence voices than to enable communication. Yuyachkani, by its very name, introduces itself as a product of a history of ethnic co-existence. Its self-naming is a performative declarative announcing its belief that social memory links and implicates communities in the transitive mode of subject formation.

There is a continuum of ways of storing and transmitting memory that spans from the 'archival' to the 'embodied,' or what I will call a 'repertoire' of embodied thought/memory, with all sorts of mediated and mixed modes in between.

'Archival' memory maintains a seemingly permanent core – records, documents, archaeological remains, bones – that, because it is fairly resistant to change, serve as some kind of 'evidence' of past events. What changes, over time, is the meaning of the 'evidence' – its value, relevance, how it gets interpreted, even embodied. Bones might remain the same while their story may change – depending on the paleontologist or forensic anthropologist who examines them. *Hamlet* might be performed in multiple ways, while the unchanging text assures a stable signifier. Insofar as it constitutes a core that endures, the archive exceeds the 'live.'

The repertoire, on the other hand, stores 'embodied' memory – performances, gestures, orature, movement, dance, singing – in short, all those acts usually thought of as ephemeral, non-reproducible knowledge. Unlike archival knowledge and memory, the *thing* does not remain the same. Dances change over time, even though generations of dancers (or even individual dancers) swear they're always the same. But even though the embodiment changes, the meaning might very well remain the same. Traditional dances, for example, might communicate stable meaning and relevance even with modified moves. However, there is a long tradition, which in the Americas dates back to the Conquest, of thinking of embodied knowledge as that which disappears because it cannot be contained or recuperated through the archive. Part of the colonizing project consisted in discrediting autochthonous ways of preserving and communicating historical understanding. As a result, the very existence/presence of these populations has come under question. The *Huarochirí Manuscript*, written in Quechua at the end of the sixteenth century by Friar Francisco de Avila, sets the tone: 'If the ancestors of the people called Indians had known writing in early times, then the lives they lived would not have faded from view until now' (p. 41). The very 'lives they lived' fade into 'absence' when writing alone functions as archival evidence, as proof of presence. Certainly it is true that individual instances of performances disappear and can never be 'captured' or transmitted through the archive. A video of a performance is not a performance, though it often comes to replace the performance as an object of analysis (a film, a documentary) in itself. Embodied memory, because it is 'live' and uncapturable, exceeds the archive. But that does not mean that performance – as ritualized, formalized, or reiterative behavior – disappears. Multiple forms of embodied acts are always present, though in a constant state of again-ness. They reconstitute themselves – transmitting communal memories, histories, and values from one group/generation to the next. Embodied and performed acts, though they belong to the repertoire, in themselves record and transmit knowledge through physical movement.

In-between and overlapping systems of knowledge and memory constitute a vast spectrum that might combine the workings of the 'permanent' and the 'ephemeral' in various different ways. Innumerable practices in literate and semi-literate societies entail both an archival and embodied dimension – weddings need both the performative utterance of 'I do' and the signed contract. The legality of a court decision lies in the combination of the live trial and the recorded outcome. Claims are performative as well as legal. We have only to think of Columbus planting the Spanish flag in the 'New World' or Neil Armstrong planting the U.S. flag on the moon. While non- and semi-literate societies have long validated the legitimacy of the performed act (the Mexica married by literally tying the knot between the robes of the bride and groom), the emotional force of the act continues to carry power in literate societies. Same-sex marriages in the U.S., for example, rely on the performative utterance to bring about the social recognition of a very real union that is not legally recognized as 'contractual.' We transmit events, thoughts, and remembrances not only through our literary writings and documented histories but also through our bodily acts and performances. The techniques of storing, transmitting, and decoding these materials differ, of course, as do the possibilities of access.

Focussing on Yuyachkani's political performance practices, this essay teases apart several interconnected questions central to Performance Studies and Latin American Studies. What is at risk politically in thinking about embodied knowledge and performance as that which disappears? Whose memories 'disappear' if only archival knowledge is valorized and granted permanence? Should we simply expand our notion of the archive to house the mnemonic and gestural practices and specialized knowledges transmitted 'live'? Or is there an advantage to thinking about a 'repertoire' of knowledges performed through dance, theatre, song, ritual, witnessing, healing practices, and the many other forms of repeatable behaviors that build on past materials while allowing for the new as something that cannot be understood in terms of the archive? Perhaps the inability to analyze embodied memory as distinct from (though not necessarily oppositional to) archival knowledge has resulted in the eclipse of the former.

For the past 500 years, both writing and embodied performance have often worked together to layer the historical memories that constitute community. Local scribes in the Andes have been keeping written records in Quechua and Spanish since the sixteenth century. Even so, historical and genealogical information has been, and continues to be, performed and transmitted through performed 'memory paths,' as anthropologist Thomas Abercrombie puts it, that access ancestral stories, hearsay, and eye-witness accounts.[2] And as the percentage of literate persons in the Andes has actually *decreased* since the sixteenth century, the need to recognize cultural transmission through embodied knowledge becomes even more pressing. The archive and the repertoire have always been important sources of information, both exceeding the limitations of the other, even in the most literate societies. The relationship is certainly not a straightforward binary – with the written and archival constituting hegemonic power and the repertoire providing the anti-hegemonic challenge. The modes of storing and transmitting knowledge are many and mixed, and embodied performances have often contributed to the maintenance of a repressive social order. We need only look to the broad range of political practices in the Americas exercised on human bodies from pre-Conquest human sacrifices, to Inquisitorial burnings at the stake, to the branding of slaves, to contemporary acts of state-sponsored torture and 'disappearances.'

The relationship between the 'archive' and the 'repertoire,' rather than antagonistic or oppositional, is often mutually sustaining. Ritual specialists and specialists in embodied culture often look to extant documents to substantiate claims that certain practices pass or fail the 'traditional' legitimacy test. Change within 'traditional' embodied practices, moreover, often comes about by turning to ancient records. Women in some Andean fiestas, such as Paucartambo for example, who have been excluded from active participation since anyone can remember, have started their own *cofradía* based on assertions that these existed in the distant past.[3] Nonetheless, written documents have repeatedly announced the disappearance of the performance practices involved in mnemonic transmission. Writing has served as a strategy for repudiating and foreclosing the very embodiedness it claimed to describe. Friar Avila was not alone in prematurely claiming the demise of practices, and peoples, that he could neither understand nor control. Yet, there was no doubt in the minds of any of the early evangelists that performance practices efficaciously transmitted collective memories, values, and belief systems. Fray Bernardino de Sahagún, in his sixteenth-century *Florentine Codex*, states that he needed to write down all the indigenous practices in order to better eradicate them: 'It is needful to know how they practiced them in the time of their idolatry, for, through [our] lack of knowledge of this, they perform many idolatrous things in our presence without our understanding it.'[4] An ethnographic approach to the subject matter offered a strategy for handling dangerous practices. It allowed for a simultaneous preservation and disappearance – the accounts preserved 'diabolic' habits as forever alien and unassimilateable, even as they transmitted a deep disgust for behaviors condemned to erasure.[5] 'Preservation' functioned as a call to erasure. Yet, even after fifty years of compiling the massive materials on Mexica practices, Sahagún suspected that they had not completely disappeared. The Devil, he concluded, hates transparency, and takes advantage of songs and dances and other practices of indigenous people as 'hiding places in order to perform his works ... Said songs contain so much guile that they say anything and proclaim that which he commands. But only those he addresses understand them' (58). The colonist's claim to access met with the diabolic opaqueness of performance. 'And [these songs] are sung to him without its being understood what they are about, other than by those who are natives and versed in this language ... without being understood by others' (58). Shared performance and linguistic practices, this statement suggested, not only transmitted cultural memory – they constituted the community itself. The spiritual conquest, these friars feared, was at best tentative. The Devil awaits the 'return to the dominion he has held ... And for that time it is good that we have weapons on hand to meet him with. And to this end not only that which is written in this third Book but also that which is written in the first, second, fourth and fifth Books will serve' (59).

Clearly Father Avila and Sahagún and others were ambivalent about preserving information about certain kinds of ritualized behaviors through writing. They wanted to understand these practices in order to stamp them out – that is, put an end to idolatry. Conversely, they want to 'preserve' information about performance practices that would be lost without writing – a preview to 'salvage' ethnography. These early colonial writings are all about erasure – either claiming that these practices are disappearing, or trying to accomplish the disappearance they invoke. Ironically, they reveal a deep admiration for the peoples and cultures targeted for destruction, what Sahagún refers to more than once as 'the degree of perfection of this Mexican people' (47). And these writings have become invaluable resources as archival data on practices since extinguished. During Sahagún's lifetime, in fact, the Office of the Holy Inquisition decreed that the books were dangerous indeed. Instead of serving as 'weapons' against idolatry, as Sahagún had claimed, they in fact preserved what they attempted to eradicate. The prohibition was outright: 'with great care and diligence you take measures to get these books without there remaining originals or copies of them ... you will be advised not to permit anyone, for any reason, in any language, to write concerning the superstitions and way of life these Indians had.'[6]

Yet for all the ambivalence and prohibitions, these sixteenth-century writers begrudgingly observed something again and again: these practices were not disappearing. They continued to communicate meanings that their nervous observers did not understand.[7]

Yuyachkani's work has drawn on Peru's archive and repertoire not only to address the country's many populations but to elucidate the multiply constituted history. Some dance, sing, speak, or otherwise perform historical memory, while others access other versions through literary and historical texts, maps, records, statistics, and other kinds of archival documents. Nonetheless, contradictions abound. How can a group, made up predominantly (but certainly not exclusively) of urban, white/mestizo, middle-class, Spanish-speaking professional theater people think/dance/remember the racial, ethnic, and cultural complexities and divides of the country without minimizing the schisms or mis-representing those who they are not? Who exactly is thinking whose thought? Thought and remembrance, as the name 'Yuyachkani' makes clear, are inseparable from the 'I' and 'you' who think them. As a group made up predominantly of Limeños, does Yuyachkani have access to the memories of the Andean communities? Can it celebrate their fiestas or perform their rituals? Can Yuyachkani tell their story of accumulative social trauma? How to avoid charges of cultural impersonation and 'appropriation?'

One obvious response to this danger of cultural trespassing that threatens practitioners lies in simply turning one's back on the rural indigenous and mestizo populations and tacitly accepting that 'performance' is a European practice carried out by and for white urban audiences in the Americas. The indigenous and mestizo practices, one can argue, belong to a self-contained, parallel circuit of cultural (and economic) transmission – oral, mythic, calendar-based fiestas, rituals, and festivities. 'Theater' practitioners, then, might decide to stick to European repertoires and archives. There are all sorts of staging, lighting, and acting traditions, methods and theories of professional training to choose from. By sticking to this pool, practitioners might either want to distance themselves from the 'non-educated' elements of the population, or signal their fear of appropriating artistic languages that are not their own. Why not do Brecht, still the most honored theater practitioner in Latin America and – ironically – the world's greatest borrower? After five hundred years of colonialism, many Latin Americans, especially those from middle-class, urban backgrounds and education, are far more familiar with 'first world' cultural materials that are readily available through the media and publishing circuits than those 'non-reproducible' performances from their own countries. Some acts of 'appropriation' are safer, and potentially less offensive, than others. Class, racial, and linguistic affinities often supersede bonds that grow out of geographical and national interconnectedness.

If, conversely, one acknowledges that indigenous and rural mestizo populations also have deep performance traditions that make up part of the rich repertoires of the Latin American countries, then how do artists from all ethnic backgrounds approach their multiethnic, transculturated traditions? Can they draw from these diverse cultural backgrounds with the same ease with which contemporary European practitioners draw from their recent and distant past? Is this, or any, 'borrowing' unburdened by the political, historical, or aesthetic baggage of 'value' attached to 'style?' Do *criollo* (European Americans) or mestizo performances that include indigenous elements in their work risk turning them into exotic, folkloric add-ons? Performing 'Indian' often reveals some kind of romantic notion of authenticity in festivals, pageants, and national spectacles.[8] It's not difficult to see the dangers of separating performance practices from the people who perform them and from the ideological framework that gave them rise. How can a theater group such as Yuyachkani dream of avoiding all the representational pitfalls?

Thinking about how performance participates in and across these networks of social memory might allow us to consider cultural participation more broadly. While criollo, middle-class Peruvians share innumerable artistic traditions with Europeans, they also clearly participate in the reality of Peru's social, racial, linguistic, and political cacophony. The very categories – 'criollo' and 'Indian' – are a product of that conflict, not its reason for being. 'Indians' were invented, not discovered. 'The people called Indians' are a product of naming. It is through this performative invocation by the colonist that 'Indians' enter the world stage. Their lives, 'faded from view,' become suddenly visible as something else. Performance becomes itself, paradoxically, both through disappearance and reappearance. Again, it is simplistic to think of 'performance' as somehow embodied and liberating, in opposition to a hegemonic, archival non-performative. The archive, like the repertoire, is full of verbal performances – some that disappear, some that evoke, some that invent their object of inquiry. The naming of the 'people called Indians' both conjured up and disappeared a people. While claiming to give life to a 'fading' population, the naming was an attempt at annihilation – verbally performing the leveling and non-differentiation that the conquest aspired to militarily. The Incas, the Mexica, the Mayans and innumerable other groups suddenly become 'Indians.' The label 'Indian' also erroneously connotes an uncomplicated homogeneity that belies the reality of extensive racial and cultural mixing both before and after the Conquest. The manuscript invokes the past of the 'people called Indians,' firm in its belief that social memory is preserved through writing and history and not through orality and embodiment. Their story was the Europeans' to tell, to preserve, to fit into their biblically informed narrative of universal History. Were the 'natives' from India? Were they the lost tribes of Israel? Or even migrant Moors? The same 'scenario of discovery' created the 'white' conquerors – themselves a mixed grouping who came to the Americas only to find the ghosts of their enemies – Jews and Moors – there to haunt them. The conquest in Spanish America continued the *re*-conquista against the Jews and the Moors back home – a performative resuscitation in the face of very real racial and ethnic diversity. Converted Jews (conversos) and free and enslaved Africans swelled the ranks of newcomers to the American shores. The 'criollo' colonizers proved a mixed group indeed. These antagonistic positions have been polarized and cemented into the social imaginary as biological 'fact.' This way of thinking of lineage and tradition would certainly insist on keeping the various circuits of memory and transmission separate – to each their own. But there is a competing imaginary – that of the nation-state, conjured into being in Latin America during the nineteenth century. National identity, theoretically, supersedes regional or ethnic difference. This model assumes that 'Peruvians' (for example) are a product of, and participants in, mutually constituting historical and cultural processes such as those I just outlined. However, the national imaginary is shaped not only by what it chooses to remember, but also by what it chooses to forget, as Renan observed over one hundred years ago.[9] '*Perú es un país desmemorizado*' (Peru is a de-memorized country), Teresa Ralli, an actor of Yuyachkani, told me, and the 'de' captures the violent refusal at the heart of a country that does not recognize or understand the realities of its many parts.[10] Peruvians participate by forgetting, not just by remembering. Therefore it's not a question of *if*, but rather how, they participate.

'Yuyachkani,' Peru's internationally acclaimed collective theater group, actively stages Peru's social memory. It is a product of a complicated national, ethnic, linguistic, cultural memory, and thought. The group includes actors Teresa Ralli, Rebeca Ralli, Ana Correa, Débora Correa, Augusto Casafranca, Julian Vargas, Amiel Cayo, the director Miguel Rubio, and the technical director Fidel Melquiades, most of whom have been in the group since it started in 1971. By now, they have worked together close to thirty years, a momentous achievement, given the severe economic and political hardships they have faced. Only a couple of other Latin American collectives – La Candelaria and Teatro Experimentál de Calí, both from Colombia – boast similar accomplishments.

This group of nine members has made visible a series of survival struggles culminating in the recent atrocities associated with *Sendero luminoso* (Shining Path) that left 30,000 people dead and 80,000 homeless. Perhaps as daring, however, Yuyachkani has insistently re-membered Peru as one, complex, racially, ethnically, and culturally diverse country. The White, Westernized Lima, built with its back to the Andean highlands, affords Yuyachkani one of the spaces to stage this re-membering for urban audiences. They perform throughout the city, staging 'public acts' on streets, in schools, on the steps of the national Cathedral, in orphanages, cemeteries, and government buildings. They also stage street performances in non-theatrical spaces throughout the country, starting conversations, participating in protests and celebrations. Recognizable characters from traditional and popular culture – musicians and masked figures on stilts – parade through the streets inviting spectators to join in. These parades, as Ana Correa describes them, end in a fiesta in which participants start talking and getting to know each other. Drawing from Western models (Brecht's political theater) and Boal's 'theater of the oppressed' as well as Quechan and Aymaran legends, music, songs, dances, and popular fiestas, Yuyachkani asks spectators to become participants in Peru's rich performance traditions. Thus, their work asks spectators to take seriously the co-existence of these diverse ethnic, linguistic and cultural groups and to bear witness to Peru's history of extermination and resistance, alienation and tenacity, betrayal and remembrance.

When Yuyachkani began working in the early 1970s, the members of the group saw themselves as politically 'committed' popular theater practitioners. Popular theater in the late 1960s and early 1970s, with its *by* the people *for* the people ethos, challenged the systems that placed 'Theater' with a capital 'T' and 'Culture' with a capital 'C' in lofty, aesthetic realms, beyond the reach of working-class people and racially marginalized communities. Popular theater groups in Latin America and the U.S. (Bread and Puppet, San Francisco Mime and Teatro Campesino, to name just a few) tended to work as 'collectives.' The members of Yuyachkani, for example, meet every morning at their 'Casa Yuyachkani' and work on developing new material and ideas. They have lunch together in their communal kitchen and meet again in the afternoon to rehearse or warm up for an evening performance. Like all collective theater, they rejected the playwright and 'star'-driven theatrical models that dominated high-brow and commercial theater.[11] They took the theater out of elite spaces, staging free performances that had to do with the real life economic and political conditions of working people. Political and economic issues took precedence over aesthetic concerns. They toured their shows to rural communities that never really had access to theater, and involved spectators in many aspects of the productions. Working under the Brechtian influence, popular theater in Latin America was closely linked to strikes and other class/ labor struggles.

As I have argued elsewhere, there are some fundamental limitations and built-in contradictions to 'popular theater,' no matter how important and laudable the projects have been in general.[12] Popular theater at times presented an over-simplified and programmatic view of conflict and resolution. In Latin America and elsewhere, popular theater was often animated by Marxist theories. Progressive, at times militant, university students and intellectuals instructed the disenfranchised about how to improve their economic lot or lead a more productive life. Because Marxism privileged class, anti-capitalist, and anti-imperialist struggles to the expense of racial, ethnic, and gender conflict, its implementation in popular theater groups in Latin America ran the risk of reducing deep-seated cultural differences to class difference. In Peru, and other countries with large indigenous and mestizo communities, the 'proletariat' in fact consisted of indigenous and mestizo groups who lived on the margins of a capitalist society for various reasons – including linguistic, epistemic, and religious differences not reducible (though bound into) economic disenfranchisement. A call for solidarity organized around anti-capitalism allowed for rampant, unthinking trespassing on cultural, ethnic, and linguistic domains. Furthermore, the 'popular,' as understood by some of its activists, became entangled with fantasies of a simple, pure world existing somewhere beyond the grips of capitalism and imperialism. The less the practitioners truly knew the communities they were engaging, the more the discrepancies in power and the lack of reciprocity threatened to place them in positions of moral superiority reminiscent of religious proselytizers.

These problems plagued the initial endeavors of Yuyachkani. The marginalized groups they were addressing in their own country had their own languages, expressive culture, and performance codes that the group knew nothing about. Miguel Rubio recalls how during that first play, *Puño de Cobre* (1971), in which they performed for miners, the actors dressed in jeans and played a variety of roles and characters. After the performance, one miner commented: 'Compañeros, that's a nice play. Too bad you forgot your costumes.'[13] Unlike some of the other popular theater groups of the period (both in Latin America and the U.S.), who set about to enlighten an exploited population, Yuyachkani realized that they needed enlightening: 'Much later,' Rubio continues, 'we understood why the miners thought what they did. We had forgotten something much more important than costumes. What they wanted to tell us was that we were forgetting the audience that we were addressing. We were not taking their artistic traditions into consideration. Not only that, we didn't know them! The miners came from rural areas rich in cultural traditions. They were right. How could they imagine a play about them that did not include their songs, or the clothing of the women who so proudly conserve their traditional dress, or the figures who tell stories as they dance?'[14] This became the beginning of the ongoing education of Yuyachkani. Their theater no longer became 'about them' but about a more complex reflection on Peru's ethnic and cultural heterogeneity. They added members from these rural communities to their group; the actors learned Quechua; they trained in indigenous and mestizo performance practices that included singing, playing instruments, dancing, movement, and many other forms of popular expression. They expanded the notion of theater to include the popular fiesta that emphasized participation, thus blurring the distinction between actor and spectator. Performance, for Yuyachkani as for other popular theater groups, provided an arena for learning – but here it was Yuyachkani learning 'our first huaylars, pasacalle, and huayno dance steps ... between beers and warm food, we started to feel and maybe to understand the complexity of the Andean spirit.'[15] Performance did indeed offer enlightenment and inter-group under-standing – but Yuyachkani admits to having taken the first steps in learning about rural populations by participating in their cultural practices. According to Hugo Salazar del Alcazar, this was the first phase of Yuyachkani's development, which focussed primarily on political issues.[16]

Since those beginnings, Yuyachkani has continued to train in various linguistic and performance traditions to offer a deeper vision of what it means to 'be' Peruvian, one that reflects the cultural, temporal, geographical, historical and ethnic complexity of that articulation. There are many tenses involved in 'to be,' and various ways of situating the 'pre-' and 'post-'markers depending on who does the telling. For Yuyachkani, this performance includes the layering and juxtaposition of the diverse traditions, images, languages, and histories found in the country. Poised between a violent past that is never over and a future that seems hopelessly pre-scripted, their performances re-present images and scenarios that live and circulate in a variety of systems and forms – from the media, children's stories, martial arts, and silent movies, to indigenous myths.

This second phase of Yuyachkani's development, according to Salazar, focusses more on the cultural debates around 'lo nacional.' The group studied José María Arguedas's work on Andean myths and performances to understand the ancient traditions that persisted in contemporary cultural practices. A play such as *Los músicos ambulantes* (The Travelling Musicians, 1983) draws from the famous folktale *The Musicians of Bremen* and Arguedas's *Todas las sangres* to tell a humorous and beautiful story of homelessness, social injustice, and the importance of working together. In an aesthetically rich performance full of masked figures, music, dance and comic routines, the little red hen, the mangy dog, the wily cat, and the limp donkey realize that for all their differences and incompatibilities, they're better off together than apart. The play also works on different levels for different audiences. In one sense, the play is an important reflection on Peru's racial make-up. The dog represents the Creole Limeño, from the barrios altos or poor sectors of the city. The hen stands for the Afro-Peruvian populations. The cat comes from the *selva*, or the Peruvian Amazon valley, while the donkey represents the *cholo serrano*, the mestizo from the Andes. These figures, all of whom have been persecuted, beaten, and exploited, come together to rebel exuberantly against the *patrón*. The negotiation among them requires that they get to know each other – to recognize each other's strengths and what each contributes to the group. But it also requires that the group respect each member's individuality. On this, more personal level, the play summed up Yuyachkani's predicament at the time –

how, as Miguel Rubio asks, does the group allow each member to flourish individually without threatening the existence of the whole? Yet, even for those who do not get the racial or personal subtext of the performance, the play is enormously appealing – sparkling with humor, energy, music, and intelligence. This play rejoices in the fact of transculturation, for the only music these characters can create requires a bringing together of the various distinct elements and traditions. The music from the jungle harmonizes with that from the Andes, the coastal plains, and the Afro-Peruvian communities. The play's national and international popularity has enabled Yuyachkani to buy their cultural center – Casa Yuyachkani. Because this play is so well known, moreover, these characters can intervene in the national drama. When the economic situation in Peru gets particularly critical, the little red hen of the production (Ana Correa) performs an *'acto público'* by joining the line of retired people waiting for social security monies to complain about being penniless. *'Cómo como?'* (How am I to eat?) she demands impatiently, as she clucks and struts about. And Teresa Ralli, the mangy dog, visits children at an orphanage.

Yuyachkani has developed more troubled plays to think through the civil violence and the apparent impossibility of respectful co-existence in a country torn apart by injustice and rage. *Encuentro de zorros* (1985) draws from ancient myths of *'el zorro de arriba'* and *'el zorro de abajo'* preserved both in Peru's repertoire and archive.[17] The legend of the two foxes was already considered ancient when it was first written in the *Huarochirí Manuscript*, and it was reworked in Arguedas's famous *El zorro de arriba y el zorro de abajo* (1968). The foxes, symbols of change, appear in moments of extreme social crisis. In their first apparition, some 2,500 years ago, they met to decry social injustice. Their challenge, as they describe it, is to devour the world and create a new one. Yuyachkani uses the myth to again think through Peru's geographic, ethnic, and linguistic schisms – *el zorro de arriba* represents the populations from the Andean highlands, while *el zorro de abajo* typifies those from Lima's coastal region. The fractured country comes together once again in the violent throes of mass migration due to Peru's civil war of the 1980s and 1990s. Beggars, thieves, and drunken clairvoyants push a Mother Courage-type cart and offer a grim perspective on Peru's urban landscape. Rather than a respectful co-existence, these characters show a world devastated by criminal violence, displacement, and unemployment. The world is turned upside down, 'parents against children, children against parents, the living against the dead and the dead against the living.' *Retorno* (1996) shows the aftermath of Peru's 'dirty war.' People have been left stranded and disoriented; the villages destroyed, the harvest lands burnt. A re-envisioning of Beckett's *Waiting for Godot*, *Retorno* stages the despair and isolation of those who have nowhere to go. There is no going forward, no going back, no home to return to.

Two of Yuyachkani's best-known pieces — *Contraelviento* (1989) and *Adiós Ayacucho* (1990) — combine moments from Peru's remote and recent past to reflect on the transmission of traumatic social experience. Developed and performed during the conflict between the military and *Sendero luminoso*, these works specifically engage with the questions I posed earlier — how does the repertoire store and transmit social memory? Whose memories/traumas disappear if we privilege the archive over the repertoire of embodied experience/knowledge?

Contraelviento, one of Yuyachkani's largest and most spectacular pieces, re-enacts the testimony of an *indígena* survivor of a massacre in which peasants were forced off a cliff to their deaths. Coya, in a trance, revisits the scene of devastation. Her body shudders as she re-experiences the intrusive image. An entire community has been annihilated by armed forces. Is that vision an unsolicited re-apparition of a traumatic event situated firmly in the past? Is it a witnessing of an atrocious episode in the here and now? Is it the here, now, and always of a violent history of the exploitation and extermination of indigenous peoples? Is it a vision of a future catastrophe? The body responds to and communicates a violent occurrence that may be hard to locate temporally or spatially. Coya's sister and father listen to her testimony. They all understand that the approaching storm will scatter them. Huaco, raging against the violence she sees coming, joins the guerrillas, fighting fire with fire. Papai stays firm to his commitment to find the seeds of life by practicing ancient, invocational practices. Coya runs to the courts, hoping to find redress through the justice system. The judges — farcical, aged, bent figures with oversize hats — perform a vaudeville version of the pre-Conquest comic dance of 'los viejitos' and speak broken English. They pretend not to understand her. Her language, represented as flute music, needs to be translated by Peru's famous sell-out character, the *Felipillo*, translator to the conquerors: 'This woman says that she comes from far away to tell us that her ancestors have told her that the Caporal is killing them ... She says too that everyone's life is in great danger and that the seeds of life are being destroyed.' The judges dismiss her with a good beating — 'if that woman can't speak, it's because she has something to hide.' This scene elucidates several points in my argument: the courts, an 'archival,' document-producing system that in Latin America serves the interests of the powerful, cannot encompass or 'understand' pleas from the poor. (Official documents, records, and figures relating to genocidal practices hardly ever make it into the national archives.) Institutionalized circuits of memory and transmission keep the Europeanized sectors of the population walled off from the rural mestizo and indigenous populations. Expressions of trauma might just as well be delivered in a foreign tongue.

Contraelviento was performed at the peak of militarized conflict in Peru.

'Disappearances' and mass murder had become common political practice in Latin America during the 1970s and 1980s. How, Yuyachkani asked itself, can theater compete with or elucidate the theatricality of political violence? Miguel Rubio sums up the challenge: 'Nothing that you create on stage can be compared with what is happening in this country.'[18] Furthermore, the heightened spectacularity of political terrorism, as I argue elsewhere, forces potential witnesses to look away.[19] It blinds the very spectators that theater calls on 'to see.' What role do artists have when, as Adorno asks, genocide is part of our cultural heritage?[20]

In the most lyrical of forms, *Contraelviento* succeeds in posing the most urgent questions. How can indigenous and mestizo communities address genocidal policies and practices that are often not acknowledged by the national or international community? How can atrocity be 'remembered' and 'thought' when there are no external witnesses, or no recourse to the archive? What is the relationship between the theatrical representation of trauma and the traumatic 'repeat'? Whose memories disappear when scholars and activists fail to recognize the traces left by embodied knowledge?

Adiós Ayacucho takes the question of witnessing further – the dismembered victim of torture and 'disappearance' is forced to act as sole witness to his own victimization. As the play begins, the members of the audience see a ramp displaying a suit of clothing and candles laid out in a funerary ritual. Only as their eyes become accustomed to the dim light can they discern movement within a large black plastic bag behind the display. Little by little, a nameless, almost voiceless figure re-constitutes himself and breaks out of the bag. As he tells his story, his voice (at first almost non-human) begins to strengthen. He was tortured. His tormented body was cut into bits and discarded in a garbage bag, by the side of the road. In this crime without an external witness, and with no survivors, no one but he himself can demand that justice be served. No documents, photos, or gravestones attest to his annihilation. Only his bones, shoved in plastic, serve as archival 'proof' of an event that left no other material evidence. Only through performance can 'disappearance' be rendered visible.

Yet while no external witnesses exist in *Adiós Ayacucho*, the play affirms the vital role of what Dori Laub calls 'the witness from inside' or 'the witness to oneself.'[21] This witness from inside, though impossible according to Laub in the context of the Holocaust that 'made unthinkable the very notion that a witness could exist' (66), because it allowed for no 'outside,' no 'other,' is nonetheless posited as the only hope for justice in the Andean context. The victim reconstitutes himself by finding his scattered body parts. Little by little, he re-claims his human form. Finally he finds his face, finally he finds his voice that will proclaim the violence done to him and his community. He not only voices his denunciation, over and over again, but he determines to take a letter to the President of the Republic, outlining the violence he has suffered. This letter, finally, will make it into the archive, a testimony that even the President might acknowledge of the erasure of mestizo and indigenous populations. This haunting image from *Adiós Ayacucho* suggests the way in which Yuyachkani layers its approach to representing violence. The clothes laid out in memory of the dead re-presents the missing body of the victim of disappearance, even as it echoes an ancient burial practice. These practices are alive; other bodies will perform them just as the man fits himself back into the waiting clothes.

Yuyachkani's most recent production is the extraordinary one-woman *Antígona* (2000), acted by Teresa Ralli and directed by Miguel Rubio. The spectators readily follow the well-known story as Teresa Ralli acts out the various figures – Antigone, Ismene, Creon, Hermion, Theriseus, the messenger – using only a chair as a prop on the otherwise empty stage. Her exquisitely precise and eloquent movements transform her outfit, a simple tunic over a pant and bodice, into numerous costumes. With a clap of her hands she conjures up the various characters, pulling them out of the archive to incarnate Peru's current woes. Unlike others, such as Anouilh or Griselda Gambaro, however, Yuyachkani does not invoke Antigone primarily to tell of a state divided against itself. As both Miguel Rubio and Teresa Ralli tell it, no doubt this too would have been their rendition of the play if they had developed it in the 1980s. In the late 1990s, the issues have changed. Now in Peru, as in other countries dealing with the long-term effects of trauma, people struggle to come to terms with their own strategies to survive in a dehumanizing environment. Yuyachkani asked Peruvian poet, José Watanabe, to write a text based on their understanding of the play at the end of the twentieth century. Ismene, the sister who failed to act in defense of Antigone and her brother, becomes the narrator. She re-enacts the story, not as an outsider, looking back, but as a witness who had blinded herself through fear. 'This is my own story,' she says, as she belatedly assumes her role in the drama, apologizing to her sister and burying her brother. She promises to remember every day, as she re-enacts her story, again and again. Through performance, Ismene will complete the actions she could not undertake the first time around. *Antígona* offers the hope to those witnesses and participants who were unable to respond heroically in the face of atrocity. Their story continues. The fact that there is 'no over' attests to the continuing effects of trauma, but it also offers the opportunity of accepting one's responsibility, no matter how overdue.

These performance practices, whether drawn from age-old repertoires or marginalized traditions, continue to allow for immediate responses to current political problems. Every response to political violence carries with it a history of responses, conjured up from a vast range of embodied and archival memories. For Yuyachkani, performance is not about going back, but about keeping alive. Its mode of transmission is the repeat, the reiteration, the yet again of the twice-behaved behavior that Richard Schechner defines as 'performance.'[22] The violence of the past has not 'disappeared.' It has reappeared in the violent response against the miners' strike (1971), the massacre of Soccos (1986), in the displacement of local populations caught between *Sendero* and government forces, on the empty streets of Lima in the 1980s and early 1990s, torn and made strange by the violence. The remembering was always past, present, and seemingly future. As Rebeca Ralli puts it, their work represents the struggle for survival of the Peruvian people even as it represents their own struggle to survive both as individuals and as a group. 'We put up with so much just to be able to live, just to be able to create.'[23]

Yuyachkani's performances make visible a history of cumulative trauma, an unmarked and unacknowledged history of violent conflict. As in *Adiós Ayacucho*, the attempts at communicating an event that no one cares to acknowledge need to be repeated again and again. For members of traumatized communities, such as the Andean ones Yuyachkani engages, past violence blends into the current crisis. As in *Adiós Ayacucho*, trauma becomes transmitable, understandable, through performance – through the re-experienced shudder, the re-telling, the repeat.

The re-telling and re-enactment, however, pose problems of legitimacy. While the performances capture the ongoing nature of the violence against indigenous peoples, it complicates a historical accounting. What is time without progression? What is space without demarcation? What happens to a people's concept of history when markers are few, or known only through a performative repeat?

The undifferentiated, reiterative nature of Peru's traumatic history folds seamlessly with the Andean paradigm of memory (summed up in the Inkarrí cycle), which defies the fixity of a before and after. 'Inkarrí's dismembered body (whose severed head has been taken, variously, to Cusco, Lima or Spain) is coming together again, underground ... The lower world, region of chaos and fertility, becomes the source of the future, an extension of the belief that the dead return to present time and space during the growth season.'[24] Faced with the consciously deployed strategy of colonial dis-memberment, the myths offer the promise of re-membering: 'Perú es un país desmemorizado.' Who can say, after five hundred years of ongoing conquest and colonization, where the memory of trauma is situated, whether trauma affects 'the subject' or the entire collectively, if it is experienced belatedly or continually embodied, whether it resides in the archive or only in the repertoire, and how it passes from generation to generation? We only know from myths and stories that Peru's indigenous populations see themselves as the product of conquest and violence. Violence is not an event but a world-view and way of life.

Yuyachkani, it seems to me, intervenes in this problematic in two fundamental ways – one having to do with the transmission, the other with the role and function of witnessing.

In regard to the first: Yuyachkani understands the importance of performance as a means of re-membering and transmitting social memory. Its use of ethnically diverse performance traditions is neither decorative nor citational – that is, Yuyachkani does not incorporate them as add-ons to complement or 'authenticate' its own project. The group's commitment to enter into conversation with rural populations has led them to learn the languages, the music, and the performance modes of these communities. Rather than attempt to restore specific behaviors, that is re-creating museum pieces that somehow dislocate and replicate an 'original,' they follow the traditional usage of reactivating ancient practices to address current problems or challenges. Moreover, Yuyachkani does not participate in the reproduction and commodification of 'popular' culture. Their texts do not circulate. Other actors or companies do not perform their plays. The only way one can access their work is by participating in it – on the streets as bystander caught up in the action, in Casa Yuyachkani as spectator and discussant, or in the many workshops open to students from around the world. New, younger members are joining the group and they, too, are Yuyachkani. They will not act 'like' Yuyachkani, but 'be' Yuyachkani, adopting and adapting the character of the group itself. Their performances, just like the performances they draw from, are inseparable from them as people. The 'I' who thinks and remembers is the product of these collective pre- and post-colonial performances.

Furthermore, unlike groups that appropriate the performance practices of others, Yuyachkani's work does not separate the performances from their original audiences but, rather, tries to expand the audiences. The productions are not about 'them' – the indigenous and mestizo 'others' – but about all the different communities that share a territorial space defined by pre-Conquest groups, colonialism, and nationalism. Yuyachkani attempts to make their urban audiences culturally competent to recognize the multiple ways of being 'Peruvian.' In addressing Lima audiences, however, Yuyachkani feels it has to start 'from zero.'[25] The country's theatrical memory, much like its historical, cultural, and political memory, has been deracinated. These performances remind urban audiences of the populations they have forgotten. Storing and transmitting these traditions proves essential, because when they disappear, certain kinds of knowledges, issues, and populations disappear with them. These traditions – the street procession, fiestas, songs, masked characters – bring together criollo, mestizo, Afro-Peruvian, and indigenous expressive elements, each vital to the deeply complicated historical, ethnic, and racial configuration of the actual political situation. Performance provides the 'memory path,' the space of reiteration that allows people to replay the ancient struggles for recognition and power that continue to make themselves felt in contemporary Peru.

This brings us to a second point: looking at performance as a retainer of social memory engages history without necessarily being a 'symptom of history' – that is, the performances enter into dialogue with a history of trauma without themselves being traumatic. These are carefully crafted works that create a critical distance for 'claiming' experience and enabling, as opposed to 'collapsing,' witnessing.[26] This performance event has an 'outside,' which is what, according to Laub, allows for witnessing. Yuyachkani, as its name indicates, hinges on the notion of interconnectedness – the 'I' who thinks/ remembers is inextricable from the 'you' whose thought 'I' am. The 'I'/'you' of Yuyachkani promises to be a witness, a guarantor of the link between the 'I' and the 'you,' the 'inside' and the 'outside.' Yuyachkani becomes the belated witnesses to the ongoing, unacknowledged drama of atrocity, and asks their audience to do the same. For this reason, no doubt, Yuyachkani was awarded the highest national honor for human rights in 1999. The group's practice points to a radically different conclusion than the one Adorno arrived at in 'Commitment.' Representation, for Yuyachkani, does not further contribute to the desecration of the victims, turning their pain into our viewing pleasure.[27] Rather, without representation, viewers would not recognize their role in the ongoing history of oppression which, directly or indirectly, implicates them. Who, *Adiós Ayachuco* asks, will take on the responsibility of witnessing? The hope offered by *Antígona* is that the spectator, like Ismene, will say 'I.' The witness, like Boal's 'spect-actor,' accepts the dangers and responsibilities of seeing and of acting on what one has seen. And witnessing is transferable – the theater, like the testimony, like the photograph, film or report, can make witnesses of others. The (eye-)witness sustains both the archive and the repertoire. So rather than think of performance primarily as the ephemeral, as that which disappears, Yuyachkani insists on creating a community of witnesses by and through performance. The group counters the performance-as-disappearance model of colonialism that pushes autochthonous practices into the oblivion of the ephemeral, the unscripted, the understudied, the uncontrollable. For many of these communities, on the contrary, when performance ends, so does the shared understanding of social life and collective memory. Performances such as these fiestas, testimony, and theatrical productions warn us not to dismiss the 'I' who remembers, who thinks, who is a product of collective thought. They teach communities not to look away.

As the name Yuyachkani suggests, attention to the interconnectedness between thinking subjects and subjects of thought would allow for a broader understanding of historical trauma, communal memory, and collective subjectivity.

This piece, of course, is destined for the archive.

NOTES

1. Hugo Salazar del Alcazar, 'Los músicos ambulantes,' *La escena latinoamericana*, número 2, Agosto 1989, 23.
2. Thomas A. Abercrombie, *Pathways of Memory and Power: Ethnography and History Among an Andean People* (Madison: University of Wisconsin Press, 1998, 6).
3. Gisela Canepa, public lecture. Hemispheric Institute of Performance and Politics, University of Rio de Janeiro, July 2000.
4. Bernardino de Sahagún, *Florentine Codex*, edited and translated by Arthur J. O. Anderson and Charles E. Dibble (Santa Fe, New Mexico: School of American Research and University of Utah, 1982). Book 1, Introductions and Indices, Prologue to Book 1, 45.
5. See Steven Mullanay's *The Place of the Stage* (Ann Arbor: University of Michigan Press, 1988) for an analysis of 'the spectacle of strangeness' and the politics of repudiation (particularly Ch. 3, 'The Rehearsal of Cultures').
6. Bernardino de Sahagún, *Florentine Codex*, edited and translated by Arthur J. O. Anderson and Charles E. Dibble (Santa Fe, New Mexico: School of American Research and University of Utah, 1982). Book 1, Introductions and Indices, 36–7.
7. Again, let me stress that this repudiation of practices under examination cannot be limited to archival documentation. As Barbara Kirshenblatt-Gimblett makes clear in *Destination Culture* (Berkeley, CA: California University Press, 1998), exhibitions, model villages, and other forms of 'live' display often do the same. We need not polarize the relationship between these different kinds of knowledge to acknowledge that they have often proved antagonistic in the struggle for cultural survival or supremacy.
8. See, for example, the essays in the issue 'Performance, Identity, and Historical Consciousness in the Andes,' ed. Mark Rogers, *Journal of Latin American Anthropology*, Vol. 3, No. 2, 1998, especially the essay by Mark Rogers, 'Spectacular Bodies: Folkorization and the Politics of Identity in Ecuadorian Beauty Pageants.'
9. Ernest Renan, 'What Is a Nation?,' in Homi Bhabha (ed.), *Nation and Narration* (London: Routledge, 1990, 11).
10. Personal interview, Paucartambo, Peru, July, 1999.
11. The anti-star sentiment was of course often contradicted in the group's make-up with the director functioning as leader and even guru. See Yolanda Gonzalez-Broyles's study on the Teatro Campesino as an example.

12. Diana Taylor, *Theatre of Crisis: Drama and Politics in Latin America* (Lexington: University of Kentucky Press, 1990, Ch. 1).

13. Miguel Rubio, 'Encuentro con el Hombre Andino,' *Grupo Cultural Yuyachkani, Allpa Rayku: Una experiencia de teatro popular* (Lima: Edición del 'Grupo Cultural Yuyachkani' y Escuelas Campesinas de la CCP, 2nd edition, 1985, 9).

14. *Ibid.*

15. In Brenda Luz Cotto-Escalera, 'Grupo Cultural Yuyachkani: Group Work and Collective Creation in Contemporary Latin American Theatre,' unpublished dissertation (Austin: University of Texas, 1995, 116).

16. Hugo Salazar del Alcazar, interview in *Persistencia de la Memoria*, documentary video on Yuyachkani.

17. 'Encuentro de zorros' was based on a text by José María Arguedas entitled 'El zorro de arriba y el zorro de abajo' and was co-written by the group and Peter Elmore. 'Adiós Ayacucho' was based on a text by the same name by Julio Ortega.

18. In Cotto-Escalera, 'Grupo Cultural Yuyachkani', 156.

19. Diana Taylor, *Disappearing Acts: Spectacles of Gender and Nationalism in Argentina's 'Dirty War'* (Durham: Duke University Press, 1997).

20. Theodor Adorno, 'Commitment,' in Ernst Bloch and Ronald Taylor (eds), *Aesthetics and Politics* (London: Verso, 1977, 189).

21. Dori Laub, 'Truth and Testimony: The Process and the Struggle,' in Cathy Caruth (ed.), *Trauma: Explorations in Memory* (Baltimore, OH: Johns Hopkins University Press, 1995, 66).

22. Richard Schechner, *Between Theater and Anthropology* (Philadelphia: University of Pennsylvania Press, 1985).

23. Interview, Rebeca Ralli, Casa Yuyachkani, June, 1996.

24. Rowe and Schelling, *Memory and Modernity* (London: Verso, 1991, 55).

25. Rubio, *Allpa Rayku*, quoted in Cotto-Escalera, 115.

26. See Cathy Caruth's *Unclaimed Experience* (Baltimore, OH: Johns Hopkins University Press, 1997) and Dori Laub's notion of the 'collapse of witnessing' in 'Truth and Testimony,' 65.

27. Adorno, 'Commitment.'

4

Re-imagining the stage: tradition and transformation in Native theater

Jaye T. Darby

The stage is dark, lights slowly rise and a spiritual leader and traditional dancers come on to transform the stage into a sacred space, creating an aura of spirituality that will remain for the duration of the performance. Later in the production, a bare-footed young man dressed in black shorts and a tank top performs a new rendition of the fancy dance. He does scoops, dives, squats, dips, twists, leaps, and pirouettes which follow an intricate choreographed pattern. At the end, as the dancer freezes in a stylized pose, his performance has deconstructed mainstream perceptions of Native performing arts as folkloric and has taken back the stage from centuries of mainstream social constructions of Indianness and cultural stereotypes. It is 1997 in the high-speed world of Southern California at the California Center for the Arts in Escondido. Tradition and transformation co-exist in a dynamic performance of the American Indian Dance Theatre, under the direction of Hanay Geiogamah.

This production, as do others by contemporary Native theater artists, exemplifies a creative process – re-imagining – which has been taking hold in the Native theater creative community since the 1970s.[1] Re-imagining, which I will explore in this chapter, is a creative approach that negotiates new artistic spaces and integrates political, cultural, aesthetic, and spiritual dimensions. I first briefly locate discussions of this direction in Native theater within broader historical and intercultural issues. I then discuss efforts by Native playwrights Hanay Geiogamah, Kiowa-Delaware; Marcie Rendon, White Earth Anishinaabe; William Yellow Robe, Jr., Assiniboine/Nakota; and Drew Hayden Taylor, Ojibway to re-imagine theater in terms of both traditional performance and contemporary transformation.

Lloyd Kiva New, Cherokee artist and the first president of the Institute for American Indian Arts, recently reiterated the reciprocal relationship between art and culture, one that remains a contested site in Native American arts and theater studies. New particularly challenges Western efforts to dismiss Native traditional art forms simply as crafts or community activities and to deny the vitality of the arts in traditional Native societies. He argues that this problem is one of categorization between three distinctive Western disciplinary 'categories of Art, Science, and Religion,' on the one hand, and the Native integration of 'a wide range of creative expressions (the Arts) to give meaning to all aspects of their lives,' on the other (2000: 9).

New's point is particularly pertinent to discussions of recent developments in Native theater, beginning in the 1960s, which is sometimes construed as Western literary theater with Native themes.[2] New argues instead that 'Theater' existed in traditional communities well before European encounter: 'Dance, music and creation myths came together in dramatization of the spirituality of Native Americans and their relationships with their universe: Earth, Sun, Sky and a panoply of supernatural go-betweens. Storyline, Music, Costumes, Lighting (firelight), Performers and Audience all came together in ways that would equate to Theater in today's terms' (2000: 10). While recognizing the unique differences among Native peoples, Paula Gunn Allen in her seminal book *The Sacred Hoop: Recovering the Feminine in American Indian Traditions* articulates the richness of the oral tradition in Native cultures, which included Creation stories, tribal narratives, songs, music, dance, and ceremonies, as an integrated tradition of performance and literature that spans thousands of years before European encounter (1986: 54–101).

INTERCULTURALISM AND SOCIAL CONSTRUCTIONS OF INDIANNESS

While Native peoples trace their origins back to Creation stories, which vary from group to group, the European (mis)naming and (mis)representation of the original inhabitants began with the arrival of Christopher Columbus and his mistaken geography, resulting in the designation 'Indians' from the Spanish *los indios.* And as the history of Native images attests, the names and constructions of the Europeans, and later European Americans, have dominated mainstream American history, popular culture, and the media, not the names and descriptions Native communities give themselves. As Robert Berkhofer suggests in *The White Man's Indian,* dominant perceptions until the 1970s have viewed Indians as one monolithic group, not as many nations with unique cultures and histories; a variant of either good (noble) or bad (blood thirsty) savage; and a general assessment of deficiency in terms of European values and standards (4–111). Implicated in these early European notions of 'Indianness' are colonial constructions of dominance and legitimacy fueled by Spanish, English, and French conquests.[3]

Furthering compounding these views of Indians, as Philip J. Deloria discusses in *Playing Indian*, enacting Indianness has played a determining role in shaping American consciousness and constructions of American identity, modeling 'a characteristically American kind of domination in which the exercise of power was hidden, denied, qualified, or mourned,' and serving as 'an equally opaque vision of power' (1998: 187). According to Deloria, a defining moment was the Boston Tea Party. Dressing up as Indians and embodying their notions of Indianness as outside the law, the American revolutionaries enacted a sense of freedom and difference as an act of redefinition against the King and British rule as they hurled tea into Boston Harbor. And playing Indian with its inherent contradictions and contests of power, from this point on, according to Deloria, far from simply occurring on the stage, continues to be performed in all aspects of American life and remains 'one of the foundations (slavery and gender relations being two others) for imagining and performing domination and power in America' (1998: 186). Thus, in the eighteenth and nineteenth centuries, as numerous nations fought to keep their lands, Deloria states: 'The reality of native resistance, however, came to be defined through the ascendant ideology of the vanishing Indian,' that asserted 'Indians had a predestined doom, and that knowledge helped erase or justify the later military campaigns against them' (186–7). In the twentieth century, the mainstream media often perpetuated this insidious construction – vanishing, vanished, now invisible.

In the academy, constructions of Indianness – especially those supporting deficiency and invisibility – have too often been reproduced by what Henry Louis Gates, Jr. calls 'the paradigm of disciplinary essentialism: imagining the boundaries of disciplines as hermetic, imagining our architectures of knowledge as natural or organic' (1992: 115) and the dominance of contemporary Western theories, scholarship, and aesthetics, which tend to privilege secular and ideological interpretations and limit what constitutes as spiritual knowledge or even art. Sharing similar questions raised by Barbara Christian and Tey Diana Rebolledo about African American and Chicana/o works, leading Native scholars and authors Paula Gunn Allen, Laguna Pueblo, and Elizabeth Cook-Lynn, Santee/Yankton Dakota, express particular concern in Native studies about critical approaches that distort, obfuscate, marginalize, or even colonize the work of Native artists and writers.[4]

Scholarship that privileges written literary traditions, critic-driven analysis, ideological interpretations, and postmodern views of discourse are particularly problematic for approaching works that are grounded in oral traditions, including many forms of Native theater, which stress the inherent power and meaning of words and performance. In the oral tradition, according to Paula Gunn Allen, no binary opposition exists between literature and performance as in twentieth-century Western criticism. Rather, both are holistically integrated in storytelling, dance, music, song, ritual, and ceremony (1986: 60–3). In some ways, then, while vastly different in form today, Native theater and literature have their epistemological, aesthetic, and spiritual roots in the same oral tradition. Therefore, Gunn Allen calls for scholarship that centers the work within the traditions, epistemologies, narratives, and perspectives of Native communities and what's at stake in the specific work(s) involved. In addition, she gives equal weight to the creative and academic (54–75). Generating this kind of nuanced, contextualized scholarship poses no small challenge given the diversity of Native nations, histories, narrative and performance traditions, cultural and spiritual perspectives, and intercultural encounters and interplays. Yet this challenge is especially pertinent for scholars, particularly those from different cultural backgrounds, such as myself, in order to avoid com-pounding this long history of constructions of Indianness, stereotypes, and misperceptions.[5] This approach is supported by a cognitive view of culture, which R. A. LeVine identifies 'as a shared organization of ideas that includes the intellectual, moral, and aesthetic standards prevalent in a community and the meanings of communicative actions' (1986: 67).

RESPONSE – RE-IMAGINING

It is against this historical background that recent proponents of Native theater since the 1960s reclaim and take charge of their stage. While the Red Power movement did not create this rise of contemporary Native theater, it did open up spaces. Unlike the Civil Rights movement, which called for equal rights under the law, the Red Power movement's emphasis was on sovereignty, the recognition of treaty rights, and the unique government-to-government rights American Indians and Canadian Natives have in the United States and Canada as nations within a nation. But sovereignty was not an isolated political goal. Integral to calls for sovereignty were calls for cultural autonomy. Inés Hernández-Ávila articulates this important point: 'Sovereignty encompasses the cultural, spiritual, economic, and political aspects of the life of the communities and of the individuals who comprise them' (1995: 492). Pressured by Native activists, tribal leaders, and communities, Congress finally passed the Indian Self-Determination and Education Assistance Act of 1975 (Public Law 93–638), giving individual nations more autonomy over tribal community and education programs, which was later followed in 1978 by the signing of the American Indian Religious Freedom Act (Public Law 95–341), important legislation for Native religious and cultural expressions (Fixico 486–92).

Thus, Native theater today has many expressions – from the hard-hitting grittiness of Bruce King, Oneida, to the poetic lyricism of Diane Glancy,

Cherokee – and often defies categories, as the work continues to evolve as an art form. Reviewing this multiplicity of performance traditions is well beyond the scope of this essay. Rather, I want to focus on one direction in Native theater, 're-imagining.' Like 'third wave' Native fiction that simultaneously embeds ancient ritual traditions from the oral tradition, integrates them with contemporary forms of Native and Western expressions, and explores current experiences, re-imagined Native theater goes one step further and re-integrates performance and narration on the stage. In doing so, such theater pieces usher in a 'fourth wave' of Native work. According to Paula Gunn Allen in her introduction to *Song of the Turtle*, 'first wave' Native writing, which dominated the first half of the twentieth century, focussed primarily on mainstream publishers' constructions of Indianness, especially the vanishing Native, and often reinscribed mainstream society's message of death and dying. In the 1970s a shift occurred, and 'defining characteristics of second wave' writing included 'a sense of renewal and hope; reasserted often deeply angry, Native identity; and incorporation of ritual elements in both structure and content drawn from the ceremonial traditions' (1996: 8). Gunn Allen argues that questions of identity in the second wave tend to center around victimization, and often the 'Native protagonist was also required to "fall between cultural chairs,"' caught between the two worlds of mainstream society and traditional Native life (10). However, for the most part, first and second wave work follows a more Western narrative structure, and Native life remains primarily on the margin.

Third wave fiction, exemplied by N. Scott Momaday's Pulitzer Prize-winning novel, *House Made of Dawn* (1968), and by more contemporary works by Louise Erdrich and Sherman Alexie, change both the locus and form of the narrative from European American perspectives to tribal ones, utilize Native ceremonial traditions, including mythic forms that move beyond linear time and space, and fuse them with contemporary issues and styles. Fourth wave Native work as I suggest in this chapter moves third wave literary considerations of tradition and transformation from the page to the stage. As Gunn Allen points out, these waves of work are not necessarily chronological but rather represent 'significantly different approaches,' all of which are still being employed by Native writers (1996: 14). Because of their performative elements, works of Native theater belong primarily in the second, third, fourth waves, but they are not a perfect fit. Often works blend characteristics of two waves. Furthering complicating these issues are the multiplicities of Native theater expressions, which do not fall neatly into any of these categories.

By way of example of fourth wave work, which spans several decades in Native theater beginning in the 1970s, I have selected a diverse range of plays: *49* by Hanay Geiogamah, *SongCatcher* by Marcie Rendon, *The Independence of*

Eddie Rose by William Yellow Robe, Jr., and *alterNatives* by Drew Hayden
Taylor. While very different in approach, each playwright reconceptualizes the
theatrical experience by re-imagining the terms of theater – the purpose, space,
narrative traditions, and vocabulary. Certainly, as the earlier description of the
American Indian Dance Theatre attests, re-imagining is not limited to these
four productions. In a recent essay, Ann Haugo provides a thoughtful
description of two other examples – *1992: Blood Speaks* by Elvira and Hortensia
Colorado, Chichimec/Otomi, and *Power Pipes* by Spiderwoman Theater, Kuna/
Rappahannock. Collaboratively developed and performed, these two innovative pieces transform colonial patriarchal structures, reclaim female agency to
heal, and ceremonially restore contemporary Native women to the sacred
circle. I believe that discussions of this broad range of works open up a
dialogue about the complexity and artistry that Native theater affords.

The power of re-imagination in these works comes from Native conceptions
of 'the way of the imagination,' described by Paula Gunn Allen as 'the way of
continuity, circularity, completeness.' This is in contrast to the Western 'way of
the intellect' as 'the way of segmentation, discontinuity, linearity' (1987: 563).
Embedded in this conception of imagination is an acknowledgment of the
wholeness and sacred connectedness of all life. Creation stories, while varying
from group to group, share a common view of humans and animals as co-
creators with the Creator. In the Cheyenne tradition, for example, according to
Gunn Allen, Maheo, the All Spirit, calls on the animals to help create the rest
of the world. She explains, 'For the American Indian, the ability of all creatures
to share in the process of ongoing creation makes all things sacred' (1986: 57).
Thus, conceptions of imagination, creation, and creative process that inform
these plays are understood in this deep sense of sacred generation.

Re-imagining also confronts mainstream tendencies to view Native tradition
as something static and inherently frozen, belonging in a museum. Rather, such
a view of theater is grounded in ancient conceptions of ritual that
simultaneously perpetuate and transform. Central to maintaining balance and
harmony at all levels from the tribal to the cosmic are Native ritual and
ceremony, traditional components of Native performance. According to
Kenneth Morrison, 'Whatever the symbolic orientation to the world's persons,
Native American ritual action aims for balance, cooperation, and mutual
interdependence' (1994: 639). This process is inherently dynamic. Consequently, such views do not constrain Native peoples to the past. Rather, as
Paula Gunn Allen writes, 'We are ritual, sacred-centered peoples who reside
equally in the modern and the ancient worlds. Liminality is our chronic state,
and transformation is our daily enterprise' (1996: 11). Or as Monique Mojica,
Kuna/Rappahannock, explains about Native artists: 'We are fertile minds from
a living culture – ancient as well as contemporary' (1991: 3).

In each theater piece, the playwrights make what Paula Gunn Allen calls a 'post-Columbian move,' in which they change location from the Western world to the tribal world, shifting from a 'Western definition to Native definition of whatever it may be – ambivalent, ugly, sacred, embedded in a Native community – multivocal' (1998a). Native people take center stage, and the White world, if present, is seen against the normative position of a tribe or community. By centering the work on living Natives and their experiences, whether the young people at a 49, a post-powwow party, in Oklahoma, an urban couple in an inner-city apartment in Minnesota, a brother and aunt struggling to keep a family together on a Plains reservation, or three upwardly mobile twentysomething Ojibways at a dinner party in Toronto, each of these productions confers the status of subject to the Native characters involved and gives back the power of story and performance. In doing so, each one also takes back the stage from centuries of stereotypical performances on North American stages and in the media and, equally important, from the multiple instances of 'playing Indian' that permeate North American life. From this creative move and the myriad possibilities for Native artistic expression arise both the excitement of this theater and many of the complexities for mainstream audiences and critics.

This theatrical process of re-imagining is inherently traditional and transformative, as complementary, not oppositional elements. As Linda Jenkins and Ed Wapp, Jr. point out, Native theater companies have been 'influenced by literary drama styles, but through them may be seen the workings of Indian ways, consciousness, values, traditions, stories and conventions' (1976: 12). While often contemporary in content, Native theater that re-imagines draws on ancient traditional conceptions of story, communal structures, performance, ritual, and ceremony and their multiplicities in terms of the diverse Native communities. As I will discuss in more detail, *49*, *SongCatcher*, *The Independence of Eddie Rose*, and *alterNatives*, while taking very different approaches, transform contemporary theater through a reworking of performance, narrative, spiritual, and aesthetic elements drawn from the oral tradition.

Fourth wave Native theater, like other forms of Native writing that have their roots in Creation stories and the oral tradition, draws on Native ritual transformation to achieve wholeness as well as on more contemporary efforts of self-determination and ongoing cultural creation. In doing so, the playwrights assume responsibility to use words and performance in 'good' or healing ways. As Joseph Bruchac explains, 'Our abilities as writers – as novelists and poets, playwrights and essayists – are a gift given to us by the Creator. It is our obligation to return that gift, to make use of it in a way that serves the people and the generations to come' (1998: xix). Thus, the purposes of Native theater in such productions as *49, SongCatcher, The Independence of Eddie Rose,* and *alterNatives* are not mimetic in the Western tradition or fragmented in recent modernist and postmodernist endeavors, but rather experiential, communal, integrative, and healing. As Joy Harjo explains, 'In our tribal cultures the power of language to heal, to regenerate, and to create is understood' (Harjo and Bird, 1997: 21). By embodying these older traditions based on healing, community, integration, and responsibility while addressing contemporary Native experiences, each production affirms life and thereby re-imagines one of the most powerful master narratives in American history and in the media – that of a vanishing race.

In discussing the vision of the Native American Theater Ensemble, Hanay Geiogamah recounts its transformative purpose: 'The stage therefore seemed to offer Indians – provided only that they could control it – a means of self-realization and of presenting culturally authentic images of themselves' (1980: 4). Originally produced for an American Indian audience in Oklahoma City on January 10, 1975, *49* reflects this intertribal orientation, drawing on the Plains and Navajo traditions, as well as Geiogamah's commitment to culturally authentic performance elements.[6] In the early workshopping of *49* as musical theater at La MaMa in New York along the lines of *Hair* or *Godspell,* Geiogamah realized that the inherent spirituality in the piece pushed well beyond mainstream conceptions of popular musical comedy (personal interview, November 23, 1994). Geiogamah and the members of the Native American Theater Ensemble worked collaboratively to develop *49* into a ceremonial theater piece in which the central theatrical vocabulary draws on Native performance traditions of ceremony, ritual, storytelling, dance, music, and song through two distinctive frames: alternating scenes between Night Walker and the Young People of the past in the late 1800s and the Young People of today at a 49. The White world is represented only through police voices and lights as the police try to stop the 49. This fusion arguably makes *49* the first work of fourth wave Native theater.

While respectful of those sacred ceremonies that belong only in tribal contexts, the performance turns on Night Walker's vision quest to help the Young People maintain their cultures, theatrically realizing the power of vision in Plains life. In the first production, the embodiment of Night Walker by a fully qualified spiritual leader, Gerald Bruce Miller, Skokomish, reclaimed the stage as a sacred space. The production countered stereotypical conceptions of Native ritual, popular in the 1970s, which Geiogamah defined as something perceived to be 'mechanical, something that you can diagram and codify' (personal interview, December 6, 1994). In addition, as the actor/spiritual leader purified the space for the vision quest, he was actually purifying the stage and making it a sacred circle for the duration of the production, a tradition Geiogamah continues today with performances of the American Indian Dance Theatre.

The spirit world evoked onstage in Night Walker's vision in Scene 3 leads him to the understanding that, even in the face of terrible adversity, 'We will live and walk together for a long time. All of us will live and walk together for a long time' (1999: 206). Based on this vision, which sets the rest of the piece in motion, he brings the Young People of the past together in a circle and ceremonially prepares them for the darkness that he sees coming at the end of the late 1800s in terms of almost complete cultural annihilation. He thereby lays the foundation for their descendents – the Young People of today – to stand up to the police and reclaim their heritage. In Scene 6, the staging evokes both this devastating vision of death through projected images of buffalo skeletons and the more powerful vision of life through Night Walker's giveaway of gifts of cultural continuity: 'a drum, a fan, feathers,' followed by the Young People joined together in a round dance (1999: 210). As a healing ceremony, scene after scene like this one responds to the devastating effects of the U.S. government's educational policies and the larger society's attitudes towards Indian children, who had been and often continue to be cut off from their rich cultural heritages through assimilationist goals and policies encouraging cultural eradication.

Staging *49* on the same sacred ground as Night Walker's vision quest ties it to the past and locates it within a specific geographic location, on the WhiteHorse family's grounds, about 45 miles from Rainy Mountain, sacred to the Kiowa people, and within a ceremonial circle on stage. Through synchronic and diachronic time shifts between the alternating scenes with the Young People of the past and those of the present at the 49, all played by the same actors, and the later fusion of the two groups into one onstage, the performance of *49* moves the audience from temporal time into mythic time and into the tribal world of circularity and wholeness, away from the Western world of linearity and fragmentation, signaled by the disembodied police lights and voices.

Onstage during Scenes 8, 10, and 12, Night Walker, Singing Man and Weaving Woman, and the arbor ceremony re-enact the traditional transmission of knowledge by elders and render visible the power of storytelling, song, dance, ritual, and ceremony in the Plains tradition. The stage space becomes a site of community, continuance, and renewal when the entire cast joins in a song that Singing Man helps the young man learn, and later the Young People ceremonially engage in rededicating the arbor, the sacred center of the tribe, with Night Walker. Just as the lost children in the parable Night Walker tells are found, so are the young 49ers metaphorically found as they stand up to the police, their bodies forming a beautiful bird of solidarity near the end of the play, driving the police lights off the stage.

The performance ends as ritual elements coalesce to send the Young People on the stage and those in the audience into a future of possibilities, one grounded in the experiential knowledge that 'We are a tribe!' (1999: 225). In a direct address to all the young people present, Night Walker stands alone in the sacred circle and affirms their new-found strength. Then, in an elaborately choreographed climactic moment, the lighting and sound signal a storm as Night Walker chants an affirmation for tribal continuity and spins his bull-roarer, each spin thrusting a young person into the sacred circle. He then guides the Young People in forming their own circle and blesses them once more. As the Young People leave the stage together, now united as a tribal community, they sing 'The Pollen Road Song' and summon forth the power of Navajo Beauty Way. They thereby bless and purify the road and, in doing so, make the roadways in life good for everybody on the stage and in the audience. Night Walker remains onstage and faces the audience, acknowledging for the last time their participation in this healing ceremony. He then exits. As the lights slowly fade, the arbor remains lit on center stage, a visual affirmation of Native spirituality and intergenerational continuity. In the face of Brother Death, *49*'s theatrical response is life: life through the stories, the songs, the ceremonies, and communal values.

SONGCATCHER

Marcie Rendon's *SongCatcher*, subtitled *A Native Perspective on Frances Densmore, Ethnomusicologist*, was produced in 1998 by The Great American History Theatre. *SongCatcher* also draws on the ceremonial performance tradition. However, in this case, rather than an inter-tribal emphasis, Rendon locates her work within Ojibwe traditions, especially those surrounding sacred Midé songs in the 'Midéwiwin, or the Great Medicine Society' (Vizenor, 1984: 26). Like *49*, the performance opens in the past with Spirit Woman moving through an Ojibwe camp at night in the 1800s, singing bits of songs to individuals in Ojibwe.[7] The staging of the traditional encampment filled with Spirit Woman's songs provides a geographic and spiritual landscape on stage and grounds the performance in the sacred homeland and ancestral voices of the people, connections that continue throughout the production as she sings to those living today.

In the next scene, set in an inner-city apartment, Jack, a young Ojibwe man, and Chris, his girlfriend, are indicative of over 50 percent of Native Americans living in urban areas, many pushed to the cities through relocation policies. Chris has managed to maintain her cultural ties, but Jack's sharpness with Chris suggests he is displaced from the past, particularly the traditional method of learning the songs from Spirit Woman and in dreams. Impatient with Bill, his friend who is an elder, and Chris's urging for him to wait to receive his song, he seeks an outside source, a book and tape from the anthropologist Frances Densmore, who had recorded a number of songs, including sacred Midé songs.

The rest of the performance returns Ojibwe cultural authority and interrogates the privilege of anthropology to define the Ojibwe people as well as Densmore's cultural misappropriation of sacred material. Just as the form of 49 turns around the power of a vision quest in Plains traditions, *SongCatcher* theatrically sanctions the importance of dreams and assistance from the spirit world in finding knowledge and songs in the Ojibwe tradition. As Vizenor explains, 'Tribal words have power in the oral tradition, the sounds express the spiritual energies of woodland lives' (1984: 24).

Spirit Woman repeatedly comes on stage to try to give Jack his song in the traditional way, but he repeatedly rebuffs her attempts and ignores Chris's warning about the dangers of using Frances Densmore's book. Then Spirit Woman, Old Man Spirit, and the spirits of Frances, her mother, her sister Margaret, and friend Lizzie inhabit the stage and intrude on Jack's life, fill his dreams, and finally, rendered visible, occupy the apartment. The dream sequences juxtapose Frances's collection of songs with those of the Dakota, Winnebago, and Ojibwe.

Thus, the stage world of *SongCatcher* integrates the dreaming and the waking, the spiritual and physical. It is through the embodied presence of dreams and ceremony on stage that the destructive history of Densmore's work becomes manifest. As Jack becomes more and more intertwined with Frances's spirit, a spiritual imbalance permeates his life and the apartment. Out of work, he fights with Chris. The performance culminates in Bill performing a healing ceremony. As the actor playing Bill prays in Ojibwe, the stage becomes a sacred space. Old Man Spirit and Spirit Woman stand by Bill, now an Ojibwe elder in the past, who prays to cleanse Frances Densmore's misappropriation of sacred Midé songs and the subsequent reprisals for Main'gans, who sang the songs for Frances, now played by Jack. Spirit Woman's song fills the stage with the power and continuity of the sacred songs. After the ceremony, Jack is finally able to hear Spirit Woman sing, receives his song, and joins her onstage, the two side by side, semiotically offering intergenerational continuity and cultural continuance through tradition and song.

THE INDEPENDENCE OF EDDIE ROSE

An enrolled member of the Assiniboine tribe who make their home on the Fort Peck Reservation in Montana, William Yellow Robe, Jr. writes that he had a 'very simple' goal for working in theater: 'I wanted the name of my family, my relatives and my people to be heard. "Assiniboine." That was it. It was my way of telling this country: "See, we are still alive"' (1999a: 41).

The Independence of Eddie Rose, which premiered in 1986 at the University of Montana, provides a new form of Native social activist theater that transforms expectations of traditional Western naturalism through the enactment of Native narrative forms and focusses on issues of survival facing young Indians. In this case, the production probes highly dysfunctional family relations, alcoholism, and violence that often dominate reservation life as a result of despair, privations, and extreme poverty.

While initially somewhat reminiscent of Maxim Gorky's *Lower Depths* and nineteenth-century naturalism, *The Independence of Eddie Rose* quickly changes the terms of the work. For while the audience encounters the characters Bobby and his Aunt Thelma struggling against a hostile environment, far from victims in the Darwinian sense, they are active agents who have control over the environment and through choices can and indeed do change their lives. This shift resonates with the powerful sense of agency inherent in the Native traditional origin stories. As Louis Owens explains: 'According to the Darwinian origin myth, as conveyed to the modern mind through the vehicle of naturalism, powerless humanity inhabits a world antithetical to that evoked in the Native American origin myths in which men and women share responsibility for the creation and care of the world' (1992: 234). While this work is not based on any particular origin story, the performance rests on the re-enactment of these tribal values of spirituality, responsibility and care. For a modern-day re-creation of the world takes place onstage during the performance as the characters move out of a world of incest, violence, and alcoholism in the opening scenes into a new world they help create.

The dysfunction in the Rose home on stage reflects a deep spiritual imbalance. In the early scenes, Bobby and his sister Theia's mother drinks and parties, focussing on her own needs and desires, not her children's and the community's. As in *49* and *SongCatcher*, an enactment of a traditional ritual on stage furthers the performance and transforms the terms of the work from tragedy to one of potential healing. Recognizing that the 'house is dead' (Yellow Robe, Jr., 1999b: 74), Aunt Thelma, in a climatic point, prays with sage. She then assumes the traditional role of an elder and teaches Bobby to wash himself with the smoke and to pray to protect himself from the spiritual death of his alcoholic mother's, Katherine's, lifestyle. Together on stage, they ritually enact the possibility for transformation.

The performance, however, does not spare the audience the horrifying violence of Theia, a young girl, brutally attacked by Lenny, her mother's boyfriend, indicative of child abuse that too often results from the breakdown of traditional values. Yet, rather than having tragic consequences, this vicious act catapults Eddie and Aunt Thelma into a final conclusion and subsequent action: Katherine Rose in her present alcoholic condition is an unfit mother, and new family alliances must be formed, alliances offered through Aunt Thelma's traditional ways and reservation social services. No longer co-dependent, and now fortified by traditional values, at the end of the performance, Eddie confronts his mother and claims his independence by telling her that he wants his life back, asking her to sign complaint papers against Lenny for brutalizing his sister and custody papers for Bobby and Theia to live with Aunt Thelma.

In this effort to save his sister and himself, by physically confronting his mother, Eddie rejects the brutality in his life and his mother's alcoholism. In the face of intense violence, Bobby and Aunt Thelma claim agency and power to create a new community and family arrangements based on love, care, protection, and spiritual balance. Bobby's offer to pray in the traditional way for Katherine and Theia at the end of the play affirms the spiritual 'relational laws in the universe' that seek 'collective order in the face of individualistic chaos' (Morrison, 1994: 640). Eddie, Theia, and Aunt Thelma can be a family and with help, perhaps, Katherine can join them. The performance of *The Independence of Eddie Rose* thereby reasserts the deeper meaning of the Assiniboine community and the spiritual tradition of healing and integration.

alterNATIVES

Drew Hayden Taylor, one of Canada's leading Native playwrights, considers Native humor and storytelling to be important aspects of his work (1996: 29–36). Consistent with this emphasis, when I told Taylor about this chapter, he asked to be described in the following way: 'Drew Hayden Taylor is an Ojibway writer of plays, television, short stories and essays. He also makes a mean spaghetti sauce' (e-mail February 15, 2000).

As a contemporary trickster comedy, *alterNatives*, which opened on July 21, 1999, at the Bluewater Summer Playhouse in Kincardine, Ontario, departs from the more ceremonial performance styles in *49* and *SongCatcher* and the hard-hitting social activism in *The Independence of Eddie Rose*, the three other plays under discussion, and re-imagines the genre of comedy within Native terms.

Set in an upscale Toronto home where Angel, an Ojibway science-fiction writer, lives with Colleen, a European Canadian academic, *alterNatives* opens with the briefest suggestion of a romantic comedy as this couple prepares for their first dinner party together. Then Angel, somersaulting onto the stage, quickly disrupts these expectations, suggesting that something is on the move, often the beginning of a trickster tale. As he tries to seduce Colleen, his subsequent Nanabush story of this woodland trickster traveling as a porcupine, then changing back into a man in search of salt, further invokes the Ojibway trickster tradition. Angel responds to Colleen's Eurocentric puzzlement over Nanabush's remarkable capabilities with 'Why a porcupine? Who knows. You'd have to be a trickster to figure out a trickster' (Taylor, 2000: 13) and 'He's a trickster. He can do anything' (14).

In this opening scene, the performance and dialogue move the play, set in Colleen's upscale home, into the liminal space trickster tales afford and symbolically back to the forest, where the mythic Nanabush lives. Nanabush, or 'Naanabozho, the compassionate woodland trickster,' as Vizenor describes, 'wanders in mythic time and transformational space between tribal experiences and dreams. The trickster is related to plants and animals and trees; he is a teacher and healer in various personalities ...' (1984: 3–4). But as Vizenor further describes, 'More than a magnanimous teacher and transformer, the trickster is capable of violence, deceptions, and cruelties: the realities of human imperfections' (4). As such he plays a major role in traditional Ojibway culture and humor as 'an existential shaman in the comic mode, not an isolated and sentimental tragic hero in conflict with nature' (4).

Thus, through dialogue and form *alterNatives* draws on the Ojibway trickster tradition that Owens suggests 'ceaselessly dismantles those imaginative constructions that limit human possibility and freedom' and 'mediates between oppositions' (1992: 235 and 238). The performance thereby offers a new Native comedic approach that holds contradictions in balance, one that is fundamentally different from the Western comedic struggle of good over evil or love triumphing over adversity. And given the tremendous oppositions between Natives and European Canadians in the early years of the twenty-first century, the subject of the play, this contemporary use of the trickster tradition is a highly innovative response to Native/White relations.

The dialogue in the first act of *alterNatives* hilariously probes the ambiguities and contradictions of identity politics as three twentysomething Ojibways – Angel, Bobby, and Yvonne – and three thirtysomething European Canadians – Colleen, Michelle, and Dale – try to socialize and have dinner together. Sparks immediately start to fly when Yvonne and Bobby enter, and Colleen realizes that, in trying to get to know Angel's friends and his life on the Reserve, she has inadvertently brought his former girlfriend to her home and has gone to great efforts to purchase a moose roast, a traditional Ojibway dish, for the event that no one seems to expect or even know how to cook, except Dale, who is now a vegetarian because of Michelle.

Disrupting monolithic views of Indians, Angel, Bobby, and Yvonne through rapid-fire delivery of one-liners top the three European Canadians with their erudition, wit, and humor, asserting that they do not need anyone to speak for them, exemplified by Yvonne's reworking of Descartes, with 'I am, therefore I think' (Taylor, 2000: 48). But far more is at stake than simple dinner conversation and rapid repartee at this party caught in the spell of trickster. Human imperfections – both Native and European Canadian – become increasingly apparent as Michelle becomes drunk, staggering across the stage, the only alcoholic on the stage; Bobby quarrelsome, taunting Michelle; Angel edgy, snapping at Colleen; Yvonne jealous, needling Angel, and Colleen possessive, seeking Angel's attentions. Only Dale in his good-natured politically correct blundering about *Dances with Wolves* seems immune to the imperfections so rampant at this party until he too slips and commits the unpardonable in Michelle's eyes. Off stage Michelle's voice of anguish rings out, and she drives the guilty Dale into the living room for sampling a bite of the moose roast. This climatic point leads to further recriminations and heated debates over whose values should prevail – vegetarians or meat-eaters, indicative of larger cultural conflicts.

Central to the performance are Ojibway responses to Colleen's efforts to create Angel in her own image of what an Indian writer should be – a construction the play exposes to be a product of Western scholarship and colonial power relations. Confident that she knows the Ojibway people and can speak for them based on her own research as a Native literature professor, Colleen happily prepares for the party, seemingly secure in her relationship with Angel and secure in her academic position. An oversized dream catcher hangs on the wall, a visual correlative of this confidence. In the trickster tradition, during the rest of the performance, Colleen's assumptions are constantly undercut – all Indians cook and eat moose, Native writers should only write about their people, all stories told are true.

Finally, in a face-to-face confrontation, Bobby and Angel reveal the truth of her early research on Ojibway legends as stories made up by boys – Bobby and Angel. As they confront her, Colleen almost collapses with the news. But she is now forced to accept that much of her career, and *Legends of the Ontario Ojibway*, a book used in Native literature courses now in its seventh printing, are based on tales of 11-year-old boys. Her horrified look of recognition to this unexpected turn of events reveals that she has become caught in the very trickster tales she collects and studies, a powerful irony. Here as does *SongCatcher*, *alterNatives* confronts mainstream academic misappropriations of Native culture. As Bobby tells Colleen, 'Our legends are none of their business,' his emphasis on 'our' (Taylor, 2000: 129). After reassessing his relationship with Colleen, Angel confronts her again and forces her to reflect on why she knows more about his culture and language than her own. Thus, through the trickster tradition of reversals, the performance destabilizes the hierarchy of power in Western scholarship and turns questions of identity and culture back on European Canadians.

But where the spirit of trickster dwells also exist spaces for possibilities. As Vizenor notes, the woodlands trickster 'represents a spiritual balance in a comic drama rather than the romantic elimination of human contradictions and evil' (1984: 4). As the evening progresses, Michelle, Bobby, Yvonne, and Colleen eventually exit through the front door. And new alliances emerge between Angel and Dale over a humorously ritualized traditional moose meal. The Native and the European Canadian men, both abandoned by their women, having nothing to comfort them but a succulent roast and their own company, finally sit down to dinner together. It is an uneasy alliance and certainly rife with contradictions. After dinner, urged by Dale to tell him one of his science-fiction stories, Angel sits on the couch huddled in a blanket and ends the performance with a story in which a Native astronaut in the twenty-first century learns that all the Native–White land claims have been resolved on Earth only to discover that 'Somebody's just bought the solar system.' Wearied by centuries of colonialism, his response is 'Not again,' which ends Angel's story. As the two men 'clink glasses' (Taylor, 2000: 144) and the lights slowly go down, this *tableau vivant* of Ojibway and European Canadian holds solidarity and dissension in balance, a fitting place to start a real dialogue between the two cultures at the beginning of a new millennium.

THE NEXT WAVE

Fourth wave Native theater, a recent artistic direction beginning in the 1970s, represents a significant departure in Native theater as a contemporary art form by re-imagining the stage through a holistic fusion of tradition and transformation. Grounded in the oral tradition and the generative power of Creation stories, such theater integrates ancient conceptions of story, community, performance, ritual, and ceremony with contemporary issues and more recent performance styles. While reflective of the great diversity among Indian nations and the multiplicity of cultural expressions, re-imagined Native theater shifts location to a Native stage world and reconceptualizes the theatrical experience by placing Native values, aesthetics, traditions, and issues at the core of each performance and employing theatrical vocabularies and narrative forms intrinsic to these values. In doing so, this recent direction in Native theater simultaneously gives back the power of performance to Native peoples and takes back the stage from centuries of Western constructions and stereotypes.

The plays *49*, *SongCatcher*, *The Independence of Eddie Rose*, and *alterNatives* discussed earlier in this chapter each re-imagine the stage and engage in sacred play in highly innovative ways, integrating tradition and transformation. Each performance also offers a shared vision of the possibilities of community for contemporary Native Americans as Native people take center stage. Central to the performances of *49* and *SongCatcher* are ceremony, ritual, and the embodiment of the spirit world on stage to restore cosmic order and promote healing. In *The Independence of Eddie Rose* and *alterNatives*, the infusion and performance of Native storytelling traditions establishes the strength of Native narratives to transform contemporary issues facing Native communities, thereby disrupting Western genres of tragedy and comedy, respectively.

Kenneth Lincoln describes the 'the fulcrum' of tribal as 'a sense of relatedness.' To Indians tribe means family, not just bloodlines but extended family, clan, community, ceremonial exchanges with nature, an animate regard for all creation as sensible and powerful (1983: 8). These traditional underpinnings embedded in ceremony, ritual, storytelling, and responsibility that these performances and others like them embody are highly complex concepts and much needed re-imaginings. To respect their viability accords this work and many other works of Native theater their power, artistry, and authority. By re-imagining the stage, such theater nurtures Native peoples. By centering performance on tribal values and what's at stake for communities, it also has the potential to nurture all audiences. *Aho.*

ACKNOWLEDGMENTS

For their inspiration and insights at various stages of this work, I wish to thank Hanay Geiogamah, Paula Gunn Allen, Lloyd Kiva New, Stephanie Fitzgerald, Pamela Munroe, Drew Hayden Taylor, Edit Villarreal, Arif Amlani, Pamela Grieman, Ken Wade, and Diane Weiner. My sincere gratitude also goes to the W. K. Kellogg Foundation for its generous support of Project HOOP (Honoring Our Origins and People through Native Theater, Education, and Community Development), of which this scholarship forms a part.

NOTES

1. I am indebted to Hanay Geiogamah for the term 're-imagine' and the many conversations we have had about Native theater.

2. See C. W. E. Bigsby, *A Critical Introduction to Twentieth-Century American Drama: Beyond Broadway*, Vol. 3 (Cambridge: Cambridge University Press, 1985), 365–74; *Modern American Drama, 1945–1990* (Cambridge: Cambridge University Press, 1992), 333–6.

3. For thoughtful analyses of the constructions of 'Indianness,' see also S. Elizabeth Bird (ed.), *Dressing in Feathers: The Construction of the Indian in American Popular Culture* (Boulder, CO: Westview, 1996); Vine Deloria, Jr., 'The American Indian Image in North America,' *Encyclopedia of Indians of the Americas*, Vol. 1 (St. Clair Shores, MI: Scholarly, 1974), 40–4. For a detailed discussion of stereotypes, see also Gretchen M. Bataille and Charles L. P. Silet (eds), *The Pretend Indians: Images of Native Americans in the Movies* (Ames, IA: Iowa State University Press, 1980); Rayna Green, 'The Pocahontas Perplex: The Image of Indian Women in American Culture,' *Massachusetts Review*, 16 (1975): 698–714; Jacquelyn Kilpatrick, *Celluloid Indians: Native Americans and Film* (Lincoln: University of Nebraska Press, 1999); Devon A. Mihesuah, *American Indians: Stereotypes and Realities* (Atlanta, GA: Clarity, 1996); and Raymond William Stedman, *Shadows of the Indian: Stereotypes in American Culture* (Norman, OK: University of Oklahoma Press, 1982).

4. See Barbara Christian, 'The Race for Theory,' and Tey Diana Rebolledo, 'The Politics of Poetics: Or, What Am I, A Critic Doing in This Text Anyhow?,' in Gloria Anzaldúa (ed.), *Making Face, Making Soul/Haciendo Caras: Creative and Critical Perspectives by Feminists of Color* (San Francisco: aunt lute books, 1990), 335–45, 346–55; Paula Gunn Allen, *Off the Reservation: Reflections on Boundary-Busting, Border-Crossing Loose Canons* (Boston: Beacon, 1998), 132–78, and Elizabeth Cook-Lynn, 'Who Stole Native American Studies?,' *Wicazo Sa Review*, 12, 1 (1997): 5–28.

5. As a European American scholar and co-director with Hanay Geiogamah of Project HOOP (Honoring Our Origins and People through Theater, Education, and Community Development), a recent initiative funded by the W. K. Kellogg Foundation to advance Native theater artistically and academically, I am acutely sensitive to these issues. I am indebted to the work and vision of Paula Gunn Allen, Hanay Geiogamah, and Lloyd Kiva New. I also acknowledge that much of my knowledge of Native theater has come from the experiential and communal – attending powwows, dances, and gatherings since I was a small child in Arizona; spending time on Native homelands, including those of the Apache, Tohono O'odham, Diné, Santa Clarita, Chumash, Kiowa, and Lakota; engaging in numerous conversations with Native playwrights, actors, directors, writers, elders, and community members, seeing productions – and above all, listening, watching, participating, and honoring. For all the years I have spent in this effort, I know that I am a guest and am very thankful to be invited to share in this work.

6. This section is based on a more in-depth discussion of this play by the author, '"Come to the Ceremonial Circle": Ceremony and Renewal in Hanay Geiogamah's 49,' in Hanay Geiogamah and Jaye T. Darby (eds), *American Indian Theater in Performance: A Reader* (Los Angeles: UCLA American Indian Studies Center, 2000), 195–223.

7. Note that Marcie Rendon uses an alternative spelling of Ojibwe to Drew Hayden Taylor, who uses Ojibway. Both are correct and reflect regional differences. Throughout this essay, I respect each playwright's preferred spelling.

BIBLIOGRAPHY

Allen, Paula Gunn, *The Sacred Hoop: Recovering the Feminine in American Indian Traditions* (Boston: Beacon, 1986).
— 'Bringing Home the Fact: Tradition and Continuity in the Imagination,' in Brian Swann and Arnold Krupat (eds), *Recovering the Word: Essays on Native American Literature* (Berkeley, CA: University of California Press, 1987, 563–79).
— 'Introduction' in Paula Gunn Allen (ed.), *The Song of the Turtle: American Indian Literature 1974–1994* (New York: Ballantine Books, 1996, 3–17).
— Lecture, English 258 (University of California, Los Angeles, April 28, 1998a).
— *Off the Reservation: Reflections on Boundary-Busting, Border-Crossing Loose Canons* (Boston: Beacon, 1998b).
Bataille, Gretchen M. and Silet, Charles L. P. (eds), *The Pretend Indians: Images of Native Americans in the Movies* (Ames, IA: Iowa State University Press, 1980).
Berkhofer, Jr., Robert F., *The White Man's Indian: Images of the American Indian from Columbus to the Present* (New York: Vintage Books, 1979).
Bigsby, C. W. E., *A Critical Introduction to Twentieth-Century American Drama: Beyond Broadway*, 3 vols (Cambridge: Cambridge University Press, 1985, 365–74).
— *Modern American Drama, 1945–1990* (Cambridge: Cambridge University Press, 1992, 333–6).
Bird, S. Elizabeth (ed.), *Dressing in Feathers: The Construction of the Indian in American Popular Culture* (Boulder, CO: Westview Press, 1996).
Bruchac, Joseph, 'The Gift is Still Being Given,' in Janet Witalec (ed.), *Native North American Literary Companion* (Detroit: Visible Ink, 1998, xvii–xix).
Christian, Barbara, 'The Race for Theory,' in Gloria Anzaldúa (ed.), *Making Face, Making Soul/Haciendo Caras: Creative and Critical Perspectives by Feminists of Color* (San Francisco: aunt lute books, 1990, 335–45).
Colorado, Elvira and Hortensia, '1992: Blood Speaks,' in Kathy A. Perkins and Roberta Uno (eds), *Contemporary Plays by Women of Color: An Anthology* (London and New York: Routledge, 1996, 82–9).
Cook-Lynn, Elizabeth, 'Who Stole Native American Studies?,' *Wicazo Sa Review*, 12, 1 (1997): 5–28.
Darby, Jaye T, 'Come to the Ceremonial Circle: Ceremony and Renewal in Hanay Geiogamah's 49,' in Hanay Geiogamah and Jaye T. Darby (eds), *American Indian Theater in Performance: A Reader* (Los Angeles: UCLA American Indian Studies Center, 2000, 195–223).
Deloria, Philip J., *Playing Indian* (New Haven, CT: Yale University Press, 1998).
Deloria, Jr., Vine, 'The American Indian Image in North America,' in *Encyclopedia of Indians of the Americas*, 7 vols (St. Clair Shores, MI: Scholarly, 1974).

Fixico, Donald L., 'U.S. Indian Legislation,' in Duane Champagne (ed.), *The Native North American Almanac: A Reference Work on Native North Americans in the United States and Canada* (Detroit: Gale Research, 1994, 486–92).

Gates, Jr., Henry Louis, *Loose Canons* (New York and Oxford: Oxford University Press, 1992).

Geiogamah, Hanay, *49*, in Hanay Geiogamah and Jaye T. Darby (eds), *Stories of Our Way: An Anthology of American Indian Plays* (Los Angeles: UCLA American Indian Studies Center, 1999, 195–226). Originally published in Hanay Geiogamah, *New Native American Drama: Three Plays* (Norman, OK: University of Oklahoma Press, 1980, 84–133).

— 'The Native American Theater Ensemble (1972–75),' unpublished manuscript, 1980.

Green, Rayna, 'The Pocahontas Perplex: The Image of Indian Women in American Culture,' *Massachusetts Review*, 16 (1975): 698–714.

Harjo, Joy, and Bird, Gloria, 'Introduction,' in Joy Harjo and Gloria Bird (eds), with Patricia Blanco, Beth Cuthand, and Valerie Martínez, *Reinventing the Enemy's Language: Contemporary Native Women's Writing of North America* (New York: W. W. Norton, 1997, 19–31).

Haugo, Ann, ' "Circles Upon Circles": Native Women in Theater and Performance,' in Hanay Geiogamah and Jaye T. Darby (eds), *American Indian Theater in Performance: A Reader* (Los Angeles: UCLA American Indian Studies Center, 2000, 228–55).

Hernández-Ávila, Inés, 'Relocations Upon Relocations: Home, Language, and Native Women's Writing,' *American Indian Quarterly*, 19 (1995): 491–507.

Jenkins, Linda Walsh and Wapp, Jr., Ed, 'Native American Performance,' *Drama Review*, 20, 2 (1976): 5–12.

Kilpatrick, Jacquelyn, *Celluloid Indians: Native Americans and Film* (Lincoln: University of Nebraska Press, 1999).

LeVine, R. A., 'Properties of Culture: An Ethnographic View,' in R. A. Shweder and R. A. LeVine (eds), *Culture Theory: Essays on Mind, Self and Emotion* (Cambridge: Cambridge University Press, 1986, 67–87).

Lincoln, Kenneth, *Native American Renaissance* (Berkeley: University of California Press, 1983).

Mihesuah, Devon A., *American Indians: Stereotypes and Realities* (Atlanta, GA: Clarity, 1996).

Mojica, Monique, 'Theatrical Diversity on Turtle Island: A Tool Towards the Healing,' *Canadian Theatre Review*, 68 (1991): 3.

Momaday, N. Scott, *House Made of Dawn* (New York: Harper & Row, 1968).

Morrison, Kenneth M., 'Native American Religions: Creating Cosmic Give-and-Take,' in Duane Champagne (ed.), *Native North American Almanac: A Reference Work on Native North Americans in the United States and Canada* (Detroit: Gale Research, 1994, 633–48).

New, Lloyd Kiva, 'Defining Ourselves,' *Native Peoples*, 13, 2 (2000): 9–10.

Owens, Louis, *Other Destinies: Understanding the American Indian Novel* (Norman, OK: University of Oklahoma Press, 1992).

Rebolledo, Tey Diana, 'The Politics of Poetics: Or, What Am I, a Critic, Doing in this Text Anyhow?,' in Gloria Anzaldúa (ed.), *Making Face, Making Soul/Haciendo Caras: Creative and Critical Perspectives by Feminists of Color* (San Francisco: aunt lute books, 1990, 346–55).

Rendon, Marcie, '*SongCatcher*: A Native Perspective on Frances Densmore, Ethnomusicologist,' in Jaye T. Darby and Stephanie Fitzgerald (eds), *Keepers of the Morning Star: An Anthology of Native Women's Theater* (Los Angeles: UCLA American Indian Studies Center, forthcoming).

Spiderwoman Theater, 'Power Pipes,' in Mimi Gisolfi D'Aponte (eds.), *Seventh Generation: An Anthology of Native American Plays* (New York: Theatre Communications Group, 1999, 154–95).

Stedman, Raymond W., *Shadows of the Indian: Stereotypes in American Culture* (Norman, OK: University of Oklahoma Press, 1982).

Taylor, Drew Hayden, 'Alive and Well: Native Theatre in Canada,' *Journal of Canadian Studies*, 31, 3 (1996): 29–36.

— *alterNatives* (Burnaby, BC: Talonbooks, 2000).

Vizenor, Gerald, *The People Named the Chippewa: Narrative Histories* (Minneapolis: University of Minnesota Press, 1984).

Yellow Robe, Jr., William, 'Author's Statement,' in Mimi Gisolfi D'Aponte (ed.), *The Seventh Generation* (New York: Theatre Communications Group, 1999a, 41–2).

— 'The Independence of Eddie Rose,' in Mimi Gisolfi D'Aponte (ed.), *Seventh Generation: An Anthology of Native American Plays* (New York: Theatre Communications Group, 1999b, 43–97).

5

Notes from a cosmopolite

Velina Hasu Houston

Even as a child, my view of the world was not provincial, but cosmopolitan. Although I was living in a small town, I was part of an international family and community that exposed me in an intimate way to diverse ethnicities and cultures – Japanese, African American, Pilipino, French, Italian, White American, Chinese, Taiwanese, and so on. The cosmopolite began forming back then. The transformation, however, was made complete by my later experiences in society and in the theater community. Being different – multiracial, multicultural, and transnational – forced me onto a path that at first felt lonely, but then proved to be a path of enlightenment that led to life as a cosmopolite, a life that I relish and find infinitely rewarding to my spirit and my art; a life that demands a worldly, multi-faceted view at all times.

EARLY DISCOVERY

As an adolescent, art – particularly literary art – was my refuge from the narrow and alienating monoracial perspective of United States society and an escape from the ways in which that perspective constantly attempted to challenge, diminish, and denigrate my identity as a multicultural, transnational, multiracial Amerasian. An antidote for this reductive perspective was to read novels, plays, and poetry that allowed me to breathe and that helped keep hope alive. I was able to create a space of precision, power, and confidence that allowed me to begin to hear my muses and to be able to survive, both as an artist and as a human being in general.

Initially, I believed that becoming involved in the theater would allow me to create a public space that could be parallel to that private space – a sphere in which I could navigate, at least in certain ways and at certain times, without thought to race or gender. In the midst of my artistic expression, I could, at times, be colorless and genderless due to the liberated universe of art. I could simply be a playwright whose work could be judged and presented on its artistic merit alone, not based on whether or not it fit into the definition of political correctness (meaning White and male) that is the standard for United States mainstream theater.

I soon discovered, however, that the nature of theater in the United States in the 1980s would not allow me to be merely a playwright. The cinnamon brown hue of my skin, my 'exotic' visage; and the fact that I had breasts, ovaries, and a womb denied me that hailing (not always, but often enough that I could not ignore it). In the early 1980s at a women's theater conference in the San Francisco Bay area, White playwright Marsha Norman was not only surprised to encounter a *hapa* female playwright, but also any women playwrights of Asian descent in general. After she acknowledged the work of White and African American women playwrights, she was asked by a group of Asian American female theater artists not to exclude Asian American women playwrights. Her response was: 'I didn't know there were any.' Hopefully, she and other White women playwrights have come a long way (baby) since that time. I learned, however, that if she and her comrades thought of women playwrights as only coming in two colors – Black and White – that the trail I had to blaze was going to be even more challenging than I initially had believed. Even today, too many White theater colleagues who meet me for the first time comment that I do not look like a 'real playwright.'

'REAL'

Although I am comfortable with and confident about my hapa identity, perhaps the world has such strict definitions of what is a Real Something (a real playwright, a real African American, a real Asian, etc.) that, in the perceptions of others in society and in the global village, I am never seen as a Real Anything. When I was living in Kyoto in 1999, my children and I had just left a *soba* restaurant and were seeking relief from the criminal humidity by standing on a bridge by the Katsura River. A Japanese man walked by us, stopped, smiled, and stated, 'You are from Ceylon, yes.' It was not a question, but I tried to answer it anyway. He plowed on, 'Yes, Ceylon. I lived there for a year. Nice, nice.' Before I could tell him that I was not Sri Lankan, he was gone. Throughout my Japan Foundation residency in Kyoto, I was declared 'Ceylonese' by every Japanese person who was cosmopolitan enough to initiate a conversation with me. One person asked me if I was 'Oriental' or 'Occidental,' my phenotype being so confusing that I was not real or authentic-looking enough to be categorical. I came close to being perceived as a Real

South Asian, except for that inquiry and one from a Japanese woman who asked me if I was Venezuelan.

When I returned to the United States, many Americans commented that living in Kyoto must have been 'interesting' or 'challenging' because I look so different. Difference is a peculiar notion when applied to me because, as a multiracial individual, particularly an AfroAsian *hapa*, I am always different culturally and phenotypically, no matter the geographical context. Perhaps looking different is a euphemism for not being a Real Anything, when it comes to race and culture. Like an optical illusion, I mutate (by others' misperceptions) into a Sri Lankan in Kyoto, a Venezuelan in Osaka, a Colombian in Tokyo, a Pilipina or Pacific Islander in California, a Latina in New York, or a Cambodian in Dallas. Only in Hawaii am I perceived as being 'local,' which is the term that Hawaiians apply to people whom they think are native to Hawaii and of mixed Asian/Hawaiian ancestry. Most Hawaiians think I have come home, and the White and African American tourists ask me for directions – but in that hesitant way that people do when they think I cannot speak English (even though, of course, Hawaii is part of the United States, as am I).

'LOCAL GIRL'

I am local to another nation as well: the nation, if you will, of theater art; which is actually more like a universe. Aforementioned, I am not always perceived as being local to that community, but I feel a sense of belonging there just as much as I feel a bond with the *hapa* community. Within the universe of theater art, however, my difference is perhaps even more pronounced than it is in society-at-large because theater in the United States reflects society's racial tribalism in a way made more intense due to the small size of the theater community and also due to the competitiveness of the arts. Theaters and theater scholars tend to think of theater either as mainstream (read White) theater (that can allow for a little color and a little female-ness, but not too much), women's theater (that can allow for a little color, but not too much), and ethnic theater (that allows only for the four traditional ethnic minority factions: African American, Asian American, Native American Indian, and Latino).

As a dramatist with a multiracial, multicultural, and transnational voice who cannot be placed neatly into any of these racial categories, I often find myself being perceived by society as not American enough, not Asian enough, not Black enough, not White enough. With regard to ethnic theaters, the exclusionary hailing of being not right also extends to my stories and characters as well. Odd comments or questions arise such as: Are these characters Black enough? Are these characters Japanese enough? This Black man's language isn't jive enough. Japanese people don't talk like this. Japanese people would never do such things (as if being African American or being Japanese were monolithic). These criticisms are akin to male writers saying that women cannot write male characters effectively, and vice versa. Sometimes the people asking the questions or making the comments reflect a very stereotypical and limiting attitude of what it is to be Japanese or African American; and sometimes these self-appointed regulators have no authentic or direct understanding of the very cultures they criticize or attempt to represent. Yet they still feel compelled to present themselves as authorities despite my intimate connection to the cultures explored in my stories.

When it comes to me, mainstream theater, just like society and ethnic theater, often does not know what to do with me either. They cannot relegate my multiethnicity easily to any specific racialized artistic ghetto because they cannot categorically racialize me. I am a conundrum in that respect. When you do not know what to do, one tends to invent a new way of doing something. Thus, what is interesting is that, given that, most mainstream theater personnel with whom I work tend to navigate in a very enlightened way. They judge the universal rather than the racial/cultural in my work and they judge me by the same measure. Instead of being a double other, I am accepted on my own terms as an artist and individual. This may seem like a contradiction, but it is not. It is actually a situation of cause-and-effect. The desire to categorize is defused by the inability to categorize. When I cannot be pigeonholed, theaters stop trying to categorize me and move on to what is truly important – the work, which is why we got together in the first place. I may not be Japanese enough or Black enough for the ethnic theaters, but I am artist enough for the mainstream theaters.

THE COSMOPOLITAN PERSPECTIVE: WHOSE MULTICULTURAL DIVERSITY IS IT ANYWAY?

In this way, being 'different' to everybody has proven to be fortuitous for me. I was forced to strike out on an independent path and develop an independent voice that is informed with the vigor and wisdom that such challenges deem inescapable. In so doing, acceptance has come in the mainstream theater, perhaps the arena that I considered to be most unlikely to embrace my work when I was starting out in the 1980s. My perspective has been enriched even beyond the multiple views that are innate to my multirace. In effect, being cosmopolitan is the consequence of needing to understand what is inside every house, not just my own. This kind of transcendence is reflected in the careers of other multiracial theater artists as well, such as Sandra Tsing Loh. While her work is informed by all of who she is (ethnically and otherwise), Loh is a cosmopolite of the first order. She is an original and her worldly outlook only fortifies the originality of her vision. Other such multiracial artists of Asian Pacific heritage include Amy Hill, Brenda Wong Aoki, Nobuko Miyamoto, Paula Weston Solano, Leilani Chan, and Alison de la Cruz.

As a hapa – the daughter of a Japanese immigrant and an African American and Blackfoot Indian father – the very nature of my earlier work was informed by my background, as has been the case with many playwrights. Perhaps this led the powers-that-be of theater to attempt to assign me to Asian American sites and, to a lesser extent, to African American sites. *Asa Ga Kimashita (Morning Has Broken),* my thesis play at the University of California at Los Angeles, garnered two national first prizes – the Lorraine Hansberry Playwriting Award and the David Library for American Freedom Award – from the John F. Kennedy Center's American College Theatre Festival. These awards recognized this play set in the provinces of southern Japan in 1946 as being not only about the Japanese experience, but also about the African American experience and about American freedom in general. Its sequel, *American Dreams,* focussed on an African American bringing his Japanese bride home to meet his family, only to discover that the United States motif of the great melting pot was in actuality just a myth. In 1984, each of these plays premiered, the former at an ethnically specific Asian American theater and the latter at an ethnically specific African American theater.

It took me years to realize that the theaters' interest in the investigation of interrace and multirace had less to do with a sincere desire to include such stories as part of the pantheon of African American or Asian American experience than I had originally believed. Rather, these intersections merely may have been mostly novelty, a sidecar freak show for the status quo of blackness and yellowness. The African American company folded, so it is difficult to say if it would have changed its colors and expanded its vision of what blackness can be. The Asian American company is still functioning today, but has yet to expand its vision of what Asian American-ness can be with regard to multirace and *hapa* identity, particularly when it comes to the inclusion of African ancestry.

In surveying the stage offerings of an ethnically specific Asian American theater over a 12-year period, the two instances of representations of blackness I encountered were negative. One referred to African Americans as *kuro-chans,* which means 'niggers,' and characterizes them (through the voice of an Asian American male) as being the only ones poor, dim, and desperate enough to eat old carp. In the other instance, the theater's play selection offered a dismal and degrading portrait of interracial marriage, *hapa* identity, and African American identity in the representation of a beer-swilling, underachieving African

American male whose Japanese wife's subconscious loathing of blackness was so severe as to make her avoid having children with him. It is so infrequent that we see representations of Asian-ness in African American theater or representations of blackness in Asian American theater that I cannot help but hope for a more enlightened perspective.

Many ethnically specific theaters often have a tendency to re-visit the same comfortable and representative themes and stories without exploring the new territories of their ethnicity – which might include interracial marriage and multiracial individuals. Perhaps a lingering issue for monoraces of color is that they have a hard time understanding or accepting that the embrace of multicultural diversity was (and is) not merely a challenge for Whites, but also for people of color. Diversity exists within and between monoracial groups of color. Beyond the diversity of monoracials exists the diversity of multirace versus monorace, and the diversity of multirace within its own ranks. It is a brilliantly complex nexus of realities that is not as easy to digest and process.

BOTH *HAPA* AND HUMAN

Although I feel viscerally connected to all of my ethnicities, particularly in terms of my politics, the fact that the nurturing parent in my family was and is my mother, a native Japanese born and reared in the provinces of Matsuyama and Imabari, is profound in terms of cultural influence. Had my mother been African American and my father Japanese, perhaps I would have been more culturally African American and perhaps 'Black enough' for all my critics. My mother, however, was not African American. She was Japanese and I make no apologies for that or for the cultural life she instilled in me. In fact, I celebrate it because it is part of my amalgam; part of my organic, authentic self. I have lived my ethnic totalities since childhood, rejecting nothing and turning over every stone. I sustain my affiliations – some spiritual, some political, some academic – with individuals or groups within my various communities, but, in the theater, a subliminal marginalization has occurred that has allowed me to exist as a free spirit writing my own unique brand of magic realism that is informed by everything that I am.

It is a marvelous path of discovery and growth, a journey that has allowed me to transcend being simply a 'woman writer of color.' Yes, I remain staunchly *hapa* in my actual and political identities, but, as an artist, I am a cosmopolite traveling the universe without tethers. The stories that I am compelled to write reflect my cosmopolitan existence, embracing a diversity of experiences: those of maids, heiresses, housewives, executives, prostitutes, doctors, soldiers, princesses, queens, nomads, immigrants of every ilk, and my favorite – ghosts. Furthermore, my work traverses myriad cultures such as Japanese, Italian American, Hawaiian, Anglo-American, Norwegian, Hungarian, Jewish, African American, German, Native American Indian, and Chinese. In a word: transnational. And another word: universal. The universe is my hometown.

As the new millennium begins, I am fortunate enough to have my plays *Kokoro* (*True Heart*), *Shedding the Tiger, Waiting for Tadashi,* and a commissioned one-act at Sacramento Theatre Company; *Tea* at Barrington Stage Company and at Pittsburgh Public Theatre; *Ikebana* (*Living Flowers*) at the Pasadena Playhouse; *Waiting for Tadashi* at George Street Playhouse; and another commissioned work, *The Lotus of the Sublime Pond,* in development with the Jewish Women's Theatre Project. In the past, I have worked with Manhattan Theatre Club, the Old Globe Theatre, Syracuse Stage, Whole Theatre, Theatre Works, the Negro Ensemble Company, A Contemporary Theatre, and other respected theaters. The journey has rarely been about race or about how 'exotic' I am or the subject matter is. As playwright Paul Zindel (*The Effect of Gamma Rays on Man-in-the-Moon Marigolds, And Miss Reardon Drinks a Little*) once said to me years ago with regard to my signature play *Tea* when he was mentoring me in a playwriting workshop at the Actors' Studio: 'Thank God you didn't try to seduce me with the exotic, only the story, only the story.' That was an artistic rite of passage for me. It is about the story or there is no story, not for the stage or for telling at tea time.

I was born to write. I am compelled to write. I want my writing to remind us all that we have souls that require nurture in order to discourage us from figuratively or literally destroying each other or ourselves in what is an increasingly complex and sometimes brutal world. Although I may face alienation at many turns, this remains my calling and I cannot refuse it or be deterred from it by race, racism, or any other hurdles or closed doors. Art is the medicine and, when it is able to stave off the demons or cure or save, it is as colorblind as justice is supposed to be. The gift of this multiracial, multicultural, transnational artist is that my soul comprises such a multiplicity of perspectives that I must see wider, longer, broader, and deeper. I am that real. I have no choice. The cosmopolite's vision must be infinite.

6

Towards a new territory in 'multicultural' theater

Harry J. Elam, Jr.

There are many ways of defining Blackness and there are many ways of presenting Blackness onstage. The Klan does not have to be outside the door for black people to have lives worthy of dramatic literature ... And what happens when we choose a concern other than race to focus on? What kind of drama do we get? Let's do the math: ... BLACK PEOPLE + x = NEW DRAMATIC CONFLICT (NEW TERRITORY).

Suzan-Lori Parks, 'An Equation for Black People Onstage,'
in *The America Play and Other Works*

The staging of Suzan-Lori Parks's play, *In the Blood*, at the Public Theater, New York City in 1999 thrusts the audience inexorably into the world of Hester, a Black homeless woman, and her wild brood of children, Jabber, Bully, Trouble, Beauty and Baby, who live underneath a bridge. Director David Esbjornson places the action on a trough-like divide with audience members on either side. It is a space of liminality betwixt and between the two embankments of audience. The proximity of the audience to the actors and to each other encourages the spectators' active engagement with the action. The intimacy of the space is conducive to or perhaps even licences other intimacies as the characters share moments of confession directly with the audience. Hester's tale is a poignant, contradictory conjunction of suffering and survival, betrayal and stubborn complicity, institutional neglect and individual abuse.

As evidenced by the quote above, Parks's creative interests lies in developing 'new territory' beyond the conventional binary of Black and White. Hester's children are a multicultural lot, Black, Latino, and White, played by adult actors who also portray the children's fathers and other significant figures in Hester's life. Within her portrait of these children and of Hester's world,

Parks questions what is 'in the blood.' Hester's problems simultaneously involve and obscure race. She is a victim but also tragically complicit in her own oppression. Parks constructs complex interactions between performance, race, sexuality, economics, and culture. While these complexities are particular to this work, they also are exemplary of the current dynamics of American racial politics. For in America today, the definitions, implications, and meanings of race have certainly entered 'new territory.'

W. E. B. DuBois famously proclaimed in *The Souls of Black Folk* that the primary problem of the twentieth century was 'that of the color line' (54). If this in fact was the question of the twentieth century, what now of the twenty-first? Where shall race and American racial politics figure in the new millennium? How will new understandings of race factor into theatrical representation? How do we read the meanings of race in works such as *In the Blood*? How can we achieve Park's call for diverse images of race and new dramatic territory? How does America's changing racial demographics figure in this effort? Certainly the new millennium will continue to usher in significant changes to the notions of racial hegemony, minority, and majority status. For, like Hester's children, the 'American people' is now an even more 'multicultural brood.' Soon, in fact, the United States will not have a White majority. Paradoxically, while we have watched America become increasingly multi-cultural, we have also witnessed the rapid rise and equally expeditious decline of the policies, platforms, and promotions of 'multiculturalism.' The overuse of this term 'multiculturalism' within the politics of social reform in education, in the work environment, and even in the American theater has emptied it of any meaning. In meaning everything, it comes to mean nothing. In fact, multiculturalism has become a bad word, attacked by critics from both the left and the right, replaced by the new code word, 'diversity.'

Certainly, within the American theater strategies of multiculturalism have helped affect a decentering of the established norms, produced a more inclusive canon of plays, increased opportunities for playwrights, such as Suzan-Lori Parks, and performers of color. Funding sources have offered grants for theaters to diversify audiences and for regional theaters to incorporate works by authors of color previously excluded into the seasons' offerings. New theaters of color have emerged and existing regional theaters like the Public Theater in New York and the Alliance Theater in Atlanta have or have had Black artistic directors, George C. Wolfe and Kenny Leon respectively. Others have established laboratories and training programs to develop artists of color. While, on the one hand, this evolving diversity needs to be celebrated for enabling new voices to be seen and heard, it also needs to be interrogated. Visibility is often not enough. Despite these advances entrenched systems of power and oppression can remain invisible and intact. The increased visibility of minorities in the theater does not necessarily translate into more harmonious artistic or social circumstances. It does not necessarily mean that artists of color operate within an equitable playing field or now can assert more authority over their cultural capital. Peggy Phelan so effectively points out in *Unmarked* that the unremarked is often more powerful than the marked. Phelan argues, 'Gaining visibility for the politically underrepresented without scrutinizing the power of who is required to display what to whom is an impoverished political agenda' (26). Questions remain as to how cultural diversity operates in relation to the power of the dominant cultural imperative. Has the development of specific ethnic theatrical projects and companies increased the balkanization of American theater? As works of different groups reach the stage do they offer the possibility not only to express cultural difference but also to build cross-cultural interchange, examination and intersection, or to develop new territories? Does the production of theatrical diversity disrupt existing artistic hierarchies and the dominant cultural hegemony?

Too often the production of a single work by a playwright of color represents a regional theater's one and only excursion that season into the realm of diversity. Staged within such constraints and structures, multicultural theater cannot alter but only reinforce cultural and social norms, a separate and unequal economy. Una Chaudhuri argues in *Staging Place*, 'The fact that all multicultural drama shares the difficult condition of being marginal to mainstream American drama threatens to homogenize the self-construction of the drama, forcing it into single undifferentiated "minority" identity' (214). Such homogenization of minority identities within the American theater threatens to undermine the projects of diversity that originally spawned increases in productivity by artists of color. Moreover, if the works of artists of color are branded only as different, as other, as outside of the traditional or the normative, then implicitly they reinforce the power of normative Whiteness. Whiteness stays at the center of aesthetic standards and artistic control as artists of color can only fight amongst themselves for the limited 'diversity' slots that are open to them. New territory in the theater for artists of color, then, demands a new commitment to politics.

And yet, recent critiques of the identity politics and cultural nationalist performance practices of Black and Chicano artists in the 1960s and 1970s have shown that a focus on the politics of oppression in some ways limited artistic expression at that time. As the Parks quote suggests, 'the Klan does not have to be outside the door for Black people to have lives worthy of dramatic literature.' She points out that theatrical responses to White racism may not liberate Black cultural expression at all but actually restrain it. When works of color emerge only in reaction to dominant representations that deny or subordinate them, they may fail to disrupt and can even replicate these systems of subordination. A question then for artists of color, such as Parks, is how can you express the diversity of cultural experience while at the same time remaining conscious of the political dynamics and White hegemony that still constrain American theater and social life? Can you find new territory for multicultural theater and still be political? One of the most significant criticisms of multiculturalism by the left has been in terms of its politics. Leftist-minded critics have argued that multiculturalism's celebration of cultural difference has too often ignored the unequal distributions of power, authority, and privilege. In the name of cultural tolerance, multicultural difference has at times been used to justify gender oppression or to embrace diversity without interrogating the politics that inform it. Angela Davis asks, 'Ultimately I want to pose the question of whether, or what kind of multicultural approaches can potentially take on the political task of challenging the gender class, and race hierarchies and continue to shape the institutions of this country' (1996: 42). Davis calls for a multiculturalism that is 'liberated from historically outmoded ways of conceptualizing race' (48), that recognizes that issues of gender, sexuality, and class and culture all disrupt unified notions of race and complicate constructions of racial identities. Thus the dialectical challenge for such new multiculturalism is to be able to champion racial difference and diversity, while at the same time acknowledging the constructed nature of race and building new politicized cultural coalitions.

This challenge has a particular resonance for current politically active theater practitioners of color, like Cherríe Moraga, who are aware of the seductive power and romantic allure of 1960s style cultural nationalism and identity politics. Moraga writes, 'I mourn the dissolution of an active Chicano Movement ... I cling to the word "nation" because without the specific naming of a nation, the nation will be lost' (1993: 150). Moraga seeks a politicized theater that can capture the spirit of the past but not its constraining exclusivity. But can such a theater reflect a radical pluralism even as it represents diversity? Can it articulate cross-cultural commonalties and new possibilities for social change? Can a theater of multiculturalism expose the 'unmarked,' and question regimes of cultural power and authority even as it reveals and celebrates racial difference? Is such a new territory in multicultural theater possible? Perhaps this is too much to ask of any theater or any production. Perhaps another question to ask is how as theater critics, interested in the changing dynamic of multiculturalism and multicultural theater, can we expand our critical vocabulary into new territory? What tools can or should we use to best articulate the interplay of gender, race, sexuality, class, and culture that occur in the space of contemporary theater of color? My approach to answering the last questions – and through them to address in turn the earlier questions – is to begin by examining the relationship between performance theory, cultural identity, and race.

PERFORMING CULTURAL IDENTITY

A notable trend in recent scholarship around race has been the appropriation of theories of performance and performativity. Scholars, some even as they denigrate and deny the social power of theatrical performance, have considered whether and how race is 'performed.' Outside as well as inside the theatrical arena, the application of performance theory to the subject of race raises awareness of the contingency of race and of the ways in which race is cited, embodied, and enacted. Race becomes understood like a performance, as a doing as well as a thing done. Conceiving race as a doing enables us to examine how subjects repeat or perhaps even subvert established gestures, behaviors, linguistic patterns, cultural attitudes, and social expectations associated with race. The doing produces effects even as it is disrupted by issues of class, gender, and sexuality. While theorizing race as performance opens up new critical territory, it is not an unproblematic journey. Questions remain as to how performance accommodates the lived experience, the visible markings, the historical baggage or the personal agency of racialized subjects. Moreover, the seductiveness of performance as mode of criticism and analysis has produced a critical excess. As a result, the term performance, like multiculturalism, has lost its meaning. Everything has become performance.

Prompted by such concerns, aware of the dangers of the over-exposure of performance as well as by the questions about new directions in multi-culturalism raised in the earlier sections of this essay, I want to turn to the subject of cultural identity. The critical foundation I hope to establish here is not one of whether or not race is performed but more particularly how cultural identity is performed and performative. For my contention is that a conscious thinking and theorizing about the performance of cultural identity can help determine how the radicalized multiculturalism and new conceptualizations of race that Angela Davis advocates might be accomplished. I will argue that performances of cultural identity inform racial constructions, interactions, and perceptions. The connections between race and culture have been and continue to be the subject of scholarly and political debate. At times they have been taken to be synonymous. Such a conflation is clearly problematic and limiting as cultural practices can both work within and outside of constructions of race. While Black peoples may be said to be of one race, they are certainly products of many cultures and cultural experiences. Culture is not simply a static set of shared beliefs and customs inherited by people of the same ethnic decent. Culture rather references contested practices and processes, modes of behavior and consciousness through which communities are defined and differentiated (Donald and Rattansi, 1992: 4). Following Raymond Williams, Baz Kershaw defines culture as a 'signifying system':

> I will adopt his [Williams's] notion of culture as a 'signifying system,' by which he means the system of signs via which groups, organizations, institutions, and, of course, communities recognize and communicate with each other in the process of becoming a more or less influential formation within the society. In other words, 'culture' is the medium which can unite a range of different groups and communities in a common project in order to make them into an ideological force operating against the status quo. (Kershaw, 1992: 36)

Kershaw asserts that culture, as a signifying system, can be a site of collective resistance. Also inherent within his definition is the notion that culture is contingent and dynamic. Following this conception of culture, cultural identity, as Stuart Hall (1996) would argue, concerns not a cultural essence but a 'positioning' (6). This positioning is political and occurs on and through difference. Lisa Lowe (1997) claims that 'just as the articulation of identity depends on the existence of a horizon of differences, the articulation of differences dialectically depends on a socially constructed and practiced notion of identity' (83). Thus what we perceive as different depends on how we construct and perceive identity. We position ourselves in relation to others. The collisions between past cultural traditions and the concerns of the current historical moment are critical to this process. Cultural identities negotiate with the presence of the past as well as with the forces of progress. They confront the particularities of language and location all in a concept that is strategic and positional. Furthermore negotiations of cultural identity I would contend are performative and are constituted on and through performance.

In making this argument, I turn not to contemporary theories of performance or performativity but back to social anthropological theories on cultural performance and to the intersections of ritual and drama articulated by anthropologist Victor Turner (1957). Such a move might seemed dated or regressive. Recently some theater scholars as well as anthropologists have questioned the relevance of Turner to our postmodern condition (Diamond, 1996: 6). Yet, I would concur with the assertion of David Parkin that Turner's work is particularly relevant and that his theory of the social drama is 'ideally compatible with the presentation of society as fragmentary as founded on fictions more than facts of social perpetuity' (Parkin *et al.*, 1996: xviii). Turner's concept of the 'social drama' is extremely useful in considering the construction and performance of cultural identity. He delineates the process of 'social drama' as follows:

> a social drama first manifests itself as the breach of a norm, the infraction of a rule, law, morality or custom or etiquette in some public arena. This breach may be deliberately, even calculatedly, contrived by a person or party disposed to demonstrate or challenge entrenched authority, for example, the Boston Tea Party or it may merge from a scene of heated feelings. Once visible, it can hardly be revoked. Whatever the case, a mounting crisis follows, a momentous juncture or turning point in the relations between components of a social field at which seeming peace becomes overt conflict and covert antagonisms become visible … In order to limit the contagious spread of the breach certain adjustive and redressive mechanisms, informal and formal are brought into operation … The mechanisms may range from personal advice and informal arbitration to formal juridical and legal machinery, and to resolve certain kinds of crisis, to the performance of public ritual. (1982: 70)

As evidenced in Turner's example of the Boston Tea Party, the breach phase of a social drama can be a highly performative moment. Such performative moments, borrowing from both Richard Schechner and Joseph Roach, foreground 'restored behaviors' and/or 'surrogacy.' Furthermore, it is within this performative breach phase that the cultural identities of the participants are constituted. The public act of throwing tea into the Boston Harbor constructed those involved as radical activists willing to resist the tyranny of the British rule. Interestingly, these White revolutionaries needed to 'color' themselves as Indians in order to implement this performative strategy. In *Playing Indian*, Philip Deloria (1998) terms the Boston Tea Party 'a generative moment of American political and cultural identity' that was not 'the manifestation of a purely American way of performing identity' but a 'collision of various traditions from the colonies, themselves transformed by older European antecedents' (9).

The Middle Passage, the Japanese American internment, and the Chicano grape workers' strike orchestrated by César Chávez all constitute social breaches that resulted in certain cultural responses and performances by African Americans, Japanese Americans and Chicanos respectively. In each of these occasions, cultural identity is performed and constructed in and through the breach phase of social dramas. These performed identities are not fixed nor totalizing but constructed in the specifics of the moment. They are continually being both constructed and contested. For cultural critics the challenge is to identify social breaches and how performances of cultural identity operate in relation to them. Elin Diamond (1996) notes, 'To study performance is not to focus on completed forms, but to become aware of performance as itself a contested space, where meanings and desires are generated, occluded, and of course multiply interpreted' (4). Interpreting cultural identities as performance foregrounds the relationship of the cultural to the political as it establishes the social breach and the political context as critical components in determining the cultural response.

The theater is an important venue both for the analysis and construction of cultural identity. The inherently constructed nature of theatrical production enables the exploration of diverse incidents of social breach and resultant performances of cultural identities. The unique conventions and inventiveness of the theater allow for provocative explorations of identity not possible in the outside social environment. *In the Blood*, for example, features adult actors as children and an interracial progeny that natural selection could never replicate. The multicultural casting stages the fluidity of race and underscores the problematic nature of racial categorizations. Hester experiences a series of social breaches, and her cultural identity as well as that of her children are constructed accordingly. The performance of adults as children raises questions about the impact that lessons learned in childhood can have on our developmental processes. Within the theatrical conventions of performances like *In the Blood* one can seemingly escape the visible markers of the body – an adult can portray a child – even as the action or content of the performance reinforces the power and meanings of the visible body. One can perform but also subvert conventional cultural roles. Theatrical performances can not only reflect the changing dynamics of cultural identity within the existent social order, but can make their own claims, structure their own circumstances, and raise significant questions about how race operates and how it interacts with issues of gender, sexuality, class, and culture. For theatrical criticism, attention to the performance of cultural identity can help illuminate the complexities of difference at play. Through isolating and clarifying the performances of cultural identity within a particular theatrical piece we can consider how culture is contested, positioned, and negotiated. We can examine the implications of these performances for strategies of resistance and for building a radicalized multiculturalism.

In order to further these contentions, I turn to a comparative examination of three recent plays by playwrights of color: *Civil Sex* by Brian Freeman, *Mexican Medea* by Cherríe Moraga, and *A Language of Their Own* by Chay Yew. These works by an African American, Chicana, and Chinese American playwright respectively explore the contingent nature of racial constructions as they foreground the performative nature of cultural identity. They examine intraracial conflict and suggest new possibilities for coalitional politics of resistance. They build on past cultural traditions even as they explode limitations of cultural nationalism and identity politics. Taken together these plays address the dilemma of celebrating particular racial differences, while attempting to represent a radical cultural politics.

Significantly, these plays deal with questions of lesbian and gay identities. They consider how sexual politics, how 'queerness,' complicates race and performances of cultural identity. Sexuality or the sex act often play a critical role in how we think about the production of raced subjects and these plays point out the inherent 'queerness' of the relationship between sexuality and race. Most specifically, they articulate how questions of gender and sexuality disrupt the essentialization of race.

PERFORMING THE PAST

Each of these three works – *Civil Sex, Mexican Medea,* and *A Language of Their Own* – collapse, conflate, and reverse time as they unfold in the performative now. They show the past to have a profound impact on the present, but they are not time-bound or linear in structure. In each work, memory and its enactments become all the more important. In *A Language of Their Own,* the main characters, two gay Chinese American ex-lovers, Oscar and Ming, speak in presentational style to the audience as they remember their love affair, their meeting, their break-up, and their subsequent relationships. As they discuss incidents the time shifts constantly between past and present. They enact selective memories and through the performance these memories become present for the audience. The play thus transcends conventional time as it works through a temporal fluidity, a language of its own.

Cherríe Moraga sets her reworking of the Medea myth, *The Hungry Woman: A Mexican Medea* in 'a near-future of a fictional past, one only dreamed in the Chicana/o imagination' (Setting, *Mexican Medea*: 294). Within this site, she imagines the political paradigms of Chicano cultural nationalism of the 1960s and 1970s carried to an extreme fruition. 'An ethnic civil war has "balkanized" the United States. Medea, her lover Luna and child, Chac-Mool have been exiled to what remains of Phoenix, Arizona. Located in the border between Gringolandia (White Amerika) and Aztlán (Chicano country), Phoenix is now a city-in-ruin, the dumping site of every kind of poison and person unwanted by its neighbors' (Setting, *Mexican Medea*: 294). Aztlán, the mythical home of the Aztecs and the symbolic home of the Chicano nation within Moraga's dramatic vision is a land founded not on cultural pride and acceptance, but on and through the practice of ethnic absolutism and essentialism. Accordingly, anyone who has not a prescribed percentage of Native Indian blood or who is not heterosexual is excluded from the homeland. It is this inclusionary/

exclusionary dynamic of the Chicano homeland that causes the tension within the play. Medea and her lesbian lover Luna have been exiled because of their sexuality. Jasón, the father of Chac-Mool, now seeks the return of his son to Aztlán because Jasón himself lacks the required heritage of indianismo and thus Chicano authenticity. Jasón needs the presence of his son to assure his belonging.

In her portrait of ethnic balkanization, Moraga reveals the inherent dangers within past systems of identity politics and cultural nationalism. Medea romanticizes Aztlán, the land of her birth, her cultural heritage, a place to which she desires to return. Yet, she also knows it is the land from which her husband Jasón exiled her after he discovered her involvement with Luna. Thus, she is personally divided on how she needs to respond to Jasón's demands. Within the work, cultural identity and affiliation remain problematic territory that must constantly be interrogated. In *Mexican Medea*, border guards literally patrol the 'cultural borders' protecting against the entry of those who do not belong.

The action of the play moves between the present with Medea in a cell in a psychiatric hospital after the death of her son and the events that transpired prior to his demise. Given our knowledge of the classic Medea story and the reoccurring image of Medea as prisoner in the hospital ward, the tragic fate of her son Chac-Mool is never in question. Rather the play explores the personal trajectory and social circumstances that lead Medea to act. The play unfolds as a ritual sacrifice and a requiem not only for Chac-Mool and Medea, but for the lost urgency and direction of the Chicano Movement. The personal collides with the political as the characters perform Medea's memories and inner turmoil.

Civil Sex similarly enacts memories of personal and political import as it explores the intersection of Bayard Rustin's legacy as a leader of the 1964 March on Washington with his own precarious status at that time as a Black gay man. While *Mexican Medea* restages the Medea myth and actualizes the mytho-historical Aztec homeland of Aztlán and *A Language of Their Own* enacts the memories and histories of a fictive couple, *Civil Sex* explores the history of an actual figure, Rustin. Using personal interviews with friends, scholars, and Rustin himself as text, Freeman stages the interactions of memory and actual history. The characters perform the recollections of real people as well as the transcripts from Rustin's television interviews, congressional testimony, and personal appearances. As a result, the play functions as what Pierre Nora (1994) refers to as 'lieux de memoire,' sites of memory where history and memory congeal (284). This play is purposefully not a historical biography. Rustin's name does not appear in the title. Rather, the title implies the collision between issues of sexuality and Civil Rights. It provokes the question: what sexualities are in fact, civil or natural or deviant?

In Freeman's *Civil Sex*, memory, history, and performance all purposefully interact. The onstage characters function as surrogates as they stand in for actual figures and perform remembered moments from the past. Joseph Roach (1996) notes that the processes of performance and memory share vexing affinities: 'Selective memories require public enactments of forgetting ... performance offers a substitute for something else that preexists it. Performance, in other words, stands in for the elusive entity that it is not but that it must vainly aspire to both embody and replace' (3). Performance re-enacts, represents or substitutes for memory within the immediate present, the performative now. In *Civil Sex*, the embodiment of the past in the present makes public Rustin's private life and makes political his personal sexuality. Within the realm of performance Freeman, like Moraga and Yew, interrogates the complex interactions of race, sexuality, and gender in the formation of identity.

QUEERING RACE AND NATIONALISM

Freeman asks that the *Civil Sex* actors in performance shift rapidly between a variety of roles. This staging convention reinforces the fluidity of identity. It focusses attention on the dynamics and meanings of gender, power, and privilege. Certainly, as reflected in *Civil Sex*, Rustin's identity and cultural performances exemplify notions of contingency and positionality. He was a Black man from Philadelphia with a British accent. A Black gay man whose sexuality raised questions about the relationship between heterosexuality and black oppositionality. The politics of the Civil Rights Movement often connected masculinity to the objectives of Black liberation. At Civil Rights marches protesters held up banners declaring 'I AM A MAN,' thus announcing their claims to manhood denied them by years of oppression and White racism. Implicitly and explicitly such strategies promoted a heterosexual vision of masculinity that constricted or negated the presence of Black gay men. With the advent of the Black Power Movement the sentiment against homosexuality became virulent. Black Power activists argued that homosexuality was a form of racial genocide and a disease that weakened the oppositional agency of Black masculinity. Strategies of Black cultural nationalism, espoused by activists such as Amiri Baraka and Eldridge Cleaver, conceived of the Black nation as a collective Black body, united and whole with one common purpose of liberation in mind. Homosexuality, Black nationalists maintained, fragmen-ted the Black body and raised anxieties about potential racial cohesion. Such homophobia restricted possibilities of sexual liberation and of new conceptions of race.

Freeman's play, however, repositions homosexuality in relation to revolutionary Blackness. As Freeman uncovers the personal history of Rustin and his sexual identity, he decenters heterosexist, essentialized narratives of Black identity. Rustin's status as both a gay man and a key player in the March on Washington challenges conventional images of Black masculinity, as well as the naïve association of the Black freedom struggle with heterosexuality. Rather than antithetical to Black liberation, Freeman posits the fight for gay rights as a critical corollary to Black resistance efforts. In a scene in *Civil Sex* that stages an interview with sociologist Kendall Thomas, Thomas relates:

> We cannot afford – if we expect an anti-racist project to be successful, uh, to accept the demonization of any Black that are consensual – and black sexualities ... Black straight people share interest with Black gay men, Black bisexuals, Black transgendered persons in fighting this demonization of Black sexuality. (6)

According to Thomas, racism and racist policies have demonized Black masculinity and Black sexuality. Thomas goes on to argue that 'all Black sexualities are queer.' He equates the prejudice and threats against homosexuals with those against all Black people. This act of queering Black sexuality complicates it and reinforces how Black sexuality is inherently political, complex, and even contradictory.

Through the interview with Kendall as well as throughout the staged memories and images of Rustin's life, Freeman explores how race is sexed and sex is raced. Freeman suggests that Rustin's queer sexuality informs his blackness and his radical politics. And yet, because of the times in which he lived, Rustin lived a closeted gay existence. The play in effect 'outs' him while at the same time exposing further his involvement with and commitment to activism and social change. Amy Abugo Ongiri (1998) argues that 'A cultural politics and expression that is then self-consciously both Black and gay exists in an often ambiguous space within either of these arenas, sometimes floating in an equally ambiguous space between the two discourses' (237). *Civil Sex*, however, posits Black and gay not as ambiguous but as complementary discourses. The play demonstrates how the politics of sex have profound personal and collective implications for efforts toward Black liberation and for a radical multiculturalism. Rustin's long-time lover, Davis Platt, is White. Platt's whiteness is implicated in the systems of White oppression that Rustin fights against as well as the integrationist policies that Rustin hopes to affect. Freeman's depiction of Platt and his memories of his union with Rustin shows the dynamism of desire that disrupts the borders of racial categories. As filmmaker Isaac Julien suggests, 'desire across racial and sexual lines ... causes anxiety, disrupts binary notions of self/other, Black/White, straight/queer' (in

Onigiri, 1998: 231). In *Civil Sex*, the desire of Platt, a young White college student, and Rustin, an older Black activist, challenges such binaries. They share a 'queer' identity, a sameness in their sexual difference that opposes strict boundaries of culture and behavior and celebrates the freedom of desire. Their relationship symbolizes the potential for cross-cultural exchange. *Civil Sex* offers a place for Black resistance within a politics that is racially inclusive.

The interplay of sex, race, and the politics of masculinity are also critical to Yew's *A Language of Their Own*. The two lovers Ming and Oscar break up in large part due to Oscar's status as HIV-positive. Unlike Tony Kushner's *Angels in America*, where Louis leaves Prior because he is unable to cope with Prior's HIV-positive status, Oscar, who finds he is HIV-positive, is the proactive one. He forces the split with Ming because he is unwilling to compel Ming to deal with his illness. When Ming gets tested and discovers he is HIV-negative, the couple grows further apart as Ming confronts his feelings about the disease, relationships, culture, and Oscar. David Román in his important work on AIDS and performance, *Acts of Intervention*, argues:

> What distinguishes *A Language of Their Own* from other plays that address AIDS is that Ming's struggle remains central to the unfolding of the drama. Unlike other AIDS plays where the HIV-negative character is seen only in support of the character who is HIV-positive or who has AIDS, or where HIV results resolve the drama of the play, *A Language of Their Own* focuses on both the HIV-positive character and the HIV-negative character. Even after they split up as a couple, Oscar and Ming remain the dual focus of the plot. (1998: 258)

The play is not simply about AIDS but about the evolving relations and relationships of these men and the socio-cultural dynamics that shape their interactions. As with Freeman's Rustin, Yew's Ming and Oscar must confront cultural and racial perceptions of their sexuality and the relationship of race and culture to sex.

Within Ming's and Oscar's evolving relationship, sexual identity and desire complicate issues of cultural identity:

OSCAR:　The only thing that binds us together is being Chinese.
MING:　The only thing that pits us against each other is being Chinese.
(*A Language of Their Own*: 132).

The play problematizes what it means to 'be Chinese.' As a consequence, race is queered. At one point Oscar calls Ming the 'Whiter one' because in contrast to the Chinese stereotype, Ming is physically demonstrative. He explains to the audience that the name 'Ming' is not Ming's real name. 'He picked up a Chinese name because he wanted to be in touch with his cultural roots' (147).

Ming speaks out against Oscar's need to categorize things in a way that reflects how the play disrupts fixed racial categories: 'He [Oscar] likes categorizing people. Boxing things into their rightful places. This is White. This is Asian. This is gay. This is straight' (139). The play crosses and queers these categories as it reveals that different permutations are possible in the intersections of Asian American identity and homosexuality.

The concept I am employing here of 'queering race' borrows from the notion that Eve Kosofsky Sedgwick terms 'definitional panic' (167). Queerness she argues has the potential to disrupt conventional gender and racial classifications causing panic and reassessments. Consequently, heterosexual and homosexual boundaries can collapse and racial borders blur. As Susan Gubar (1997) argues: 'Racial ambiguity, in other words attends to sexual ambivalence and vice-versa … "queerness colors me"' (176). In *Mexican Medea*, Moraga colors queerness or queers color as she challenges notions of family, race, and gender. Rather than the traditional nuclear family unit, the lesbian pair of Medea and Luna have raised the son Chac-Mool during his formative years. This is the family unit he has known and loves. His grandmother, Medea's mother is also a lesbian exiled to Phoenix. Thus, Moraga reconfigures the Chicano family and questions the relation between sexuality, gender, and cultural identity.

Significantly, Medea's sexual relations have racial ramifications. Jason throws her out of the Chicano homeland for sexual betrayal. Still, throughout the work Medea's position as desiring subject and subject of desire continually shifts. She remains the embodiment of ambiguity. She replaces the male Jason with Luna in her bed but never fully declares herself a lesbian. Her bisexual status causes disruptions in both of her relations. Sex continually challenges simple alignments with race. Moreover as Chicana, as a 'mestiza,' a woman that is inherently of mixed blood, she fundamentally confounds simple racial categorization. Alicia Arrizón (2000) writes, 'Neither Anglo-American nor indigenous, the *mestiza* body troubles the borders of feminist practices, nationalism, and colonial discourses' (31). Medea in this play represents what Arrizón terms the 'native woman': 'The body of the native woman does not necessarily assert the presence of an authentic self because it challenges cultural "purity." The "native" body's presence in Chicana (and Latina) cultural productions and critical theory becomes a metaphor for the process of the political unconscious' (32). Moraga's Medea as native woman wrapped in her racial and sexual ambiguity and ambivalence resists and challenges conventional ideas of Chicano identity and authenticity.

Moraga in *Mexican Medea* decrees Chicano identity politics that structure particular gender roles and promote a heterosexist paradigm that excludes gay and lesbian presence. As Arrizón (2000) relates, Moraga deconstructs 'the male-centered, nationalistic vision of space that perpetuates a specific hierarchical order where race *should* matter more than feminist epistemologies and sexual identities' (48). Early in the first act, Medea's mother reports the history that resulted in the exile of queers from Aztlán.

MAMA SAL: Pan-indigenismo tore America apart and Aztlán was born from the pedacitos. We were happy for a while.
SAVANNAH: Sort of ... And then en masse, all the colored countries –
MAMA SAL: Threw out the jotería.
SAVANNAH: Queers of every color and shade and definition.
MAMA SAL: Y los homos became perigrinos, como nomads, just like our Aztec ancestors a thousand years ago. (*Mexican Medea*: 306–7)

Purposefully, Moraga relates the migratory experience of the jotería, the Chicano queers, to that of the ancient Aztecs. She points out the contradictions inherent in the 'colored countries' ' acts of exclusion. Borrowing a phrase from Audre Lorde, there can be no 'hierarchy of oppressions' (306–7); rather there is a need for radical equivalency of oppressions, and resistance. Moraga queers Aztlán by questioning who belongs in the Chicano nation and how that nation is defined. Within each of these works sexual politics challenge identity politics and complicate notions of being Chicano, being Black, or being Chinese.

PERFORMING CULTURAL IDENTITY

In *A Language of Their Own*, Yew further problematizes questions of interracial desire raised by Freeman in *Civil Sex*. Tensions over cultural identity escalate after Ming and Oscar break up and Ming becomes involved with Robert, a White gay man, while Oscar finds companionship with another Asian, Daniel, a younger Filipino AIDS activist. Interestingly, Robert has continually been involved with Asian men and takes a Vietnamese lover, Pran, when he and Ming have problems. Jonathan Dollimore argues that 'desire for, identification with the cultural and racial other brings with it a complicated, ambivalent history' (25). In *A Language of Their Own*, past histories of Asian/white desire haunt contemporary relations and reflect the power dynamics and cultural hegemonies that are in place. Yew brings these complications to the surface as Ming and Oscar discuss Ming's new lover:

OSCAR: I thought you never dated white guys.
MING: Well I am.
OSCAR: I see.
MING: A lot of Asian guys date white guys.

OSCAR: I know all too many.
MING: Is that a problem?
OSCAR: Asians only date white guys –
MING: Please don't –
OSCAR: To assimilate –
MING: That's not fair –
OSCAR: To emulate –
MING: I'm with Robert because I love ...
(A Language of Their Own: 167–8)

Certainly, Oscar's attitudes are 'colored' by his own feelings of rejection. Still, the conversation raises oft-heard prejudices against and perceptions of Asian desire for the White other. The scene reinforces the potential power of racial histories to impact on sexual desire. Racial difference intersects the 'sexual difference' of homosexuality within the play and complicates the characters in their struggle with each other, with their cultural identities, with themselves.

One telling moment of intercultural exchange occurs when Ming discovers Robert has slept with another man, his Vietnamese friend, Pran, in the bedroom he shares with Ming. This indiscretion creates a breach, social dramatic crisis and it is within the crisis phase of this social drama that performative cultural identities are constructed. Ming becomes the abused and abusive lover as he later physically assaults Robert. He also acts to denigrate Pran and to distance Pran from himself through racial epithet:

ROBERT: Let me put this in plain and simple English: You're jealous.
MING: Jealous? Of that little Vietnamese boat person? I don't give a –
(A Language of Their Own: 199–200)

Ming performs cultural difference. He otherizes Pran and separates Pran's Asian status from his own. Ming asserts his own identity on and through his distinctions from Pran. This cultural performance and venomous attack reinforce our recognition of 'Asian American' as an inherently constructed political category that can both reflect and elide difference. Present perhaps within Ming's performance are elements of internalized racism, self-hatred, and denial. Also present within this portrait, as in *Civil Sex*, are the inevitable disruptions that desire inflicts upon conventional binaries of difference. Race is again queered. The racialized nature of the sexuality complicates and informs the contingent nature of racial categorizations.

For the other couple, Daniel and Oscar, social crisis and resultant performances of identity arise not because of racial or intraracial tensions but due to the rapid advance of Oscar's disease. Within the social crisis that is AIDS, Daniel performs the role of caregiver and lover. 'No one asks how I'm doing. Everyone assumes. That I'm fine' (A Language of Their Own: 210). In this social breach, as he watches his lover suffer, he questions his own identity as an HIV-negative gay man. David Román notes that within the new culture of HIV-positives and 'the dominant media's conflation of AIDS and homosexuality' such doubts are not uncommon.

In a culture that systematically denies their identity and experience, some HIV-negative gay men assume their seroconversion will bring meaning to their lives, as well as attention and love. HIV-negative gay men's desire to test positive results from the anxiety associated with the logic of inevitability, but it is also motivated by the desire to be seen and heard (Román, 1999: 191).

Daniel does become HIV-positive as Oscar dies. In contrast, Ming faces the crisis of Oscar's death and subsequent memorial service through performances of denial and avoidance. He does not even attend the service. 'I wanted to but – I didn't' (*A Language of Their Own*: 224). In *Mexican Medea*, the social dramatic breach involves Jason's plan to reclaim his son Chac-Mool and bring him back to Aztlán. This threat disrupts the world of Medea and affects her performances of cultural identity. This breach and the play's resulting action comment on the 'unmarked' power of the patriarchy and latent heterosexism within Chicano cultural politics. Medea laments:

> 'Politics.' Men think women have no love of country, that obsession with nation is a male prerogative, So like the gods, they pick and choose who is to be born and live and die in a land I bled for equal to any man. And I am left out here in this wasteland where yerbas grow bitter for lack of water, my face pressed to the glass of my own revolution like some huerfana abandonada. (*Mexican Medea*: 301)

Through Medea, Moraga questions the conventional position of women within the politics of Chicano liberation. She decries the devaluation of women and women's work within the Chicano cultural nationalistic espousals of Aztlán. Her Medea's personal plight links the political, racial, sexual, and cultural. Medea recognizes and desires the security, the authority, and the sense of cultural identity that come from belonging to a homeland. Still, branded as different and deviant, as woman and lesbian, she remains a liminal outsider struggling for re-entry.

Moraga interrogates the relationship between blood, race, and nation. Aztlán in *Mexican Medea* is a space of racial purity and consequently miscegenation and interracial desire are forms of pollution that threaten to dilute it. The lesbianism of Luna, Medea, and others is another form of pollution. Samuel R. Delaney writes in 'Some Queer Notions about Sex,' 'Homosexuality pollutes the family, the race, the nation *precisely because* it appears to reduce the threat or menace of pollution to others – the mutual menace that holds the boundaries of a given family, race in tense stability'

(273). Aztlán excludes gays and lesbians not because they procreate and
produce racial impure progeny but because their sexual difference undermines
the heterosexist imperative that maintains the stability of this racialized state.
Still, Medea complicates notions of pollution and exposes the fluidity of the
borders between gay/straight and Chicano/other because she did procreate
and produce the Indio son Chac-Mool that Jasón desires.

Moraga in an earlier essay, 'Queer Aztlán: The Re-formation of the Chicano
Tribe,' idealizes an imaginary and inclusive Aztlán that accepts gay and lesbian
Chicanos even as it celebrates Chicano cultural identity: 'A Chicano homeland
that could embrace all its people, including its jotería.' With this notion of a
Queer Aztlán, she longs for and looks back to the 1960s and a time of
romanticized Chicano identity politics and political urgency. 'What was right
about Chicano Nationalism was its commitment to preserving the integrity of
the Chicano people.' At the same time she is cautious of the absolutist and
exclusionary dynamics of cultural nationalism. 'What was wrong about
Chicano Nationalism was its institutionalized heterosexism, its inbred
machismo, and its lack of a cohesive national political strategy.' She calls for
a new politics of radicalized identity, that brings people together around a
shared political ideology rather than a constrained and exclusionary identity
politics. 'But it is historically evident that the female body like the Chicano
people, has been colonized. And any movement to decolonize them must be
culturally and sexually specific' (Moraga, 1993: 148–50).

With *Mexican Medea*, Moraga calls for such a culturally and sexually specific
decolonization through the body of Medea. Moraga's Medea, caught within
the social breach and its resulting liminality, attempts to redress her situation
through cultural performance. In one moment she even plays the role of
contrite heterosexual-desiring wife. In order to convince Jasón to take both
Chac-Mool and her back to Aztlán she sleeps with him again.

JASÓN: Medea, why the sudden change of heart?
MEDEA: I want what's best for my son. He'll be forgotten here in this
ghetto.
JASÓN: I'm ... sorry.
MEDEA: Are you?
JASÓN: You don't have to stay here either, you know.
MEDEA: I don't know that.
JASÓN: You're not a lesbian, Medea, for chrissake. This is a masquerade.
MEDEA: A seven-year-old one?
JASÓN: I'm not saying that you have no feelings for the relationship,
but you're not a Luna.
MEDEA: (*Sadly*) No, I'm not. (*Mexican Medea*: 327–8)

For Luna, the spurned lover, the rupture also necessitates cultural performances. She takes on another lover, a black woman, Savannah. With this interracial relationship, unlike Yew in *A Language of Their Own*, Moraga does not highlight the complex interactions of racial and sexual difference. Rather, Luna and Savannah come together over sameness. They share a politicized cultural identity as lesbians. Medea, on the other hand is sexually and culturally uncertain. When Jason betrays her again and the loss of her son is imminent, Medea performs the act of infanticide, poisoning Chac-Mool with curandera herbs. This act immediately connects her to other cultural traditions and to other mothers in history vilified and celebrated for the murder of their children. This heritage includes Margaret Garner, the escaped Black slave, who when re-captured, killed her children rather than see them sold back into slavery. Medea's act saves Chac-Mool from returning to a politically segregated and ideologically bankrupt Aztlán. She prevents him from carrying on traditions of patriarchal oppression. Most specifically, her act joins her with La Llorona, the weeping woman of Mexican legend, whom when wronged by her young husband threw her children into the river. The La Llorona legend has been continually reimagined and reinterpreted in Mexican and Chicano history. Within more recent feminist appropriations, La Llorona symbolizes the loneliness and agony of the disparaging mother, a woman without agency in a patriarchal society. La Llorona's action drives her mad with grief. Eternally, she searches for her children and cries out for their return. Correspondingly, Medea's act places her in a psychiatric prison ravaged by the loss. Moraga asks that her Medea's relation to La Llorona, the 'Mexican Medea,' be made tangible in the stage directions after the death of Chac-Mool: '*Their lament [the choruses] is accompanied by the soft cry of the wind in the background that swells into a deep moaning. It is the cry of La Llorona. The moon moves behind the mountains. The lights fade to black*' (*Mexican Medea*: 357). Significantly, La Llorona needs the light of the moon to appear and Medea too needs her Luna.

Medea's son Chac-Mool is equally trapped within intersecting liminalities and ruptures in the play: he is in the alien space of Phoenix caught between the wills of his father and his mother; he is 13 years old, within the throes of puberty, moving from childhood into manhood. While he desires to return to Aztlán and experience the ancient cultural traditions of initiation, Chac-Mool also wants to stay with his mother and Luna. His two names, 'Chac-Mool' and 'Adolfo,' given to him by his mother and father respectively, reflect the paradoxes of his cultural identity. The nickname Chac-Mool – the name he has tattooed into his arm, etched into his being – is the name of the ancient Mayan messenger to the gods and thus a symbol of Chicano cultural heritage and pride. On the other hand, he dislikes Adolfo, the name given to him by his father, because he associates it with Adolph Hitler, with Nazism. Chac-Mool's liminality raises the question: is it possible to reaffirm cultural identity without also reinforcing exclusivity, separatism, and ethnic absolutism? His liminality is both a place of potential danger and potent possibility.

Through Chac-Mool Moraga also asks if it is possible to raise a new culturally sensitive Chicano man who does not perpetuate the sins of the father. 'The man I wish my son to be does not exist, must be invented' (*Mexican Medea*: 339–40). Significantly, the boy-child Chac-Mool is the only male actor in the piece. In *Mexican Medea*, Moraga asks that women play all the male roles, including the husband Jasón, but not the boy, Chac-Mool. She asks that an actual young man portray him. Conventional Western drama, in concert with the hegemony of the male gaze, identifies with the male figure and inevitably makes the man the protagonist. In such an economy, Chac-Mool becomes the hero and focus of the piece. Moraga exposes this malecentric prejudice in a scenic moment that breaks the fourth wall and in Brechtian fashion compels the audience to think about the meanings of Chac-Mool and gender within the production. Standing at the border between Aztlán and Phoenix, a Border Guard chastises Chac-Mool by pointing out his difference: 'It's your play ... You're the source of the conflict. You're also the youngest, which means you're the future, it's gotta be about you. *And*, you're the only real male in the cast' (*Mexican Medea*: 344). Through this explicit rupture of the theatrical convention, Moraga exposes the unmarked and interrogates the power of patriarchal authority.

In *Civil Sex*, Freeman also challenges unmarked authority as he explores and exposes the dichotomies between what acts are considered public and private. At the end of the first act, Freeman stages the 'public display of lewdness' that landed Rustin in jail and jeopardized his career as a Civil Rights activist. As 'My Funny Valentine' plays in the background, the actor portraying Rustin and two white actors engage in a homosexual 'three way' with choreographic precision. At the end of this scene, the police 'bust' the three men and escort them off to jail. This is a scene of powerful and provocative exposures. Within the intimacy of a public theater, it re-creates the act that publicly exposed Rustin's sexuality, ruptured his relations with certain social organizations, and caused him to undertake redressive performances of cultural identity. These performances included a press conference in August 1963 held to respond to charges levied by Senator Strum Thurmond. Freeman strategically replays this press conference at the climax of the play, while Senator Thurmond's attack serves as the inciting moment at the play's outset:

RUSTIN: ... Third, regarding the question, regarding the question of my moral behavior, I will let Mr. Randolph respond.
MACREYNOLDS: And Randolph said 'Well, these charges really go back

some years and Mr. Rustin has been of great service to our community and I think that I will not dignify the charges by any further comment on them.' Gone! He was suddenly respectable. No one believed Thurmond's charges. They were all absolutely true ... (*Civil Sex*, Press Conference: 1).

This scene also exposes the public/private dynamic that Freeman sees at work in Rustin's arrest and in gay male sexuality. Kendall Thomas relates 'gay male culture has been at least for the last 100 years a public sex culture. So it's not surprising he would be arrested' (*Civil Sex*, K. Thomas: 2). In a later theatricalized interview, the interview subject, Tim Bensten, a young Black gay man states: 'its [gay sex] is this very private activity that takes place in a public place' (*Civil Sex*, Tim Bensten: 2).' The public nature of these gay sex acts then – in themselves already a breach of the social norm – represent a performance of subversive visibility. They perform in public places that which even in private has been declared socially taboo. Yet, Freeman in *Civil Sex* suggests that this must not be what Phelan (1993) terms an impoverished visibility (26). Accordingly, Freeman relates the public, private revolt of gay sexual politics and cultural behavior to the fight for Civil Rights made visible through public displays, such as the 1964 March on Washington organized by Bayard Rustin. In the staged version of the play at Berkeley Repertory Theater in Berkeley, California, in February 2000, the play ends with a celebratory Gay Rights March symbolically linking Black and gay activism. The march as a conclusion triumphantly links race, sexuality, and resistance in a moment of celebratory protest.

TOWARDS A NEW AUDIENCE

All three works expose simplistic racial definitions. They raise questions about and provide examples of how sexuality disrupts homogenized racial readings. Within each work queerness and understandings of queer identities across racial and cultural borders create the potential for new coalitions and new performances of cultural identity. The performances of cultural identity in each of these works reveal the contingent nature of culture, the presence of intraracial differences, and the potential new cultural coalitions. By exploring diverse representations of sexuality, these plays open up new dramatic territory. These works reflect the potential of a new multicultural theater to articulate problems but also for it to raise awareness of the continued need for racial reconceptualizations and for social change. Like Suzan-Lori Parks's work addressed at the outset of this chapter, these plays reveal that race is not simply 'in the blood.'

While each of these works focusses on particular racial groups and specific cultural experiences, they do not simply represent these groups in isolation. Rather they queer race and show ways in which the very queerness of race necessitates new political strategies. These works evacuate the exclusivity of identity politics even as they assert productive tensions around identity positions. They help us view racial, sexual, and cultural identities as constantly producing and produced rather than fixed and immutable categories. As José Muñóz (1999) suggests, such a new multicultural theater 'calls attention to the conflict and strife between identity components, refusing to whitewash such complexities' (167). If these plays exemplify a move towards new territory in multicultural theater, then such a move requires that we push beyond previous homogenization and conventional limitations on multicultural theater. And yet, within such works, vestiges of the past histories of racial oppression and resistance must not be forgotten. They are present but now reconfigured. A new multicultural theater opens up, as Muñóz notes, 'worlds of transformative possibilities ... that alter the present and map out a future' (195). An investigation of these three works also begs a series of critical questions at the core of this chapter but not yet addressed: Who will be the audience for this new multicultural theater? Do these three works because of their queer politics re-territorialize minority theater and find only audiences attentive to gay issues? Can the politics of these works attract and engage diverse, multicultural audiences? As I sat observing the audience on the other side of the narrow stage for *In the Blood*, I reflected on such questions of spectatorship. That December night, the audience embodied a wide spectrum of gender and racial diversity as manifest in the cast of *In the Blood* and in Artistic Director George C. Wolfe's cultural mandate for the Public Theater. And yet, there were also empty seats across from me that night. Despite stellar critical reviews, *In the Blood* at the Public Theater was not a commercial success. Although the work is more linear and accessible than other Parks plays and even though it featured the virtuoso acting of Charlayne Woodard as Hester, the play did not appeal to a mainstream clientele.

Who should be the audience for a new multicultural theater? A paradox perhaps remains in our desire for new dramatic territory and in how we seek out an audience, determine public approval and critical acclaim. New territory for multicultural theater requires new audiences, different and diverse spectators, and new cross-cultural connections. And yet, the economics of theater demand success in the existing commercial mainstream. Can or should work that emanates from the margins, minority voices, and experiences be mainstream? How do we further decenter and explode the definitions of what constitutes the mainstream? We must push for new critical territory of analysis, but also for new territories of recognition and standards of theatrical legitimacy. New audiences must be both educated and engaged. They need to see themselves on stage but also to appreciate the potential for new cultural, social, sexual, racial, political understandings outside their immediate circumstances. These are lofty goals but we are in a new time of possibility to achieve them.

ACKNOWLEDGMENT

Special thanks to Landonia Jones for her inspiration on this piece.

REFERENCES

Arrizón, Alicia, 'Mythical Performativity: Relocating Aztlán in Chicana Feminist Cultural Productions,' *Theatre Journal*, 52 (March 2000: 23–49).

Chaudhuri, Una, *Staging Place: The Geography of Modern Drama* (Ann Arbor, MI: University of Michigan Press, 1997).

Davis, Angela, 'Gender, Class and Multiculturalism,' in Avery F. Gordon and Christopher Newfield (eds), *Mapping Multiculturalism* (Minneapolis: University of Minnesota Press, 1996; 40–8).

Delaney, Samuel R., 'Some Queer Notions about Sex,' in Eric Brandt (ed.), *Dangerous Liaisons* (New York: New Press, 1999, 259–89).

Deloria, Philip, *Playing Indian* (New Haven, CT: Yale University Press, 1998).

Diamond, Elin, *Performance and Cultural Politics* (New York: Routledge, 1996).

Donald, James and Rattansi, Ali, 'Introduction,' in *Race, Culture and Difference* (London: Sage, 1992, 1–16).

DuBois, W. E. B., *The Souls of Black Folk* (New York: Penguin, 1969).

Freeman, Brian, *Civil Sex* (unpublished playscript, 1998).

Gubar, Susan, *Racechanges* (New York: Oxford University Press, 1997).

Hall, Stuart, 'Introduction: Who Needs Identity?,' in Stuart Hall and Paul Du Gray (eds), *Questions of Cultural Identity* (London: Sage, 1996, 1–17).

Kershaw, Baz, *The Politics of Performance: Radical Theater as Cultural Intervention* (New York: Routledge, 1992).

Lowe, Lisa, *Immigrant Acts* (Durham, NC: Duke University Press, 1997).

Moraga, Cherríe, 'Queer Aztlán: The Reformation of the Chicano Tribe,' in *The Last Generation* (Boston: South End Press, 1993, 145–74).

— *The Hungry Woman: A Mexican Medea*, in Caridad Svich and Maria Teresa Marrero (eds), *Out of the Fringe: Contemporary Latina/Latino Theater and Performance* (New York: TCG P, 2000, 289–364).

Muñóz, José, *Disidentifications: Queers of Color and the Performance of Politics*, (Minneapolis: University of Minnesota Press, 1999).

Nora, Pierre, 'Between Memory and History: Les Lieux de Memoire,' in Genevieve

Fabre and Robert O'Meally (eds), *History and Memory in African-American Culture* (New York: Oxford University Press, 1994, 284–300).

Onigiri, Ami Abugo, 'We Are Family: Miscegenation, Black Nationalism, Black Masculinity, and the Black Gay Cultural Imagination,' in Kostas Myrsiades and Linda Myrsiades (eds), *Race-ing Representation: Voice, History, and Sexuality* (Lanham, MD: Rowman & Littlefield Press, 1998, 231–46).

Parkin, David, Caplan, Lionel, and Fisher, Humphrey (eds), *The Politics of Cultural Performance* (Oxford: Berghan, 1996).

Parks, Suzan-Lori, *The America Play, and Other Works* (New York: TCG Press, 1995).

Phelan, Peggy, *Unmarked: The Politics of Performance* (New York: Routledge, 1993).

Roach, Joseph, *Cities of the Dead* (New York: Columbia University Press, 1996).

Román, David, *Acts of Intervention* (Bloomington, IN: University of Indiana Press, 1998).

'Negative Identifications: HIV-Negative Gay Men in Representation and Performance,' in Michal Kobialka (ed.), *Of Borders and Thresholds: Theater History, Practice and Theory* (Minneapolis: University of Minnesota Press, 1999, 184–213).

Turner, Victor, *Schism and Continuity in an African Society: A Study of Ndembu Village Life* (Manchester: Manchester University Press, 1957).

— *From Ritual to Theater* (New York: Performing Arts Press, 1982).

Yew, Chay, 'A Language of Their Own,' *Two Plays by Chay Yew* (New York: Grove Press, 1997, 117–228).

7

Sour grapes: the art of anger in América[1]

Cherríe Moraga

> Here is a fruit for the crows to pluck
> for the rain to gather
> for the wind to suck
> for the sun to rot
> for the tree to drop.
> Here is a strange and bitter crop.
>
> 'Strange Fruit', as sung by Billie Holiday[2]

But for the shared history of miscegenation, Pulitzer Prize-winning playwright August Wilson and I have little in common, at least at face value. He is a man, a man of large stature (he must be over 6 foot 2 and 200 lbs). He is an African American, a heterosexual, born in the East. I am a short, half-breed Mexican woman (I won't note my weight), born and raised in the Southwest. I am a lesbian. And yet, sitting in the last row of the packed 500-seat McCarter Theater at Princeton University, I cried and called him 'brother' out loud. I cried as he said to an audience of theater professionals, overwhelmingly White, 'I am a race man.' 'The Black Power Movement ... was the kiln in which I was fired.'[3] I cried out of hunger, out of solidarity, out of a longing for that once uncompromising cultural nationalism of the 1960s and 1970s that birthed a new nation of American Indian, Chicano, Asian American, and Black artists.

I describe here my experience of August Wilson's keynote address at the Theater Communication Groups conference in June 1996. My unexpected tears forced me to acknowledge my longing for a kind of collective mutual recognition as a 'colored' playwright writing in White America. It is a longing so wide and deep that every time Wilson mentioned 'Black,' I inserted Chicana. With every generic 'he,' I added 'she.' When he named Black artists who insisted on their own self-worth in what he referred to as the 'culturally imperialist' world of American theater as 'warriors on the cultural battlefield,' I knew he wasn't thinking of me guerrera and embattled; but I knew I carried the same weapons (more crudely made than his) and the same armor (mine surely more penetrable in my colored womanhood, in my sexuality). I knew, whether he recognized me or not among the ranks, that I was a 'sister' in that struggle against a prescription for American theater that erases the lives of every one I call my 'pueblo.'

In his address, Wilson went on to cite the history of slavery, distinguishing between those slaves who entertained in the big house for the master, versus those who remained in the slave quarters, creating song, dance and story for one another. He proclaimed, 'I stand ... squarely on the self-defining ground of the slave quarters.' Wilson writes unequivocally for a Black audience. The day before, I had gone to see his latest play, *Seven Guitars*, on Broadway, surely the 'big house' by mainstream theater standards; still, the language – of word and body – in the play, as is the case with all Wilson's plays, reflected an 'un-translated' conversation among African Americans (especially men), one which White audiences may be privileged to witness, but are prohibited from shaping, even as they 'consume' it through their ticket purchase.[4]

As a Black *American* writer, Wilson sees himself in the trajectory of Western theater, that finds its foundation in the Greek dramatists and Aristotle's *Poetics*. Possibly this shared 'foundation' is what makes Wilson's work, although challenging in content, accessible in form to Euro-American audiences. Still he 'reserve[s] the right,' as he puts it, '... to add [his] African consciousness and ... aesthetic to the art [he] produces.' A right he freely and powerfully employs.

The American theater establishment enjoys using August Wilson as the example of the ultimate democracy of American theater, that even a one-time member of the slave-class of this country can make the 'big time.' Meanwhile the aesthetics of Euro-American theater – what is considered 'good art' – remain institutionally unaltered and secured by the standard theatergoer who pays 'good money' to see it; that is, a theater which reflects the world as Middle America understands it, a world which at its core equates free enterprise with freedom. As Chicano theater historian Jorge Huerta puts it: 'If theater is a temple, it is now dedicated to corporate greed.'[5] A few 'darkies,' 'commies,' and 'perverts' may slip through the cracks, but the gestures are token attempts to keep the marginalized in this country – that growing discontent 'minority' – pacified. Exceptions to the rule never become the rule.

Sometimes I marvel at my own naïveté. Throughout my 12 years of writing for the American theater, over and over again I am referred to the Aristotelian model of the 'well-made play.' So, good student that I am, I track down Aristotle's *Poetics*. I read it, re-read it, take copious notes. But not until I read the Marxism of Brecht, then Augosto Boal's *Theater of the Oppressed*, does my discomfort with the Aristotelian system begin to make any sense. Aristotle created his poetics within the context of a slave-based economy, an imperialist democracy, not unlike the corporate-controlled democracy we are living under in the United States today. Women and slaves were not free citizens in Aristotle's Greece.[6] I am reminded of my own character's words in a recent play, as she struggles to remember the dance of her O'odham ancestors: 'I just keep moving my feet like this ... ignorant feet ... in order to do something other than theirs on this stage.'[7] What does the theater of the oppressed really *look* like? Can the forms of our theatrical storytelling take on a shape distinct from the slave-master's stage? Today, the very people (Mexican *and* American at once) who take center stage in my plays daily have their citizenship denied, questioned, and/or inauthenticated. These are me, my mother, my cousins, my ancestors, and my children. These are my characters, like Wilson's, the children of slaves. And when the children of slaves become playwrights, even our literary ancestors are proffered freedom.

I'm watching this freedom struggle take space on stage. I'm watching history in the making, watching child-of-slave-little-brother-son take pen in hand and write. For us.

In *Fed Up: A Cannibal's Own Story*, Chicano playwright, Ricardo A. Bracho, gives voice to whom he refers to as 'the first woman of color of the outer colonies of Western Theater,' Sycorax of *The Tempest*:[8]

> You know (silence) goes way back. ... I used to think that was my name, but it aint. ... The name's Sycorax. Silence. Silence. Sycorax. Close, huh? Particularly when you're not allowed the chance of sounding it out. See on account of one whiteboy who went by the name of William Shakespeare I been ... shut-mouthed for centuries. He wrote a play about me n mine (indicates the 'Cannibals'). My island. My sex. And this fantasy he and his call my race.[9]

When the children of slave women begin to speak, they point fingers as deadly as knives. The knives pierce to core depth of silence. It hurts all around. And they will care more passionately about their love for one another than their hatred for their one-time 'master.' Bracho's play attests to this colored-centric passion. In *Fed Up* his 'cannibals' (i. e. modern-day Calibans and the children of Sycorax whom the playwright characterizes as gay men of color) make a meal out of the body of the Dead White Writer, a gay man. Historically the White man's prey, the 'Cannibals' revolt in their ritualistic consumption of the writer's remains. A rage generated by the colonization of the colored body motivates the writing of the play and the action of the characters.

CorporateAmerika is not ready for a people of color theater that holds members of its audiences complicitous in the oppression of its characters. *Who would buy a ticket to see that?* Audiences grow angry (although critics as their spokespeople may call it 'criticism') when a work is not written *for* them, when they are not enlisted as a partner in the protagonists' struggle, when they may be asked to engage through self-examination rather than identification, when they must question their own centrality.

The next day, at the same TCG conference, I was on a playwrights' panel where we were to discuss the motivation or inspiration for our playwriting. Without hesitation, I responded 'absence.' Like in those children's games where you are shown a picture, you study it, then turn the page, and you are shown the same picture again, but this time you have to figure out what is missing. You are asked, 'What's missing in this picture?' That question sums up my entire experience as a Chicana feminist playwright. With every play produced whether on Broadway or in the barrio, I ask the question, what's missing in this picture? And the answer is invariably, 'we.' Suzan-Lori Parks echoes this sentiment in a 1995 interview in *The Drama Review*: 'It's a fabricated absence. That's where I start from ... It's the hole idea ... It's the story that you're told that goes, "once upon a time you weren't here ... and you didn't do shit." '[10]
I don't go to the theater looking for other Chicana lesbians. (Or at least I don't look for them *on stage*.) But I do look for glimpses of colored-woman-centered realities without White male translations. Stories of colored womanhood that are complex, contradictory, and compelling told by equally complex, contradictory, and compelling colored women writers. Certainly in the late 1990s, we can witness some of this on the pages of a book, but theater remains what seems to be the last bastion of cultural imperialism in the American art world, with the visual arts a close second. Is it because it is a three-dimensional live form which, like film, requires real live women of color as actors, writers, and directors? The novel requires only one tenacious colored woman and some significant support along the way. The collaborative art forms require a small army.
I most viscerally experienced this 'what's missing in this picture?' phenomenon as an audience member of Tony Kushner's *Angels in America* on Broadway. Of course, I loved the play, as did most of the audience that Sunday matinee, as has most of the theater-going public of the United States in the last few years. The play is undeniably and unabashedly queer and dangerously 'commie' in perspective, which I relish and respect about Kushner's work. But what I anticipated would make the audience uncomfortable was precisely what made the audience hysterical. Every dick joke, even every *Jewish* dick joke, even every *homosexual* Jewish dick joke, tore the audience up. They weren't offended. They were entertained. So, I thought to myself well, Jewish humor is synonymous with New York and so even non-

Jews 'get the joke' on Broadway. The same is true, to a certain degree, across the United States, where prime-time TV abounds with Jewish and 'kind of' Jewish guys cracking jokes, written by Jewish writers. To the degree that a Jewish sensibility – the exquisite timing in the telling of a joke, the witticism, the occasional Yiddish term, the sharp-tongue, the self-denigrating comment, and so on – has penetrated the family evening TV hour, Kushner's *Angels* has to do little cultural translation to be understood by mainstream audiences. (Except for the fact that the playwright is better read than 99 percent of most Americans.) I would also interject here that Jewish-American *drama* is another story all together, where Jewish culture for the most part remains 'ghettoized' within the genre of comedy. Further, I must also add before any inferences of 'Jewish conspiracy theories' be extrapolated from this writing that I make the comparison with a leftist queer Jewish writer precisely because he is *not* a WASP. Because he is specific about his cultural 'otherness' from WASP Amerika and the history of genocide that prohibits his complete assimilation. Because this comparison is the closest I, as a Chicana lesbian playwright, can get to a mainstream counterpart, like August Wilson, which still is, of course, very far away.

OK, so culturally, *Angels* is translatable. Everyone's laughing at the Jewish jokes, but the dick jokes? The homo jokes? I look around at this Broadway audience, mostly straight, overwhelmingly White, upper middle class, of course: your typical theater crowd, and again, I can't believe it, they're all laughing. Are they laughing because the play is a Tony Award winner and they think to be cool and hip, they better laugh? Maybe. Still, to my amazement two guys start to 'fuck' on stage (as Kushner describes it in the stage directions: 'They fuck.') and everyone is fine with it. Of course, we know theater is not real life and those same laughing lawyers and stockbrokers in the audience may very well cry at the *real* news of having a *real* gay son. But theater is what I am looking at here. So, I did a little private experiment. Every time I heard the word or a reference to 'Jewish dick,' I replaced it with 'Mexican pussy.' Jewish dick ... Mexican pussy. Jewish dick ... Mexican pussy. Jewish dick ... Mexican pussy. And nobody was laughing. That's me on Broadway. That's my people on Broadway. That chilling silence. Nobody is laughing. Pussy ain't funny unless a man tells the joke. Mexican ain't funny unless a gringo's talking. Put a Mexican woman downstage center having and wanting some pussy and nobody's gonna laugh ... unless she is laughed at ... i.e. ridiculed, objectified, scorned. *And who the hell's gonna translate that Spanglish those Chicanos speak anyway?*

Of course, prick like pussy is always racialized and, therefore, politicized; and not for a minute do I imagine Kushner is not critically aware of the racialized history of Jewish genitalia and the sexual exploitation and distortions suffered by Jews (male and female alike) through anti-Semitism. Nevertheless, in contemporary U.S. mainstream society, there is also a profound identification with dick, from both men and women, and a comfort in the 'normalcy' of its Whiteness. After all we aren't talking Black dick here, which is, Eurocentrically speaking, altogether more dangerous.

'Sour grapes,' this is what the little diablito (internalized-racist) voice keeps whispering in my ear, throughout this writing. 'Ah, Moraga, this is all just sour grapes.' And I think, 'Yes, exactly.' Sour grapes: the bitter fruit artists of color are forced to eat in this country.

Zoot Suit, by Luis Valdez, the only Chicano work that ever made it to Broadway was a sold-out long-running success in the late 1970s in Los Angeles, but it only lasted a few weeks on Broadway. Why? It was not culturally translatable. Even the play's concessions to the mainstream, including a few redeeming and redemptive White characters to whom the typical theatergoer might relate, weren't sufficient to 'de-Chicano' the play. Who would pay for it? Not New York. New York won't even pay to see Puerto Ricans, whom ostensibly they should know better by sheer geographic proximity and demographic representation. (Of course, there is always the occasional revival of *West Side Story*.) The reviews killed *Zoot Suit* because the reviewers were being asked to step outside their cultural myopia in order to not only evaluate a work, but actually 'see' it.

If the agreed assumption is that good theater is a good time, a good cry, a good laugh, then writers must create characters with whom their audience can identify to create that emotional connection. And the reviewers, representing the concerns of the typical audience, are being entrusted with that responsibility to ensure a 'good time' to their readers and ward off the 'bad.' Although the majority of theatergoers are White middle-class *females*, the producers are overwhelmingly White and *male* who expect all of us cultural consumers to digest the works we witness on stage as they do, that is as White men. This doesn't require great cross-cultural leaps for most viewers, regardless of gender or race. We know how White men think because White men have had the privileged opportunity to tell us so through our educational system, every manner of media, all forms of literature and the arts. Similarly, the White-male-minded writer has to do little cultural translation to elicit his audience's identification and sympathies. We slide effortlessly into the well-worn shoes of his protagonist. The story moves us. Leaving the theater, we feel better. Again, Aristotle's theater of catharsis.

When the subject of a work is a woman of color, however, a poor or working-class woman, maybe even a lesbian, and the character is *not* constructed within the White male imagination (neither exoticized, eroticized or stigmatized), how much harder must the playwright work to convey the character's humanity, for she is from the onset perceived as 'other,' that is not a suitable subject for identification. In this case, playing before a mainstream theater audience, how much more difficult it is to establish that emotional connection with the audience. The spectator and the reviewer don't care about her life. She is foreign. The play is judged as inferior. 'I wasn't moved,' writes the critic. Chicanas' multi-generational conversation sitting around a kitchen table is referred to as 'banter' because the critic isn't interested in it. The only significant male figure in an otherwise all-Chicana play, *Shadow of a Man*, is mistakenly viewed as the protagonist because he's the closest the male reviewer can get to caring. 'He's a weak character,' the reviewer states. 'He doesn't hold the play together.' He wasn't supposed to. In *Shadow*, the father's (intentional) weakness as a character is fundamental to the plot; it is the women who must hold the family *and* the story together. But the reviewer wasn't following the plotlines of those whom he was accustomed to viewing as auxiliary to the 'real' (the man's) story.[11]

I have never felt so strongly about the cultural tyranny of theater reviews as with the premiere production of my play, *Watsonville: Some Place Not Here*.[12] Probably more than any other of my works, *Watsonville*, to the credit of Brava Theater Center (the producer), generated in its six-week run in San Francisco the most diverse audience I have ever witnessed. It included the mainstream theatergoer, all the major press, the 'art' community, the politically active Chicano community, student groups, youth groups from the barrios of San Francisco and Watsonville, queers of all kinds, feminist activists, women's groups, and a steady base of Mexican immigrant workers from the greater Bay Area. Each audience created a different gestalt, each new configuration of all the sectors mentioned above made for a different experience of the play. This is, I'm reminded, the marvelous beauty and danger of theater: the audience as collaborator in the experience. Teenagers snickered nervously at the lesbian kiss. Cannery workers from Watsonville whispered in Spanish to their comadres, 'Así se sucedió.' ('It happened like that,') referring to the 18-month strike upon which the play was based. Chicana lesbians laughed out loud when the heterosexual cannery worker, a single mother, wants to know how you can tell who's who in a lesbian relationship: 'If some women are your friends and some are your lovers, how do you know when to be celosa [jealous]?' Her innocence is familiar and familial; we see her in our cousins, our aunts, the young women of our barrios. Lefties found resonance in the middle-aged drunken nostalgia of two Chicano organizers who mourn the increasing poverty and isolation of Cuba due to the U.S. embargo. 'Ay pobre de Cuba. The only island left in the world.'

Journal entry. May 27. The morning after.
I don't remember the opening night party, I only remember the performance.
What was on a different night too long, last night captured all our attention,
our minds & hearts — those of us so hungry to see our lives, our people reflected.
I felt vindicated. Yes, I believe that is the word: 'vindicated.'

'You see. Ya ves,' I want to say to all those who doubt us, our complexity,
render us invisible. 'We exist ... y más.' The reviews tomorrow, no doubt, will
say they saw something else. But, I must remember the work. I am getting
closer, I hope, to some more profound portrait of who we are as a people. That's
all that really matters: the writing.

My journal entry predicted correctly. When the reviews for *Watsonville*
came out, the only official judges on the play's significance were middle-class
Euro-Americans who regarded the play as outsiders, without once questioning
the cultural bias and ignorance that influenced their opinions. The play's
structure didn't adhere to the requirements of a 'well-made play,' they
complained. (Otra vez, Aristotle.) 'Who *is* the main character?' 'Too many
stories.' 'Epic in dimension,' but 'the playwright just doesn't pull it off.'

OK, who needs them — these reviewer guys and (sometimes) gals?
Progressive theater needs them because they bring in the middle-class ticket
buyers, those who can afford to pay full price on a Saturday night and cover
the cost of all the group rates and freebies that bring in the audiences who *do*
see their lives reflected in the work. Without governmental support for the
arts, community-based theaters striving to create an art of integrity and beauty
are forced into dependent relationships with whiteuppermiddleclassamerica.
Still, this is not just a question of exploiting the monied classes for the
advancement of the disenfranchised; there is also a moral and aesthetic
obligation here. If critics refuse to learn the traditions, the languages, the
sensibilities of the artists they critique how are they then to educate their own
readers? As August Wilson states: 'The true critic does not sit in judgment.
Rather he seeks to inform his reader, instead of adopting a posture of self-
conscious importance in which he sees himself a judge and final arbiter of a
work's importance or value.'[13] Simply put, how can a critic judge a work he
knows nothing about? And how can s/he call something representative of
American theater when his definition of 'American' remains a colonial one, that
is White America perceiving Blackness through the distorted mirror of its own
historical slave-owner segregationist racist paranoia and guilt, while all other
people of color remain racially invisible.

Sour grapes? Oh, most definitely.

I attended that TCG conference in Princeton one week before the closing of *Watsonville* in San Francisco. In the best of scenarios, we'd hoped the play might run all summer. Due to the lukewarm critical reception of the play, ticket sales dwindled and the play closed after the sixth week. In retrospect, I understand that the proximity of my disappointment in the reviews is one reason August Wilson's words brought tears to my eyes and the shape of an 'old-fashioned' raised fist to my hand. Few theater professionals really comprehend the obstacles to creating a colored (and I would add female) theater in White America, except those who have suffered at its hands. I do not turn to this writing to discuss the merits or weaknesses of my dramatic works, for I know the body of my writings contain both. I turn to these words to discuss the politics of trying to write and produce theater in a country where the people you speak of, with, and for are a theatrical non-event or worse in 'real life' and the object of derision and scapegoating.

This is real life.

I am a half-breed Chicana. The difference between my gringo immigrant side and my native Mexican is that when gringos came to the United States they were supposed to forget their origins. My whitedaddy isn't quite sure what he is. Orphan son of a British (maybe changed-his-name-Irish) Canadian, he thinks. His mother ... French, yes French for sure, cuz there was some French grandmother somewhere, but Missouri is where they all end up. She meeting my grandfather whom I only met once ... they say ... I was too young to remember ... my Dad's history too vague to remember because they came to this country to forget.

Mexicans, however, don't forget. Anything. We remember our land daily in the same smells, same seasons, same skies, same sierras, same street signs ... San Francisco ... Alameda ... El Presidio ... the Spanish sounds slip and slide away. It is a colonial language, but of an Indian people. And the measure of our 'Americanism' (in U. S. terms), the testimony to our acculturation to U.S. culture, is our eventual forgetting.

But I remember ... one smog-laden sticky-thighed childhood afternoon, sitting inside the cool stone walls of the Old San Gabriel Mission, our parish church. The nun tells us, 'There are dead Indians buried down there, too.' She said this 'too' like an afterthought, after roll-calling the rolling r's of each of the Spanish friars' names carved into the man-sized floor plaque filling the center aisle floor. 'Down there,' she said. Down there under my white Oxford mission schoolgirl soles, shuffling against the creaking wooden pews and a buried history.

I am neither Spanish friar nor mission Indian, but it's Indian history I'm diggin' up, diggin' for, thirty-five years later. Or maybe I'm just hunting for some woman somewhere some breed some mixed-blood mixed-up mess of a woman-loving-woman like me.

I am once twice three times removed. But I know, I ain't all immigrant.

To me, one of the greatest and most bitter ironies is that the Mexican immigrant daily reminds us Chicanos (or U.S.-born Mexicans) that we are not really immigrants at all. What most immigrants from Mexico share is poverty and what most poor people share in the nation-state of México is their Indianism. They may be calling themselves 'Mexican,' but their blood is speaking indigenous American. And the shape of the head, the nose, the cheekbones, the shade of skin is talking back.

So, I'm angry and I write about it. I write when little in the national picture reflects back anything I understand as common sense. What was initiated by the California's Proposition 187[14] in the mid-1990s and nationalized in Congress is the lie in the line, the borderline. When I first began this essay in the Fall of 1996, Congress had already made recommendations that would require a national ID, repeal the 14th Amendment's guarantee of citizenship to U.S.-born children of undocumented parents, limit due process for asylum seekers, deny undocumented children a public education, and increase, yet again, border patrol enforcement. Ironically, this turn-of-the century 'witch hunt' against 'illegal immigrants' is being mounted primarily against Mexicans and Central Americans, people with roots in this continent that surpass the Anglo-American by millennia. The real truth is Americans are being kept out of América. As the century comes to a close, California emerges as the brainchild of a legislation of fear and scapegoatism. 187 laid fertile ground for the unrestrained xenophobia and racism of Propositions 209 and 227,[15] which followed a few years later. The combination of the abolition of affirmative action and bilingual education in our public schools ensures that the Latino/a student, in particular (the largest minority in California), will remain firmly situated in the underclass of this country. We will remain 'illegal' and 'illiterate,' which is exactly where CorporateAmerika prefers its working poor, if not in prison. In the meantime, U.S. corporations, thanks to NAFTA, can cross the border, without restraint, in order to exploit Mexican labor and land. The maquiladores are a case in point, but Mexicans cannot return the favor by freely seeking a livable wage in the U.S.

Generated by the same cultural arrogance and greed exhibited by U.S. corporations and their legislators, the so-called progressive American art world inflicts admittedly more benign but equally insidious acts of exclusion on Chicano/a and other 'colored-identified' Latino artists.[16] It is precisely the indigenism of Chicano art and its opposition to Euro-American cultural dominance that renders it 'foreign' and of little interest to the dominant U.S. culture, a culture of European immigrants.[17] Ironically it is the same indigenism that makes much of Chicano culture fundamentally 'American' in the original *native* sense of the term, not the constitutionally constructed one. While regional theaters complain as federal legislators hack away at their government funding, those very institutions subscribe to the same narrow definition of American culture that their so-called enemies on Capitol Hill do.[18] They want us to forget our origins and, in the act of forgetting, make our work palatable to an American consumer culture. But I/we are not so easily eaten.

I am a third-generation Mexican born in the U.S. My mother was born in Santa Paula, California, in 1914; my maternal grandmother was born in the Sonoran desert in 1888. Was it Arizona then? Was it México? In the nineteenth century, borders were drawn like fingered lines in the sand, and erased with every wagon wheel. In the 1840s, U.S. land had been Mexican land; a generation before that, it was Spanish territory; and before that and always Apache, Yaqui, Seri, O'odham. Same land. Same folk. But shifting geopolitical borders, slavery, rape, intermarriage and Catholicism name the land and its dwellers differently and our identities change along with the changes. But never never thoroughly.

This is the American landscape: this califaspomo land upon which the United States imposes itself; this 'nation' born in 1776; this 'frontier' appropriated in 1848; this 'New Spain' stolen in 1519. The history of conquest in América constitutes so little time compared to the indigenous history that preceded it. And yet this is all América (even liberal América) seems to remember. To counter the racism laid bare by recent national anti-immigrant measures, progressives assert, 'but it was immigrants who built this country.' In order to justify the integration of new immigrants into U.S. society, liberals portray the United States as a nation constructed exclusively by immigrant labor, while slavery, the contributions of Native peoples, and the theft of Native lands are conveniently ignored. Further, there is little public discussion about which immigrant groups are made welcome in the United States and when? What does economics and politics have to do with it?[19] What does U.S. intervention in the Third World have to do with it?

Five days and five hundred years ago in América, immigrant Whites and their ancestors considered themselves welcome in this continent. Call it manifest destiny, call it the gold rush, call it the godly-thing to do, call it convert los indios, call it sugar cane, banana plantations, call it Phoenix-Arizona and Club Med, the dot-com gentrification of La Misión de San Panchito, call it New Age Spiritualism, call it whatever you want, Indigenous Americans continue to suffer as a consequence of European-immigrant cultural and political domination. Witness the neo-colonization and cultural appropriation of the U.S. Southwest by East Coast immigrant artists: the 'New New Mexico.'

How quickly we Native-born and immigrant people of color are required to forget our place of origin as guarantee of our Americanism. But what does a culture of forgetfulness produce except suburban shopping malls and more and more violent video games? True, every nation of people living within U.S.-imposed borders must reckon with the monolith of the nation-state, but we do not have to believe that a 'nationality,' a monoculture of people, was invented with the signing of the declaration of independence. If the Bill of Rights could be altered to give human rights to a U.S.-conceived fetus, while denying those same rights to a U.S.-born child of an undocumented immigrant, how much confidence should we put into the constitution as a reflection of the cultural/ethical values of the peoples of the United States of America?

On my more lucid days when my ideas are less controlled by prescribed modes of conventional thinking, I ask myself how it could happen that a new nation was invented to hold complete dominion in a land where verifiable nations already existed? How is it that the spiritual practices, ethical beliefs, systems of government, gender roles, and ecology of the original peoples of this land, as well as the peoples themselves, were not elemental to the construction of this invented nation? The Iroquois influence in the writing of the constitution seems thoroughly remote in its implementation. These are purposely naïve questions because the answers are equally simple. Such co-existence requires a humility of spirit and a sense of communal responsibility with other living beings which totally counters what we've come to understand as American culture.

Sour Grapes. The fruit of the labor del pueblo mechicano.

Highway 5, heading north from L.A. to San Francisco. I am on cruise-control, speeding through the California landscape. Grapes growing, thinking . . . Mexicans dying.

Cruising . . . and vineyards turn to endless miles of yellow dirt and graying tumbleweed. The backdrop: sentinels of electrical towers. There is a faint, very faint, mirage-like outline of what could be the Sierras, somewhere east of this cloudless central valley white-blue stillness. It's not desert here exactly, too much food growing, but the same trucks barrel through I-5 as I-80 with their oversized loads of trailer houses split into two for transport.

Five miles later, I can't name what crop borders the stone river of this highway, yellow-flowers blooming from irrigation, then fruit trees . . . almonds? Back to yellow dirt. Broken barbed wire and stick fences hold in fields of burnt brush.

Cruising . . . I pass a sign reading, 'Pleasant Valley State Prison,' an institutional oxymoron, then pull into an Arco station. A man hops out of the late model van next to me and slides open the passenger door. And I find the woman I have been looking for.

The van is packed hip-to-hip with Mexican farm workers coming back from the fields. It is the end of the day. She is squeezed among them, the only woman. She is the face of the best looking of us Mexican women. Her body draped in a loose flannel shirt and oversized khaki trousers. She is covered from shoulder to delicate wrist to ankle, I can't see her ankles, but want to. She could've been my mother sixty years ago. Same black eyes, black rope of hair. 'You don't belong here,' I hear my mother's words rise to the surface of my own lips. I want to tell her, 'you don't belong here.' Meaning out there, in the fields. Like they told my mother, her delicate-boned back bent over the potato, the cotton plan, the brussels sprout. Her artist's hands hooked into the shape of hoes.

The native beauty of this land reduced to labor undersold and stolen. The native beauty of this land reduced to labor: parceled plots of pesticide poison.

Land has memory. And the original peoples of that land, and those who daily live its lessons, are the memory carriers. The failure to remember, failure to respect and defend the memory carriers, destroys cultures, ecological environments, destroys lives. The United States' record of genocide against the original peoples of this land and the ecological devastation it has wreaked upon it are testimony to this fact.

Today, our memory carriers, often removed from their place of origin, are more and more difficult to encounter. If we are fortunate, we may find elders in our own families who still carry stories with them. Our storytellers are the chief purveyors of memory and, as a consequence, vision. But the memory carriers are also our youth, if they can find form in which to express it. And this is where Art comes in; for through Art cultural memory is transmitted and our stories are told. I do not want the Vietnamese, the displaced Palestinian, the Jew or Gypsy, the Quiché Maya to forget their cultures when they take residence on this North American continent. And with even greater passion I do not want their artists to forget. I want this country to remember its origins and its peoples to remember theirs.

Recently, I saw a rerun of an interview with Toni Morrison on public TV, which had taken place a number of years ago, upon the publication of her book, *Beloved*. As always, Morrison's eloquence awed me. But what most astounded were her words: 'What is really infinite is the past.' And I thought of how un-American that way of thinking is, for this 'nation' was built upon the belief that one could and should forget the past and invent a future.[20] By contrast, Morrison spoke of the future as something finite; and indeed it is, from an artist's perspective. Because history in all its limitlessness determines the future. And unraveling history, the multitude of versions of the story, the story from multifarious perspectives, this is limitless. And how great is our task to remember if we are people of color artists, if we are artists without a *written* history, if we are artists who have been forced into exile (three or three thousand miles) from our ancestral lands.[21]

Finding the path to memory is my task as an artist. Writing for the 'Ancestors' as playwright August Wilson has said. That's my job. To remember ancestral messages, to counter the U.S. culture of forgetfulness. Sometimes memory is no more than a very faint scent. You sniff it, take a step, stop and sniff again, and gradually make your way along a path to a people. You are blind and hand-and-tongue-tied. You just keep sniffing toward the warmth of the light on your face, the scent of heat on the stone-packed dirt beneath your feet, the cooling of a summer central valley evening drawing a sudden chill to your skin. You go backwards in time. You write. You're right. Even if you never read it in a book, saw it on stage or at the movies, you're on the right road.

'Bitter Fruit.'
We are 'a strange and bitter crop,' Billie.
We, the children of slaves, the survivors of genocide.

And we don't forget how we got here.

NOTES

1. This essay was first published in the second edition of *Loving in the War Years: Lo que nunca pasó por sus labios* (Cambridge, MA: South End Press, 2000). Copyright Cherríe L. Moraga.
2. 'Strange Fruit,' original words and music by Allan Lewis.
3. August Wilson's address was delivered on June 26, 1996. It is entitled 'The Ground on which I Stand' and was first published in the September 1996 issue of *American Theater*, pp. 14–16 and 71–4.
4. A major factor in Wilson's ability to maintain an African American aesthetic in his plays is his insistence on working with Black directors, which he has consistently been able to actualize. Wilson's gift as a playwright was first nurtured under the guidance of African American director, Lloyd Richards, which begin in 1984, when Wilson, a virtual unknown, submitted *Ma Rainey's Black Bottom* to the National Playwrights Conference at the Eugene O'Neill Memorial Theater Center. The play caught the attention of Richards who served as the conference's Artistic Director. As the Dean of the Yale School of Drama and the Artistic Director of Yale Repertory Theater, Richards directed the premier production of *Ma Rainey* at Yale. He would go on to direct the play's première on Broadway and would serve as director for the next six of Wilson's play premières both at Yale Rep and in New York.

5. Jorge Huerta, 'Looking for the Magic: Chicanos in the Mainstream,' in Diana Taylor and Juan Villegas (eds), *Negotiating Performance: Gender, Sexuality, and Theatricality in Latino America* (Durham, NC: Duke University Press, 1994): 37–48.

6. Ancient Athenian (aristocratic) women were never considered citizens of Athens. They were excluded from *all public activities* (politics, the law courts, the Olympics and other Games, the army, navy, and war, from agriculture and trade) and restricted to the private sphere of the home where their primary purpose was to bear children and maintain the household (of goods and slaves). Slaves were both laborers and a central part of the Greek household. An aristocratic household could own fifteen to twenty slaves who functioned as servants, tutors, and guardians. They were not considered citizens of Greece, only living possessions – property. Greeks strongly believed that nature intended certain humans to be subjugated from the very moment of their birth. The presence of Athenian women or slaves in attendance at the performances of tragedies during dramatic festivals of the fifth century is a hotly contested historical debate.

7. *Who Killed Yolanda Saldívar? Prison Correspondence between the Poet and the Pervert* was first presented in a staged reading at the Lesbian Playwrights' Festival at the Magic Theater of San Francisco on January 13, 2000. It was directed by Irma Mayorga.

8. Euripides' Medea, however, may qualify as the first 'woman of color' in all of Western theater. In terms of Hellenic society (500–300 BC), any person not of direct Greek origin was considered a foreigner and therefore a 'barbarian,' an uncivilized 'Other' in relation to the cultural norms (superiority) of the Greeks. In many traditions of her story, Medea was originally from the city of Aea in a region known as Colchis on the eastern end of the Black Sea. Ethnically speaking, the Greek historian Herodotus describes the Colchians as 'black Egyptians.' On the other hand, *The Tempest*'s Sycorax, mother of the 'uncivilized' Caliban (usually seen as a figure who represents the 'savage natives' of the 'New World') and, like Medea, a wielder of magic, does not make her appearance in drama until 1611.

9. *Fed Up: A Cannibal's Own Story* premièred at Theater Rhinoceros in San Francisco in the Spring of 1999. It was directed by Reginald McDonald.

10. Suzan-Lori Parks and Liz Diamond, 'Doo-a-Diddly-Dit-Dit,' *The Drama Review: A Journal of Performance Studies*, Fall 1995, 39(3): 56–7.

11. *Shadow of a Man* premièred in San Francisco at the Eureka Theater in a co-production with Brava Theater Center in 1990. The play was directed by María Irene Fornes.

12. *Watsonville: Some Place Not Here* premièred at Brava Theater Center on May 25, 1996, directed by Amy Mueller. The play is scheduled to be published in 2002 in a new collection entitled *Some Place Not Here: Five Plays by Cherríe Moraga* (Albuquerque, NM: West End Press). It also appears in *Plays from South Coast Repertory: Hispanic Playwrights Project*, ed. Juliette Carrillo (New York: Broadway Play Publishing, 2000).

13. Wilson, 'The Ground on Which I Stand', p. 74.

14. Passed as an initiative statute in November 1994 by California voters, Proposition 187 (sponsored primarily by the then California Republican Governor Pete Wilson) was designed to deny illegal immigrants access to public social services, health care services, and all levels of public school education. As touted in the ballot's official language, the initiative was to be 'the first giant stride in ultimately ending the illegal alien invasion.' Pandering to a tide of xenophobic hysteria, Prop. 187 argued that undocumented immigrants arrived in the U.S. solely to exploit public social services. It maintained that cutting off public aid and access to education to undocumented immigrants and their families would save Californian taxpayers millions of dollars. Conveniently, proponents of the proposition ignored the impact immigrants' labor, spending, and taxation has on the overall health of the U.S. economy. Furthermore, the statute required a wide variety of state agencies and local officials, including public school employees, to report persons to the INS who were merely *suspected* of having entered the U.S. illegally, encouraging rampant racial discrimination based solely on appearance or circumstance and converting school teachers, among others, into a kind of unofficial 'border patrol.' Once passed in 1994, Prop. 187 was quickly diffused by the work of civil rights groups who succeeded in blocking its enactment through four years of lawsuits and litigation. It is still a contested piece of legislation that continues to divide public opinion and policy.

15. Proposition 209. Passed in 1996, California Proposition 209 or the 'California Civil Rights Initiative,' supported, of course, by Governor Pete Wilson, negated the crucial links between racial bias, gender bias, poverty, and equality, and proposed that color-blind and gender-blind measures would ensure equality for all citizens. Defenders of the proposition argued that since 1964 the 'playing field' (of business and educational opportunities) for minorities and women had been successfully leveled; therefore, affirmative action equal opportunity programs should be eliminated. In language that echoes the Civil Rights Act of 1964, the initiative prohibits 'discrimination' or 'preferential treatment' in public employment, public education, or public contracting on the basis of race, sex, color, ethnicity, or national origin. After a series of legal actions designed to stop the enactment of 209, in 1997 the Supreme Court cleared the path for 209's enforcement by refusing to hear an appeal filed by the ACLU that offered a broad challenge to 209's constitutionality. Meanwhile, at least 25 other states have proposed or plan to propose laws or initiatives similar to Prop. 209.

Proposition 227. Led by ultra-conservative Ron Unz and passed in November 1998, California Proposition 227, the 'English Language in Public Schools' initiative, proposed to radically reconfigure the teaching of English in the California public school system for bilingual students. Aimed mostly at the children of Latinos (the soon-to-be-majority population in California), the initiative requires all public school instruction to be conducted solely in English. The proposition offered the installation of a 180-day English immersion program, at the end of which students, regardless of English proficiency, would be funneled into English-only classrooms without further aid in language development in either language. The 'sink or swim' based program refused to recognize the importance of bilingual proficiency, individual learning impediments, or successful bilingual programs already in place at many schools. 227's singular and monolithic model of learning English worked to placate xenophobic fear caused by California's growing immigrant population – a population that actually speaks over 140 languages, not solely English or Spanish. The enforcement of English in the effort to acculturate and assimilate children (and in essence wipe away any identification with their ethnic origins) was espoused as the best possible way to guarantee a successful future for bilingual (non-white) children. The truth is that it secures the privileged position of the monolingual Euro-American student, in what has become an increasingly competitive job market. Second-class students will become second-class workers, i.e. working *for* the Euro-American student turned businessman. Ironically, the initiative advocates monolingualism in an era when global markets, along with networks of communications (inherently multilingual), are expanding at an unprecedented rate. In short, English-only speakers (White students) acquiring a second language (Chinese, Japanese, German) in order to compete more effectively in twenty-first century global economy is seen as 'good,' while children of color, already in possession of a first but 'un-American' language, are viewed as deficient and a deterrent to the overall efficacy of California's next generation workforce.

16. I make a distinction here between Chicano, U.S. Latino, and Caribbean artists, who posit their work in resistance to Western aesthetic dominance, and 'Hispanics' who identify with Whiteness and situate themselves culturally as any other European immigrant to the U.S.

17. The situation for North American Native artists within the art world is distinct from Chicanos and other Mexican Native artists. Within the plastic arts, there are more opportunities for exhibition and sale for Native American artists than Chicano/as. But the Euro-American interest in contemporary Native American art, traditional work, and Native spirituality often reflects a kind of perverse romantic fascination, which sometimes results in the outright theft of imagery, language, and religious practices. At such times, invisibility seems preferable. In the mainstream theater world, however, both Chicano and North American Native theater artists suffer from virtual disregard by the regional theater community.

18. At the initial writing of this essay, the NEA was being dismantled in Congress. In 1995, the agency's $175 million budget was cut by 39 percent to 99.5 million, causing 89 staffers, nearly half of the agency, to be laid off. In 1997, the Republican House voted to abolish the agency, but the Senate rescued it at the last moment.

19. Consider the now-famous case of Cuba's unwitting émigré, Elian Gonzáles. In casual conversation among friends, we joke: 'Good thing he's White (and cute) or nobody'd give a damn.' We aren't exactly kidding. We remember the brutal 'welcome' the mostly Black and often gay Cuban Marielitos received upon their arrival to 'freedom' in the early 1980s. We remember the Haitian detention

camps, the Senate bill outlawing HIV-infected immigrants entrance into the U.S. We know INS break-ins against undocumented Mexicanos occur without warrant or warning and with considerable more violence than we witnessed on CNN in the Miami home of Lázaro Gonzáles in spring 2000. We know Mexican kids are separated from their parents (just like Elian) daily in Migra raids along the border and there is no public outcry.

20. Clinton's acceptance speech at the 1996 Democratic National Convention illustrates this perfectly. His 'Bridge to the Twenty-first Century Speech' was completely devoid of historical reference. No man was mentioned beyond the last four years of his administration.

21. Many North American Native nations still reside within the same basic geographical area of their pre-Conquest ancestors. But the harsh socio-economic conditions of most Native communities, on and off the reservation, can certainly be described as a kind of internal 'exile' imposed by the U.S. government.

Part III

Interviews

Ellen Stewart
Photo by D. E. Matlack

8

'Some place to be somebody': La MaMa's Ellen Stewart

Alvin Eng

'Eighty percent of what is now considered the American theater originated at La MaMa,' playwright/performer Harvey Fierstein once said. Composer/playwright Elizabeth Swados describes La MaMa as a 'Marx Brothers version of the United Nations.' As such, everyone and, ahem, their mother has a mythological story about La MaMa and its founder and Artistic Director, Ellen Stewart. And like most larger than life legends, Ellen is all of these myths and none of these myths. But while the truth of these myths may always be questioned, her legacy of being a singular maverick pioneer of the theater is never questioned. Not one iota. In fact, one could expound upon the Fierstein and Swados testimonials by saying that before Ellen founded La MaMa in 1961, there was no place to see theater by people of all colors – from around the block as well as from around the world – on a consistent basis under one roof. In fact, those places are still few and far between.

Ellen and La MaMa are regularly, and rightfully, celebrated for offering early, and in most cases, first New York or American stagings of ground-breaking work by the likes of the aforementioned Fiersten and Swados as well as playwrights Sam Shepard, Harold Pinter, Adrienne Kennedy, and Lanford Wilson, director-creators Tom O'Horgan, Jerzy Grotowski, Peter Brook, Andrei Serban, Joseph Chaikin's The Open Theatre, Tom Eyen's Theatre of the Eye, and Mabou Mines among scores of others.

But La MaMa is heretofore less celebrated for being the first to give full-time homes to American theater troupes of color such as: La MaMa Chinatown, founded by Ching Yeh and Wu Gingi (out of which grew the Pan Asian Repertory Theatre, H. T. Chen & Dancers, and, eventually, SLANT); Ping Chong and Co.; the American Indian Dance Troupe, founded by Hanay Geiogamah (which later became the Native American Theatre Ensemble); the Duo Theatre, founded by Manuel Martin; the La MaMa GPA Nucleus (out of which grew the Jarboro Troupe that featured playwright Ed Bullins and directors Hugh Gittens and Allie Woods, among others). La MaMa was also instrumental in the development of playwright Leslie Lee, performance artist Winston Tong, and The Nuyorican Poets Café, among many others.

Ellen has also applied this new world border-less order to her own directing – decades before 'non-traditional casting' was even a glimmer in Actors Equity's eyes. Under Ellen's directorial tutelage, it was common to see Asians in Greek tragedy, Middle Eastern performers in Yiddish theater-inspired works and much, much more. Her usage of music and dance likewise reflects her pan cultural instinct that has paired Butoh and tap dancers in a production whose orchestra featured a Tibetan and Balinese percussionists' score alongside an Australian didgeridoo player that was narrated by African Griots.

Although details about Ellen's childhood are sketchy, several accounts trace her year of birth to 1919, and that she was the older of two children, whose father was a tailor and mother a schoolteacher. In 1950, Ellen moved from Chicago to New York City to become a fashion designer. Soon thereafter she became the first black woman to run a fashion design department at Saks Fifth Avenue. This job financed her first forays into theater producing in the late 1950s.

Café La MaMa was born October 18, 1961 at 321 East 9th Street in Manhattan's East Village. On that night, Ellen rang her bell to welcome the audience and raise the curtain on their first 'official' production, an adaptation by Andy Milligan of the Tennessee Williams short story, 'One Arm.' In 1964, Café La MaMa moved to 82 2nd Ave., and became La MaMa Experimental Theater Club (hence, the E.T.C.). La MaMa E.T.C. would have two more East Village addresses, 122 2nd Ave. and 8 St Mark's Place, before settling, in 1969, into their permanent home at 74-A East 4th Street, which houses a 99-seat theater, a club/cabaret space, offices and living spaces. Over the next few years, La MaMa would also renovate a building a few doors away into their 299-seat Annex, and on East 1st Street open its Galleria, a poetry/play reading space and art gallery. La MaMa still simultaneously operates all of these spaces.

The 2000–1 season was La MaMa's 40th year with some 2,000 productions to its credit. During those four decades, Ellen has received almost every award and citation imaginable including 15 honorary doctorate degrees, three OBIE awards, two MacArthur Foundation 'Genius' Fellowships, and official decorations by the governments of Korea, Japan, France, the Ukraine, and the Philippines for her outstanding achievements in bringing world theater to New York and vice versa. In 1993, Ellen Stewart became the first off-Broadway producer to ever be inducted into the 'Broadway Hall of Fame.'

Of course, all these accolades and accomplishments did not come without their share of intense struggles. For while Ellen may appear to always have a *laissez-faire* air to her in public, she did not get to where she is without being strong willed. Just as her stages have always given forum to many and very varied unsung voices, her life has also been a place of unique experiences – not all of them nice. Among the latter, and most pertinent to this book, is her struggle with intra-racial tensions. While inter-racial tensions have long been explored, if not become commonplace in the theater world, on stage and off, significantly less has been said of intra-racial tensions. For Ellen Stewart, this has meant a most complex relationship with some parts of the African American arts community.

Ellen, as always, spoke most eloquently and candidly on this issue and many others during a conversation held on a late April afternoon during the first spring of the new millennium. We spoke in her living and office space above La MaMa's theaters on E. 4th Street.

ALVIN ENG: When you started out, you were one of the few, if not the only Black woman theater producers –

ELLEN STEWART: *(Interrupting)* I never called myself a 'Black woman theater producer.' I'm Black and I'm a woman. But I don't going around talking about how 'I'm some Black woman and Black this and Black that.' Some people keep trying to put me in a 'Black box' and I tell them, 'You can't put me in a "Black box."' I told them that a thousand times. It's very racist, I think. The only people, who I guess you could say, wanted to put me in a box were people who have nothing to do with La MaMa. They come from somewhere else, they want to meet me and when they meet me, they're shocked that it's me.

(As if staged, Ellen diverts her gaze down the hall to an adjoining office and calls 'Michael?' Michael Arian, a featured performer – often in drag – of the legendary 1960s/1970s La MaMa troupe, The Play-House of the Ridiculous, *directed by John Vocarro, enters.)*

ES: Michael. Since you've been with me since 1965, have you ever seen me in a 'Black box'?

MICHAEL: You? No. We could never even put Ellen in a category much less a box.

(Ellen smiles and acknowledges 'you can go.' Michael exits.)

ES: And he's been with me 35 years – in my ups, in my downs, in my go-arounds. Some other people who categorized me were The Negro Ensemble. In the 1960s, they forbid anybody in their group to walk on my side of the street. Because if they did, they were automatically eliminated from The Negro Ensemble. Now I don't know what kind of 'box' they were putting me in.

AE: Why were they doing this?

ES: Because I wasn't a Black theater. And this was only from the blacks. Like I didn't know until after [the fact], that I was on the 'hit list' for the Black Panthers. McNeil Lowry, who was then the head of the Ford Foundation,[1] 'put two detectives on me to follow me around for two years to protect me – I didn't even know I was being protected – because I was supposed to be destroyed because I wasn't doing 'the black thing.' I was doing my 'people thing.' The only other person who tried to put me in a box was Mayor Lindsay, who offered to build me a Lincoln Center uptown if I would relocate and move uptown and just do Black things. I refused. This was about 1968.

AE: Did you have a confrontation or issues with the Panthers?

ES: No, no, no, no, no. Nobody ever talked to me. I don't know how they categorized me, dear. All I know is that they wanted to get rid of me as an example. I don't know how The Ford Foundation got its information. All I know is that they protected me for two years. McNeil Lowry told me later.

AE: What was your reaction to being told about being on the Panthers' 'hit list,' and what the Negro Ensemble were doing?

ES: I didn't have any reaction because I've been criticized by many Black artists because La MaMa is not a Black theater. And that still goes on. It hasn't stopped. And I haven't stopped being what La MaMa's always been which is a people theater for all of the people.

AE: Did you ever have a dialogue with your detractors?

ES: I didn't because they just hate me *(laughs)*.

AE: Why do you think they hated you?

ES: It was because of you.

AE: Because of me?

ES: Yes. They didn't like me because I had people like you [non-Blacks] at La MaMa, and they didn't want any people but Blacks.

AE: So would you say that, perhaps they felt 'betrayed' by you?

ES: There, you got it. Whatever I had, it should be for them, it shouldn't be for you [non-Blacks].

AE: Was your vision for La MaMa always consistent with –

ES: Dear, wait a moment. I didn't have any vision. There were two people: a Black one who was like a brother to me and a White one. Fred Lights was the Black one and Paul Foster was the White one. If you know anything about American playwrights you know that Paul Foster is one of our foremost playwrights. He wrote *Tom Payne, Elizabeth.* Those two people wanted to do theater. [Lights was also a playwright.] I didn't know anything about theatre. But certain things that happened to me, made me decide that I would try to make a little theater for them. I didn't know what that meant, but I decided to help them out. I thought to have a play be theater, you just have a place, you write the play, you have some of your friends be in it, your friends will come, and that was doing theater. That's all I knew about it. So I made this little basement to do just that.

AE: How did you meet them?

ES: My mother had helped to raise Fred Lights in Chicago. And Paul Foster I met after I came here to be a fashion designer and moved down here [East Village] in 1958.

AE: Before that, you never had any ambition to do theater?

ES: I still don't have any ambition to do theater.

AE: What made you decide to continue?

ES: Well, I just never decided to stop.

AE: If you were starting La MaMa now, would you do anything differently?

ES: No, I would do it exactly the same.

AE: How do you think the climate for starting this kind of a theater is different today?

ES: But I am doing exactly the same thing now. Everybody now is doing what they call ...

AE: Multiculturalism?

ES: We've been multicultural, baby, I just never thought of it in those terms. We've just been that. I started Asian American theatre in New York. Everyone thinks its [Pan Asian Rep. founder] Tisa Chang, but Tisa started here at La MaMa and got great training from all the La MaMa groups like Mabou Mines. But in 1970 we had La MaMa Chinatown. Ching Yeh and Wu Gingi, who were a part of La MaMa, told me that they wanted very much to have something in Chinatown. They said that the only thing in Chinatown was an occasional traveling troupe doing Beijing opera and would I come and do something? So I did, and that's how La MaMa Chinatown got started, and much later on, Pan Asian grew out of that. But back then, there I was; a Black woman in the middle of that park in Chinatown [Columbus Park] asking people to please come to La MaMa. And it was hard because the Chinatown audience wouldn't come and the mainstream White audience wouldn't come. I also started H. T. Chen. He couldn't speak a word of English. That boy washed dishes to put himself through N.Y.U.

In 1972, I started the first Native American theater troupe, the American Indian Dance Troupe with Hanay Geiogamah. I introduced 'Shango de Ima' to this country. Now in the 1980s and 1990s, the Blacks tried [to claim this], but it was done here first in 1970 from Cuba by Pepe Carille, translated by Susan Sherman. .

I was also the first to bring [director Jerzy] Grotowski to America. These Polish officials down in D.C. saw our tiny ad in the *Village Voice* for [Polish playwright]

Thadeus Roseweiz and they sent me a large bouquet of flowers and said they wanted to meet me. Remember, this was during the Cold War and they were trying to break the wall and bring anything Polish to America. So we met and they asked me if I wanted anything else from Poland. I said I would like to have Grotowski. So they said if you have someone to sponsor the money, you will be the artistic sponsor and I will do the rest. And that's how Grotowski first came to America in 1967.

AE: Going back a step, how did you get Thadeus Roseweiz to La MaMa?

ES: I was in Warsaw in 1965, and after they got over seeing a Black person for the first time in their life, the young people there were all talking about Thadeus Roseweiz, the first young playwright to be produced in Poland since the war.

AE: And how did the American Indian Dance Troupe get started?

ES: Hanay also just found out about La MaMa and wanted to meet me.

AE: How did La MaMa come to be such a magnet, or Mecca even, for experimental artists from all over the world?

ES: How people knew, I don't know. They just came to me. Young people heard about me and felt attached to me and La MaMa. We had La MaMa Paris, La MaMa Copenhagen, and even La MaMa in a kibbutz in Israel and we started this exchange. Not meaning to be anything.

AE: Were you looking for any specific type of artists?

ES: I just wanted to include people who could do the work and were interested. It was international without trying.

AE: You primarily relied on instinct?
ES: That's all I've ever done.

AE: So most of your criticism comes from Americans?

ES: I'm not criticized outside of America. America is very prejudiced in both ways. We couldn't get critiques in America but I figured if we went to Europe we could get critiques. So in 1965, I put 16 people on a boat with one-way tickets *(laughs)*, and off they went to Europe with 22 plays.

AE: Did you ever want to leave America?

ES: I was leaving America.

AE: I meant permanently.

ES: I was going to move to Germany because the Germans invited me to move there in 1967, because I was having so many problems. But then that same man, McNeil Lowry, gave me money to buy this building [74-A East 4th St.] and fix it up in 1968. We moved here in 1969. But if that didn't happen, we were going to move to Germany. Because we played in Germany and the people in Munich really liked us and invited us to live there.

AE: What kind of problems were you facing?

ES: Everything. I had the police chasing me because they said that what we were doing was illegal. I didn't have money and I was working five jobs at the time to keep La MaMa going. I had other people that just weren't nice to me.

They didn't try to kill me, but there were racial incidents. Like in a rehearsal, one Black actor knocked all the teeth out of one of the White actresses because he said 'That White bitch was looking at me.' We had to pay for all her dental work and there were always things. I was introducing Black musicians on East 3rd Street where the Nuyorican [Poets Café] is. I gave that building to them [the Nuyorican Poets], to Miguel Algarín, because they had no place. So I would have theater and jazz workshops there. Many of the Black musicians would play and practice there, then we would have the shows over here. Then they would come on the night of the shows and they wouldn't let anyone but Blacks walk down this block. They beat up a few of the White persons who tried to come to the shows. And this was my show! That was my workshop, I paid the rent and everything so they would have some place to work. Finally I had to stop. I tried to talk to them and get them to stop this but I didn't get anywhere because I was a sister.

AE: If you were a 'brother' would that have helped the situation?

ES: Nothing was going to help that situation! The only thing that was going to help that situation was if I threw out everybody who was White and only had Black folks here and that wasn't going to happen. So I had to tell them to stop performing here.

AE: Could you have a dialogue with these musicians?

ES: *(Long pause)* They're telling me that they picked the cotton . . . OK? Well I had picked cotton! I had been a slave. I was still a slave to the White man . . . that's enough. That's not me. I don't want to dwell on this stuff.

AE: We are just interested in hearing some of this so we can appreciate your struggles and accomplishments even more.

ES: Well you heard some of this! I had a lot of Blacks here. I just went by my instinct and that's all I've ever done.

AE: Because of your criticisms within the Black community, was it almost dangerous for Black artists to work with you?

ES: They had to show their loyalty so they couldn't [work with me]. That's why the Black theater, *per se*, that was here – the group [Jarboro Troupe] that I took to Europe and all – they stopped coming to La MaMa and I could understand it. They were going with the brothers.

AE: Did this make you feel isolated?

ES: Not at all. By 1970 and 1975 I had people all over the world supporting me. I was not here alone, not at all. I had all these arms around me and I still do. This meant people from Asia, Africa, from Eastern Europe, Israel, the Arab countries . . . the whole world. So I didn't have a problem. It would have been nice if there would have been more blacks, but I certainly had plenty of Black artists here like Bill Duke, Garrett Morris, Adrienne Kennedy, Ed Bullins, Loretta Devine.

AE: Before you said that you still get criticized to this day, and I find that shocking. What sort of criticisms do you get?

ES: Well, I can't tell you what this one said and that one said. But I hear things. Like the man that publishes the *Amsterdam News* once wrote a favorable article about me and then, boy, the hate mail he received! He lives down the block and he was always apologizing that he didn't help me, but he couldn't.

AE: Going back to the beginning of our conversation. While you've never defined yourself as a Black woman in theater, I would think that the Black theater community would like to define you that way. Have you ever been asked to speak at Black theater conferences?

ES: Are you kidding? OK, listen: I've been decorated by the Emperor of Japan. This is my second award from Korea. I have been decorated by the President of the Philippines. I have been decorated by the French. *(Long pause)* But I have never been in *Essence Magazine*. I have never been in *Jet*. I have never been in *Ebony*. I have never been invited to any Black awards ceremony. My name is never mentioned. I don't know what you call that. But I'm not looking back. I'm just looking at today. God gives us this day and that's what it's all about. My mother raised me to see that you are me and I am you. You're no better than me and I'm not any better than you. So I'm all those rolled into one. I'm happy with the world and I'm happy that the world loves me.

AE: How would you like to be remembered?

ES: I hope I am remembered as a human being in God's world. That's all I want to do. I have never felt that I was in one category or the other. I don't want to be in any box, I don't want to be itemized. I just want to keep doing what I've been doing, which is to do art with the people – and by that I mean everybody in the world – and that's what makes me happy. I don't intend to change this.

AE: What do you see in the future for you and La MaMa?

ES: La MaMa's an experimental theater and our goal is communication. And plays that are very traditional, i.e. talking on the stage and very literal and heavily dependent on their language is not what we usually do. You may see one or two of these types of plays a season, but that's all. It has been 40 years, and I don't intend to change because I tell everyone who works at La MaMa: 'Just remember that I'm Chinese. And if I can't understand you, what does your work mean?'

NOTE

1. W. McNeil Lowry was hired by the Ford Foundation to direct its education program in 1953. He developed the Foundation in arts and humanities and became its first director in 1957, serving until 1964. He retired from Ford in 1975.

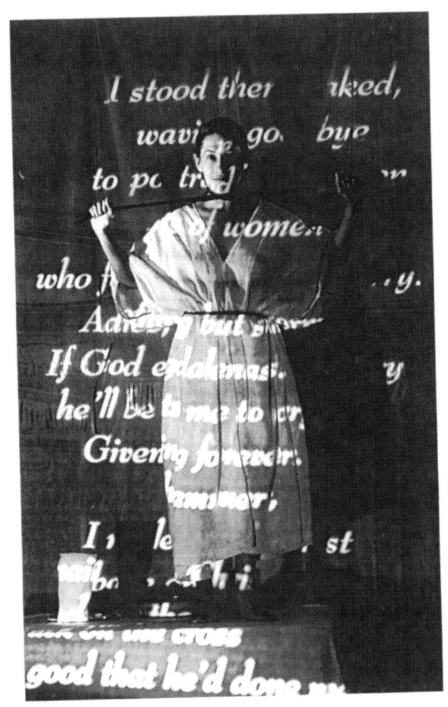

Jesusa Rodríguez
Photo by Julie Archer

9

Uncovering and displaying our universes: Jesusa Rodríguez in/on Mexico

Roselyn Costantino

The search for knowledge of our myriad interior and exterior universes takes Mexican actress, director, writer, and activist Jesusa Rodríguez (b. 1955, Mexico City) on an artistic, political, and personal journey that continues to treat and challenge spectators in Mexico and abroad. The interrogation of corruption, neo-liberalism, democracy, the Catholic Church, ignorance and censorship, and homophobia and machismo occurs simultaneously with the search for pleasure, desire, and love on Rodríguez's stage, as likely to take the form of an opera as to appear as cabaret, classic Greek theater, indigenous ritual, puppetry, film, or performance art. In general terms, the preferences of this 'chameleon' of Mexico's artistic community evolve from the practice of theater, spectacle, and theatricality in Latin America's history rather than from theoretical discussions. Humor, parody, and biting satire are constants. Rodriguez's central tool: the human body, often feminine and at times nude. This body is never taken as value free but as a primary signifier across which she exhibits the markings of history, politics, economics, and social institutions that have everything to do with achieving and maintaining power and little or nothing to do with exploring or expressing individual and collective experiences. While highlighting the constructed nature of its identity, there is no attempt to negate or erase the 'real' body or the reality of its lived experiences. Since the early 1970s, Rodríguez has been exploring the problematics and possibilities of representation in a developing country catapulted into a global economy, and opts for a strategy of visibility – that which has been kept in the closet, the kitchen, the mountains, the barrio, the confessional is 'made seen' on the body, on the stage, and in the streets of Mexico.

Rodríguez tells of writing and directing plays at home for her family since she was a child. Born in the 1950s, a decade that produced some of Mexico's most important and active women writers and theater artists, she began formal training as an actress at Mexico's National Autonomous University where she studied and worked with one of Mexico's most important directors, Julio Castillo. At a time when the director was considered the ultimate authoritative voice over the written and performative text, Castillo's collaborative and co-operative theater style deeply influenced and inspired Rodríguez. According to Castillo, the theatrical experience is enriched by the full participation of each member of the 'team' which includes the actors, playwright, director, and light and set designers. Castillo's model continues to influence Rodríguez's approach to her work. After his untimely death, she quickly realized that the survival of artistic autonomy and creativity demanded complete independence from, in her words, debilitated and debilitating official cultural institutions that fund the arts in Mexico. For that reason, in 1980, with her partner and collaborator, Argentine-born composer Liliana Felipe, she opened her own theater-bar, El Cuervo, and then, in 1990, the cabaret-bar, El Hábito, and theater, La Capilla, in Coyoacán, Mexico City. From 1990 to 1997, directing the collaborative theater group, Las Divas, that she formed in 1983, Rodríguez produced some 200 shows including 68 farces and 75 'musicals', and, from 1993 to 1995, she directed and acted in 30 cabaret shows for which Liliana wrote and performed the music. A few examples of the works that Rodríguez wrote or adapted, directed, and appeared in include adaptations of Shakespeare (¿Cómo va la noche, Macbeth?, 1981); Mozart's opera Donna Giovanna (1983–7); a filmed adaptation of Così fan tutti (1997); pastorellas – short Christmas stories (Fue niña, En el pesebre con Madonna, 1993); cabaret (Víctimas del pecado neoliberal, 1994); Greek-style tragedy (Crimen, an adaptation of Marguerite Yourcenar, 1989, 1992); revue and sketch (Diana casadera, 1993); melodrama (El conde del orgasmo, 1996); traditional theater (El concilio de Amor, 1988, 1994 – an adaptation of Oskar Panizza's play which was immediately banned upon publication in Bavaria in 1894); as well as unclassifiable pieces like Cielo de abajo. Cabaret prehispánico (1992) and Güevita (her response to Hollywood's Evita, 1997). Presently, she is directing a cabaret show, Regina Global, starring opera singer Regina Orozco, with plans to take the show on the road to the central plazas of cities and town throughout the country, plus Prometeo en el desierto, to be presented outdoors, in the desert of San Luis Potosí, a project in which she is working with over 100 Mexico City street children.

Rodríguez emphasizes that equally important to her growth and vision is her international collaboration, most recently with Ruth Maleczech and the New York-based performance group Mabou Mines. After two years of preliminary work in Utah, Mexico, Italy, and New York, Las Horas de Belen. A Book of Hours debuted in Mexico City's Historic Center Festival, and then opened for an extended run in New York City in May, 1999. The piece was inspired by the history of Belen, an infamous sanctuary/prison for women in Mexico City (1683–1935) founded by the Catholic Church, as well as the grim reality of *maquila* factories in U.S.–Mexico border towns and recent news of unsolved rapes and murders of hundreds of young women there.

The numbers or titles of shows do not, however, accurately reflect the depth and breath of Rodríguez's artistic production and the central role she has played from the margins, for more than two decades in the artistic, cultural and social landscape of Mexico.[2] What follows are highlights of conversations in which Rodríguez talks about her craft, her passion, and the ever-more urgent need to express herself on the public and theatrical stage. All translations are mine.

ROSELYN COSTANTINO: Jesusa, what are the driving forces behind your work and your choices of form and content? How, if at all, has censorship in Mexico affected those choices?

JESUSA RODRÍGUEZ: For me, it is the search for universal knowledge, or the general knowledge of the different universes, whether that be the universe outside or the one inside the human body, the one you carry inside, which is you, your universe. In art we focus on the amazement we feel when faced with the observation of these two universes. I believe that throughout humankind's history all efforts are geared toward devising instruments to observe this phenomenon which is these distinct universes. Sometimes we need to observe the stars, so we make telescopes; sometimes we need to observe the interior of the body, so we make surgical knives and open that body; at times we need to observe the phenomenon of the universe of emotions so we make works of theater, we use distinct forms of art to observe these other universes. My father was a surgeon and when I was a child he took me to see human bodies opened up. It occurred to me that looking at the body from the inside was like looking outside at the universe of the stars. What we carry in the interior of our body is equal to the infinite universe outside. The world of emotions is an infinite universe. For me, these planes were never separated and were an endless source of amazement. I am just as amazed to see yesterday's eclipse or the movement of the stars, as the movement of a person or a society. So, in many ways I correlate this with my way of working. I think for me cabaret is a precision instrument to study social events and why we live together in this manner. Theater is an instrument of observation of humans as a race; opera is for emotions – if you wanted to observe some crater on the moon, not the moon or the planets, but the crater, then opera is the way. Theater serves to observe the moon, and cabaret serves you to study how all the planets function among themselves. Like a telescope and a microscope, they are similar objects of observation, only they observe from distinct points of view.

With respect to censorship, I believe, for example, there can be censorship of a nude, but one would never think to censor a biopsy of a kidney or a probe in an operation; the interior of the human body is not censorable. We only censor the surface, its most immediate appearance, or the behavior between us. Censorship serves to produce ignorance, because when you enter the world of knowledge, of science, censorship doesn't function. And since I believe human life is nourished by instruments of knowledge, the instrument of ignorance that is censorship is one I never use. It doesn't serve me in any way.

RC: It doesn't affect you in Mexico, what you can and cannot do?

JS: It affects as it might affect the enormous world of ignorance as it grows. I think you run up against your own ignorance, for in one way, the limits of my ability to know are the limits of my ignorance. We travel through life precisely in this fight against ignorance, in search of knowledge, crashing against our own ignorance. And it's there that censorship begins to draw its limits, it begins to be useful so that we see ourselves. The instrument of ignorance, however, is used to manipulate, to control, to gain power. In the moment I keep you ignorant, I control you.

RC: Would you talk about your personal journey in the evolution of an artistic language? What have been the influences?

JR: I depart from the same place, facing the amazement of the world, inside and out. I think the departure points of this path that you call 'artistic' are very diverse. From childhood, you are influenced by the culture that imposes itself from the outside, which in my case was obviously a Western, European culture – art forms from the Egyptians to the Greeks to medieval Europe, all the aesthetic movements from the Renaissance to now. You then face the reality that you live in a country whose departure point is the cosmovision of Mesoamerica – another culture, with nothing to do with the West except that they were human beings and they felt similar things, but from a different world-view. So I feel that even though my education is 'Westernized,' the daily influences of living in Mexico make you look at other universes – from the conceptualization of your body to the concept of the world. As occurred with the Conquest, suddenly there is an explosion between, a merging of, two very different cosmovisions that might lead to the same point. I'm now reading a book about the Olmecs that says that for the West, the working of metals, the wheel, and even writing are the three basic points of what we call civilization. If you look at the Olmec civilization which developed to a level as sophisticated as the West, but whose writing we don't know, who didn't use metals, who didn't use the wheel, then, it isn't true that *those* are the origins of civilization. In the final analysis, they are the origins of *Western* civilization, but not points of arrival in the civilization of Olmec culture. I can't say that an Olmec temple is less 'developed' or 'advanced' than a Greek temple. If you compare an Olmec and an Etruscan figurine, there's nothing that lessens the value of one or the other. On the contrary, the value increases. If you have both Etruscan perfection and Olmec perfection, it increases the possibility of approaching that knowledge, or even the world of aesthetic harmony. I believe that with these mergings one can, suddenly, even lose oneself, because the stimuli are so many. When I was a child, Egyptian culture influenced me tremendously, from the beauty of the bust of Nefertiti to the pyramids and the emblematic hieroglyphics. But then, still a child, I came face-to-face with the ruins of Cuicuilco [Mexico] and, although as a child you are so unaware of science, it talks to you, it is alive, and it proposes ideas to you. The same with the statue of Coatlicue or all of that world that we see here in Mexico – it is a tremendous influence, perhaps even greater because it is what you are touching, walking on, what appears to you in the faces of the people, when you go into the street, in how the people walk and speak, it is in your language. Although we speak Castillian Spanish as the official language, how many *Aztechismos*, how many *Náhuatlismos* are in our language! My influences come from those two cultural sources, the Western, which is taught at home, and the Mesoamerican.

For that reason, my body of work has been very scattered, very diffused. Without the academic rigor or discipline of, say, the French school of drawing, I began to draw and make theater from what I saw, be it Shakespeare or Coatlicue – each one giving me entry into a different universe. Perhaps the Western entrance is much more rational, and the Mesoamerican more direct. It's what you touch, what you put in your hands whereas the other is what you put in your head. I don't know the Egyptian pyramids, I haven't climbed one, but I have climbed many Mexican pyramids. They are two different aesthetic forms learned through different means – one is the map and the other, the Earth. For me the West has been the map, Mesoamerica the Earth. In my work, the two mix to form a single idea of the universe.

For a long time one of my great obsessions has been with all that is underneath prehistory. You find no difference between the human being who lived in a cave in Mexico, Ireland, Africa, or in Central Europe. There is a human substratum in prehistory in which it seems we all shared the same worries, the same forms of 'arriving.' Prehistory is for me the only synthesis of all that baroqueness in which Mesoamerica and the West mix. In prehistory I find things in which we coincide, in which all cultures move toward the same funnel, and so you extract from prehistory the most essential human being, who later expresses himself/herself through language, through stone or dreams, through pure fantasy, or the Earth. The primordial human then breaks off, disperses, into other aesthetic or cultural forms. In the final analysis, I don't think that the emotions of a prehistoric human have changed much. Things have changed: owning a telephone makes one feel differently, but the feeling of, say, jealousy is the same for the cave couple as for the virtual couple. Evidently, we are different in terms of the instruments we use to approach these other universes.

So I believe theater is the best of all possible worlds because you construct it as you want, or at least in a way permitted by the compact world of theater. Theater is the great laboratory where you can create a prehistoric universe. And so, to do a tragedy is to find the substratum of the West, of thousands of prehistoric families who lived in Greek cities and were summed up in Agamemnon or Oedipus, in archetypes. Theater permits you to set a tragedy in prehistory or put the same tragedy in cyberspace. It is an extraordinary instrument of approximation to different historic moments, it has no limits of time or space or of material because, in theater, a brick can represent the door to the cave of Alibaba, and we, the audience, will believe it. For me, that's the world of theater. I was an introverted and easily frightened child. So while the real world is so complicated and difficult, theater provided me with the opportunity to explore other universes that, any other way, implicated relating to a lot of other people.

RC: And how does the material body figure into all this?

JS: In my opinion it is precisely in the theater where the central point is not only the scenic objects but also the actors, the live bodies there. Unlike in film or television where the body's presence is not live, to have a real body there, in front of you, speaking, moving, feeling, transforming him/herself into whatever, creates an absolute bodily presence. And as I said, if the body is central, that is because it's we humans who are making theater.

The concept of the body is very influenced, however, by Western thought. Most work with nudity, I think, is very Western ... this idea of nudity as something reproachable. The West is accustomed to join these ideas: the body is the most beautiful thing, but it's the most shameful. It's like the revolutionaries. Take Che Guevara – you have to shoot him up so that he can be converted into a poster in everyone's rooms; Jesus Christ has to be crucified to be able, then, to hang him in the dining room. Emiliano Zapata had to be shot up by that strange, bourgeois, comfortable society, they had to see Zapata's bloody, mangled body to be able to put his picture in their houses and say, Zapata, what a great hero. That very Western double-morality.

RC: Which affects women in a big way. It's either La Malinche or the Virgin Mary.

JS: It's the same thing. Women are the most sublime and they are diabolical. I think it's a very Judaic-Christian mode of thought widely accepted in the West, one that the Church has exploited quite a bit. Things are dual, but their duality is of opposition, it's black or white. Different, for example, from the Nahuas, for whom everything is dual, but it's not good *or* bad. In Mesoamerica everything is what you know and what you don't know, or something that you see and something that you don't see. Which is very different. It's never occurred to me that a nude is something unsettling, shameful, provocative, or that you would propose to put your body there to see who you could move. It's so strange to me that people would do that. It's like censorship, except that there are people who do this to make money or to gain power or some other benefit. I've never been able to understand how a scenic nude, like in painting, could be an element of 'use.'

RC: But those attitudes form part of daily life, like it or not. What do you do with those of us who come to your show with all the cultural baggage of seeing things in that way?

JS: I believe the enormous difference is in the convention that we establish, of the instrument of knowing through which we work. If you are doing theater, you establish that this is theater, a space in which anything and everything can occur. If not, you don't do it. Or you don't go to the theater. There can't be, then, that attitude, 'Oh! What's this! They're naked!' which was the response in Mexico to the first works by Jodorowsky where the actors emerged naked. Or the opposite, the way they react to those places where they do burlesque, where women are used as objects, like stripped lamps. It's all garbage. Yet, morally, everyone has the right to see whatever they want. The immorality for me falls directly in the content of the show, in the objective which is none other than to make money by using others. *Punto.* Not even to entertain the people who are there, only to make money. I think that, perhaps, there's something totally visible, which is money, that drives *everything.* People kill for money, die for money, prostitute themselves for money, do whatever is necessary for money. And no one proposes to make money illegal, to treat it like a drug, the greatest addiction of all. I don't see any drug more addictive and dangerous than money.

RC: And it reaches cultures throughout the world, now, with the diffusion of technology. Your piece *Victims of Neoliberal Sin* (1994) comes to mind. At that moment everyone was asking what would happen to Mexico with NAFTA. Would it dissolve in the overwhelming influence from the outside? How, five years later, does Mexico imagine itself at this moment? What is its concept of itself as a nation?

JS: At that time, we were in the middle of *Salinismo* [the presidency of Carlos Salinas de Gortari], the moment Salinas made changes to the Mexican constitution. These included two very basic modifications that, for me, put us inside the problem of national identity: changes of Article 27 of the Constitution which called for the end of the *ejido* [communal lands], that is, to sell that land; and modification of Article 130 which meant opening once again the doors of Mexico to the Vatican. I asked a friend and scholar, what do these 'reforms' mean to you? He said that they are Mesoamerica's *tiro de gracia*. What a commentary, no? Why the *tiro de gracia*? It's a question of culture: Mexican campesinos and their relationship to the Earth — culturally, it's their Mother. You work the Earth which is your Mother. The moment that is no longer yours, you sell your land, it's no longer your Mother, you don't treat it as your Mother. The cultivating is for another; it's not your Mother, it's land, it's an object. When you work on your land, it's the sacred filial relationship between mother and child, whom you would never harm. A Mexican is capable of doing everything but to his mother, never! The moment you remove that relationship, effectively, you give the *tiro de gracia* to an entire culture. Regarding Article 130, how many thousands of people died to remove the weight of the Church from the nation and its people, to end the oppression of over 500 years!

Suddenly one man arrives [Salinas] and re-opens relations with the Vatican under the pretext that we are all Catholics although we pretend not to be, that we are all raising our children as Catholics, which is not true. And Salinas opens up a space again for the entire bunch of authoritians, of these assassins. Now they've gotten involved with textbooks, with abortion, with condom use. So, the influence of NAFTA coincides with Salinismo, economic neo-liberalism, the break with our ancestral traditions, and the elemental equilibrium of our country. Open ourselves up to the Vatican – there couldn't be anything more anti-Mexican than that. For that reason we asked, what will happen to Mexico in the moment that you close off the source of your knowledge of original inspiration and you open it to the oldest authoritarian movement – two thousand years – of the Western world? These are two movements in exact opposition to the possibility of the consolidation of a country and a culture that is, also, pressured by the far-reaching influence of the United States, by all that is implied in the arrival of U.S. imperialism.

RC: Returning to your work, what has been for you the most satisfying, interesting, illuminating or defining artistic experience or event?

JR: For me, at a very personal, not shared, level … I remember one day when we were in Germany, doing *Don Giovanni* [*Donna Giovanna*], artistically, something very surprising happened. I had one of the most incredible experiences in my life. The audience arrives, the show starts. Of course, Mozart's music is alchemic; it transports you to other levels, the sounds transport you, move your organs, your feelings. Then, something strange happened, as if I were in a trance for two hours, like I had never imagined. I was playing Don Juan in the first scene, I kill the commendatore and I began to feel as if I were living the real experience, absolutely real, and to top it off, very pleasurable and very brutal. Sinking the sword into the French lace, I experienced with total clarity the assassination, with absolute veracity. At that moment I knew what it is to kill someone, to experience perfectly the feeling. I began to cry, remaining totally within the story. I didn't move outside to see if I could continue the show or not; to the contrary. I said to myself, I'm the assassin, now I know what it is to kill, I just killed a human being … with the feeling and the music, and someone speaking, another singing, agonizing. We run off because immediately I have to come back as Doña Elvira. Then, a strange alchemy off stage. I take off this shoe and I see Don Juan leave me, I feel him go over there. I put on Elvira's shoe and she enters in that instant, here (*Jesusa points to her body*). Suddenly I am Doña Elvira, in an absolute way, the woman who abandoned the man that I just killed, the father of Doña Ana. It goes on like that for two hours, an experience of one second after another, a total emotional and physical experience. I understood in that moment what theater is and what it isn't.

And so I began and continue to work with another departure point for acting, *Nahualismo*. From the cosmovision of Mesoamerica, *Nahualismo* is to act from the liver and, so, to experience something that with Western methods of acting I could have never achieved. It had happened at other moments of my work, but never so continuously and with such intensity. It's not that you *represent* Doña Elvira or Don Juan. I try to understand it from a Mesoamerican cosmovision. In the liver there is a soul, the *ihiyotl*, that only leaves the body when you die although, according to the Nahuas, there are people who by disguising themselves are capable of taking out this soul during life, along with essences of other characteristics of other entities. They bite that essence and make that character/soul grow through their own essence, parting from their essence, not mine which they've robbed. So it's not me, representing you, but it's what I robbed from you that expresses itself. It's another approach to acting that is not that I possess you or you possess me but I rob a piece of your substance and make that substance grow in me and it expresses itself, to whatever point. Your substance, not mine, is expressing itself through me. To work in this way, in this line of inquiry, has been very useful. Suddenly you begin to think like that other, because it's not just you who are thinking, the other is thinking within you, moving, feeling within you. How interesting, as we were saying at the beginning, that knowing another cosmovision makes you see other techniques of acting that complete the experiences in a way the methods of Stanislavsky or others don't permit. As someone living here in Mexico I feel I need these Mesoamerican techniques of acting because it's where I live, it's my land and world. I began to discover these qualities of the liver that for the Mesoamericans are most obvious. As a Westerner would say that the hypothalamus has the function of emotions, a Mesoamerican would say that the liver has the function of acting. It's the most natural thing although, for me, it was an important discovery. I know that night, in that German theater, what happened to me is that my substance was robbing and sharing substances, and, for that reason, I was able to live integrally what was occurring. In reality, if there existed at one time a being who killed the commendatore, that being expressed himself in me, and he made me know what murder is. Theater permits you to have experiences that you will never have in your lifetime, as if you had lived them.

Another thing about the liver that I discovered many years ago is that ire/wrath is a great detonator of theatrical expression. When you get really angry outside the theater and you arrive on stage, you can do it all. Why does ire open to actors their entire emotional being? I found it curious that ire is generated there, in the liver.

RC: Since when, and in which works, have you been utilizing this method?

JR: A lot. Over the last years almost all the time. It's not something you do apart from yourself, consciously.

RC: It's interesting to learn of your methods because in my writings about your work I've commented that when I see your body on stage, no matter what your function or role, or which character, myth or icon you bring to life, you never are totally not you, you never stop being you, as if you/your body were giving the 'other' an opportunity, the space, the material being to be present.

JS: But you never are absent. You can't erase yourself. I remember when I saw *The Lion King*, how wonderful to see Julie Taymor's proposal, visible throughout the play, the mask is placed above the face, the face always present. Both exist, one does not disturb the other, the mask doesn't hide the face of the actor nor the actor hide the mask. When you leave the theater you remember both, you leave with both experiences. Work is the most important thing in life, it's what I do every day, it's my entire life, it's what gets contaminated by all the influences of all my experiences, it has to do with what I see all day – for me, it's sacred. Years back, in this medium, I felt incredible hostility and aggression from those people dedicated to theater. I'm weak, I don't have the strength to resist aggressions of the medium. I become defensive or aggressive or cynical because they want to win by grabbing at your heart. Better for me to escape. That distancing created an ever greater need to work independently. On the other hand, and another theme behind my work, is what's going on now in Mexican society. Why do the collective art groups fail, in theater, film? What is it to work collectively? How do the systems of government, the way politics and economics are conceived of in a country, condition the collective groups so that they crash, individuals wound each other, they eat each other up? And I see that more in Mexico now; it's more difficult than ever to integrate individuals into a theater group, to work deliciously in the grand pleasure of making theater because it seems that everyone detests you because you were able to get money to do something. This is another awful topic. That's why I don't do theater, I just create and hope people come to see. I want people to come but I don't want newspapers to say that I've done anything or critics to think this is theater, even better. It's gone to an extreme, Mexican society is living a very profound decomposition and we can't imagine that a political system doesn't affect the daily life of its citizens and their work! In that way, it's great to speak about the direction of one's work. But also, my work is a way to justify my life in Mexico. It's the only place in the world where I can live, where I want to live, because I love living here. At the same time, I'm ashamed to live here, each day more. I ask myself, if some day I run into the son of the assassinated union leader, sitting down, what can I say to him? Damn! They killed your father, it was a dirty death, and what did we do? My mouth gets dry, and I ask myself why do I live in Mexico? Yet with age, your tolerance grows. In the U.S. it's different from what goes on in our countries. In my opinion, we have been elected as the 'garbage' countries, the countries selected for experiments of corruption and shams, it's terrible. If I go to live in Helsinki, I can be sure that according to the laws, certain rights will be respected; it's structured so that it's really that way. So you say, damn, I want human liberty to grow to such a point! But when you are born in those countries where you know things are planned so that you are constantly butting up against corruption and overlooked dignity, you begin to feel something horrible.

I don't know if it's from the Mexican, or that maybe it's the indigenous side of us, to just lower the head and keep going. I know I'm hitting against an apparatus that's perverse and that perverts you. When I go to Europe, I go because I'm drowning in shame from living in this country, one that is marvelous, so extraordinary, in which so many incredible things happen all the time. But this feeling inside squeezes me. At times, I have to escape.

RC: One thing I wanted ask about is the reality of your theater-bar, El Hábito, here in Coyoacán, which is rather expensive, limiting your audience.

JS: A lot of things come together. I was born on the corner and as I child I was fascinated by this house, of Salvador Novo, who scared me. It only had wrought-iron gates – we added all these windows and doors. He would be entertaining the dogs, one a German shepherd, so when we as kids went by, I was scared. I jumped over the dogs and we always passed terrorized. They seemed like strange people, it's a strange place. We played in the street along Río Churubusco with the neighborhood kids. My Mom and Frida Kahlo called the same plumber, it was a different world. So for me getting this house was like destiny.

I rented the theater in 1980. We began to work here, and many people have commented that it is elitist, it's very expensive, and I thought so, too. Theater is a germinal phenomenon. You plant a seed that expands, you don't know where it goes. If I wanted to do popular theater, for a lot of people, by necessity I would have to submit myself to the government, to public officials who don't understand anything about the apparatus although they create bureaucracies. To what point is a project elitist if you are able to develop yourself to your fullest capacity? It's a lot of work, you have to work excessively, but you are free. It's the great thing in this country, where you can say, let's do popular theater! But can you do it seriously? Many years ago I decided that I would do it when I am able produce popular theater in the best of conditions and quality, so that the audience could be comfortable. Not in Plaza Solidaridad burning in the sun, sitting on the ground, seeing a terrible production that can't even be heard. This work has a lot of conditions, that go far beyond me saying that I'm going to put an exquisite theatre in Coyoacán for the beautiful people. And also, I feel that theater is a local phenomenon, through which you are able to talk about what's going on here in the neighborhood. At times I think that some particular work should be presented in a particular place, that the story needs to be there. At the same time, I know that being here reduces the audience, but only to a point. Yes, a student who can't afford the ticket can't enter nor a taxi driver who thinks this place is only for 'beautiful people'. But the gain is that you can plant a seed that then can explode to other channels without limits. Until now, I've been able to work with freedom and independence. To not have to censor even half a word. They've offered me T.V. shows, but I know that they'll take it off before it ever even airs! I refuse to go down that road of censorship, in T.V., in those media that are perfectly limited. And neither am I a genius, like Gasai in Argentina who does marvelous things on T.V. in spite of the Church and the military in Argentina. And I'm not against the medium itself, it's very important. If there are no campaigns against AIDS on television, we're not doing anything. The problem is how T.V. is managed. The same things happen to me in theater. I have so much freedom working in the margins.

RC: Isn't included here the idea of expanding civic participation, of expanding a civic consciousness?

JS: Many people believe that there's been a growth in Mexico's collective consciousness, but I think Mexico is very strange, as we have this other ingredient which is is our ability to forget.

RC: Carlos Monsiváis says that the capacity of Mexicans to forget is as great as the number of Mexicans.

JS: Exactly. People can't remember what the PRI (Institutional Revolutionary Party) was like in Federal District's government of only three years ago, what the PRI with Oscar Espinosa did. They criticize Cardenas, say he and the PRD don't know how to govern Mexico City, and they don't remember what the PRI did. We forgot in less than 400 years where was the Templo Mayor located, we didn't remember where the center of the universe was for our culture ... at least the Templo Mayor was the center of the universe of 500 years ago. We forget what was the center of the universe. Also, I imagine that the Egyptians forget why the pyramids were constructed. We have great capacity to forget and rapidly.

In relation to the collective consciousness, beyond the efficiency of the strategy of the system to brutalize the people, to terrorize them, the second big blow that has been delivered on Mexico is FOBAPROA [the government bail-out of the failed private Mexican banking system], a fraudulence the magnitude of which is unmatched. But if you grab people in the pocket, you paralyze them enormously. We are now in this drama. It comes down to that drug, money. On the other hand, the authoritarian system pays you for the terrorism you can cause, to be a paramilitary, beat people up, to be a bastard politician – they pay you.

For money we kill daily. We exploit people. Make them sick, abuse them. I've not seen a campaign against the addiction to money. Or hospitals that cure you of that addiction. They all offer to cure you of drug addictions. If we see money as a drug, so efficient, so used, why isn't it attacked? That's why theater is generous, because it's one of the art forms that needs the least amount of money, not like film that requires millions to produce. Theater is not subject to the laws of this drug ... and that makes you want to stay and dedicate yourself to work. You've got to find a way to do it, to survive.

NOTE

1.   For an analysis of Rodríguez's work, see Roselyn Costantino, 'Jesusa Rodríguez's Body in Play,' in Coco Fusco (ed), *Corpus Delecti. Performance Art of the Americas* (London and New York: Routledge, 1999).

Petrona de la Cruz and Isabel J. F. Juárez Espinosa of La FOMMA
(Fortaleza de la Mujer Maya)
Photo © 1992 Macduff Everton

10

Gendering Chiapas: Petrona de la Cruz and Isabel J. F. Juárez Espinosa of La FOMMA (Fortaleza de la Mujer Maya/ Strength of the Mayan Woman)[1]

Harley Erdman

The Chiapas-based theater collective La FOMMA draws upon the rich performance heritage of Mayan Mexico and the techniques of Latin American *teatro popular* to create an accessible people's theater, based around vignettes that combine broad comedy, vivid melodrama, and piercing social commentary to depict the struggles of everyday life for the region's indigenous peoples. Unlike most other practitioners of *teatro popular*, La FOMMA stands out because it is a women's collective. Its pieces, created and performed by the ten indigenous women who currently comprise the company, are directed at an audience made up primarily of women and children. The company is trilingual: depending upon the venue, La FOMMA presents its work in either Spanish or one of the region's native languages, Tzotzil and Tzeltal.

The two founding members of La FOMMA, Petrona de la Cruz (a native Tzotzil speaker) and Isabel J. F. Juárez Espinosa (a native Tzeltal speaker), got their start in the late 1980s in the newly founded acting troupe of the Sna Jtz'ibajom ('House of the Writer'), an organization in San Cristóbal de las Casas, Chiapas, dedicated to the creation and fostering of Mayan cultural expression, including writing and theater. At the time, it was the only such theater company operating in Chiapas. Aside from La FOMMA, it remains so. The acting company of Sna Jtz'ibajom, along with its complementary puppetry troupe, explores and theatricalizes Mayan myth and reality, reinvigorating and reinventing pre-Columbian performance traditions for which the ancient peoples of the region were celebrated and which their descendants today continue to enact in their rural *comunidades* (villages).[2]

After gaining experience and acclaim with Sna Jtz'ibajom, de la Cruz and Juárez Espinosa left the troupe in the early 1990s because, among other reasons, they found it was not adequately addressing issues of concern to women.[3] After a period of transition during which de la Cruz and Juárez Espinosa laid the groundwork for their own company, La FOMMA was officially incorporated in 1994.

If de la Cruz and Juárez Espinosa are exceptional, as Tamara L. Underiner has written, for the way their work frames social reality from the 'perspective of women and children,' using cross-gender casting 'to refashion a whole tradition that has historically mocked and excluded them,'[4] La FOMMA also takes its place in a venerable counter-tradition of extraordinary female voices within Mexican theater, from the seventeenth-century prodigy Sor Juana Inés de la Cruz to contemporary urban playwrights like Sabina Berman and performance artists like Jesusa Rodríguez. Within Chiapas, they also have the example of Rosario Castellanos (1925–74), the renowned poet and novelist who not only occasionally turned to playwriting but, in the 1950s, headed a puppet company for the National Indigenous Institute of San Cristóbal. While Castellanos wrote movingly of the exploitation of the region's indigenous population, she (like Sor Juana, Berman, Rodríguez, Luisa Josefina Hernandez, and other Mexican female writers for the stage) hailed from Mexico's more privileged classes. For this reason, de la Cruz and Juárez Espinosa are heralded internationally today as pioneers: the first female indigenous playwrights in Mexico. Their growing reputation has resulted not only in tours of the United States but also in featured articles in *Ms.* magazine and the *New York Times.* Meanwhile, de la Cruz and Juárez Espinosa continue to skillfully juggle roles as producers, writers, directors, and actors.

While La FOMMA was created the same year as the Zapatista uprising, both women are careful to distance themselves from the guerrilla movement. Both La FOMMA and the Zapatistas are responding to the same material conditions of struggle and exploitation – the brutal reality of five centuries of colonial and postcolonial domination of the region's indigenous peoples – but the women assert their neutrality in the ongoing conflict. While such a public stance of 'neutrality' may be a necessary survival strategy, particularly given the company's need to avoid harassment from the Mexican government, it is probably more useful to see La FOMMA's work as providing a different perspective on injustices endemic to the region rather than one that is merely 'neutral.' As symbolized by the charismatic figure of Comandante Marcos, the rebellion in Chiapas is often viewed abroad (as well as in Mexico City) in terms of military and political confrontation between starkly opposing forces, as part of a sensationalized narrative palatable to middle-class, urbanized sympathizers. La FOMMA's work, in contrast, delves into the personal, domestic foundation that supports and perpetuates the exploitative system that has spurred the rebellion. La FOMMA for the most part resists detailing conflicts between guerrillas and government, between *comandantes* and *fuerzas armadas*. Nor do they buy into discourses of the 'noble savage,' replete with romanticized idealizations of a happy, innocent Latin American folk peasantry. Their plays, in other words, are not the commodified Chiapas, the 'public face' of a region that finds its ways into the evening news and tourist promotional material. Rather, their work paints a rich and disturbing tableau of everyday life, often using conflicts within families to stand in for – with startling clarity – larger regional struggles.

La FOMMA's approach to theater is evident from the plotlines of some of their major plays. *Migración*, for example, depicts the plight of a rural family whose father, against the better judgment of the mother, relinquishes their meager landholdings in search of what he hopes will be a better life in the city. Things go wrong, friends go back on their word, and the family ends up rootless, dispossessed, and abjectly poor – with the father having become an alcoholic. *Madre olvidada* dramatizes the situation of a widow harassed and abused by her own son, who acts like a tyrant and has appropriated family lands for himself. With the help of local indigenous authorities, two of his sisters go behind the brother's back to thwart his efforts and rescue their mother; in the end, the brother repents. In *Desprecio paternal*, a controlling widower alienates his daughters enough to force them to run away to the city to seek careers as teachers. He is left bitter and alone, eventually attempting suicide, only to be saved at the last moment by his daughters, who take him off to the city to find a doctor. *La tragedia de Juanita* tells the story of a wealthy light-skinned landowner who targets a nine-year-old indigenous girl for a wife. Despite misgivings, the girl's parents – their judgment clouded by alcohol and fear of the powerful landowner – give in. The landowner, himself in an alcoholic stupor, ends up raping and murdering the girl. The local authorities are unable to give the landowner more than a slap on the wrist as punishment.

Together, these plays, along with many others by La FOMMA, paint a stark yet startling vision of contemporary Chiapanecan reality. The judgment of women is shown as being more valuable than the dreaming and scheming of patriarchs, whether husbands, fathers, brothers, village elders, or landowners. Children are depicted as being wiser than their elders, either suffering for their parents' sins or, in some cases, redeeming their parents through their own suffering and exile. Modernity, as represented by the city, holds promise but also presents dangers. If the men sin, it is frequently because they are under pressure from the material conditions of their existence: land that is worth little, farms that don't produce much, life that represents a daily struggle for subsistence and that presents them with humiliation after humiliation, especially given the tremendous power and prestige of the Spanish-descended *caciques* who preside paternalistically (but not benevolently) over the region. The overall portrait is of a region full of desperation, brutality, suffering, and rage, where the main hope for salvation and social change comes from women and children. La FOMMA insists that their spectators see the struggle from this domestic perspective: that the injustices of sexism intersect with those of race, class, and culture with which the region is commonly associated. And if the circumstances of the plays seem melodramatic, one should compare them to the circumstances, for example, of de la Cruz's own life story, recounted in this interview. Besides, like other practitioners of *teatro popular* throughout the Americas (including such companies as the San Francisco Mime Troupe), La FOMMA embraces melodrama as perhaps the most enduring, accessible, and powerful popular performance traditions, widely recognized and understood by audiences of many different backgrounds.

An incident just prior to the taping of this interview, alluded to in the transcript that follows, pointedly reminded me of the power issues at stake when community-based performers from a remote, impoverished area come into contact with international scholars interested in promoting or critiquing their work. On the day of the interview, I received in the mail the issue of *Theatre Journal* with the above-cited article by Underiner. It featured a section on La FOMMA, along with a prominent photo from the company's production of *Migración.* I shared it with de la Cruz and Juárez Espinosa, thinking they might already be familiar with it in some form. The women were taken aback. They said they were not aware of any such pending article; in fact, they were initially somewhat unsure about who had written it. After the interview, I translated the section on La FOMMA for them, and both women were greatly relieved, even proud of it – they felt the author had been meticulously accurate and fair in describing their work. I cite this anecdote in a self-reflexive spirit: to express wariness about the practice of intercultural scholarship. Differences in power, distances between cultures, and difficulties in communication require those of us with privilege to be constantly vigilant about the ultimate goals and uses of our work.

HARLEY ERDMAN: Could you talk a little about what you did before founding La FOMMA?

PETRONA DE LA CRUZ: I finished primary school at age 15 and went on to start the *secundaria.* My mother wanted me to learn tailoring, alterations, so I was sent to stay at the house of a woman in San Cristóbal who could teach me. That's when it happened. I was 17 years old. I was raped, kidnapped, and I ended up pregnant. A man from one of the *comunidades* did it. It had to do with politics. They held me for a few days. I was so terrified I couldn't bring myself to tell anybody what happened.

Nobody knew I was pregnant. The man who kidnapped me paid a lot of money to the authorities. He told me never to tell my parents – if I told anybody, he'd kill my father. So when the baby was finally born, it was such a terrible shock for my mother – she got sick and died six days after. My family didn't know what had really happened, I was too scared to tell them, and since I wasn't living at home when it happened, they had no reason to suspect I'd been kidnapped. They blamed me for my mother's death and threw me out of the house, along with my infant son.

So I went to work as a domestic servant. After that, I went from *feria* to *feria*, selling tacos. My son – he was three or four years old by then – got lost a few times. Once he was missing all night, we didn't find him until five o'clock in the morning. That made me realize it was time to go back home again. I had an aunt who let me stay with her. She watched my son while I finished my *secundaria*. *Then* I found out about a theater company that was looking for women: Sna Jtz'ibajom. Isabel was the only woman in the group. I was 23 years old.

ISABEL JUÁREZ ESPINOSA: This was a group that used to compile stories and tales from the surrounding *comunidades*. They sent me into my *comunidad* to speak with old men and women, to hear them talk about their lives. Later, in 1987, this organization decided to form a puppeteering group, and we started to tour all over Mexico. After a while, we thought of producing our plays with real actors and decided which of our stories to adapt for the stage. In 1988, when our first play was produced, we as a group liked it and decided to produce a new play every year. But in these new plays other actresses were needed, because I was the only actress in the group. The rest of the actors were all men.

HE: What was it like being the only woman in the group?

IJ: At first, my relations with my colleagues at work were good, since we only had to compile stories, make puppets, make their clothes. However, a woman's voice is unmistakable, isn't it? And the way she moves her hands ... When we had to perform in front of an audience and play women, my male colleagues didn't want to dress as women, so they decided to look for other women. That's when I met my *compañera* Petrona. Most of the women didn't like it, couldn't feel comfortable in an environment so dominated by men, and they started to leave. Petrona and I were the two women that stayed the longest with this group. In 1992 I decided to leave the group, before Petrona did, and work in other jobs, but then, a little later, Petrona left the group as well, and we formed another theater group ...

HE: ... that was *not* La FOMMA ...

IJ: ... it was not La FOMMA – it was nothing. It didn't even have a name! And then we starting thinking about forming another group – about how to organize it. 'Why don't we form another group, composed mainly of women? If men can, so can we.' So we began our travelling theater company in 1993. We started to seek out *compañeras* who were willing to participate voluntarily – because we didn't have any money, we were only doing it because we liked it. We were invited by seminarians and other groups, by groups of women, not native but mestizo, and by some universities. These places paid us a little and gave us all the materials that we needed at no charge. We'd collect the materials and keep the money, with the goal of legally constituting our association.

Once we had enough resources, we started to send out brochures with the support of some American friends, especially the anthropologist Robert Laughlin and his wife Miriam. We advertised this way, and responses started to come back. And that's how we created La FOMMA. By February of 1994, we had done all the necessary transactions with an attorney to legalize the association.

HE: So you had to struggle for a number of years before founding the company?

IJ: Yes. For a long time we were working independently for another institution and would meet only in our spare time. Later, when we had a small office and enough resources that we felt that it was possible to work mostly with women, we did look for more supporters, as well as *compañeras* to join our group. We started with literacy workshops in our native tongues. And then theater, and then plastic arts, and then all the things that theater involves.

When we started, we saw that many women came with babies and small children, saying, 'Well, I do want to learn, but I don't have anybody to take care of my child.' So we opted for starting a day-care center for the children while the women attended the workshops. That's how La FOMMA started to grow. We had to look for another house because the house we had was too small. That new house is where we're located now. Our workshops continue to grow. But it's not easy getting funds.

HE: I notice you've had to travel a lot to raise money. It must be difficult being away from your organization for long stretches of time.

IJ: Yes, indeed, especially because there are new chores to do, and we're a small group. Our *compañeras* support us in the workshops, or teach the classes. We've distributed all of our work. We also have families, and sometimes it's a little difficult being without our families for such a long time. But it's our work, and we like to do it.

HE: Did you encounter resistance from men when you created La FOMMA?

IJ: It was a surprise for them. They never thought that a woman, even two women, could initiate a group like this and recruit so many women. Many men were against us. They thought we were feminists, or that we didn't like men.

HE: The word 'feminist' in Mexico is more or less a curse, isn't it?

IJ: That's right, or at least that's what men mostly think when they hear the word. But our organization does not mean that we despise men or that we won't give opportunities to men. Our starting this group meant telling women how valuable they are, how they have their rights. It meant showing them they can solve their problems. And men must understand that we have to support each other. There are still men who don't understand. We've had *compañeras* whose husbands wouldn't let them join us or told them bad things about our organization. But there are some young men working with us now. They've seen the work we do, and there's no problem. Most men by now are aware of what we're doing with our group. I believe that in any country, any new group will be either admired or despised, and people will wonder 'Why start it at all, why start this new fight?' But then when people see the work we do, they realize it's about everyday human life.

HE: How has attending conferences and visiting universities in the United States impacted your work?

PC: It's very important for us. We get to know the work other people do, see other workshops, learn about new problems. Sometimes we, as Chiapanecas and Mexicans, think that only Chiapas has problems. Being at a conference unites us. It lets us come in contact with many other cultures and persons.

HE: It must be unusual to come here, open up a journal, and see pictures of yourselves and scholarly writing by professors from the United States.

IJ: It surprised me. I didn't know that article that had been published. Many people have taken pictures of us, so many universities everywhere might have pictures of us. It's possible we're in other books, in other countries, and we don't even know about it. I'd like it if the person that publishes the journal or book or the person that took the pictures would send us a copy to put in our library. We have a library too! Then our *compañeras* could see the work that we're doing, far from our workplace. Because it's good for us to have publications, even if we can't follow very well what's written because we don't speak English. Everything is fine as long as it's accurate. Sometimes people misunderstand us. Or maybe we didn't express ourselves well enough.

HE: I'd like to know a little more about the process through which you create a work like the one you presented last night [*Esfuerzos y llantos de la selva*].

IJ: The play was written collectively by our *compañeras* at La FOMMA. We were told that we had to have a production ready. We had some plays in our repertoire, but thought, 'Why not bring a new play?' Of course, there are many theater performers and companies that have produced plays about the Zapatistas and their strife, but they have another vision. As a theater company composed of women, we have a different vision. We're the ones that suffer. We're the ones that live through the worst situations. Sometimes there are people or men who do not understand us. For example, if there's a rape, you tell them about it, and they accept it naturally. But for women, it's traumatic to suffer incidents like that. And when we put them on stage – maybe our lesson is a little comic, but it also has a message. We show what's really happening everywhere in Mexico, not just in Chiapas.

HE: And how are plays like this developed. Do you talk? Do you write?

IJ: We write. All of us . . .

HE: . . . the ten of you . . .?

IJ: . . . together.

HE: All of you?

IJ: Each one of us gives her point of view. Later, when we're on stage, rehearsing the play, if there's any point we don't like, we change it depending on the performers we have. We often 'dress up' the characterization, adding *colorido* [local color].

HE: So you have ten people in the same room, all writing at once?

IJ: Yes, at a table just like this one. We work on our viewpoint, or the characters, and on everything else.

PC: Take my *compañera* and me. We're both writers, so each of us writes sometimes by herself, in a separate room, so she can concentrate and write in her own personal way. But when we write collectively, we all write together. Then, when we get to a point when we have enough ideas, my *compañera* and I create the final script. Once the script is ready, then we take it back to the women and revise it collectively.

Whatever we're doing, La FOMMA is the livelihood for all of us. We work together all day, rehearsing, writing, making scenery. If we have a new show, we might perform it twice a week, taking it to various schools or *comunidades*. For the women taking workshops, it's different. Almost all of them are *indígenas*, single mothers. We have to find scholarships for them to participate in the workshops.

HE: How did you find the other eight women who make up La FOMMA?

PC: Many times, especially at the beginning, when we were touring *comunidades*, people didn't understand our theater. They discriminated against us, said bad things about us, said it was shameful what we're doing. It was just so different for them – they had never seen theater. But there always would be a few women who'd come up and say, 'How courageous of you to stand up before an audience this way. I'd like to get involved.' So we'd invite these women to our workshop and see if they wanted to join our group. At times we haven't been able to accommodate all the women because there isn't enough room in the workshops!

María was the first *compañera* to join us – this is about five years ago now. She came on her own, we didn't know her. Next came Francisca. Then Faustina. She wanted to work with us but her husband wouldn't let her. She'd go running home as fast as she could at 3 p.m. so her husband wouldn't be furious. She's a different person now. She's left her husband, lost her fear. And she has a new husband!

HE: Petrona, in both pieces I've seen you perform, you played men. You play these roles very well, with a great sense of comedy. What's it like to perform these roles?

PC: I think I've always liked to play men because I've always had to play men. In this group, we've always had very short *compañeras*, like my *compañera* Isabel here. It falls to the taller among us to play the men. And we like to do it. It's theater. Isabel, on the other hand, plays young girls because she's a little short and she fits the roles well.

HE: That reminds me of Sna Jtz'ibajom, which you were invited to join because the men didn't want to play women. Is it hard for you to play a man in front of a Chiapas audience? The act is very subversive, challenging.

PC: I like to play the character I have to play because I like to do theater, because the theater to me is something good, beautiful, and fun, and carries a message. In my case, I like to play all characters. I'll play an old lady, a woman, a man . . .

IJ: I've played an old lady. I've played a young girl. I've played mothers. I don't think there's a specific kind of character that I prefer to portray.

HE: What has been your most difficult moment while performing a play?

IJ: The most difficult moments for me on stage came when I was just starting out as an actress. I felt physically weak, that I was going to forget my lines. I felt I couldn't do it as well as during rehearsal. These days, I still feel a little nervous when I first meet the audience. I'm thinking the audience may not like the play, the audience is going to be aggressive, the audience may interrupt you in the middle of a scene. But later, when I'm acting, I have no fear: I feel free to do whatever I want. I ignore the audience because I can't see them watching me. I have no problem then. I'm acting. I'm expressing what I feel.

HE: Last night, you were very close to the audience: two or three feet away from the front row. Do you often perform on stages like that where you can look the audience so directly in the face?

IJ: As far as I'm concerned, I ignore the audience, whether they're close or far. Otherwise I can lose my rhythm or forget my lines. I think it's better to look away and pretend you can't see.

PC: I do the same. I think I felt a little fear when I started doing theater because we used to go on tour all around Chiapas, and almost everybody in the group was male. Because of the kidnapping, I was full of tension inside. There was a time once when I was so destroyed mentally, so terrified, I couldn't even speak with a man. I felt that tension whenever I was about to perform. I would step on the stage full of nerves, wondering what would happen. At some point, though, I somehow realized this was my opportunity to talk and to draw out into the light what's inside me. Then, I starting feeling a mixture of nervousness and strength whenever I performed in public. That's the moment when I started to lose my stage fright. I even stopped being scared of men. I started to trust them, to approach them. The theater has changed me. It's given me confidence. It's helped me get stronger.

HE: Your work addresses controversial cultural, political, and social issues in a region that's been torn apart by violence. How do you express your point of view on these explosive topics in front of an audience that may not be sympathetic and that itself has been divided by these issues?

IJ: We are very careful then. For example, last night's play cannot be performed as easily in Mexico as it can be here. We still perform the play there, but in front of people we already know, in front of certain groups with whom we feel confident. Even in this country, we ask ourselves, 'What if a Mexican sees us and he or she disagrees with everything that is going on in Chiapas? What if people who don't like us are waiting for us at the airport?' For us, it's just a play, and nothing more. We're not against anybody. We're only expressing our point of view about what is going on in Chiapas. But there are people who interpret it in a different way.

HE: Do you get tired of people in this country assuming that you must be linked to the Zapatistas because you are activists from Chiapas?

IJ: Many people believe that we're Zapatistas. Actually, we don't even know *who* is a Zapatista. We do our cultural work. We support women in the city, but we don't know what is happening within the Zapatista organization. We know that there are problems in the *comunidades*, that there are murders and rapes, that children are being kidnapped. But we don't know who is actually doing anything. We cannot lie. We cannot say 'The government is doing this or that' because then we would be wrongfully branding a person without being sure.

HE: Do you have a vision for La FOMMA ten years from now?

IJ: I've set my hopes on La FOMMA. We don't know whether we personally will continue with La FOMMA or find work somewhere else doing what we like. But ten years from now, whether we are part of it or not, I'd like La FOMMA to still be there, organizing workshops, supporting women and children.

As I said last night at our show, we do theater, but we do not dedicate ourselves exclusively to theater. Only some people like to perform. Others are afraid of acting, afraid of leaving their *comunidades* or their homes, afraid of being in front of an audience. If we ever have more workshops for our students, or when I am old – if I ever grow to be old – I would love to have a space there in which to work.

PC: I agree with my *compañera*. I don't know if we'll reach old age. I don't even know if we'll be alive next year. Only fate knows that. But, for my part, I'd like my other *compañeras* to have the willpower we had, that dream, that hope of supporting women and children. That strength we had – I hope that stays with them.

NOTES

1. The interview was conducted in Spanish on October 24, 1998, at the Department of Theater, University of Massachusetts at Amherst. I am grateful to Juan Pablo Fernandez of the UMass Translation Center for his work transcribing and preparing the initial translation of the interview. Some additional material has been added based upon Roberta Uno's interview with de la Cruz in Mexico City in November, 1999.

    At the time of the original interview, de la Cruz and Juárez Espinosa were on campus to perform *Esfuerzos y llantos de la selva*. A few weeks earlier, they had performed a scene from *Víctimas del engaño* as part of a showcased presentation at the Intersections conference.

2. For more on Sna Jtz'ibajom, see Donald H. Frischmann, 'New Mayan Theatre in Chiapas: Anthropology, Literacy, and Social Drama,' in Diana Taylor and Juan Villegas (eds), *Negotiating Performance* (Durham: University of North Carolina Press, 1994, 213–38). Also see Frischmann, 'Contemporary Mayan Theatre and Ethnic Conflict: The Recovery and (Re)Interpretation of History,' in J. Ellen Gainor (ed.), *Imperialism and Theatre: Essays on World Drama and Performance* (New York: Routledge, 1995, 71–84).

3. For more on rupture with Sna Jtz'ibajom, see Cynthia Steele, 'A Woman Fell into the River: Negotiating Female Subjects in Contemporary Mayan Theatre,' in Taylor and Villegas (eds), *Negotiating*, 239–56.

4. Tamara L. Underiner, 'Incidents of Theatre in Chiapas, Tabasco, and Yucatan: Cultural Enactments in Mayan Mexico,' *Theatre Journal*, 50 (1998): 358, 360.

Brian Freeman
Photo by Peter L. Stein

11

'Who's doing it now?': conversations with Brian Freeman on the politics of Black gay performance

Marlon M. Bailey

We constitute the invisible brothers in our communities, those of us who live in the life ... The Black homosexual is hard-pressed to gain audience among his heterosexual brothers; even if he is more talented, and he is, he is inhibited by his silence or his admissions. This is what the race has depended on in being able to erase our recorded history. But these sacred constructions of silence are futile exercises in denial. We will not go away with our issues of sexuality.

'Loyalty,' by Essex Hemphill[1]

Black gay poet Essex Hemphill eloquently articulates the significant role that Black gay cultural production plays in claiming and affirming our complex identity in the face of hostility. Accordingly, versatile artist Brian Freeman has produced the kind of artistic work throughout his extensive career that engages Black gay men and their complex lives on the mainstage of social discourse. And he's still doing it. In many cases, Black gay voices are muffled by the confluence of racial and sexual hegemony. In the midst of this current reality, Freeman's work reminds us that our relentless examination of what it means to be Black and gay is essential.

In their writings, several Black gay scholars explicitly describe an insidious form of racism that pervades in White gay communities. It is this racism that rules out any political coalition between Black and White gays to challenge homophobia and heterosexism. As David Frechette argues in his 1999 article 'Why I'm Not Marching,' Black gay men are subject to similar kinds of entrenched racial prejudice within the gay community as they are in the larger society. Therefore, many Black gays are either excluded from or are resistant to

White gay political agendas (131). This reality is compounded by the pervasive homophobia in Black communities. For instance, many Black leaders believe that homosexuality collides with the collective Black socio-political agenda and that heterosexuality is the only legitimate form of Black sexuality. As a result, Black communities are continuously indifferent, at best, or totally opposed, at worst, to the inclusion of Black gays and lesbians as a part of an overall Black cultural vanguard (Hutchinson, 1999: 28). Our attempts to galvanize intellectual, political, and even economic resources to actively resist dominant social inscriptions, and to mobilize around our racially and sexually convergent identities, grow increasingly complicated in such a hegemonic matrix. Yet, if we don't collectively claim our Black gay identities and tenaciously challenge racism and homophobia in tandem, we are complicit in society's efforts to render us silent and invisible – erasing our history and culture, our very being. I believe a central imperative to combating invisibility and silence is cultural work. Our literatures, our dramas, our music, our films, and our performance traditions are effective cultural tools that document experiences, histories, traditions, politics, and collective struggle. Black gay artists today stand on the traditions of the past, where earlier cultural workers took on the responsibility of protecting our stakes in both our cultural and sexual identities (Román, 1998: 164).

When I moved to the Bay Area in 1999, I had several conversations with Black gay men who have lived here for a long time. They lamented what they viewed as the passing of the politically fervent years. These were times where many Black gay artists' works were consistently used to shape gay liberationist discourses. During the post-Stonewall years, both Black feminists and Black gay and lesbian discourses experienced a resurgence of visibility. Black feminists helped to create a theoretical space for Black gay cultural workers to engage their concurrent racial and sexual oppression (Jackson, 1993: 131). People would nostalgically recall how politically vibrant it used to be for Black gay people, 'back in the day.' Invariably, these conversations would include the mentioning of prominent names such as film-maker Marlon Riggs, recording artist Sylvester, transgender activist Martha P. Johnson, and most of all, Pomo Afro Homos, the former Black gay triumvirate featuring Brian Freeman, Djola Bernard Branner, and Eric Gupton. In light of the unfortunate deaths of all of the former names mentioned and the disbanding of the latter group, I have often heard people ask, 'Who's doing that political artistic work now?' I immediately think of Brian Freeman who, even after the end of Pomo Afro Homos, continues to create insightful and provocative performance material that reflect the multi-dimensionality of Black gay lives, attempting to secure a space for Black gays to exist in this society, free from racial discrimination and heterosexual persecution (Elam, 1996: 7).

As a Black gay playwright, director, actor, and performance artist, Brian Freeman has spent most of his artistic career using the stage to challenge the marginalization of Black gay men. Over the last decade, his work has sought to provide clarity to an otherwise nebulous position in both the Black and gay worlds that many of us occupy. Using performance as a site of contestation against racism in the White gay community and homophobia among African Americans, Freeman has helped to shape perhaps the most emergent theoretical discourses that explore the connections between culture and performance. His work with Pomo Afro Homos and his recent contributions to the performance world take up some of the most pressing issues concerning Black gay communities such as racism, homophobia/heterosexism, Black gay images in the media, class issues, Black politics, and AIDS. Yet, in light of looming threats of invisibility and silence, surely the most important aspects of his work are those that document and retrieve Black gay history. His plays offer an opportunity for our community to recognize and honor the many people who have made enormous contributions to African American causes who otherwise, because of their Black gay identities, never receive the kind of recognition afforded to others who supposedly led more socially acceptable lives. Brian Freeman's work provides a historical foundation for Black gay people by commemorating those individuals who struggled before us.

Freeman left Boston, Massachusetts where he grew up, to attend the University of Pennsylvania for a brief stint. He then moved to New York City to work and train with the Negro Ensemble Company[2] for three seasons. He subsequently moved to San Francisco to work with the San Francisco Mime Troupe[3] where he served as a playwright, director, producer, and performer for eight seasons. After leaving the San Francisco Mime Troupe, Freeman joined Rhodessa Jones and Idris Ackamoor's Cultural Odyssey[4] as a writer/director. During this period in his career, he worked with such prominent artist as dancer/choreographer, Bill T. Jones, playwright Ed Bullins, and vaudevillian performer Derique McGhee among others.

During the late 1980s, Brian Freeman worked with Marlon Riggs as Associate Producer on the seminal film *Tongues Untied*. As he describes in the following interview, this collaboration with Riggs galvanized a whole range of Black gays who had been invisible. Along with Eric and Djola (who also performed in *Tongues Untied*), this experience motivated Freeman to start Pomo Afro Homos (Postmodern African American Homosexuals). Between 1991–1995, this trio, who first performed at the Center for African and African-American Art and Culture in the Western Addition District in San Francisco, toured all over the world. Their two provocative shows, *Fierce Love* and *Dark Fruit*, toured to England, Scotland, Cuba, Canada, and all over the U.S. The group's work garnered several awards and opportunities to perform at various prestigious locations. In just four years, Pomo Afro Homos had established itself as the most eloquent and poignant theatrical voice for Black gay men (Clum, 1996: 319).

Pomo Afro Homos enabled Freeman to engage with a multitude of political issues that reflected his complex personal experiences at that time. As evidenced by what he refers to as 'his theatrical life,' the group's unorthodox performance style and the radical racial and sexual politics that undergird its material fostered a more feasible theatrical trajectory for Freeman. His subsequent work after the closure of the Pomo Afro Homos project demonstrates his ongoing commitment to theater/performance that boldly confronts the hegemonic socio-political terrain that mainstream American theater tends to reproduce. In the same vein, and just as important, Freeman's work also resists conventional ways of staging theatrical material. Consistent with his politics, Freeman's performance style is highly integrative, deploying various art forms in one piece. His plays encompass music, dance, stylized movement, video images, slides, flamboyant costumes, along with personal narratives, testimonies, parody, sermons, poetry, rap, as well as other creative artistic devices designed to lure audiences into the world he creates. For example *Fierce Love, Dark Fruit*, and *Civil Sex* are similar in actual form. All three pieces include a variety of sketches and vignettes joined together by a common theme. Although *Civil Sex* is written in a style more reminiscent of traditional dramatic scripts, Freeman is not constrained by conventional forms of American realism.

Most of all, the actual performances are what best constitute this new way of presenting radical ideas on stage – a new kind of theater. Freeman's performances usually have either no set or a minimal one, some props, and lighting and music cues that can be easily accommodated by different venues (Román, 1998: 164). He and the other performers in his plays are highly versatile and play a variety of roles throughout the show. Many times these performers play opposite gender roles as well as use their bodies to serve as actual set pieces, while other devices are used to support the action at any given time in the production. The very nature of this performance approach represents Freeman's notions about the multiplicity of Black gay identities.

In essence, this performance approach directly involves the convergence of personal experience and politics within an American theater landscape that has failed to address Black gay issues. Ironically, as a Black artist, Freeman moved away from the traditional Black theater approaches to presenting experience on stage. In many ways, Black theater has historically used versions of theatrical realism both in style and content to challenge racism in the American theater and the hegemonic racial reality it mirrors in society. Yet in its attempt to interrogate racism through the replication of Western theatrical style, some Black theater traditions may very well re-inscribe the racist paradigm it seeks to dismantle. The racial, gender, and sexual essentialism that underlies many Black characters, and the narrowly realistic way in which these characters are constructed and portrayed, creates a myopic prism by which audiences view Black experience. Although he left the Negro Ensemble Company at an early point in his career, Freeman did not abandon the principles behind resisting racial oppression and the necessity to depict Black lives on stage. Instead he chose to expand the presentation and understanding of multiple Black subject positions and the complex experiences they engender (Mercer, 1991: 204).

An instructive example of Freeman's extensive experience with this convergent reality of politics and performance is his discussion of Pomo Afro Homos's controversial 'banning' from the National African American Theatre Festival held biannually in Winston-Salem, North Carolina. This incident, as he characterizes it, is a quintessential example of the prevalence of homophobia in the Black community that the group needed to expose and contest. Consequently, the group's continuous resistance to these acts of exclusion has opened doors for many Black gay artists to present their works at a wide variety of theaters and performance spaces.

Currently, Freeman is a freelance writer, director, performer, and founding member of the Playwrights' Lab at the New York Public Theatre. He has received numerous grants and fellowships to continue his much needed work. In his latest project, *Civil Sex*, based on the life of Black gay civil rights activist, Bayard Rustin, Freeman excavates an important part of African American history by examining the challenges Rustin faced as a Black gay cultural worker during the Civil Rights Movement. Freeman was intrigued by Rustin's very flamboyant lifestyle during the 1960s. As he points out in this interview, the more he delved into Rustin's personal history the more he realized how interesting and important this story is.

Brian Freeman is undoubtedly one of the most important Black gay cultural workers in the current theater/performance arena. As he continues the work of his contemporaries, many of whom have passed on, the politics that permeate Freeman's performances demonstrate new possibilities for a Black queer praxis that affirms Black gay identities and navigates our efforts to jettison racism and homophobia from our communities. And even though Freeman suggests that he is not motivated by a need to liberate or empower an entire community, that, instead, he focusses on the stories of individuals, I am convinced that his plays and performances indeed change people's lives. Because performance has consistently proven to be an effective strategy for raising socio-political consciousness, mobilizing marginalized people around common concerns, and inciting people to move to action, surely numerous Black gay men and women have been positively impacted – indeed entire communities. Those who have witnessed his performances, read his plays, or worked with him on projects, all become an integral part of efforts to ensure our perpetual visibility and socio-political presence. So, now when someone asks me 'Who's doing it now?' I emphatically say, 'Brian Freeman is.'

MARLON BAILEY: I am interested in the breadth and scope of your work over the years. First I would like for you to talk about how you got involved in the kind of writing and performing that you do. What I find most intriguing is your journey from a more traditional theatrical tradition to your current work that merges the personal and the political.

BRIAN FREEMAN: It's really just the history of my theatrical life. When I first started working professionally in theater, I started as a stage manager with the Negro Ensemble Company, Off-Broadway. I was really kind of an intern and then an assistant stage manager. It was very traditional play work, really only family dramas, complete with the kind that George Wolfe makes fun of in his show *The Colored Museum*. But there was a time during the sixties and seventies where audiences were really starved to see themselves on stage in family, or familiar situations. A perfect example of this would be plays like Leslie Lee's *The First Breeze of Summer*, Steve Carter's *Eden*, and some of Charles Fuller's early works such as *Waiting for Mongo*, and of course, *A Soldier's Story*. Although it was a very hierarchical kind of organization, it was a wonderful place to be around. Many of the people there were doing all kinds of professional work. It was a really great time, but after three seasons of that stuff, I really knew that it was enough family drama – for a lifetime! That form ceased to inspire me, and I had gotten interested in dance at that time, in ballet and jazz dance, modern dance, which was just much freer in the way it would take on things. I loved the musicality, the abstraction, and it really got me started into really looking for another way of making theater.

MB: So, you began to visualize a more artistically holistic approach to performance that inspired you to move in another direction. Since what you described was a very popular form in Black theater at that time, did this move you away from theater at all to a more performance art genre?

BF: No, not quite in that sense, I always knew theater would be the field I would work in. So, I left New York and went back to Boston. Then I moved from there to San Francisco, and it was there that I saw this group performing in pubs in San Francisco, the San Francisco Mime Troupe. They perform these very big, very comic, musical satires about whatever the issues of the day are. They've been going since the late fifties, and they're still going now. I signed on there, first as a stage manager and then I started performing and studying there. Eventually, for me, it became one of those great environments where you could get to do anything. I studied various performance styles, and really learned how to make plays. I started writing for the stage there. I was with them for eight years. We toured all over the place, all over the world, across the U.S., performing many times in Europe, Canada, Cuba, East Germany – when there was an East Germany. It was great fun.

But then I grew tired of it. I liked the style and the broad strokes, but by then I grew tired of always viewing the big issue and not looking at personal ones. And as a gay man, it was difficult working within the company that was not particularly open to dealing with anything related to gay issues. I think a lot of it is kind of grounded in . . . well, there's a lot of homophobia along the left, along with these sort of antiquated notions that homosexuality is the by-product of a bourgeois society or something. No one has ever openly said anything, but it was rooted in that.

MB: So, this became a hindrance for you and your work. Did you feel like this situation was no longer conducive to your overall artistic growth?

BF: Yes, I just got tired, and this is about '85. At that time, I was living in San Francisco, of course, and the AIDS epidemic was really, really just wrecking the city. Frankly, part of me just couldn't reconcile traveling around the country talking about 'let's get organized around this issue in theater,' while there's this issue right *in* my home, in my face, in my life, in my bed really! And so I said, 'I can't stay here.' I couldn't put the two together anymore. I did regular work for a while, and then I got more into the performance art arena in the area. I started working with Rhodessa Jones of Cultural Odyssey along with some other folks. Later, I worked with her brother, Bill T. Jones, a dancer, on a collaborative project. To me, it was just so liberating to kind of put away the larger struggle of things, with all the burdens that come with it, and really look into some of the more complicated personal spaces, and realize the power of that kind of storytelling.

MB: When you left the San Francisco Mime Troupe, your subsequent work began to engage those personal issues that are articulated in a more political performance realm?

BF: Yes, and see, I really responded to that. For example, I'm always a bit attracted to humor as a means of conveying truths and discovering the depth and complexity of that way of working. So I worked with Cultural Odyssey for a bunch of years. Then, I began to collaborate with Marlon Riggs, the film-maker. I also joined a group called Black Gay Men United. This was a support group for Black gay men based in the San Francisco area, and we'd meet about once every other week in different members' houses and just talk. We would just discuss what it was like being Black and gay. Oddly, it was really the first time we had had that kind of a space to just talk in the privacy of our homes. We used to mostly reflect on who we were and really begin to feel a power within each other. San Francisco has this very, wonderfully progressive, enormous lesbian/gay community, but it's overwhelmingly a White gay community – a Midwestern gay community made up of these exiles from the farm belt in Kansas, Iowa, and Minnesota. And these people, of course, bring all types of baggage with them. There had not been a lot of space for Black people, Black men *or* women within the gay community to speak oppositionally. You can always speak about racism in the gay community, but to really speak about ourselves – this group allowed us to do just that. There were artists in it. Marlon was already a film-maker, and he made this great film *Ethnic Notions.* He'd also made a film about the blues in Oakland. He was getting ready to work on a film about images of Blacks in television.

MB: *Black Is Black Ain't?*

BF: No, it was called *Color Adjustments.*

MB: Oh, OK. A lot of professors still use that film in their courses.

BF: Yeah, he did eventually finish it, but that was going to be his next project after the blues film, but he postponed it. He went to visit his Mom, while she was working for the military in Germany at time, and he had severe liver failure while he was over there and almost died. He came back, but in the process he found out he was HIV-positive. It took him about two or three months to recover. It was *really* a shock to him that he was positive. It really, really shook him. We'd been chatting about how nice it would be to make some kind of film about us, and so he postponed the *Color Adjustment* project because he basically was afraid that he was going to die. He said, 'I want to make this film right now.' And so we began collaborating on what eventually became *Tongues Untied.* At first I was just working with him, and then he invited me to be associate producer on that project. In that film, there's this great density to the film work; it's really very rich even apart from the subject-matter, the way the story is told is really ground-breaking. It's not a documentary *per se*; yet it has some documentary techniques in it. It also even has some performance art techniques in it, so it's really a melding of all those. So here I'm having this wonderful opportunity to create this work that my heart is totally into as well as jump in with all these amazing techniques, and this is a true success – the film did great which has its own story.

MB: What kind of response did the film receive in the Bay Area?

BF: When the film showed in San Francisco, it played at the Castro Theater, which was just the nicest thing. It played there for a week on a double bill with Isaac Julian, a British film-maker's film, *Looking for Langston*, a meditation on Langston Hughes. And the audience came out; it was a 1200-seat theater, and it was packed night after night with all these Black gay men. It was a lot of different communities, but suddenly there are all these Black people at the Castro . . .

MB: That had been invisible . . .

BF: That had been completely invisible! They were in the Bay Area, and all of us including Marlon, were shocked. In the group I said, 'Who are these folks? Where did they come from? How come we've never seen these people.' You know? Both Marlon and I had been living there for a while; it was like, where did these folks come from? And when I saw that crowd, I thought, well, you know, this is great; this is working for *Tongues Untied.* The Black folk were there; yet, why were they there? Because suddenly there was something they were interested in. This was something for them. After years and years of going to lesbian/gay film festivals, and saying, 'Well, OK, it was about the White gay men struggling to find themselves.' 'It was the White gay women struggling.' And every now and then there's maybe one Black good buddy or the Black drag queen . . .

MB: . . . who doesn't have a life . . .

BF: . . . that doesn't have a life, that just kind of scurries through like they always talk about Lena Horne in those old Hollywood musicals. She's the Black woman who comes out and sings her song out of nowhere and then disappears; she is digressive. Invariably, in gay films, Black people are relegated to being the diversion from the main story.

MB: What happened after *Tongues Untied* and *Looking for Langston*?

BF: After the film thing, a new cabaret space had opened in the Bay Area, called Josie's Cabaret, and I knew the guy who ran it. I spoke with him before it even opened, and I thought it would be really fun to do a Black gay show. I don't think there has really been one that has been done. There have been a few *very*, very small ones, I think something like poetry readings. I told him, 'It would be fun to do a little show.' He was like, 'OK. Well, we have a slot in January. Why don't you do one then?' I said, 'I don't have one. I think it would be fun to do though.' And he said, 'Just get a couple of friends and do something. You know? Maybe it should be 75 minutes long,' he says, 'And it should be funny! It's a cabaret. And if you can, put some music in it.' Now, I'm no Ellen Stewart. So, I have these parameters; nonetheless, I called a couple of guys (Djola Branner, Eric Gupton). One was a friend; and the other I had just seen around the area working as an actor. I said, you know, 'Let's get together. We have this opportunity to do this show. Would you perhaps be interested?' And so we met up at a café and just threw out story ideas, and it just clicked right away. It just went shhhhhhh! Like that. We decided to do some skit work. I said, 'I'll direct the piece, but I'd also like to be in it, and we'll all write it.' We had a friend to do the costumes; we begged and borrowed – it was really put together on no money. We got some free rehearsal time at a local space – there was this Black community center in San Francisco that, at the time, was called Western Addition Cultural Center, but while we were in there they changed it to the Center for African and African-American Art and Culture. It was very much an Afrocentric spirit there. They would kind of trip out that we were rehearsing this gay piece there. People would listen and they would hear our piece. Sometimes they'd come in and people started acting out by displaying their ignorant and backward attitudes towards our play. In a way it made the show stronger because we were operating with the understanding that this is exactly why we're doing this piece. So, it became this daily thing, while we were rehearsing. We were also trying to terrorize the people in this organization because they were trying to terrorize us out of there, but we were just not going to move to another space, so at that moment it was just like, no! We're going to do this, and we're going to do it right here! And you're all going to have to deal with us because that's what this is all about. We did this, what goes to your question, style, within a cabaret setting, that calls for something similar to stand-up comedy. The main thing about this particular event was that we would be performing for audiences that want the kind of quick, cutting kind of humor. The show had to be on its feet. I think the only time people would ever sit down in the show was when during the first skit in the show. This skit is a parody of the characters from *In Living Color*, Blaine and Antoine – 'Men on Film' – which was something that popped up onto people's televisions out of nowhere in 1990. There was a big debate going on about this in Black gay circles around the country regarding whether these were positive or negative images. And suddenly this was in everyone's face, and all of a sudden people are snapping. So imagine this skit; it's really over the top, where they would meet the other over the top thing that was happening, which was like ACT UP activism,[5] these were engaging and really bold, outrageous acts of street theater all over the country. So, imagine that they're doing their show and their show is disrupted by a guy from something like an ACT UP style. Instead, for us, we made it an 'Act Black' thing. So it's doing this like triple flip, satirizing the thing that's satirizing us, as well as satirizing us in our most serious mode. This scenario reflects our existence. Then it gets to where it begins to speak about the duality of exactly a Black, queer existence, you know. You're always a part of many different communities. Yet you're not at home in any of them. I always feel like there are these situations where I go through, where I have to *be* Blaine and Antoine in one moment, and then be this angry activist in the other.

MB: So, breaking away from the realist theatrical tradition to a more agit-prop kind of performance art is the beginning of that new style – that kind of in your face, merging of the personal and the political?

BF: This is the beginning of that style, yes. This is where the personal and political sort of merge. That's because that piece really took these outrageous, satirical things, but then grounded them. Each of the three of us did a very personal story. I did a coming out story. We knew we needed to do a coming out story, and we wanted to do a sex piece. Eric Gupton did a safe sex monologue; but he didn't want to ground it in safe sex terminology because, obviously, that's not much fun there. So, he told this great story about going to a sex club in San Francisco. Because it's in San Francisco, of course it's going to have lots and lots of White men, and in that particular moment, he expresses the desire to meet someone Black. He has this encounter with a Black stranger, but they never touch. It's all totally verbal and it's very, very sensuous. Actually, we just kept him in a spotlight, and it was really just about his words and his eyes. He has huge eyes, so he only did very little; it's a very, very quiet piece with very rich vocabulary.

MB: I want to stay with that point about personal stories a little as it relates to your own work. For example, in the piece you are currently working on about Bayard Rustin – *Civil Sex* – clearly you are driven by the need to reveal the invisible. You re-circulate those Black gay personas that have been written out of history or out of existence for that matter. Therefore, this engagement of the personal is simultaneously political because it illuminates and in some ways celebrates those lives whose identities have been rendered anonymous.

BF: Right. These people are not written about at all. You see, I was really raised as a Civil Rights baby. My parents are almost exactly the same age as Martin Luther King if he had lived. They are very much a part of the integration movement; they were integration activists in their own right in Boston, Massachusetts. Growing up, my earliest memories are marching with my parents in demonstrations in Boston. We were marching as part of the integration movement; and I met Dr. King at a talk he gave once when I was about eight years old. This was at a rally in Roxbury, the black section of Boston. So all of that has a very, very deep resonance for me. And as I grow older, it's not just a question of what do I do with all of this. It is more a question of what does this mean for me? Where does this put me? You know, these opportunities that I have, that I know my parents didn't have, are what they struggled for. This is what really haunts me. Yet as I grow older as a gay man, I'm looking for myself! I mean, where am I? What is this territory I'm in now? I'm a little over 40; and who are my peers? And what am I looking for? I don't really have the history to tell me what to expect next! But I know it's there!

MB: This is also an attempt to recuperate that history. I see what you mean. That history is really what gives us a sense of purpose, a memory – an identity really, because it is our reference. However, we find ourselves in this somewhat nebulous position because that reference is not always accessible.

BF: Right, because I know I'm not the first, you know. None of us are the first. But, for instance, I look to Baldwin in some ways, but then I see this alcoholism; I see a lot of really messy behavior that, while I admire his writing, is not my life. I'm not going to go live in some chateau in Switzerland, you know . . .

MB: Drinking and smoking every evening . . .

BF: . . . partying every evening . . .

MB: . . . and then write in the middle of the night.

BF: You know . . . that's not it! That's not going to work for me. So part of it is that I'm still digging a little bit, in a way, for what is this world? When you dig up something, go into a territory that's not familiar, you really bring it out; you bring it back to life in a way. You often get labeled by that, regardless if your interests may be that and many other things and mine are. So that's a bit of a struggle. For example, Alice Walker really brought Zora Neil Hurston back for popular consumption; she got her novels back in print, and that interest in her just grows and grows. But she really spent a number of years doing that stuff, so that's always a battle for her. You get known for one thing, and then people only want you to do that, whereas usually if you do something, then you're done with that particular aspect of your work. You want to go on to the next thing.

MB: It seems like the nature of the circumstances compels artists who create work from the margins to write about our foremothers and forefathers. Hence, we create this body of work because the people who lived at the time couldn't necessarily come out. They couldn't say who they were. Would you say that this inspired you to do this piece on Bayard Rustin in *Civil Sex*.

BF: To some extent yes. And you are right; many couldn't necessarily come out and say it, although, the thing is, a lot of them did. For example, for various reasons, Rustin was not 'in.' Rustin was 'out!' He was way out in the forties. He really *lived* in New York; he *lived* in the world. Kind of like Ellen Stewart. I suspect they knew each other, and they were both very colorful. They both have these accents. Ellen has this sort of French accent. My grandmother knew Ellen Stewart when Ellen served as an elevator operator at Saks Fifth Avenue, *way*, way back! And my grandfather says, 'She didn't have a French accent . . . she's just Ellen.' But this is like Bayard and this English accent, and in some of my research people say, 'Oh, he lived in England for years.' But we know people who did this; actually it is something that we all do. We as Black people do it, but really all Americans do it, so most people perform themselves.

MB: In many cases, class plays a role in the performance of those kinds of identities. Yet, what is the difference in that and someone being gay functioning within a heterosexual environment and having to perform an identity based on at least the stereotypical notions of heterosexuality?

BF: Well, part of it is a survival strategy, you know. You walk into a room, and you don't want to have someone throwing beer bottles at your head.

MB: Before you go on, I have to ask, why Rustin? What is it about his story that captured you?

BF: I saw an interview with Bayard Rustin in a book called *Other Countries*. It was one of the first anthologies of writings by Black gay men. It was the last interview he did before he died. In that interview, he talked about his life and he talked about his work. The thing that interested me the most was a statement that he made. In this interview he says, 'I spent most of my life looking for interesting sex, rather than relationships.' And I was like, 'What?' He said this at sixty-five. By this time, he was finally able to make a commitment with someone – at sixty-five. He found Walter, the love of his life, and he talked about that. He talked about how much happier he was then compared to his earlier life, to finally be able to be in a relationship with someone, and the joy that Walter had brought to him. I just thought that was just an incredible statement from someone like him because people always think, 'Well, if you're not married by 40, forget it! It's over.' As far as I know, they both cared enormously about each other. He was much younger than Bayard; Walter was 27 at the time they met. I just thought that was such a profound statement. 'I spent my life looking for sex.' I said to myself, 'What is that? What does that mean?' You know, because as gay men we do that. That is a part of our experience – that's the easy part of gay male culture. Go and have sex, and I don't mean that in a negative way. I'm sure you hear people even say it's hard to find deep, meaningful relationships. They're not necessarily long relationships; short relationships can be meaningful. So I thought, let's find the journey. And so that's how I came up with the words to the title, 'Sex' and the word 'Civil,' because to me, those two words, put together, interrogate each other. This is not really about just the meaning of sex, but how sex relationships and politics all fit together. And in his life, they just do. In every single interview, people ask me if I know how sexual Bayard was. This question is asked before questions about his involvement in the Civil Rights Movement, the pacifist movement or anything else – they go there first.

MB: It seems that his work in the Civil Rights Movement as an openly gay man was also a pretty salient aspect of his life worth examining as well.

BF: Absolutely. Bayard was very interesting in this respect which makes working on a show like this, uncovering all of these connections, fun. Most of all, this kind of work allows you to really show the joyousness of this individual. It is not that he was this noble hero who suffered, but this is really a person who is a major part of the American landscape. The Civil Rights Movement is written very large on the American canvas. He was very much an architect of that as a strategist and theorist. It would have been a very different struggle without him. So it's just sort of acknowledging that. But during the time this was operating, it was clearly very, very difficult for him. And we also have to recognize the very ambivalent relationship between the Black leadership and Rustin; they needed him, but he was a gay man. I always think that as gay men, we're like the lieutenants of the world. We know how to get things done. You know it's going to happen. OK? And sometimes a little too much. Whooo!

MB: That is interesting because Lorraine Hansberry, who was an 'in-the-closet' lesbian, for a while at least, was reluctant to come out because she feared exclusion from the Civil Rights Movement. Would you contend that part of our responsibility, as Black gay cultural workers, is to write our African American gay ancestors into history, using a more accurate depiction of their lives? Should this be our praxis?

BF: How can you, in researching anyone's life, ignore these essential aspects of the personal? For instance, how can someone go through a retrospective of Picasso's work without acknowledging that he painted all his lovers! There are all these portraits of his wives and lovers in there. How can you say, 'Oh, that didn't matter?' Then who are they? Granted, it's not the only thing in someone's life, but it is certainly a major part. And whether they locate themselves within the queer community or not, that's just a choice that sometimes people make. But other times it's made for them. See, it's like, with invisible lives, you've got to understand who they are, what they're doing, and how they're able to succeed. Yet, it's the fear that they will be perceived in a negative way if we tell that. Black America and these questions of sex and sexuality are a unique thing that we struggle with. I think it's because we have this legacy of slavery, of White supremacy, where Black sexuality was so much a product of sexual commodification. Black women were really regarded as hyper-sexed; they were supposed to have hotter pussy – compared to, in the most extreme terms, the kind of icy White women, Scandinavian type. With Black men, of course, it's sort of a 'Mandingo' or the hypersexual . . .

MB: ... huge penises ...

BF: ... the huge penis, hyper-stud, always ready. And we have this cultural memory of all that, of that burden, so it's difficult to discuss sexuality of any kind whether it be gay, lesbian, bisexual, whatever, on really anything but superficial levels. Under White supremacy in the South, Black men could get lynched for looking at White women, so there is still a White burden that is unfortunately still with us. A lot of times, I think it prevents us from really moving in this realm, possessing the kind of sensitivity needed. It shadows so many other issues.

MB: Sticking with this same terrain of writing ourselves into history, I want to explore Stonewall as a defining historical moment of the gay movement ...

BF: ... contemporary gay/lesbian culture ...

MB: Yes. So, in what way then does Stonewall have meaning to you as a Black gay man?

BF: What does Stonewall mean to me? During that time period, riots were pretty common in those years, '68 and '69. I remember thinking that I'd been to gay bars in Boston because they were places where you could go and get in under age and have a beer or something like that. And they were fun. And when I saw and heard about this riot and that these police were raiding all of these gay bars I was angry. I remember the police would come in and everyone would pay the police off. I remember thinking, 'This is wrong. This is really wrong.' So when the riot happened I thought it was completely right.

MB: Do you feel that the Stonewall riots and the overall gay movement have been a collective effort? The reason why I asked that question is due to the fact that Whites, politically, have led much of the gay movement. Looking at this history, isn't this why Black gays are sometimes seen as being apolitical?

BF: It has and it hasn't. If you really look at the history of the gay movement, you see men and women of various ethnic backgrounds all the way through. We never leave. It has never only been White people. At times we don't get the credit. Baldwin was one of the most brilliant novelists of our time, especially with *Giovanni's Room*, but as a gay man, being out and speaking out all around the world, he never got the credit! Audre Lorde is one who had been there all along. We're not always invited to the table. So, a lot of times, the White communities in America have more money than Black ones, and if you break it down to the gays the disparities are even greater. So, I just never buy into that, it's just never been so – the White community did this and that and the other. A lot of people did this and that and the other! A lot of the White people always try to take credit for everything. Black gay people are not really at home in the gay community, or in the Black heterosexual community, but we keep our foot in both places. All of that's sort of the nature of a lot of people in this country.

MB: In terms of your work, how would you consider class issues within Black, gay society, or gay society as a whole? We tend to ignore large sectors of Black gays, meaning the everyday working-class, gay, Black man. Because many times, in terms of political involvement, Black gay women are more involved than Black gay men. So, how do you negotiate that to empower them, if that is indeed your intention?

BF: I don't try to empower anybody. I just do it because I like stories. I think people enjoy stories, and I think sometimes the work can be a way for people to kind of come together and, you know, see each other, have something to argue about, whether they like it or not. I'm really not trying to . . . I really shy away from that empowering thing, or trying to change anyone in any way. I just don't think shows do that. I think we make an argument for people and sometimes we even challenge them. But I like it when sometimes I provide a forum for community groups to do something. Like we'll buy the house out in different cities, and then there's a chance for people to come to see theater and that's nice, but nah! People can think about empowering themselves! Because, you know, you can't focus on that.

MB: But the way that you write and perform really confronts issues that the Black community many times have a hard time dealing with, or discussing openly. You don't see this as empowering? Here you have someone who grows up feeling isolated, feeling like they can't connect with anyone, and then you produce something that they can connect with. That seems to be an important function of art.

BF: As the artist I just can't take that on. And actually I couldn't encourage or teach students, especially students of color, to work in such a way. I encourage them not to carry the burden of race. It can be a very silencing thing, *to feel* that because I identify with a community, therefore, I need to not say these things which someone might use to hurt me, my family, all of us. This is too much of a responsibility for them to take on. When I do the workshops with people, I really try and encourage people to not think about this large community. I try to get them to view their community as being very small. Being one or two friends that they know and love and feel open with. People that they feel able to share with, even if they're not real people. Sometimes it's sort of good to imagine there is someone you can speak to that you can pour your heart out to. Sometimes it works; sometimes it doesn't. But in my own work, I resist laying out those burdens even though eventually it becomes a public spectacle.

MB: What is this small community that you are talking about made of? If not the larger oppressed and downtrodden communities, what set of conditions or what collective experiences motivate your work? Don't you write to and for Black gay communities?

BF: I try to not think of it that way. When I write, I usually will have specific people in my mind. For instance, I have a friend who has a way of laughing that I like, and when I'm working on something that I want to be funny, I think of what will crack him up. This is an example of how I really try to encourage people to recognize that the kind of work that requires you to take on such a burden as a community can just be *so*, so awful! A few years ago, I was in Chicago for this conference. It was a Chicago Area Black Lesbian/Gay Conference where I was judging a poetry slam. It was this Black lesbian poetry thing, and some of these women were getting up there and doing these poems that were like 'I am Mother Africa,' or 'Black Woman I am!' And the crowd was kind of like, 'Ummmm.' They're doing it because this is what's easy; this is what's familiar. Well, this drag queen gets up there and does this 'Harriet Tubman in Drag' thing. He sprays the audience with rose petals to finish, and totally steals the show. Both the men and women went crazy mainly because he had twisted all of that other stuff into a really fresh way of thinking. We always respond to that.

MB: That's a good example of a different way of thinking. I hear you saying this over and over again as an idea to live by or an objective. Yet, how does your experience as a gay Black man change? I know that's a huge question.

BF: Honestly, I don't think of it that way. I'm just me! It's Brian.

MB: So do you think that your acknowledgment of who you are, proudly proclaiming your gay identity, is an act of resistance in such a racist and homophobic society?

BF: I resist that because that's the handle that people like. People always love to say, 'Well, you know, he's in this little box over here.' I think if we're doing that work, then, OK! Let's just do it, and then all this other stuff we'll have for ourselves. I want to do this here, *and* I want to play with all of that other stuff over there! So, yeah, I'm a Black, gay man. I'm a middle-aged man. I'm from a middle-class family. I'm an artist, and I'm very educated. But I like lots and lots of other people and lots and lots of other things. I like to play in a lot of different ponds. But that's the handle I often get just because there aren't a whole lot of other people out there (there are probably more now). This is great. However, there seems to be this thing that people always attach to you. So, no, I don't like being the Black gay spokesman. I can't take that on. I really try and resist that.

MB: Right. Right.

BF: I just want to continue to do work that interests me. Sometimes I do the Black gay stuff and sometimes not.

MB: OK, but I think I'm also asking about your understanding of equality and how you connect it to your art. We can assume that your understanding of the importance of equality is, at least in part, a result of your personal experiences with inequality. Surely, these experiences constitute a certain kind of knowledge for you; therefore, you have a vested interest in fighting for equality no matter what face or form it comes. These issues are not so big that they don't impact these small or more local communities of which you speak. Clearly you have been confronted with racism and homophobia because of the way you deal with these issues in your work. This reflects a kind of consciousness that many of us do not have. Wouldn't you say that your experiences give you a view of the world that is quite different from a lot of people?

BF: Well, yeah. But it's not unique. I guess it's something I really don't know how to answer. I'm not a champion for all causes. I really don't like being put in the role of being the PC police or any of that. That role is just very uninteresting to me. I'm just an artist. By the end of the day, I'm an artist. I have a boyfriend, and he has a dog. Sometimes we just go out to dinner, and sometimes we just go to see bad movies and things. So, I don't really have this continuing political existence. I work as an artist and a teacher. I'm also an arts administrator. And that's really what I do.

MB: But you're being real modest!

BF: No, I'm not!

MB: In *Fierce Love*, for example, you clearly have a political project in mind.

BF: But that was a long time ago. It's interesting, but that was a long time ago.

MB: So you are saying that there are different stages?

BF: Yeah! That's what I'm saying. By doing that it's very easy for people to try and say, 'This is what he does.' But that's not true. I do a whole lot of other stuff! *Fierce Love* is a show I wrote seven years ago, but other things interest me now. Granted, some of that will intersect with the other stuff, but some of it won't.

MB: Well, since we've started talking about *Fierce Love*, I want to ask you about your time with Pomo Afro Homos. What was the experience like working in the group for such a long period of time? And also, what's the difference in going back to doing your work by yourself?

BF: You know, Pomo Afro Homos was really this rocket ride I *never* expected to take in my life. It was something that was really done just for fun; I thought we'd do it for a couple of weeks in San Francisco and that would be the end of it. Surprisingly, it became this four-year journey with us flying all over the U.S. to places like Alaska, Florida, San Diego, Boston, Canada, and almost every major city in between. We went to Texas, Iowa, on and on. And I never even counted how many cities we went to. We also went to England four times. It was great to do it. It was really fun for the first couple of years, and then the second couple of years, it was really a struggle. It became painful. I don't think we knew what was going on because things happened so fast.

MB: What do you mean by that?

BF: Well, I specifically remember one Saturday night we played at La Peña in Berkeley, which is about a 125-seat community space. This was a fundraiser for a lesbian magazine. The tickets were very cheap, and ultimately no one was turned away for lack of funds. Then, the following Thursday, we were playing at Avery Fischer Hall at the Lincoln Center. And the tickets were like 25 dollars apiece. All of a sudden, we were in the *New York Times* and it's a 1000-seat house, completely sold out. That's not an easy leap to make! It is especially difficult physically, spiritually and emotionally. It was hard. Whereas we found a lot of common ground in the first couple of years, the lack of that emerged in the second half because in a way people started believing their reviews, which is always a dangerous thing for performers. My sense is that some of us got excited about being famous just for the sake of being famous, whereas in the first two years it had been about the work. Therefore, when we started having to go digging for truths and the hard stuff, and it was no longer about the work, that was really the time for the partnership to end.

MB: Do those challenges still affect your work now because of that transition?

BF: Yeah, sure, it's nice to have a base as an artist. It's always nice to have people that you can collaborate with freely. Nonetheless, the honest truth is it stopped working with that particular collaboration so it was time to find another way.

MB: When the collaboration was at its high point, an important institution in the African American theater community rejected you all. I read an article that stated Pomo Afro Homos was 'banned' from the National Black Theater Festival. How did you all deal with that? What was all that about?

BF: I'm writing this show about the basic struggle for human dignity, what this integration thing was all about. And, in dealing with the National Black Theatre Festival, I thought, well, 'I've been there.' The first year they had it, I worked on another show, another gay show for that matter. This was some play that I had been directing, and the show did great! And I'd met the people who run it, and I thought, well, I said, 'I'd like to bring something here next time.' Two years later, I had a friend who was working on the show, and I just thought, why not? The show had just started in San Francisco and gotten great reviews and I had a tape. So, I was thinking, theater festivals are about the exchange of ideas. You get an opportunity to see all sorts of different things you don't usually see at home. I can't really say that I thought of the show as being shocking – it was doing really well. So, I sent it, and I didn't hear from him, and I said, 'That's funny.' Then I called, 'Hello? Did you get the tape?' I asked. 'Well, we gave it to so and so to look at and he's going to report back,' he said. I said, 'Is it something you're interested in?' 'That tape wasn't good; can you send us another tape?' So I said, 'Fine.' I sent another tape. I call again, and suddenly my phone calls are not being returned. There's a silence, a *wall* of silence! Something has happened. What? I call, and call, and call – they are never returned; I sent letters; no response. What's up? Why? Friends of mine are telling me that it's nothing: 'You have a hit show, three people, it can't be the money!' What is the deal? So, after that, this reporter called them, and he got some really very hostile remarks from them. The reporter calls me back and says, 'It looks like you've been banned from this festival because of the content.' So that totally sets off this whole ordeal. Then other reporters who saw the story kept calling and, so, we didn't get in. The next time, it happened two years later, the company was still going and we sent in the tapes *way* ahead of time and I finally managed to catch up with someone. I called up the guy who ran it [Larry Leon Hamlin, Artistic Director]. I just kept dialing the number, and it was early in the morning. I figured he might actually pick up his own phone. Finally, it worked! He picked up his own phone.

MB: This must have been before caller ID was in!

BF: Yes, before caller ID was in! He picked up his own phone. His name was Larry. I said, 'Hello Larry, I don't want to accept this. I know you have the tape. I know you have the reviews. The company's been to England twice.'

MB: And all you wanted was to perform in Winston-Salem, North Carolina, at the National Black Theater Festival. After you all had tried for more than two years.

BF: OK, Winston-Salem, North Carolina. That is all. I said 'Larry, we're going to New York right before your festival, so there's probably going to be some articles about it.' We're already booked at the Lincoln Center. How are you going to justify this? You can't just go silent.' I said, 'Don't do this. We'll work it out; we're not interested in anything else; we just want to come to the festival.' He said he'd think about it. He never got back to me, and it was the same drama all over again. So this time we just handed it to the reporters. When the *Times* did it, they did the interview with me. I think that they called the Festival and they tried to say, 'They didn't send their tape.' That ordeal was so sad. Finally we actually did make it to North Carolina. We got invited to Duke University to do the show. This was in '94. There were other artists who did go to the Festival that year, like Robbie McCauley, Laurie Carlos, and others. Of course, by then, because something like that happened, they already knew about us, and so it became the thing people were discussing. It became what the Festival was about that year. People wanted to know why weren't we there? So anyway, we went to Duke and performed. Interestingly, a woman from the North Carolina Arts Council went to them and said basically, 'You're disgracing the state. You're making us look bad. You're making Black people in the state look stupid and homophobic. You need to go to that show and you need to clean it up.' So he came to the show, and he was nice. Now, I think, since then, they've been a bit more open to some other gay performances there. It hurt. It hurt to be excluded. Because it just came down to simple prejudice. That's what it was – in theater! This is theater! At a theater festival! Come on, who's running around at this theater festival?

MB: That is really tragic. Yet, this struggle apparently made an impact on the material that the festival now accepts. For example, in 1997 Cheryl West's *Before It Hits Home,* a play about homosexuality and AIDS, played there on the mainstage. That is pretty ironic in light of your experience.

BF: Yeah. I mean, wow! It's incredible!

MB: Now that you have all of these accomplishments to your credit, and now that you are pioneering a new kind of performance tradition, what is next on your artistic agenda?

BF: What's next? Well, there was a horrific scientific study done in the thirties of lesbian and gay people that tries to make a connection between people's physical traits and levels of queerness, if you will. It has all these charts and diagrams, where, for example, they compare a lesbian pelvis versus a straight or a 'normal' pelvis. They compare a sexually deviant penis versus a normal penis. I am not joking! It goes on to do finger length, skull size, etc. Of course it is a very flawed scientific study. What is interesting about this study is once you kind of look past the flawed scientific part, people tell wonderful stories in these interviews of people's struggles to find love during those very repressive times. There are all these horror stories of the people's families, discussing what they go through, and so on. So I want to take three stories and make a piece out of it. So it's going to be like a period piece.

MB: You always find these very interesting characters in your stories. From where do you get your ideas? Does it just come?

BF: I guess I go to a lot of stuff. I look in libraries, and I poke around. Some people send me stuff because they know I like weird stuff. I get all of this mail. For instance, someone sent me this book called *The Darker Brother* that was like a weird pulp novel about race and stuff. That got me kind of interested in pulp novels, so I visited a store that sold old porn and asked them where were their pulp novels. While looking through all of their old stuff, I ran across a book called *Black and Gay*. This story was set against a town in the South that was beginning to be integrated. A Black student integrates the school and is having sex with an all-American White jock student, so I just staged it verbatim. It was just hysterical! Yet it ends kind of tragically because the student ends up getting kicked out of school.

MB: Yeah, I read that! That's *Dark Fruit*. Here is an example of one of your interesting characters. Can you briefly talk about the scientist in that piece?

BF: First of all, I played both the White student and the White scientist. So, I got this White wig that looked like, you know, that hamburger chain, Big Boy. It had kind of a permanent greasy look to it. Then, I played it very straight suburban White like *Leave it to Beaver*. And then I showed his research. So I went back to the same store, and I asked for some male model slides; I wanted something like early porn slides. I wanted something that would look completely ridiculous. I got both Black and White slides. So, as he's going through the lecture, someone clicked on these slides and my friend Pam made up these phony charts, so it was so funny. Most of all, I loved the way people got so upset at that. People would get so mad at me! Usually it was like people who were in interracial relationships. I was really hard on the interracial relationship thing.

MB: It's satirical, though.

BF: It's really meant to trash the people who make up all these rationales that you are better able to deal with Black people who are in interracial relationships. They suggest that Blacks are better when they are on the White side, and it's just not true. You're in a relationship and then you have to deal with the world. So I just wanted to play with all of that. I also wanted to acknowledge that not everyone's in a White–White relationship or a Black–Black one. And sometimes people's first experience is with someone of the opposite sex too. People are in all kinds of relationships. The White gay press in San Francisco could not trash me enough for doing this show. The show was really popular so it kept running, and then they'd come back again and they'd trash it. 'Why is he doing that? He just needs to stop doing that!' They would say. I just thought it was great!

MB: At the beginning of *Dark Fruit* you interrogate these Black character tropes that appear in three very popular American plays. You set up this scenario with the Black characters in Kushner's *Angels in America,* and in Guare's *Six Degrees of Separation.* These are extremely problematic characters.

BF: Yes. So, I imagined this meeting between the three most well-known Black gay characters from American theater, Miss Raj, from *Colored Museum,* Belize from *Angels in America,* and then Paul from *Six Degrees of Separation.* They're having a tea party; it's right before they're all going to perform that night. They're just ripping the shows they're in to pieces. As a result, Kushner got really mad at me, so he calls up George C. Wolfe and George tells him to calm down. 'You're famous, it doesn't matter,' he tells him.

MB: It never ceases to amaze me when these playwrights create these roles that have problems, and when we critique them, they get angry at us for raising these issues.

BF: Clearly it is all in the fun of it, but for example, Belize is a problematic part. It is a good part, really all those parts are good, but they are all the same stuff. I mean, Belize is a drag queen and a nurse, what is that about? How come Belize is like the cleaning lady? But it's a great play. We have a lot of great plays with some really good Black characters, but at some point we need to critique those roles and then move on to something else that may better reflect our complex experience. That is what theater is all about.

ACKNOWLEDGMENT

I want to thank my colleague Xavier O'Neal Livermon for his timely assistance in the editing process on this project.

NOTES

1. This passage is taken from Hemphill's 'Living the Word/Looking for Home,' in Martin Duberman (ed.), *Queer Representations: Reading Lives, Reading Cultures* (New York: New York University Press, 1997), pp. 305–10.
2. The Negro Ensemble Company was started in 1967 in New York City. The company was established with Douglas Turner Ward as the artistic director at the

St. Mark's Playhouse in downtown New York City. The company was convened based on more inclusive premises than other Black theater companies in the 1960s. The Negro Ensemble Company's originally stated goals were to cultivate artistic excellence, generate a primarily Black audience without excluding Whites, and to broaden the scope of material produced at the theater. In addition, the theater combined with their regular theater season an extensive training program designed to develop Black talent. Various world-renowned artists such as Esther Rolle, Ossie Davis, Ruby Dee, Frances Foster, Denise Nicholas, Edward Burbridge, and a host of others trained at the Negro Ensemble Company. The Company was launched with a hefty grant from the Ford Foundation, funding its first three years. However, due to financial problems, the company closed in 1978. For more information on the company, see Ellen Foreman's 'The Negro Ensemble Company: a Transcendent Vision,' in Errol Hill (ed.), *The Theatre of Black Americans: A Collection of Critical Essays* (New York: Applause Theatre Book Publishers, 1987), pp. 270–82.

3. Plays with the San Francisco Mime Troupe: *Factwino Meets the Moral Majority* (1981) by Joan Holden with Brian Freeman, Tede Matthews and Henry Piccioto, music and lyrics by Bruce Barthol, directed by Sharon Lockwood. (A down and out 'wino' gains the superpower to shed light on Reaganomics and the rise of the Religious Right.) *Factwino Versus Armageddonman* (1982) by Joan Holden with the San Francisco Mime Troupe collective, music and lyrics by Bruce Barthol, directed by Brian Freeman. (A sequel exploring the nuclear arms race.) *Secrets in the Sand* (1983) by Joan Holden and Robert Alexander and the SF Mime Troupe collective, music and lyrics by Bruce Barthol, directed by Brian Freeman. (Based on the true story of a 1950s Hollywood epic filmed on a nuclear test site in the Nevada desert.) *1985* (1984) by Joan Holden and the San Francisco Mime Troupe collective, music and lyrics by Bruce Barthol, directed by Brian Freeman. (George Orwell's *1984* meets Charles Dickens's *A Christmas Carol* in a nightmare exploring the 1984 presidential election.) *Crossing Borders* (1985) by Michelle Linfante, Steve Most, Joan Holden, and Brian Freeman with the SF Mime Troupe collective, music and lyrics by Eduardo Robledo and Bruce Barthol, directed by Brian Freeman. Featuring Marga Gomez. (A San Francisco domestic comedy exploring immigration and alienation.)

4. Works with Cultural Odyssey: *The Rent Party* (1987) conceived by Rhodessa Jones and Idris Ackamoor, written by Rhodessa Jones with additional material by Idris Ackamoor and Brian Freeman, musical direction by Wayne Wallace and Idris Ackamoor, produced at the New Vaudeville Festival at San Francisco State University and Life on the Water Theater, San Francisco. (A late night 'rent party' set in the Fillmore jazz district of the 1940s.) *Tausundundeine Idee: A Performance Cabaret* (1988) by Rhodessa Jones and Idris Ackamoor, directed by Brian Freeman, produced at Intersection for the Arts, San Francisco. (Combining personal stories by Rhodessa Jones and Idris Ackamoor with songs.) *'I Think It's Gonna Work out Fine'* – *A Rock & Roll Fable* (1989) by Idris Ackamoor, Rhodessa Jones, Brian Freeman, and Ed Bullins, original songs by Rhodessa Jones and Idris Ackamoor,

directed by Brian Freeman, produced at the National Black Theater Festival, Winston-Salem, North Carolina, the Climate Theater, San Francisco, and La Mama Experimental Theater, New York. (A two-person musical about a performing couple on the rock and roll circuit in the 1960s, 1970s, and 1980s.) *Perfect Courage* (1990) written and performed by Idris Ackamoor, Bill T. Jones, and Rhodessa Jones with Brian Freeman, directed by Brian Freeman, produced at the Walker Arts Center, Minneapolis. (A performance piece built from the stories of the physical scars the performers bear.)

5. ACT UP is the AIDS Coalition to Unleash Power, a political street theater group largely responsible for the mobilization around the AIDS epidemic.

REFERENCES

Clum, John M. (ed.), 'Pomo Afro Homos' *Dark Fruit*: Editor's Introduction,' in *Staging Gay Lives: An Anthology of Contemporary Gay Theater* (Boulder, CO: Westview Press, 1996), pp. 319–21.

Elam, Harry J., 'Colored Contradictions in this Postmodern Moment: an Introduction,' in Harry Elam and Robert Alexander (eds), *Colored Contradictions: An Anthology of Contemporary African-American Plays* (New York: Penguin, 1996), pp. 1–16.

Frechette, David, 'Why I'm Not Marching,' in Charles Michael Smith (ed.), *Fighting Words: Personal Essays by Black Gay Men* (New York: Avon Books, 1999), pp. 131–3.

Hutchinson, Darren Lenard, ' "Claiming" and "Speaking" ' Who We Are: Black Gays and Lesbians, Racial Politics, and the Million Man March,' in Devon W. Carbado (ed.), *Black Men on Race, Gender, and Sexuality: A Critical Reader* (New York: New York University Press, 1999), pp. 28–45.

Jackson, Earl, 'The Responsibility of and to Differences: Theorizing Race and Ethnicity in Lesbian and Gay Studies,' in Becky W. Thompson and Sangeeta Tyagi (eds), *Beyond a Dream Deferred: Multicultural Education and the Politics of Excellence* (Minneapolis: University of Minnesota Press, 1993), pp. 131–61.

Mercer, Kobena, 'Skin Head Sex Thing: Racial Difference and the Homoerotic Imaginary,' in Bad-Object Choices (ed.), *How Do I Look? Queer Film and Video* (Seattle: Bay Press, 1991).

Román, David, 'Pomo Afro Homos' *Fierce Love*: Intervening in the Cultural Politics of Race, Sexuality, and AIDS,' in *Acts of Intervention: Performance, Gay Culture, and AIDS* (Bloomington: Indiana University Press, 1998), pp. 154–76.

Nobuko Miyamoto
Photo by Ed Ikuta

12

Something larger than ourselves: interview with Nobuko Miyamoto

Lucy Mae San Pablo Burns

Nobuko Miyamoto and her family were forced to leave their lives behind, like most Japanese Americans living in the United States during World War II, as a result of Executive order 9066 in 1942. Thousands of Japanese Americans and Japanese living in the U.S. were ordered to leave their homes and were interned in designated areas of surveillance in the Western U.S. She and her parents were evacuated to the Santa Anita Assembly Center and later forced to relocate to a work farm in Montana and later to Ogden, Utah. In these early years of instability, moving from one work camp to another, Miyamoto's parents instilled her passion for music and dance. This passion for the arts has since been burning and a gift that Nobuko Miyamoto has shared with others.

In 1958, young dancer Nobuko Miyamoto had made it to Broadway and film musicals, playing a Puerto Rican in the film version of *West Side Story*. Even before she had reached her twenties, with *The King and I*, *Flower Drum Song*, and *Kismet* in her list of credits, Nobuko already had a successful performing career as a dancer. Ten years later, she was singing in political protests (fighting for better work conditions for people of color, resisting the presence of the United States in Vietnam, calling for the end of oppression of brown and black people in the world), writing songs in Spanish and recording music 'for the struggle of Asians in America' (liner notes for *A Grain of Sand*).

Twenty years later, in 1978, Nobuko established Great Leap, Inc., one of the oldest Asian American arts organizations in the country. In 1999, Nobuko released *To All Relations*, a collection of songs that 'reflect the twists and turns of Nobuko's artistic journey' (liner notes). In her journey as an artist, under the shadow of the internment of Japanese Americans, from the working camps to Broadway to Chinatown, we read in this interview the continuous movement of an artist who has dedicated her work towards presenting a view in which our many cultural backgrounds and perspectives cross and transgress boundaries, arriving at something new.

Nobuko maintains the best of what she learned as an active participant in the political movements of the post-Civil Rights era of the late 1960s and early 1970s. It was during these powerful years that Nobuko came into her political consciousness. Shortly after her exposure to the Black Panther Party and the Asian Americans for Action in New York, she found a connection between her art and her then new-found understanding of social justice. In 1971, she, Chris Iijima, and 'Charlie' Chin recorded an album entitled *A Grain of Sand: Music for the Struggle of Asians in America*, now included in the Smithsonian Collection. She continues her practice as a cultural worker/cultural activist, and along the way encourages others. Nobuko has kept her artistic practice true to individual and personal voice, even when cultural workers fought for the validity of personal and individual voices within 'revolutionary work.'

The Asian America she presents to us in this conversation is one that is grounded within a multiracial and global perspective. This seems to be the Asian America that she and her co-activists understood 'back in the day,' and she remains true to this construction. Her commitment to multiracial and global politics is reflected in the works supported by Great Leap, Inc. and Bindu Records.[1] She has mentored Asian American artists, including the members of the first Vietnamese American theater troupe in the United States, Los Angeles-based Club O'Noodles. Nobuko's work also extends beyond race-based constructions of community. While Great Leap, Inc. began as an Asian American theater organization, it has shifted its focus, using 'personal stories' as a way to bridge the gaps among different groups. This was a direct response to the reality concretized by the 1994 Los Angeles riots/uprising.[2]

While some of the work she has created with Asian American communities celebrated the community's triumph over exclusion and injustice, her one-woman show, *A Grain of Sand*, challenges exclusivity and biases within Asian America, questioning the community's responsibility in the continued troubled relations between and amongst the races. In one of the scenes from *A Grain of Sand*, Nobuko reminds us of the unfulfilled promises and potential of the social and political movements of the 1970s, set against images of the burning streets of Los Angeles during the 1994 uprising/riots.

Nobuko speaks of spirituality in her artistic work that is grounded in the community, on the triumphs of humanity. What she asks of her artists is so deeply personal, though the stories are universal. She does not deny the challenge of sustaining community-based/community-centered arts and/or for social justice. She does not romanticize this work, after over four decades of practice. Through her work, Ms. Miyamoto inspires both emerging and established artists towards working with a sense of community, demonstrating the potential of theater to make us realize our own divinity. In this conversation, Ms. Miyamoto links her understanding of politics, her artistic practice, and her spiritual belief. Each of these informs the other, defining spirituality as the search for something larger than ourselves.

LUCY BURNS: Tell a little history from a few years ago, how you came into the world of theater.

NOBUKO MIYAMOTO: A few hundred years ago! I guess my first exposure to theater was actually music. It was during the war. We were relocated from Los Angeles and had to be moved inland [Santa Anita Assembly Center]. First we were at a work camp in Montana and then we moved to another work camp in Ogden, Utah. In Ogden, my father heard that there was going to be a concert in Salt Lake City, so he took me. My father was a lover of classical music. I was a little child, maybe I was four years old. And that was the first time I'd ever heard an orchestra, and the sound just encompassed me. My mother exposed me to dance, tap. My father, in his real desires, would have loved to be a musician and my mother would have loved to be a visual artist. I think, in their frustration, or their love of this, they wanted to expose me, at first. When I got interested and got serious about it, they really supported me.

LB: What was your experience as an Asian American in a performance world that barely represented Asian America, with little, if any, complexity?

NB: I had a taste, from almost every job that I did beginning with *The King and I*, at 16, and then *Flower Drum Song*, of what an Asian American cultural person working in the theater and music and dance would get exposed to. It really felt as if our representation was a tool of another person's idea of what an Asian is. Some of it was quite clever. In *King and I*, the choreography and theatricality was quite interesting. In working in a musical film called *Les Girls*, I worked for Jack Cole, who was a choreographer who borrowed from the African forms and East Indian dance and Balinese, etc. He was actually very studied in those forms, too. I learned other kinds of styles of dance, the African and East Indian, etc., from watching him. I also saw how Eastern forms and artistic practices of people of color affected the art of America. I recognized people like Martha Graham, Jack Cole, Jerome Robbins were very heavily influenced by the East, Eastern theater, Kabuki, Noh, Chinese opera. But we got it second-hand. Even the stories, we looked at it really from a Westerner's eyes in many ways. You didn't realize what *The King and I* was really saying about Thai culture – that this king was brutal and this white woman tamed and changed him, made him civilized. It was a sort of a confusing thing, growing up in this.

At the same time that I trained very hard as a dancer, and I would audition for TV shows that other dancers would go for. They would come up to me afterwards and say, 'You're a very good dancer, but we can't use you because you'd stick out.' I would go to these auditions and hear this. Anger was building up because I had been trained and trained and trained and trained in the best training, and yet I couldn't get any jobs outside of these Asian shows. The only non-Asian character I performed was *West Side Story*, and it was because Jerome Robbins had worked with me as a young girl. Several years later after those early years, actually when we were doing *King and I*, he was working on *West Side Story*.

After that though, I didn't get anything that really interested me. The movie *Flower Drum Song* came around and I said, 'Well, I did the Broadway show. I don't want to do this again.' I just felt like I was looking for something, but I didn't know really what it was.

LB: You were in all these musicals. Did you pursue a separate career as a singer?

NB: I sang in *West Side Story*, but I also realized I was fearful about singing by myself. I decided I needed to take singing lessons. Dancers usually hate to use their voice; I'd be in my lesson and if somebody from the next class would come in, I would stop singing. I just couldn't sing in front of anyone; that's how shy I was. I knew I wanted to get over this fear that I had of my voice. It's a continual thing, though! *(Laughs)* So I started singing pop songs. I figured I could choose the songs that I wanted to sing. Always it was a matter of wanting to overcome and say, 'I can, I'm just a person. I can sing any kind of song that I wanted to sing.' Here I was 21 years old, 22, 23, and at that time, Asians were about breaking the stereotypical barriers. Just breaking out from this vice that we were in, this very narrow image that we were living under. To say that we were just like any other Americans.

I got the experience of singing in a night club in Seattle. Pat Suzuki was one of the first, I would say, Asian American-born jazz singers in this country. She was really very good. She was the star of *Flower Drum Song* on Broadway. Her manager said, 'Well, if you want to learn how to sing, come to Seattle and you can sing at this club that I used to own.' I got the opportunity to sing every night, two shows a week, two shows a night, on the weekdays and three shows on the weekends. I also got the opportunity to sing with a band. This experience liberated me from the world of dance, and the world of theater, which was really controlled in its writing by the Western voice.

LB: This is during the American–Vietnam War, right?

NB: Yes. At the same time, the Vietnam War was happening, and I was afraid that my brother would be inducted. I also saw students at the University of Washington protesting against the war. At that point I thought 'What am I doing in a nightclub, singing?' I wondered if there was something else I'm supposed to do. From the time I was seven to 27, all I knew was this world of theater and dance and music. That was it! I started seeing that there was a whole world outside of that. I left Seattle. Back at home, in Los Angeles, I met this Italian film-maker who was making a movie about Black people in America, a documentary involving the Black Panthers.[3] I started moving around with him, helping him to make this independent movie. That's how I got exposed to the movement, the Black movement, basically. It was 1968, 1969. It was the middle of the whirlwind. People, Black Panthers and different people were meeting on the campuses; people were dying, getting arrested and jailed, and all of this great turmoil happening. People's Park was happening in Berkeley;[4] we were there. Everywhere there was something going on in the country, we would fly there. It was an incredible exposure. That was really my entrance into politics.

When we moved and worked out of New York City, he eventually went back to Italy. I stayed in New York. I actually went to the Young Lord's Church, when they had taken over the church in East Harlem. I was there when they were occupying it and this Asian woman, Yuri Kochiyama, at that time Mary Kochiyama, came up to me and started to say, 'Oh, who are you? What are you doing here? Do you know about the Asian groups here?' I said, 'No, I don't know anything about it.' She made me come to this meeting of Asian Americans for Action. I started attending the meetings and that was where I met Chris Iijima and his mother. That was an interesting thing, seeing Japanese Americans talking politics, with their focus around the Vietnam War and Asia. I had just walked out the Black Panther gathering, and *(laughs)* . . . I was trying to understand what was going on there! At that time I had no thought about music or theater. My goal became 'Get involved in the community; let's make revolution.'

LB: Before all this, your artistic work was really quite separate from political consciousness towards social justice. So when did the cultural meet the political?

NB: Really by chance. Chris and I and other Asians from the East Coast met at a gathering of the Japanese American Citizens' League [JACL] in Chicago. We got together with Asians from the West Coast. We were just hanging out, much like a conference. There were many different activities. We were going to protest against the war to the older people in the JACL, and one night Chris got out his guitar and just started singing. We just sat there and created a song together. It blew people's minds so much that we decided, 'Oh, we'll sing it for the protest, for the education thing for the grown-ups.' When we saw the power of the song, we realized we needed to keep doing it. It just happened; it happened by magic.

We decided that we wanted to go to the West Coast and see what was going on on the West Coast. We did a benefit for an organization called The Yellow Seas in Stockton, California. And then, we went to Los Angeles and San Francisco, where we really saw the power of music, of cultural work. All we had done in New York was write five songs and learned a couple of other songs together. Then we started moving, and from then on, we wrote. It was really driven by the momentum of the movement. We became just sort of the voice of the movement at that time. Not too many people were doing what we were doing.

LB: How long did you work together and what happened after the group stopped making music together?

NB: We worked together for about three or four years, until 1973. The last thing we did was this album called *A Grain of Sand*. We wanted to document the work and so that became the last work that we did together.

And then I moved to the West Coast to be in an Asian community, and to continue doing work. I believe that if you don't have roots, there's nothing to work from; there's nothing to gather from. I lived there and I did concerts. I started working with another musician, Benny Yee. We had a band together. Some people in the community asked me if I would teach dance. This forced me to think about dance again, which I had left and totally ignored. The Senshin Buddhist Temple, which is pretty much in the central part of Los Angeles near USC, offered their space. One of the earliest U.S. Taiko groups started there, and classes were being offered. The Temple became a kind of cultural center. And East West Players was also going on.

LB: Those were the early years of East West Players. Did you find similarities in your goals, in using cultural expressions as a way to build and strengthen community?

NB: Their situation was a little different. Here were actors who wanted to gain skill so that they could find a place in the movie industry. My concern was how do you make a voice for the community? How do you create cultural workers? Do you create them by training them from scratch? Or by finding people who are political, and training them? Or do you create them by politicizing people who are in the theater? And the people who are into dance? And the people who are into music? Trying to get them to be more political. That was sort of my question at that moment. I tried to bring in people who were dancers, into the community. We held concerts and we got them to do workshops, etc. We worked with different subject-matters that were relevant to the community. At the same time, I enjoyed working with community people. I enjoyed training them and getting them into it, creating the context for expressing themselves. At that time, it was mainly through dance. And then, when the band came into it, Mako, the artistic director of East West Players, then said, 'Why don't you write a musical?' So we did. We wrote a musical called *Chop Suey*. It was a story about a young kid growing up in Chinatown who wanted to leave and see the outside world. Her parents are very traditional, you know, an archetypal story of Asian Americans. It was done in a fun way. We integrated people, actors, or people from the community as well as sort of aspiring theater people from the East West Players. We did it at ten different parks and other places. We did two or three different versions of it, and then we even toured it to the Northwest. We performed it along the California coast and then Oregon.

LB: When did Great Leap, Inc. come into creation?

NB: In 1978. After three years of working sort of in this ad hoc way, we established Great Leap and got our first funding from the NEA. And then it became a little bit more. I never wanted to really become stable; I didn't want to have a center. I just wanted to concentrate on creating work. So, unlike East West Players or the Japanese American Community Cultural Center [JACCC], I just wanted to see how I could continue to create and get other people with me to create. First we created collectively. Benny [Yee] would write the music; I would write the words. Sometimes we would maybe get somebody to help us with the story and choreography. There were times when I directed and I choreographed. It just was a fluid kind of thing. I did that until about 1983, I think, or around the early 1980s.

    At that time, I broke away from Benny to write my own music. It was the first time I wrote my own music for all my songs. Before that, I was always depending on his musical voice. I realized I could write music too. That was a real liberating thing. I then made an album, *The Best of Both Worlds*. I made a musical by myself called *Talk Story*.

And then I started seeing there were people doing solo performance work. I had gotten tired of working and trying to corral different people into doing one thing. I got more interested in seeing all these people doing their own thing. I thought 'Why not gather them together and let's try to create a space for them to do what they do, create a context for it.' That's what Great Leap, Inc. is doing today.

LB: How does your interdisciplinary practice, the relationship between dance and the voice, the music and the dancer, the speaking dancer who acts, come into your own methodology as a teacher?

NB: Everything is in transition for me. Especially now. I don't think I could teach anybody really how to sing. What I do is I try to get people to find their voice through movement, because I think that movement through breath, first, you find movement in your body. Your body is the storage place of memory. Through the body, through the memory, the stories come out. Through the need to communicate the story. You need your voice and sometimes some people are more oriented towards music; sometimes they're more oriented towards movement; sometimes they're a better writer. My interest right now is utilizing whatever people's strengths are and trying to add to those strengths. I'm interested in getting them to explore using different elements that they might not have thought of, that they could actually utilize. I like working with people who aren't necessarily trained to find this voice. To get them started, it's like getting your engine going. And then they're going to make their own explorations after that and build on that strength.

LB: I know that you've worked with Club O'Noodles, a Vietnamese American Theater troupe based in Los Angeles. How did that relationship with emerging artists come about?

NB: The work with Club O'Noodles was the deepest and longest commitment in terms of developing artists and new work. We worked for a whole year, every week. That was a political commitment for me. I didn't get paid for it; I did it because I was involved in the Vietnam War and protesting against the war. I felt that that was part of my awakening as a political person. When I met Hung Nguyen and some of the Club O'Noodles people, I said, 'Well, these are the kids we were talking about.' I felt that I wanted to bring out that part of the story. It was walking a tightrope in many ways. Because you're talking about Southern Vietnamese people and here we were protesting against the war. They considered people like us as, you know, not being for their side. When they came to see my show and saw that I protested against the Vietnam War, they went home and they had this huge argument for hours! Some people felt that Ho Chi Minh was Hitler, and would not move from that position; other people said, 'Well, he was a nationalist.' It sparked a political dialogue within their group. Some of the positions still hold, what we consider reactionary positions.

What I tried to do in this story was to bring out their human condition, of living in a war, and then their transition in becoming American. Once they've come over that hill, we explored what we saw as Asian Americans – people not knowing how to pronounce your name, people looking at you. With *Laughter from the Children of War*, we looked at entrance into American life and being on this side of the fence! It was a way for me to bridge them into seeing how we saw. At the same time, I needed to see how they saw, from where they were when their parents were taken away from them. What they saw when their furniture was taken away from their house and there was only the picture of Ho Chi Minh. When they didn't have food. Why they felt the way they did as children. I wanted to see what that was. It helped me to see how to use bodies, stories, and movement, not put a lot of pressure on any one person to carry a story and yet, through these moments, to create a story. These circles of stories would create one story. It's not a linear story; but somehow, together, it does make the story. It started them on a process. Some of them are at work with other people and are now going in one direction. Some of them are off and doing other things, trying to find their own voices and get other training. It has been interesting to watch.

LB: You started with just the arts and then found a way to marry arts and politics, which was a product of a certain kind of urgency given the time in history. Now here we are, 30 years later, the same urgency isn't as tangible. The intensity isn't as palpable. Where do you find the source for continuing the work, the relationship between art and politics, now that we are led to believe that everything is really OK.

NB: That's a very interesting question. I think it's a very relevant question right now. I think that there were people doing work that have become discouraged. One, because the movement is not there to really support the work; and two, just the whole environment is, the economics, you have to make money, much more money, now. When we were trying to do it in the 1970s, you could live very cheaply. Now the reality is you cannot create work in the same way; you can't live, just survive. You either have to teach or you have to find some way to make a living outside of that, unless you have an organization. Then, building an organization is a whole other task. Even though you don't want to become an establishment, which I didn't want to, there is still a certain amount of demand to have an organization, an organism that will support this kind of work. It takes a lot of time and patience, because you can't always do what you want to do, follow your immediate instinct the way that we did before. You have to plan a year ahead of time, or two years ahead of time to do something bigger. Although some of this quick and dirty work can continue on. I get frustrated myself.

LB: How is your individual creative desire reflected in your organizing, producing, teaching?

NB: Sometimes also I'm interested in developing my own art, in terms of pushing my own self, I mean, that's why I did *A Grain of Sand*, my solo piece. At that time I wanted a chance to explore my own artistic boundaries and expand those boundaries, test myself and keep pushing myself. I still want to write music, but I'm looking at the source of two different things. One, I still have a community relationship with the Temple. That has also sort of given me another layer, on top of the community and political, and that is spiritual. The pieces I create with the Temple extend the Buddhist tradition and bring it into the present moment. Which is where it should be anyway. I also learn a lot and I feel like I belong to a community. I belong to a place where I can do work not judged in the larger world. They accept my work; they're glad that I'm there, and I'm glad, because I get a lot from them.

I'm interested in my spiritual growth. It is an important part of my work. I'm also seeing how the spiritual, the political, and the social part of it is all and should be one thing. I think that, in looking back, in the most basic sense, the movement was a spiritual movement as well. It was a movement that wanted to connect us with something larger than ourselves. That in itself is a spiritual thrust, to do that. But without understanding that whole thing, one's ego, the personal problems, interfere with that, keep it from truly happening. In doing spiritual work, you have to deal with those things on a personal level. If you really truly change your personal self, then those things around you will change. If everybody did that individual work. Not, say, 'I'm going to change the world and I don't care how I'm going to change it. I'm going to kill. I'm going to maim . . .' You know what I mean? Because then we have the same thing replacing the system that we wanted to destroy. We have to change the human being as we're going along. That's how I'm going. It's not easy to try to create. It's a bit schizophrenic. On one hand you want to stay true to these really basic beliefs and develop these things. At the same time, you have to go out there, you have to deal with the corporate. You have to deal with foundations. You have to deal with these things with a distance, just to get what you need. But then to bring it back into this realm where you can do work that is true to your heart. I think that's the delicate balancing game that we play and trying to stay alive and, you know, it's not so hard to do if you, if you don't mind not having money! *(Laughs)*.

LB: It's very different from when you, Chris, and Charlie were just 'hanging out.'

NB: Yeah, and it went a long way! It's so much more responsibility. It's so much easier for me to go out and just perform. Now we're doing reunion concerts, Chris, Charlie, and I. We just go out and we just play and it's very easy! That's easy! I said, 'This is easy!' But each of us have other responsibilities. Chris is now teaching law! Charlie is basically making a living through his performance and his writing.[5] Still, somewhere along the line the marketplace has to be engaged. It's a complicated process.

LB: One last question. You talked about culturally, as an adult, identifying with or being much closer to African American culture. How or where does Asia or Asian culture, whatever that may be for you, appear in your work, your creative process?

NB: You know, I ask myself that in a way. I do martial arts, Tai Ch'i and Xing Yi. I feel, although I was trained as a dancer, my later years, in doing martial arts and yoga, I'm re-learning another way of moving through my body language in learning these forms. That's one language that I've acquired more of an Asian, I think, outlook, centering and lowering the center. I think capturing the essence of what it is and not just the form is important to me. Same thing with Buddhism; I'm not orthodox anything. I have to look at it and try to find out the seed of what it is for myself. Going to India was a big turning point for me, because I'd never been in an Asian country before. I had a chance to go there to, with a singing teacher, to learn some music. I'd never been exposed to Indian music before, but I liked Indian music! I also saw that Indian classical music was used for spiritual purposes. That exposed me to the spiritual element of music.

There are parts of me, just because of my family upbringing, that I am. There are times when I'm with other Asians and I don't feel very Asian, but when I'm with other people I feel Asian. It just sort of stands out more. There are parts of me, the way I act or the way I am, that I think I learned from my parents, and the way we were taught and the food I eat.

My husband being Black and my child being half, I also embrace and I feel very comfortable in the Black community. Musically I feel comfortable in it; food-wise, except I don't eat pork. In a family situation, being culturally with a Black family is very different from being culturally with a Japanese family or an Asian family. In many ways I'm much more involved in the Black part of the family because they're just much more open and active and more engaged with each other than my family is, for some reason. Now, I'm really in my nuclear family. I'm the oldest in a very small family. Tirabu has a huge family! They had a family reunion with 150 people! I'm trying to get a small family reunion together. But most of my family members are not culturally tied; most of them are not Buddhist. I think Buddhism is not only a spiritual thing, it's a cultural thing. It tied people to Japanese culture. It's not just for the spiritual practice; it's the cultural practices. It's through the Buddhist Temple that I get more of the cultural parts of observance or traditional things. It is the essence of it that I think I take into myself.

I'm dreaming right now of going to Japan; I've never been. I have this slight fear because I don't speak Japanese. This idea just came up to go with a friend who does speak Japanese, who was born in Japan, whose father was a Noh actor and has a Noh school in Japan. I'm really thinking about this right now. Perhaps it is something I need to do to claim that part of myself. Maybe I'll make a little project of it. I don't know. I may or may not do it, but something may come out of it. I'm also going to go to my family home in Skoka and try to communicate with my relatives, to see where I am and where I'm not. Where I could touch again. That's my next dream.

NOTES

1. Great Leap, Inc. has been touring a multicultural festival of performance and public school residencies, *A Slice of Rice, Frijoles, and Greens,* with artists such as Dan Kwong, Amy Hill, Calvin Jung, Chic Street Man, Louise Mita, Arlene Malinowski, and Paulina Sahagun.

2. In 1994, civil unrest in many U.S. urban sites broke out following the acquittal of police officers accused of police brutality and abuse of force in the Rodney King trial. Rodney King is African American and the four police officers are White. The riots/uprising has been referred to as the first U.S. multiracial riots in U.S. history, which deeply affected Latino, Black, Asian, and White communities in these urban settings.

3. The Italian film-maker is Antonello Branca and the documentary film is *Seize the Time*.

4. People's Park in Berkeley, California has been a central site for protests and political gatherings since 1969. It continues to be a place to gather to address current and on-going political issues in the U.S. and globally.

5. Chris Iijima is a law professor at the University of Hawaii. Charlie Chín is an artist based in the Bay area in California.

Chuck Mike
Photo by Nathaniel Okititan

13

Theater and activism: conversation with Chuck Mike

Awam Amkpa

'The defining yardstick for the search has been the notion of deliberation, of conscious uses of the performing arts to bring about or reinforce a process of social change; changes in self-concept, attitude, awareness, skill, or behavior,' says Ross Kidd about practices of Theatre for Development.[6] The following conversation between two practitioners of this kind of theater draws specific examples from Nigeria. As a practice, Theatre for Development generally pays attention to the use of performance traditions in developing awareness of a community's local, national, and international identity. Within such contexts, issues of the community's social, economic, and political identity provide material for evolving cultural consciousness critical of power relations, as well as setting up criteria for such a community's social and economic development.

Chuck Mike is the Director of Performance Studio Workshop (PSW) based in Lagos, Nigeria. His organization trains theater artists and runs outreach programs on social and political issues, as well as producing political plays. His organization's mission is to:

> ... perpetuate the performing arts of Nigeria as a rewarding and relevant profession. PSW's relevance to society is based on the fact that it addresses issues affecting daily existence. Beyond entertainment and enlightenment the studio attempts to act as a catalyst for positive change by prodding the community through performance to recognize its power to address its own problems. In this respect the Performance Studio Workshop acts as a catalyst for the upliftment of the Nigerian society.[7]

As an affiliate organization of the Nigerian Popular Theatre Alliance, Performance Studio Workshop combines a repertory of political plays with outreach grassroots activism in the various communities they interact with. The organization's outreach activities include projects based on drug abuse, road safety, environmental awareness, and women's issues. It has collaborated with various agencies and base groups in developing such projects.

Mike's experience as a director has ranged from Theatre for Development to work on the professional stage. In the latter arena, most notably his direction of Chinua Achebe's *Things Fall Apart*, adapted by Biyi Bandele-Thomas, he has demonstrated the potential of Theatre for Development principles to offer new approaches and tools towards the development of professional stage work. Commissioned by the London International Festival of Theatre and produced at the Royal Court in 1997, the play met with critical acclaim in the U.K. and in the U.S.A. on tour in 1998. In the following conversation, Mike follows the trajectory of his involvement in Theatre for Development in regional, national, international, and intercultural contexts.

AWAM AMKPA: It might benefit those not familiar with Nigerian society if we provide a brief introduction to the context of your work and those of the Nigerian Popular Theatre Alliance. We have a country where after its political independence from the British, there was a sense of a national culture whose most visible and sustained representation is the army and its supply of military dictators. These soldiers dictated what is allowed as a national culture. They even built an architectural monstrosity called the National Theatre, which in their arrogance, is modeled on an army General's hat! It is so bizarre that whilst driving in central Lagos the sight of this structure literally follows you around. Anyway, what happens within the National Theatre, even when they appointed a National Troupe, is the production of plays from indigenous cultures meshed into the fantasy called and imposed on the nation as 'national culture.' And what happens in such designation is that the kind of work Chuck is talking about actually falls way outside this notion of national culture. Theater artists . . .

CHUCK MIKE: In that 'hat-ridden' national culture.

AA: That's right. Theater artists in that context have a peculiar problem of having to declare a stand or where their practices stand in relation to the national culture which excludes a large section of the society for gender, class, and ethnic reasons. Are their practices going to sustain the official 'national culture' or the unofficial culture of Nigerian peoples, trying to find strategies of communicating better with each other, as well as understanding the predicaments corrupt governments have put them in. It is important that we underscore what you and others are doing and its significance to the cultural history of Nigeria. Your work is a kind of theater with a huge social responsibility. At the same time, it does not underestimate the aesthetic moment. The language is the performance, so that it does not assume its work is just sociology on stage; rather it is actually saying symbolism, its beauty, and how captivating it is, is actually the first hint of the politics of its theater.

CM: That's where it all starts. It's that enjoyment; the use of cultural resources which make the political actuality possible. Once you forget that, then it's about dogma; it's no longer about theater. It's no longer about enjoying the arsenal of play. You know the social index of the dance, the song, etc. I must stress that our work is part of a larger network involving other theater and community groups catering to the development of places ignored by the official government.

But let's talk about the broader context of our work and the Nigerian Popular Theatre Alliance. You were part of the group at Ahmadu Bello University Zaria.

AA: Well, my experience in the then University of Ife Guerilla Theatre Unit led by Wole Soyinka started a process which eventually took me to community and popular theater work in Zaria. I take pride in acknowledging the hybridity of my experience drawing from traditions developed in different institutions based in different parts of the country. More importantly it is how that training and practice of theater cuts across class, ethnic, and gender differences, producing a language or forum of articulating our different if sometimes contestatory experiences of Nigerian social reality. Peasant communities had taken up the work in Zaria as they formed their own groups and evolved practices where theater addresses their social and political developments. This led to a local alliance then called Zaria Popular Theatre Alliance. Despite the differences between us, things worked out for a while until social crises led to a different tack leading to the formation of the national organization [Nigerian Popular Theatre Alliance]. I should perhaps elaborate on the crises. Like others, I learnt a lot from that history and in fact can say I am a product of the historical evolution of various groups into a regional and then national one. What was most fascinating about the history and its various projects was that social crises always fine-tuned the relationships between the different identities of various groups. I'll give you a quick example. Sometime in 1987 or so, there was a conflict leading to Moslems attacking Christian churches and homes. The difference there was not simply religious but also ethnic and class based. The conflict made everywhere unsafe, including the university. Most of us came to the painful realization that our compatriots and friends in the alliance were the same people burning down homes with our other friends and families! That created a crisis of confidence in our relationships. We came out of that experience with questions such as: 'Where do we actually stand in these relationships?' 'How do we cope with all kinds of social crises external to the group?' Some people just packed it in. It's like, 'I'm not going to stand around and wait for these guys to burn down my house,' and so on. That's where the politics becomes very important: the clarity of one's intention and the belief that politics is not a clear-cut idea that you are simply performing but that it is actually a process that keeps changing by offering new and difficult challenges.

CM: Was that also responsible for the coming together of people who were practicing Theatre for Development sometime in Zaria?

AA: Well, that particular experience was significant, coupled with the renewed energy that individuals like Oga Abah brought back to the work. We found out that our work has to continue and should not simply be regional and based only in Zaria.

CM: Hence the beginning of a national organization?

AA: Yes, and I should stress that this was merely a factor facilitating the move to a national organization; there were of course other factors. Regarding the kind of strife in Zaria, we thought focussing on a national organization means such local issues should not be allowed to destroy a work we loved so much. Coupled with other factors, Theater for Development systematically became a nationally recognized and legitimate practice leading to so many models. It became open to different practices across the country and people moved from one region to the other, and that was the moment I left the country to study alternative theaters in England.

CM: That's interesting … because as a follow-up to those, I think the Nigerian Popular Theatre Alliance came into being.

AA: That's right.

CM: For me, I came to Nigeria from the U.S. after the Civil Rights and Black Consciousness Movements. I arrived in Nigeria to study with Wole Soyinka and have never left. Like you, my current theater work is primarily informed by training in Wole Soyinka's Guerilla Theatre strategies. The Performance Studio Workshop extended mainstream theater work by initiating the first Theatre for Development workshop in Lagos and perhaps in the southern part of the country. We brought together different factions of the Nigerian Popular Theatre Alliance, potential funders, and enthusiastic theater artists in a week-long forum at Badagry, Lagos. Our intention was to attempt a broader definition of Theatre for Development by focusing on the Zaria foundational work and extending their traditions with a view to broadening our scope and range of activities. Following the various initiatives from the Zaria collective and the new national context, there was a workshop in Harare in Zimbabwe partly funded by the British Council and the Zimbabwean government. A similar forum also happened in Britain. Recently we also brought together people from all over the continent; had a few people from Britain, one or two from the U.S. as well. Again, we were looking at practice, so we went to some sites of activity and the general consensus of that meeting was that this practice must be defined here very coherently toward building some type of forum which will carry it further by a constant exchange of ideas. So, one of the definitions was that Theatre for Development is a performative forum grounded in a procedure that is participatory. Such a process should seek results, not be held necessarily accountable for it, but should seek and have tangible results at the end of the day. We are particularly thrilled by the emergence of an association of African Theatre for Development practitioners. Recently I was at a working group meeting in Ghana where a detailed directory of practitioners was initiated. So that's where we are now.

AA: I think it is important to know this work is not unique to Nigeria. Similar practices existed in Kenya, Zambia, South Africa, Tanzania, and so on. Indeed there was a previous global organization called the International Popular Theatre Alliance, which I think has literally collapsed! It's hard to articulate reasons for its collapse, but its significance kind of receded.

CM: Yes, we discussed that and assured all the funders and everyone else that our current state is a different spirit, and of course our history is different despite the fact most members of that international organization work with us. Indeed one of the objectives of creating a directory is to document and vet those of us who have been practicing very consistently and understand more of the procedure. Such exercise makes available the philosophy and various models we have developed over time. What's happening now is that international organizations are becoming aware of that specific document and they are asking, 'Who's who?' in such practices. It gives us a template of reference for the professionals. So, whether they're university professors, or working in organizations and so on, the registry offers legitimacy to the practitioners.

AA: But let's come to *Things Fall Apart*. I'm fascinated by this experiment. Apart from being a very good novel, I think the novel has different meanings for various generations of Nigerians. There are those for whom its meaning is significantly different from those of my generation of early post-independence Nigerians and Africans. For younger Nigerians, 40 years after 'independence' from Britain, the major colonial conflict between Europe and Africa is no longer the big deal. The big deal is more . . .

CM: . . . conflict within . . .

AA: . . . right . . . the big deal is the country's neo-colonial misadventures. I am fascinated by the translation of the novel onto stage. I know it has been done before, but your joint adaptation with Biyi Bandele-Thomas is remarkably and refreshingly different. Tell us about the process of devising the play, cast and rehearsing it prior to being seen by the public.

CM: It basically evolved out of a workshop instigated by Biyi Bandele-Thomas's excitement with the novel. Firstly, I believe no matter how well meaning, or well intentioned, Nigerians should continue to write about their own people, history and so on, particularly to those for whom the contexts of historical events have shifted. Biyi, of course, being two generations after Chinua Achebe's, was fired by such enthusiasm. As a person of African descent in America, I faced the same kind of re-writings and revivals of our history. In retrospect, it was a kind of activist learning, particularly of African American theatre in the 1960s. I think the same passion brought Biyi, Achebe's novel, and myself together.

As a child Biyi was highly influenced by the novel and brought the idea of a different adaptation to me years ago, when he was an undergraduate at the then University of Ife. He then took off to England, where he became a writer of serious repute. When he approached the British National Theatre about a likely project with the novel, he brought me into the process of realizing it on stage. When the National Theatre in London accepted his proposal, we set up a workshop involving a choreographer and musicians. At this stage Biyi was a writer in residence at the

National Theatre in London and had not written any part of the proposed adaptation. With a company of mostly Black British performers funded by the National Theatre, we started a series of improvisations. In a little while, Biyi had written ten pages. We went to town on those ten pages and actually put together some kind of presentation, which was viewed by an invited audience as a 'work in progress.' After the two-week workshop people saw the possibilities of this work on stage, and decided to go ahead with it. I returned to Nigeria with my troupe and six weeks later Biyi sent a full-length play that was phenomenal. He kept Achebe's language, and with a very crafty modulation of ideas introduced innovative use of scenes and multiple roles for characters. Another workshop was immediately summoned to explore the new script before establishing a full-scale rehearsal/ production.

I was slightly unprepared for what I discovered during casting. Apart from international politics, I found myself confronted by the differences of national and professional identities of the Nigerian and Black British cast. Firstly, the British group had a specialist orientation, somewhat compartmentalist in their approach, which did not make the players holistic in orientation. Nigerian artists on the other hand were generalists who danced, drummed, acted, sang, as well as possessed skills in scenery building, a phenomenon you and I are familiar with.

In any case we ended up having a fine array of people. We somehow managed to put an integrated cast together. We put together a cast of people with Caribbean as well as other African backgrounds alongside Nigerians and some Caucasian English actors. It was such an exciting mix and we had fun as we tried to get different groups to acculturate into each other's traditions. When they were in Nigeria we fashioned a program, which allowed them go out during the day, negotiate their ways through eating, cooking, and drinking palm-wine and other social interactions with people in Lagos. In terms of performance they had access to various performance traditions such as dances and songs. Despite the fact that most of the group was Black, our dance workshops revealed remarkable differences in terms of rhythm. Our speech workshop sessions also revealed linguistic differences. The challenge became how to create a community of performers out of this diasporic group. I think we managed to do so effectively with our so-called 'improvisation circle.' As a process, it streamlines the actors' attitude toward working as a company, as well as towards being flexible, more eclectic, and not dependent on the kind of fastidious planning that I found most European and Western actors do. We tried to make them simply rely on their basic instincts and to trust themselves. And between that trust and the power of the idea, the piece itself, which I believe has its own life; we had a production of merit. It bespeaks the kind of freedom that gave the project life.

We got back to the U.K. after these workshops and rehearsed, I think, for five weeks and then finally opened in London. Reactions were phenomenal. I'll never forget the reaction of one former colonial administrator who lived in Nigeria. He came up to us after a performance and said: 'You know, we just didn't know. We just did not know!' And what he saw on stage told him that when they had contact, they were completely arrogant and ignorant of the fact that there was a society in motion which had its own norms, its own educational systems, its own legal systems, its own culture intact. And this was completely ignored by that contact. But to hear this man say that he didn't know was, for me, a revelation. For him, as well as me! You know, no matter how many times you do this kind of work, when you get these kinds of reactions, you still get blown away. When the show opened at the Royal Court, which you know is a traditional theater venue for developing new work, we had a surprisingly large audience every night. The Nigerian community and their friends came out in full force. All tickets were sold. We got good reviews in the press.

After the Royal Court shows we had talkback sessions. Though their appreciation of the play was highlighted, many wanted to know what was happening in Nigeria. A common area of questioning was how we came to the decision of using female actors in gender-rotating roles. This is particularly poignant against the background of the novel, which was about a male-dominated society whose values are mostly determined by male chiefs.

AA: How did you respond to that?

CM: Well, the female members of the company earned their roles and fulfilled the artistic rendition of the story in contemporary times. Women constitute the largest part of our population and should be part of telling the stories of their societies. Apart from that they were excellent actors, and the democratic style of achieving the play made it imperative that we did not discriminate. The collective process of defining characters and how they are played became part of the show. I'm convinced that the storytelling technique in this piece, as conceptualized by Biyi Bandele-Thomas, allowed us to boldly face such challenges. The form already sets a precedent for what's going to happen. You know, you have a company of people who are at once giving dialogue, but all of them are playing instruments at one time or the other. Everyone's filling in for everyone on stage, so you have this mixture of form and attitude that, I think, beclouds any specific criticism. This process is itself influenced by our Theatre for Development principles, which sort of crossed over into producing *Things Fall Apart*. We were addressing issues of imagery and change and if such a change has to be a substantial one, the process that goes into a work should be revealed in the work. I think our production of *Things Fall Apart* speaks to that. I have been proud of the process and outcome of the show and I see it as a kind of 'homecoming' to Nigeria and Africa as a place of my symbolic and original birth.

AA: Would you like to comment on your next project?

CM: I sure would. I think this one's probably been one of the biggest thorns in my 'artistic hide' for a few years now. Some years ago, I had some funding to start some research on female genital mutilation with a view to setting up a play and series of workshops sensitizing and educating communities about its human rights context. We started doing interviews with women from various sections of Nigeria. We interviewed victims, health workers, and perpetrators of this custom. Having lived in Nigeria for so long, mostly in the south-west, I thought it was going to be easy to talk with some people, and they'd just open up. Of course it did not happen like that. People closed up immediately. We later found out that in that part of the country women disliked talking about it. In other parts of the country we found communities where women were proud of it and actually came out boldly to talk about it, particularly in the mid-west. We discovered the reasons for such practices varied from place to place. For example, in the south-west, where we are based, they cut, let's say, just the tip of the clitoris and it's a minimalist act. And they say it's to prevent promiscuity. In a place like the eastern part, they will tell you it's for cosmetic reasons and that the whole vagina area is ugly, so they 'trim' it to make it look better. In the north-east, it's some kind of a rite of passage in which they scrape out just about everything and keep a small hole there. It's called a 'fibulation,' and they patch up such women afterwards. When she has to give birth, they open her up and then close her back up, so in that part of the country it is an ongoing process.

Despite the various cultural reasons for their practice, a common denominator is the tradition's justification of patriarchy. It is about male control or power, in all cases male-driven, but executed by women and codified as a sacred tradition.

The drama created from our research was itself a form of inquiry engaging audiences with information about the subject and what their own stories were. Dance offered us a valuable vocabulary for performing. In retrospect it was a process quite similar to the one adopted for *Things Fall Apart*. During eight weeks of researching, studying our data, and devising their visual interpretations, it became clear that 60 percent of the women in our group were themselves victims of this practice. The process offered them a public forum to deal with the contradictions and oppressive nature of this tradition. I must stress that this was not our intention and it took a while before the whole company had this knowledge, and when we did, the passion with which we pursued the issue was amazing. It is probably one of the most powerful experiences I've had in the theater and one the company will want to develop further. Remember Performance Studio Workshop has a permanent company as well as training others for specific projects. The company has several main stage and community plays in its repertory and has in the last ten years been a steady group with a permanent location in Lagos.

AA: Two quick questions. Are there generational differences between the victims of female genital mutilation? Is your group aware of other women's activist groups working on the subject? I recall the group Women in Nigeria working on the subject in northern Nigeria. I also recall the not too positive response to Alice Walker and Pratibha Parmar's documentary on the subject, particularly among the activists.

CM: Our work was exploratory and will continue to develop. Yes there are vast differences between generations, ethnicity, and class. Our response is very political and we believe everybody has a role to play in eradicating not only this tradition but also all oppressive traditions. What we see now in the global movement is that everybody has their role to play. I think Alice Walker's role was really to bring public attention to the issue. I think since then she's learned from the responses and will probably revise her own strategy. I think her role has been to get support; to get people to pay attention and to fund those working to challenge and stop this and other practices of gender oppression.

We worked with other groups and indeed took our cue from working with the Inter-African Committee on Traditional Practices. Through our close working relationship with such groups, we learned more about the issue, knew areas where such traditions were prevalent, and so on. There were two phases within our work. One addressed our mainstream audiences who were mostly middle class and had a lot of social influence. The other addressed various peasant and working-class communities in rural and urban areas where the tradition is prevalent. Such people are hopelessly paralyzed by the traditions too. Our acronym for the entire project was SISTERHELP.

Collaborating with other groups gave us lots of access to communities and taught us a great deal about approaching the issue without being offensive.

AA: How did your various audiences react to the performance?

CM: Shock, anger, and disbelief in most cases. For others more familiar with the practice, it offered clarity in terms of its gender politics. For us as a group it had a politicizing effect. I recall a circumcizer from Benin who, during an interview, said: 'Come by tomorrow. I'm going to be doing a circumcision.' So I was there with this video camera and I, and I'm standing there asking myself, 'Can you do this? Can you shoot this, or should you try to stop her?' And my better instinct said 'Shoot it!' And, as sure as I'm sitting here, we did what we called an information blitz with the material we shot and its visual impact, though sensational, was immensely effective in drawing people's attention to the matter. We brought together perpetrators who had stopped the practice, those still active, victims, and other activists to confront this issue for real rather than in abstract terms. Some of these people are still active not only within campaign groups but also groups tackling other forms of gender oppression. Others have gone on to find alternative sources of income using their skills in traditional medicine for curative practices.

Our work in association with others has also intensified government interest in the subject. Public education on the subject continues to be our concern, because even if government creates a law tomorrow you still need an ongoing educational process. The piece we created is awesome! More fundamentally it is about women telling their stories. Female genital mutilation is only one of numerous harmful traditional practices in the country. We also know other societies have their own forms of marking and subordinating the female body. For instance, feet binding in China, in my opinion, was equally horrendous. A related issue we are still considering and researching are based on ideas of widowhood, especially in the eastern part of the country, where when a man dies his wife is put through all kinds of humiliating and denigrating circumstances. She is basically 'quarantined.' She's kept sitting barefoot, naked, on the floor, and in a filthy environment for a very long time. She is never allowed to touch certain foods and all because her husband dies. Like female genital mutilation this is considered a sacred rite she is expected to endure and it has devastating effects on the individual. Her husband's junior brother, who may just as well be somebody she may have actually brought up, now has the right to take her as a wife. He has the right to claim her, which now tells you that she's a possession. We also have child labor issues to deal with. The issues are numerous and we will continue to work with them within our theater practice.

AA: It is certainly an important issue. The language of decolonization must transcend negotiating independence from colonial Britain. It must be the language of democracy within which unequal relations of power are perpetually questioned and stopped. That I think is what informs popular theater and theater for development practices, particularly in postcolonial countries like Nigeria. What you have said certainly suggests theater artists have to take political action and must be socially responsible for the progress of whatever communities define their audience's reality. I hope Performance Studio Workshop continues its great work and that more exchanges within the national organizations continue to foster a culture and language of decolonization.

NOTES

1. Widely practiced in the Philippines, India, Pakistan, Botswana, Zimbabwe, Ghana, and Burkina Faso, the integration of theatrical traditions into development strategies forces significant redefinition of the term and practice of development. For countries defined at the margins of European modernity through colonial histories and postcolonial tragedies, development goes beyond providing people with water, hospitals, and shelter. In such contexts, the term assumes a cultural form through which communities define themselves internally and externally. Such critical consciousness of power relations uses theatrical performances as forums for organizing people within decolonizing discourses, thereby giving them opportunities to set up and negotiate the criteria for their own progress and description within society. Conceptualizing the drama, rehearsing it, presenting it and facilitating debates, negotiations and planning specific actions to take beyond metaphorical representations of a community's underdevelopment summarize the nature of a typical Theatre for Development practice.

    It is worth stressing that the practice has no fixed rubric; rather it allows the specific need of a community to determine its direction. Generally, the performances and their rehearsals are used not only in organizing people into political discourses that empower their communities, but are also used in evaluating development projects as well as disseminating information to other communities with faced with similar needs. Such cultural and performative dimensions provide communities with the means of sustaining the discourses of self-improvement and empowerment.

In Nigeria, Ahmadu Bello University Zaria pioneered the evolution of this theater practice by making it the focus of theater training and liberal arts education. Using residual and emergent cultural practices to provide students with a context for developing theater skills, the focus of the university's drama degree was on building tangential relationships with less privileged sections of Nigerian society. Other universities and social groups have since developed the practice of according to the specific needs of communities they work in. Keeping focus on the social responsibility of performance and its place in empowering communities with decolonizing attitudes, various groups around the country sustain such vision through a national organization called the Nigerian Popular Theatre Alliance, founded in 1988 by university teachers, social workers, and other cultural activists.

For further reading, see R. Kidd, 'The Popular Performing Arts, Non-formal Education and Social Change in the Third World: A Bibliography and Review Essay' (The Hague: *Centre for the Study of Education in Developing Countries*, 1982), p. 2.
2. Promotional brochure for Performance Studio Workshop, Lagos, 1998, p. 2.

Muriel Miguel
Photo by Richard Agecoutay

14

Weaving a legacy: an interview with Muriel Miguel of the Spiderwoman Theater

Ann Haugo

In this interview, Spiderwoman Theater co-founder and director Muriel Miguel states clearly a point that many feminist theater scholars have made as well: Spiderwoman Theater even in its infancy confronted racism and classism in their performances and within their group dynamics. Yet Spiderwoman Theater's work has become known in academic circles largely through feminist theater scholarship.[1] I find this singular direction of scholarship somewhat peculiar, as Spiderwoman Theater's work has never been solely about gender issues. As Miguel points out, Spiderwoman Theater's work has always been about gender and race and class. Yet outside of feminist scholarship, even in the growth in the last decade of critical race and class studies, theater scholarship has sidelined not just Spiderwoman Theater but Native theater itself. Could it be that their politics are still too radical for even the liberal-progressive schools of criticism? That Spiderwoman and other Native companies and playwrights force some of us to confront a deeply rooted privilege that − as non-Native peoples living in America − we would rather not have uprooted?

As an example, consider the irony of postcolonial studies in theater. Of all of the texts and anthologies published in postcolonial theater to 2000, none contains a play by an American Indian playwright or an article about American Indian theater. We instead focus our attentions on the vestiges of the British Empire, reinforcing an unfortunate belief that colonialism happened over there − across the border or across the ocean − and back then. 'Postcolonial' in its original conception of course referred to the countries once colonized by the British Empire, and for that reason, Native Canadian (First Nations) theater sometimes makes an appearance in these texts.[2] Even in the application of postcolonial theories and methodologies to work by marginalized groups of color in the United States (however controversial that maneuvering might be), American Indian theater − and indeed, one might argue, American Indian issues in general −

receives little academic attention. In our obsession with the 'posts,' we all too often avoid or ignore the ongoing material effects of colonialism in the U.S.

Spiderwoman confronts the present effects of colonialism in its performances; whether they speak of personal identity or community responsibility, they demand that their audiences hear, take account, learn, and while they're doing all that, laugh along the way. Underlining on stage the interconnectedness of oppressions, Spiderwoman cultivates a method which is at once seductive and confrontational, flirtatious and emphatic. In *Sun, Moon, and Feather*, the first piece the sisters performed as a trio, they reminisce about growing up in Brooklyn, and in one hysterical and poignant scene, re-enact their childhood love affair with Jeanette MacDonald's Indian Princess and Nelson Eddy's Canadian Mounty. Asked by the Circle of Elders to create a performance about the theft of Native spiritual ways, Spiderwoman takes on Plastic Shamans and New Age spiritualists in *Winnetou's Snake Oil Show from Wigwam City* (with Hortensia Colorado of Coatlicue Theater Company). *Reverb-ber-ber-rations* emerged in part from *Winnetou's* exploration of false spirituality, as the sisters found themselves telling stories about their own spiritual lives, celebrating and making public the spiritual gifts they received from their mother. *Power Pipes* brought more friends and family members together to collaborate – initially Hortensia and Elvira Colorado and Monique Mojica (Gloria Miguel's daughter) and later Murielle Borst (Muriel's daughter). Like all of their pieces, *Power Pipes* examines survival – the persistence of Native community. But like the piece that Spiderwoman is currently developing, *Persistence of Memory*, *Power Pipes* concerns itself with the future, with what the present generation leaves for the generations to come, a topic which Muriel speaks to at several points in this interview.[3]

Though their method pulls the audience in with humor and then forces them to see the issues, a Spiderwoman production extends beyond simple confrontation and education. When I asked Muriel about the power of their work, and Native theater itself, to heal, her answer was forthright. Like the quilt that has stayed with the company since its inception, the need to empower themselves and their audiences has stayed with Spiderwoman over the years. Muriel speaks of the power of storytelling: to give voice, to place oneself within a community, to create and re-create identity. That healing happens in the process of performance, for example, when a performer speaks on stage her autobiography or when the audience begins to see an issue from another perspective. Whether Spiderwoman asks you to confront your personal demons (as in *Women in Violence*, discussed below) or examine your place in the continued commodification of Native America (as in *Winnetou's Snake Oil Show from Wigwam City*), whether Spiderwoman celebrates Native identity with you or asks that you peel away the layers of false knowledge about Native people gained through popular culture, whether you are Native or non-Native, Spiderwoman insists that you walk away from a performance with a fuller perspective – not, as Muriel says, with easy answers but perhaps with questions.

I opened the conversation by asking Muriel what sort of reflecting she has been doing, now that Spiderwoman has celebrated its 25th year. The longest continually running Native theater ensemble (rivaled only by the Thunderbird Theater, the resident theater company at Haskell Indian Nations University) and women's theater in the U.S., Spiderwoman Theater itself has undergone many changes, and we talked about some of those changes – changes in membership, in creative process, and in the content of their work. First formed in 1975 as a six-member, multiracial, feminist company, Spiderwoman stood out among the feminist companies of that period by confronting issues of race and class head on – both in the content of their pieces and in their group dynamics.[4] That road wasn't an easy one to follow, and by 1980, the group would separate, initially by working on two separate pieces about family history. Group members Lois Weaver, Peggy Shaw, and Pamela Verge began to develop their own piece entitled *Split Britches*, about Weaver's Blue Ridge Mountain family history, and the three Miguel sisters developed *Sun, Moon, and Feather*, about sibling rivalry and racism while growing up in Brooklyn. After these performances, Weaver and Shaw left Spiderwoman and founded the performance collective Split Britches, which has become the best-known lesbian performance company in the U.S. The core of Spiderwoman Theater since that time remains the three Miguel sisters, but the spirit of collaboration has remained constant. Muriel refers to people 'passing through' Spiderwoman, and over the years, many people – designers, technicians, and other actors – have passed through, shared in, and contributed to Spiderwoman's work: daughters and nieces performed in *Power Pipes*; Coatlicue Theater Company, sisters Elvira and Hortensia Colorado, developed several pieces with Spiderwoman, including *The Three Sisters from Here to There*, *Winnetou's Snake Oil Show from Wigwam City*, and *Power Pipes*.

Spiderwoman Theater's 25th anniversary performance names the space that the sisters of Spiderwoman find themselves in now, as mothers and grandmothers, veteran performers and activists, artistic, and political leaders: *The Persistence of Memory*. They have spent this year looking into the future as much as into the past – or perhaps looking more to the future than the past. While 'anniversary' would seem to name a celebration of what has gone before, Muriel Miguel and her sisters are concerned most with what will happen: what have they left and what can they still leave for the next generations of performer-activists?

Talking with any of the sisters in Spiderwoman Theater is a bit like being an audience member at one of their performances. As Muriel explains in this interview, Spiderwoman's method grows from answering questions with stories, offering explanations and contexts, if not answers. During this interview, Muriel answered many of my questions with stories. Like any good storyteller, Muriel brings her stories back around, explaining context in answer to the question.

MURIEL MIGUEL: People have been asking us what our five-year plan is and what our ten-year plan is. And my thought is that really it's a hundred-year plan, because I really think of this as a legacy. We did a lot of work here, but a lot of work can be done now. We have all the things that make a theater. We have the name, our federal status, so now we should be attracting other younger women to come in to work. We should be attracting my daughter, Gloria's daughter to come in to work.[5] And all of us should be teaching these various ways of working. I would like to see *Sun, Moon, and Feather* done by three other women. I think that would be a gas, to see another director's take on *Sun, Moon, and Feather* and make their own film.[6]

After performances with Spiderwoman, I sometimes talk about six generations. I say you're responsible. You're really responsible for six generations. Even if you die you're responsible. That isn't such a hard concept to me.

ANN HUAGO: What has Spiderwoman already contributed, to Native theater, feminist theater, American theater?

MM: We've hit all fronts. Part of it was that in theater we were so shocking. I remember when they sent a bit of *Sun, Moon, and Feather* to PBS. The man was so upset with it. He sent it back and said, 'Nobody is interested in three older women, overweight women.' So you know, that hits everything. We're not White, we're fat, we're old, and we're not talking about what other people are talking about. So then the question becomes, 'Are we aht? Is this real theatah?' So in many ways we have broken a lot of barriers. We have also said to a lot of people, 'Yes, you can do it, too.'

AH: In part you've done this by the new works projects – like the performance project at Gila River or the At the Foot of the Mountain production *Neurotic Erotic Exotics*. What did Spiderwoman leave At the Foot of the Mountain with after *Neurotic Erotic Exotics*?[7]

MM: The important thing was that we faced certain things as we talked. There were eight women. Everyone talked. Everyone told stories. One woman, a Chicana, told a story about how she was invited to a White person's house in a fancy neighborhood. She went to this person's house. She knocked on the door and said, 'Hi. I'm so-and-so.' And they said, 'Alright.' So she came in and she sat down, and no one said anything to her. And she sat there and she sat there and she sat there. And she started to get really nervous. And then she said, 'Well, is Mary coming down?' And they said, 'Oh, she lives across the street. She doesn't live here.' But, you know, it was the opposite of neurotic and erotic. It's that you go into this other world and everyone looks alike to you. All White people look alike. You can't even tell their houses apart! But then you go to the barrio, to the inner city, and what do you have there? The White people are saying the same thing, right?

So there were a lot of stories like that, stories about surviving in all these places. It was exciting just to get people to tell their stories and to see the different ways we told the stories. We had a Chinese woman, three Indian women, two Chicanas, an African American, and a Jewish woman. And it was exciting and scary for a lot of them. A lot of them were talking about things they had never talked about before. They talked about their size, how big they were. And, to say that your people are not accepting of certain things – that's a big thing to say.

AH: And then there was the Gila River project. Why did you go to Gila River?

MM: We were invited to Gila River to do a theater piece talking about all of the things that have happened on this reservation.[8] We were working with Ak Chin and Gila River, and they hadn't worked together before on something like this. So the idea was to collect people to work on storytelling and then perform. People wanted to do things on AIDS, their own stories, all these different things. When we were there, we pulled out stories from *Women in Violence*[9] – the abuse story, Daddy's drunk, a bunch of stuff – and the people were so moved.

This is what I mean by a legacy. We went to Salt River, and in Salt River they told us, 'Well, it's just a lecture-demonstration.[10] Do what you want.' So we got there, and we realized that the whole community turned out. This was more than just a lecture-demonstration. The chief or chairperson was there, the curator. They brought food. It was a big deal. Afterwards we went into the audience talking to people. Women were coming up to me and saying, 'That happened to me.' 'That happened to me, and I got pregnant.' 'This happened.' Women were just surrounding me, and then one of the women said, 'We should really have a talking circle.' And we thought, yes, it was very important, especially if things like this were happening to their kids now.

And the day before we were to open, there was a big sandstorm that knocked down all our lights. This was all outside, and we left up our sets. Kids came over the wall and destroyed our sets. That day I was walking on my knees. We were so tired, and I thought, here we are. We have to go to a ten o'clock circle. That means that we have to get up at eight in the morning. I think it was Deborah who said, 'We have to go. We said we were going to go. We have to go.'[11] So we were late. We got there around ten-thirty, and women were waiting outside for us. They'd catered it. Women came in from Phoenix for this talking circle. They wanted to know how. How do you do this? How do you take these stories? What do you do with these stories? How do you get to these stories? But more than that, everyone talked in that circle. Everyone talked about what they were doing, where they were from. There were woman politicians there. All these women showed up. They gave us presents. And it would have been awful to not show up.

I think that this type of theater is so interwoven, like Native people, interwoven with everything. The only thing you can do is to say, 'Is it theater? Is it Native theater? Is it queer theater?' But when you get down to it, it interconnects, and that's the only way we can work, by interconnecting it.

AH: When you were talking about the talking circle and the women coming to you after the performance, I started thinking about Native theater and healing. Monique Mojica has written about this, and I was talking with Dianne Reyner about this the other day, too.[12] Do you see your work as healing work, and how does that healing happen?

MM: Well, again, a lesson learned. This same piece was done in a big theater and, to me, it was not successful, right? It was not 'successful' because everything went wrong for me [the director], looking at it. I was forgetting. These people were on stage telling their stories. They told stories that haven't ever been told. The people on Gila River have all these bird stories and bird songs and things that people have ignored. And now they're losing it. So to have someone tell these stories was wonderful. And then to have someone tell a battery story was wonderful.

When I understood it, and it took me a long time to understand it, I said, 'Oh, yes.' Now I keep on talking about them because it was so important to say what they said and to put it into a structure. So, the structure didn't 'work' sometimes because they didn't understand the structure. But what they did, whatever they communicated to other people, to Native people, their pieces – that was important.

AH: So, a mainstream critic would have looked at this and said that it was not 'great drama,' not great acting, but . . .

MM: . . . but that wasn't what we were after, were we? We were after people telling their stories, people empowering themselves. All these buzzwords like empowering – that's actually what it was. This is really what we're talking about. This is really the true thing.

AH: Why is it empowering to tell the story?

MM: Well, for instance, we have a woman tell her story, and she's doing it in third person. Finally she starts to tell it in first person, and she's scared shitless telling it in the first person. She really felt brave when she told this story on Gila River. Then she invited her mother, her daughter, and her new husband to the show, and she told the story. They were so moved. She communicated to them something that she never told them before, about all the battery that happened [in a previous relationship]. Her daughter now understands why she's so angry at the father. They were able to talk about it.

There was a powwow afterwards, and I was going around to different stands, and this guy said to me, 'Oh, you're from that group. I was the one who was yelling and yipping and carrying on at the end there. That was amazing. I never saw anything like that before. That woman told her story. Men should see this. That's what we need now. We need people to go out and talk like that.' So it isn't theatah. But it's theater. It's doing work.

I think that we had all kinds of stuff. We had storytelling. We all had storytelling. It was put in such a way that kids could listen to it. People listened to it. The usual thing I say about storytelling. You've heard me say this before, right?

Storytelling is the way you feel and know where you are within your family, your clan, your tribal affiliations, and from there into the history of how you fit into the world. Storytelling starts at the kitchen table, on your parent's lap, on your aunt's and uncle's laps. Storytelling begins there, about who you are ... Then it continues from there about who you are in the family; of where you are as a tribal member, as part of that particular nation; then where that nation is in the community; and where that community belongs in the world. There's always circles upon circles upon circles. And that's how Spiderwoman approaches theater, through circles upon circles upon circles.[13]

That's really where it's at. This is probably the way it was done many years ago, centuries ago. Then the creation stories were stopped, the stories that told where we came from. The tribal historians, or whatever they were called, were the people who had the knowledge and couldn't pass it on. That's one of the things that I feel responsible for, passing the knowledge on about how to do that, how to get it out of people, how to put it together.

AH: You use a quilt as a backdrop for all of Spiderwoman's performances. What does that quilt represent for you?

MM: That's our history. It really is our history. For me, it's all the things that were important to me, and all the people that were important to me that went into that backdrop. At the giveaways at my first Sun Dance, I was given all these quilts. I came back to New York City with quilts and pieces of calico that people gave me. And I remember saying – because we had said that we needed something to use as our background – that I had these quilts and I was going to use these quilts. So we then took all this material, put it all out on a Westbeth floor someplace at one of the galleries there, and we organized it. Gloria had a huge mola, and she put the huge mola in the middle. In the beginning there wasn't anything except the molas and the quilts and the material. Later on we started to add more things to it. A lot of people who passed through Spiderwoman started to put their things into it. So sometimes you'll see a Japanese square, and so on. It means our history. That thing is 25 years old. It means everything we've ever done. It's in there. We've carried it all over Europe, New Zealand, Australia. It went to China. It has been all over the place. It's our trademark.

AH: The quilt seems like something that has been sustained through Spiderwoman's history? Some things have changed; the quilt has stayed the same.

MM: The quilt stays the same, because it's significant in many ways. The tapestry of the quilt, right? It's what we do. We do this layering; we put things together; we piece things together. We piece a lot of things together to make a whole. I like to see the whole thing. From there I dive in.

AH: So in creating the performance you try to see a whole fabric in order to develop the work?

MM: Yes, well, the whole fabric is whatever the idea is: the persistence of memory, three sisters growing up in Brooklyn. So I start with 'It would be great to have film in it.' And I think about that a while. With *Sun, Moon, and Feather*, I suddenly thought, 'I have fifty cans of tape, of film, at home.' I knew that I wanted to have us superimposed on it, I wanted us coming through it, I wanted us talking with it on, and that it was like another thing that was really part of us. The same with the audio. In the beginning there's all this talking and a couple of women, perfectionists, you know, were all upset because they couldn't understand all the words. To me it didn't matter. You got the idea pretty much about what was going on, about how we were talking to each other. And it's just another sound, just another facet. You hear all these things. I call it the poverty tape because we're talking about how poor we are and everything.

AH: Where does art meet politics? We're talking in artistic terms about seeing the whole fabric, what ideas you start with. Where does art meet politics? Your work is very political.

MM: I think that if you write and perform about what's bothering you now, at that moment, it's going to be political. I am writing and performing about certain things. It's going for that kernel. And if you don't go for that kernel, that's when you get sidetracked. I guess it doesn't matter if we're on our feet or if we spend days talking. That doesn't matter as much as going for the kernel and trying to find out. It's like following the pain. When you have a headache and you have it at the front of your head, you put something there. It goes to the back of your head, you put something there. It goes to your shoulder, you put something there. You know what I mean? That's what the kernel is. And you have to follow it. If – and this is where the politics happen – if you're talking about certain things and certain things are bothering you, and if you follow it, it becomes political. Fat is political. Being big is political. Being old is political. We're not even touching here on the stuff that Spiderwoman talks about – battery and violence and incest and drinking and drugs. If you go to any of those reservations where they give all the commodities out, you find that if you said, 'This is the oppressor's food.' Well! I remember saying that to someone. They were all eating frybread and I said, 'It's the oppressor's food.' And people thought I was nuts. I said, 'Well, think about it.'

AH: Right – why do you have that? White flour . . .

MM: . . . lard . . .

AH: . . . the cheap food that the government could give you when . . .

MM: . . . you were starving. I mean, not to say that Native people aren't great for being able to do that, to take these things and make it into this great thing. It has changed at a lot of the powwows, especially up north, where they're selling wild rice, buffalo, corn soup, and not selling the tacos. People are starting to become aware of healthy eating. Same way with tobacco. People are growing their own tobacco; that's a strand from centuries ago. To me, everything is political.

AH: So in some ways you've thrown the question back at me: how can Spiderwoman not be political?

MM: Yes, and for us it will always be that way.

AH: Do you think that this is true for Native theater, considering its place in contemporary theater?

MM: This is probably being hard-core: I like trickster stories. I like old stories. I like creation stories. But I don't think it stops there. I think that if we just give creation stories or we just give trickster stories, if we give what people want to see, we will always be, 'Oh, those wonderful Indians. Aren't they wonderful? They tell these stories and they're so colorful and they can sing so.' And that's not where I want to be.

AH: Do you think of that consciously when you're creating work, or is that something that's just kind of always present in your mind?

MM: It's always present in my mind. I don't want to give pretty pictures for no reason. And sometimes we get all messed up in that because we want to look beautiful on stage. Or we want to be perfect on stage. And all of a sudden I say, 'What the hell are we doing?'

AH: Other artists might be trying to find a more mainstream home.

MM: Spiderwoman will never be mainstream.

AH: Since that space is already there, to perform the old stories and be a storyteller, is it seductive? To believe you're contributing that way?

MM: Well, you are contributing. Just the fact that you're on stage telling these stories is political. Just the fact that you're there. But I think you have to go past that. People have seen blankets and beads, and they want to see more blankets and beads. It's like they're going to the circus. And we have to be aware of that because we've been a part of that circus. We've been a part of sideshows. We've been in Wild West shows. When we did *Winnetou's Snake Oil Show*, all of that stuff came from our backgrounds. The whip. The sharpshooter. The horseback rider.[14] All of that. All of that we've seen. So we just kept on layering it. Like my nagahyde, when I said, 'You know how many nagahydes I killed for this?' (laughter) Well, people think that that's the way you look. All of those old movies. That's the way they looked, with fake braids. But under it there's the real thing.

AH: Academia encourages us to define and describe, for example, what constitutes Native theater. It's a problematic question, and I'm never exactly sure how to best avoid, as a non-Native person, being put into the position of defining what Native theater is or isn't.

MM: Was Spiderwoman Theater in the beginning a Native theater?

AH: Sure, we can start there.

MM: When I approached this whole idea of making a theater group, it was because I kept my life compartmentalized that way. I had my life as a Native person and I had the life as an actress. Then I started to work with another group, more of a consciousness-raising group, but it was theater-orientied.[15] These women asked me questions. There was a certain assumption about me and an assumption in the feminist world that I didn't exactly fit into here in New York City. I wore make-up, I had a husband, I had children – and radical feminists were not doing that. I was different, really different. At the same time I was interested in what these women were talking about, really interested as a feminist. I realized that I was a feminist, but I was a Native woman also. My reaction to the mainstream feminists was: 'You're the ones that also degrade the Native men. You're part of that. You're not separated from that, you know. A White woman cop is just as much going to beat up on a Native man as a White male.' So I had to keep on shifting my sides and how I looked at things.

When I started my own group, it was definitely as a feminist group. And that's because of how I compartmentalized everything. And then it became obvious, even within the women in the group, that we, all of us, were not living middle-class lifestyles. We were all struggling women and all of us were outcasts within the feminist movement. 'Is this acting? Is this theatah? Are you women who are actresses, or actresses who are women?' But that was not going to push us out. We were here, we were telling stories that were important stories. So we had to stand firm on who we were.

So we started to define ourselves. We were not White people. We were women of color. We were women. And that is the reason why it eventually turned into a Native theater, because we had all these things happening to us. We didn't look like anyone else. We didn't look like the ones in our group, so we were pulled out because they wanted to take pictures of us. I think that we were trying very hard to be a group, and it was an exciting group but it was a very difficult group. We were all sizes, we were all colors, we were all ages, we were all gender-bending, we were grandmothers, some were married. We were all of those things, and there were 13 of us screaming and yelling across Europe. When you think about that, it was exciting but we did have huge fights. And a lot of the stuff we thought was racist. And a lot of the stuff, we thought, was classist.

AH: When you say 'a lot of the stuff,' are you talking about relations within the group, too?

MM: Yes, relations within the group. And I'm not saying it was just the Indians going after the Whites. It wasn't only one way.

Spiderwoman wasn't started to do cute little revues. So [we had to remember], what is the question? That's what my kind of director does, ask the question 'What are we asking and telling? What are we asking ourselves that makes us perform the things that we do?' We had said in the beginning that we would not let the ratio go low, that there would not be more White people than Native people or people of color in the group.

AH: This is something that I find interesting about Spiderwoman in the context of feminist theater of that decade. I won't go so far as to say that you were the only group but you were one of the only who made race and class a part of your content, consciously. Those were the fights that brought about the end of some of the theaters.

MM: It was very important to us. We were talking about this, and that was one of the things we said we should really make sure of. And that's what happened. There were four of us and there were, like, seven of them. We're talking about stage managers, costumers, business manager. Everybody was White. And they were saying, 'It's not fair.' And finally I was saying, 'I don't give a shit if something is not fair.' Then I was a bad woman.

By the time it came to *The Three Sisters from Here to There*, it was definite.[16] Now, all of our pieces were about racism. In *Fittin' Room*, when we had Nadya, we did 'Oh, Them Golden Slippers.'[17] They did a minstrel show, but when Nadya left, we couldn't do a minstrel show without Nadya (who was African American). We could only do what we consisted of. That's how we felt. I know there are other groups that don't feel that way, but we certainly felt that we could not do that. We ended up with 'One little, two little, three little Indians.' And we used to come out doing this crazy little Indian dance. We did Indian jokes.

We were changing. We kept adding more and more Indian-themed things like that. Things started to get really narrowed down. It wasn't an everything feminist group. It was quite obvious that there were three of us; then there was Nadya, and two other African American women who came in. And at one point, it was just a woman of color group, for *Lysistrata Numbah*. And then the group changed again when we started to look at *Winnetou's*. *Winnetou's* came out of the Elders' Circle and the Elders' Circle being really worried about all of this stuff. They approached us; we didn't approach them. They said, 'We think you should do something about this.'

The Elders' Circle meets around the country in the summertime and they talk about what's of concern in Indian Country. Usually it's a mixture of elders and young people, and a way of connecting young people and elders together. This was one of the questions that was coming up about what was happening in Indian Country. This whole New Age thing happened, with shamans and smudge sticks and crystals and vision quests.

The Elders' Circle decided they were going to do a conference on plastic shamanism and a lot of people came. They brought medicine people from around the country. What was so interesting was that Buddhist monks came. They were really interested in what was being said. And I thought that was so interesting because they really wanted to support Native people. And to listen to men and women talk about how they feel as medicine people – you don't just wake up a medicine person someday. To be a medicine person, you really do a lot. Some of these people were people who never come off the reservation.

[With *Winnetou's*] we weren't thinking of any other people except Native people, partly because it was quite obvious to us in our community that people wanted to see us as Native people in our community telling our stories because *Sun, Moon, and Feather* had happened right before this. When we started to show *Winnetou's* around in Canada, we realized how people really wanted to see us, hear our stories.

AH: The piece is in part a deconstruction of the novel. You sort of send up the novel. But it's also very personal at points.

MM: At points we tried to talk about real stuff that happened. Real things that are actually Native, like talking about Mama and the caul and how she doesn't get any money for this. She's done this all her life. They called her a wise woman, but people gave her food. That was one of the things that we tried to say to Lynn Andrews. You don't charge for this. You should be honored that people come to you, not they should be honored that you're talking to them. And you as a medicine person take anything that those people give you. One time I went to a woman and all I had was two cans of salmon that someone had put up. They had caught it themselves, and to me it was really precious. So I gave her two cans of salmon.

Anyway, what happened after that: We worked on *Winnetou's* serious parts, we talked about the journey of Hortensia's father, where he came from, where he went, and how she was always looking, looking, looking. This whole thing with the bones. It's about digging and looking for the bones. And that thing about this face. This is an Indian face, because that's another thing that we're confronted with all the time. 'You're not going to share this? You're so mean.' At the same time we look at you – out there – and see all these faces wanting to be Indian. But we can't be in the same places with these people. We couldn't go into their community and easily adapt because they don't want us there. We'll always be the oddity. It's the paradox that they want what we have but they don't want us. So that Indian face thing speaks to that paradox.

All of this to me is Native theater, from the beginning, because people didn't want to accept us as grassroots people and that there were Native women there. The White women were there being cutesy and beautiful, and because of the way we looked we were not accepted. 'What? You're actresses? You studied? You can sing? Isn't that amazing?' That's the stuff that was dropped on us. Damn right. No matter what you say and no matter what we produced, we're Native theater. Damn right. If someone says it isn't Indian theater, how dare they? This is our point of view. This is us. And they're going to turn around and tell us that this can't be? That's what I say to the academics. How dare you tell us what can be Indian theater and what can't be? We came at it the hard way, 25 years ago, and to us, this is hard-won, being Native theater. We did all the other things, and of course it wasn't as interesting to us.

And you have to think of it across borders. That's another thing that's thrown at me – well, you're an American Indian. No, I'm a Native person, and you throw these things around: Is it American theater? Is it Canadian theater? For me it feels like trying to pull us down again. We get up there, and you're trying to pull us down again. You know when you're having a fight and you start cursing, and the other person says, 'Oh, what foul language.' My mother used to do this. Your point doesn't get across because all you can then talk about is that. That's what I feel like – they throw all this other stuff in: Is it theater, is it this, is it that? It clouds the issues. But at the same time I think that Native people have to do Native theater. Sure you can go out and do other theater, but I'm interested in control of your product, your production. I'm interested in doing it all the way, Native playwright,

Native actors, Native director, and then see what happens! When we're talking, a lot of times people get angry at us: 'Well, you can only do Indian theater.' But a lot of times we hit people because it is universal, it can be universal. But no one allows us to be universal.

I've stood by and watched non-Native directors, famous directors, open [Native actors] up, take things out, examine them, and put them back in a different way and not in a good way. There was no taking care of these Native people. So, if you opened them up and you showed everything, then you expected them to show up at ten o'clock the next day and you're shocked that they went on a drinking spree? You had no idea who these people were.

AH: So the need to control your own work grows out of not just the content of the pieces themselves, but a need to safeguard against processes that don't honor who you are?

MM: I had to learn my lesson many times before I said, 'Oh, I understand this.' But it took a long time for me to figure that out.

The way I see it is that we can only control our own work. We can't control what other people do and what other people think. Our problem of course is not that we can't control that; it's that because they are the ones in control of a lot of stuff, people will accept and listen to [their version] easier than what we are saying. So we really have to be out there saying our things in all kinds of different ways so that it's heard. And sometimes it's good work, sometimes it's cheesy work, sometimes it's 'Indian lore.' White people do sitcoms, television, and they write short plays, revise things, they write good plays, they write bad plays. Whatever. No one says that you shouldn't do that, and they have control of their stuff. It's always the indigenous people, us, Maoris, and Aboriginals – we're the animals you have to control, and we're only one-sided. In order to move past that, some of us go astray. Some of us hang in there. Some go into the popular culture.

We have special things because we are closer to the earth, we are closer to whatever that realm is. But at the same time we are living on this sphere, so we share a lot of things that everybody else shares. To me, to say that we can't do this or we can't do that is wrong, as well as feeling bad when my type says they sold out. That's wrong, too. What I like and what I dislike and what I see and what I want to see – all those things come under the heading of Native theater.

And even the ones that are living, like my tribe [Kuna] really does live in centuries back. They still live in thatched houses. They're near Colombia, and drugs and things are coming through and it's a worry. The young men want to leave. They want to go to the barrios of Panama. That's much more exciting than living on an island. This is about that persistence of memory that I talk about all the time. That persistence of memory, we have to drag it from centuries back to bring with us. No matter where we go, what we do, we are different. We are different because we were here first, and that is something that people don't want to touch with a ten-foot pole.

NOTES

1. See Charlotte Canning, *Feminist Theaters in the U.S.A.: Staging Women's Experience* (New York: Routledge, 1996); Sue-Ellen Case, *Feminism and Theater* (New York: Routledge, 1988); Jill Dolan, *The Feminist Spectator as Critic* (Ann Arbor: University of Michigan Press, 1988); Rebecca Schneider, *The Explicit Body in Performance* (New York: Routledge, 1997).

2. For example, W. B. Worthen includes Tomson Highway's *Dry Lips Oughta Move to Kapuskasing* in *The Harcourt Brace Anthology of Drama, 3rd Ed.* (New York: Harcourt, 1999); Helen Gilbert and JoAnne Tompkins analyze Monique Mojica's *Princess Pocahontas and the Blue Spots* in *Post-colonial Drama: Theory, Practice, Politics* (London: Routledge, 1996). For a bibliography of critical resources on Native theater, see the 'Resources' section of Hanay Geiogamah and Jaye T. Darby (eds), *American Indian Theater in Performance: A Reader* (UCLA American Indian Studies Center, 2000).

3. This is only a brief summary of some of their work, limited to those performances which have been published. For more details (though still in summary form) of their recent work, as well as the work of other Native women playwrights, see Ann Haugo, ''Circles upon Circles upon Circles': American Indian Women in Theater and Performance,' in Geiogamah and Darby, *American Indian Theater.*

4. Founding members were Muriel Miguel, Gloria Miguel, Lisa Mayo, Lois Weaver, Pamela Verge, and Nadya Beye.

5. Muriel Miguel's daughter is Murielle Borst, an actor and playwright who works out of New York City. Gloria Miguel's daughter is Monique Mojica, an actor and playwright who works out of Toronto.

6. Developed in 1980, *Sun, Moon, and Feather* was the first performance piece in which the Miguel sisters — Muriel, Gloria Miguel, and Lisa Mayo — performed on their own as Spiderwoman. A 30-minute video-cassette of the performance, directed by Muriel Miguel, is available from New York's Cinema Guild, and the script has been published in two anthologies. See Hanay Geiogamah and Jaye T. Darby (eds), *Stories of Our Way: An Anthology of American Indian Plays* (Los Angeles: UCLA American Indian Studies Center, 1999) and Kathy Perkins and Roberta Uno (eds), *Contemporary Plays by Women of Color* (New York: Routledge, 1996).

7. *Neurotic Erotic Exotics* was developed while Spiderwoman was in residence with the Minneapolis-based feminist theater company At the Foot of the Mountain. The program lists Muriel Miguel as director, with Lisa Mayo and Gloria Miguel as co-directors. The performance ensemble was made up of seven women: Antoinette Biami, Shirley Duggan, Sophronia Liu, Esther Ouray, Ramona Rivera, Carmen Valenzuela, and Angelita Velasco. Spiderwoman and At the Foot of the Mountain collaborated to explore the connections between and differences among women of color.

8. Spiderwoman's residency at Gila River and Ak Chin was sponsored by Atlatl, Inc., (the National Service Organization for Native American Arts) and Arizona State University as part of an audience development project, 'Drawing the Lines,'

funded primarily by the Lila Wallace Arts Partners program. Spiderwoman is sometimes invited by educational or community/reservation organizations to complete a residency which includes performance-building in the community. In addition to the project at the Gila River Reservation, for example, they have done work for the Minnesota American Indian AIDS Task Force's Ogitchigag Gikinooamaagad (Warrior/Teacher) Peer Education Program, working with urban Native youth. Out of this residency grew a performance entitled *Ni Nokomisug Zahgay* (*My Grandmother's Love*). In this piece, which was part education about protecting oneself from HIV and part reminder of community responsibility for all members, children constructed a shield, at the center of which were pictures of their grandmothers. (Thanks to Sharon Day, founder of the Ogitchigag Players and sponsor of Spiderwoman's residency there, for help with the Ojibwe titles.)

9. Spiderwoman's first piece, *Women in Violence*, premièred in January 1976 at New York City's American Indian Community House (AICH), which was then located on 38th Street. Then called 'Spiderwoman Theater Workshop,' the ensemble included Muriel and Gloria Miguel, Lisa Mayo, Pamela Verge, Lois Weaver, and Brandy Penn. For this piece, the performers each found within themselves a personal clown, a persona which reflected something about their identities and which helped to reveal to the audience – and in some cases, to the performer herself – personal violences she had confronted. For more information on *Women in Violence*, see Canning, *Feminist Theaters*, and Ann Haugo, 'Native Playwrights Newsletter Interview: Lisa Mayo,' in Geiogamah and Darby, *American Indian Theater*.

10. Spiderwoman has in their repertoire a lecture-demonstration which they perform for community and academic audiences, particularly during long residencies when they're called upon to do many things, from workshops and performance facilitation, to performances of their own. It is a fluid piece which they are likely to adjust for each audience, depending on demographics.

11. Deborah Ratelle, Spiderwoman's stage manager.

12. Monique Mojica (Kuna/Rappahannock), Gloria Miguel's daughter, is a Toronto-based actor and playwright. She edited a 1991 special Native theater issue of *Canadian Theatre Review*. See her introduction to that issue, entitled 'A Tool towards the Healing' (68, Fall 1991). Dianne Reyner (Kiowa) has developed a website for Native theater: http://www.haskell.edu/playwrights/playwrights.htm

13. 'Storyweaving: Storytelling, Oral Tradition, and Collective Creation,' Miller Comm Lecture at the University of Illinois – Urbana-Champaign, 2 October 1996. The quotation is reprinted from Haugo, ' "Circles upon Circles upon Circles".'

14. The Miguel sisters grew up performing in sideshows with their father and uncles. In some performances, they use images from this period of their lives, superimposing their live bodies, on stage, over slides or film of the sideshow performances.

15. Before Miguel organized Spiderwoman, she had created another performance group called Womanspace. See Canning, *Feminist Theaters*, pp. 94–5.

16. A retelling of Chekhov's *The Three Sisters*, Spiderwoman's *The Three Sisters from Here to There* (1982) relocated the story to New York City, where three Native sisters dreamed of getting from Brooklyn to Manhattan. See Dolan, *The Feminist Spectator*, pp. 111–12.

17. Created while Spiderwoman was on tour in Europe, *Fittin' Room* premièred in New York City in the fall of 1980 and would be the last piece that the full company created together. The next pieces were the separately conceived productions of *Split Britches* and *Sun, Moon, and Feather*. *Fittin' Room* explored categories which women were 'supposed' to 'fit.'

Chay Yew
Photo courtesy of Northwest Asian American Theater

15

Los Angeles intersections: Chay Yew

David Román

Chay Yew and I met in his West Hollywood home on January 16, 2000 to talk about his work in the theater. I first met Chay when I was living in New York and his production of *A Language of Their Own* was playing at the Public Theater in 1995. That production, which was directed by Keng Sen Ong and performed by a quartet of excellent actors – B. D. Wong, Alec Mapa, Francis Jue, and David Drake – marked the first time I had seen one of Chay's plays staged. I've been lucky enough to see various productions of Chay's work since the New York performance of *Language*, including Tim Dang's intensely powerful staging of Chay's *Whitelands* trilogy at East West Players in 1995. *Whitelands* comprises *Porcelain*, *A Language of Their Own*, and *Half Lives* and was staged by East West Players in repertory to mark their 30th year anniversary season of producing and presenting Asian American theater. The three plays in *The Whitelands Trilogy* are lyrical and dramatic meditations on the nature of desire and sexuality, on the fragmentation of identity and community, and on the often dangerous friction between our private and public selves. Together these plays significantly shifted the poetic and political landscape of both Asian American theater and gay theater.[1] This trilogy was followed by three new plays: *Red*, which premièred in 1998 at Seattle's Intiman Theater and was directed by Lisa Peterson, *A Beautiful Country*, which was produced in 1998 in Los Angeles by Cornerstone Theater Company and was directed by the playwright, and *Wonderland*, a complete reworking of the earlier *Half Lives* play, which premièred at La Jolla Playhouse in 1999 and was also directed by Lisa Peterson.

Chay's work is distinguished for its poetic meditations on difference, for its haunting ruminations on home, for its aesthetic innovations on tradition. Chay's plays have been produced by a diverse range of venues, from established regional theaters, such as those mentioned above, to community-based theaters throughout the United States such as Northwest Asian

American Theater, Theater Rhino, and the Group Theater. Since the première of *Language* at the Public, Chay has emerged as one of the most significant new playwrights in American theater.[2] However, what most people don't realize is that he is also a producer and director of Asian American theater. We spoke just before the opening of his latest directorial undertaking, a revival of David Henry Hwang's *Golden Child* at East West Players. He was also in the midst of moving the successful run of Alec Mapa's solo *tour de force, I Remember Mapa*, which Chay directed, from San Francisco to Seattle. I asked him to begin by talking about his work with other Asian American artists.

DAVID ROMÁN: We know you primarily as a playwright but you are also a Resident Artist at the Mark Taper Forum and the Director of the Asian Theater Workshop there. You're also the Resident Director at East West Players. Tell us a little about these roles. Let's begin with the Asian Theater Workshop at the Taper. How would you describe it?

CHAY YEW: The Asian Theater Workshop's genesis was five years ago when the Taper offered me an artistic residency through the Andrew W. Mellon Foundation fellowship they had received. At first, I felt it in my skin that it was simply an affirmative action gesture to include an Asian American in their artistic staff. In our initial meetings, I told them I was only interested in being a part of the Taper if I was able to found a theater lab that developed Asian American theater. To my surprise, they readily agreed. The grant has since expired. However, the Taper has continued its steadfast support to the lab. I designed ATW to develop new work and plays by emerging and established Asian American playwrights. Our program includes commissioning new plays, developing and workshopping plays and performance pieces, and producing new work. I also mentor young playwrights and directors who intern with me, and dramaturg emerging writers' new plays. We have a public reading series where we showcase new Asian American plays written by Han Ong, Alice Tuan, Diana Son, Sung Rno, Elizabeth Wong, and David Henry Hwang. Their plays have ultimately gone on to be produced at Seattle Rep, Public Theater, East West Players, and many theaters in the country. We also produce the Black Box Series where we have free-to-public workshops of performance work. Past participants included performers Leilani Chan, Justin Chin, Noel Alumit, and Dawn Akemi Saito, theater composer Nathan Wang, and poets Chungmi Kim and Russell Leong, to mention a few. This series allows the performer an opportunity to incorporate audience response into their works-in-progress. Inversely these workshops allow audiences to understand the creative process of theater artists. Once in a while, we hold the Lounge Conversation Series where we invite Asian American theater artists to speak about their craft and process. Guests have included set designer Loy Arcenas, playwright Philip Kan Gotanda, and actors Tsai Chin and Sandra Oh.

DR: Aside from developing new work, does the Asian Theater Workshop also mount its own productions?

CY: It was not my original intention for ATW to produce. The Taper does have a mission to represent the diverse communities of Los Angeles on its main stage. However, like any other theater institutions without a second stage, the economics and aesthetics of the theater rarely afforded more Asian American plays to be given productions. There had not been any Asian American representations on the Taper main stage for many years, and that is a poor record.[3] Part of my mission at ATW is to develop a pipeline of potential Asian American plays for the main stage. I was also unwilling to be held hostage by the dreaded regional theater play development machinery. I didn't see the point of it and didn't have the patience for it. I strongly felt that creating and developing all this work only to see it languish on the shelves of my office was an utter waste of my time and the artists'. I decided to produce some of these works via ATW and to forward the work to other theaters around the country. Hence, I produce Asian American work on the periphery of the Taper. We try to. One every year at least. And given a very small annual budget, I try to be entrepreneurial by partnering with the smaller 99-seat theaters and East West Players to produce new theater work.[4] This allows ATW to produce new work cost efficiently, and in turn, gives the partnering theater a new production enhanced technically and financially with help from the Taper. In 1996, we produced *Hymn to Her*, a celebration of the voice of Asian American women in the theater. That festival included performance, a reading of monologues written for Asian women and music. Margaret Cho, Lauren Tom, Jude Narita, Jennifer Paz, and Jacqueline Kim were some of the participants. The following year we produced *Two at the Too*, a double-bill of solo works from Sandra Tsing Loh and Alec Mapa. The year after that, we collaborated with Cornerstone Theater and East West Players to produce *A Beautiful Country*, a documentary theatrical project that explored the 150 years of Asian American immigrant history. This past year, we presented *Word Up! A Festival of Asian American Performance*, which was a festival of solo work by Dan Kwong, Denise Uyehara, Alice Tuan, Eric Steinberg, Amy Hill, Dennis Dun, and many others. We managed to give four shows a world première run and others a workshop that eventually led to productions at Highways Performance Space and East West Players later that year. We continue to produce work every year given our very finite budget.

DR: What's remarkable about this work is that it diverts from the idea that work should only – or even primarily – be developed for the main stage. Anyone who's lived in Los Angeles knows by now that the Taper is not the place to see the works of playwrights and performers of color staged with any regularity. Here, instead, we see how you've been able to use your position at an elite theater institution to generate new work and stage it throughout the city with the Taper's imprint. This seems to be a mutually beneficial system for everyone: the theater, the artists, the audiences. Rather than simply waiting around for a mainstage production, a production that may not even happen, and placing all of one's energy there, ATW has found a way to use the resources of the Taper to the advantage of the artists and the Asian American community. I'm not suggesting that Asian American artists – or any other artists for that matter – should relinquish mainstage ambitions. ATW seems to have come up with a way to both develop new work for potential productions on the regional theater circuit and stage actual theater and performance events in Los Angeles.

CY: I hope to continue offering resources and support. It's something that I would've wanted to have when I started out as a playwright, and now that I have an artistic home at the Taper, I feel it is vital to open the doors to other performers, playwrights, and actors in the city.

DR: It's important that the Taper, as the premier regional theater in Los Angeles, help support artists of color. And it's clear that the Asian Theater Workshop has done lots of interesting work precisely through its affiliation with the Taper. But, as you know, most people know the Taper primarily through their mainstage productions.

CY: The Taper has been nationally known for their diverse artistic staff and play development programs. While it is easy to point the finger at the Taper for not producing plays of color on the main stage, much of the work that has been developed and produced in the Taper's more intimate venues, for example the 'Taper, Too' season, which I am producing, starting June 2000, includes the world premières of *Black Butterfly, Jaguar, Piñata Woman, and Other Superhero Girls Like Me*; *Drive My Coche*; *Weights*; and *The Square*, all of which have been written by a slew of Latino, Asian American, Black, White, and gay playwrights whom the Taper has commissioned and developed. Next season, we will present on the main stage August Wilson's *King Hedley II*, Charlayne Woodard's *In Real Life*, David Henry Hwang's rewritten book of *Flower Drum Song*, Marc Wolf's *Another American*, and John Belluso's *Body of Bourne*. I believe this is diversity at work in American theater. Aside from the Public Theater in New York and New WORLD Theater in Amherst, there are very few theaters in this country that can boast of such a multicultural palette.

DR: That's certainly true, although most of these works you mention are the works that will circulate nationally. But, you're right, the Taper's peer institutions – Manhattan Theater Club, Lincoln Center, American Repertory Theater, even Berkeley Rep – are stunningly conservative on this issue of diversity and these are theaters that are located in racially diverse cities! It's really amazing when you think of it. If it weren't for George C. Wolfe, the color of theater in New York would be strikingly different. Not that it's only George Wolfe who's doing the work – but as a producer and as a director, we need to give him credit for significantly changing the landscape of theater in New York City and by extension the rest of the country. Let's not forget that he offered you your first New York production.

CH: He's been an influential mentor and supporter. I admire his commitment to theater and to making theater relevant to the community.

DR: You seem to follow in those footsteps. The Asian Theater Workshop also produces other kinds of cultural events that educate audiences about larger social and political issues. Tell me about the Workshop's presentation of Wei Jingsheng's *The Courage to Stand Alone*, which you directed in the summer of 1997.

CH: At the time, Wei Jingsheng was an imprisoned Chinese political dissident. Nominated numerous times for the Nobel Peace Prize, he was kept in jail for many years for criticizing the Communist government in China in his writings on the Democracy Wall. Wei was recently released to the U.S. for medical care but I hear he's already planning on slipping back into China, risking further imprisonment, to stir up the democracy movement there. During his imprisonment he had written many letters to the late Deng Xiaoping, China's Premier, urging and challenging him to reform China into a democratic state. On the anniversary of the Tiananmen Square riots in 1997, we presented a reading of his inspiring letters with a dramatization of his life and struggles at the Taper.

DR: Many people went to the Taper that night to become educated around the issue. There was a panel discussion afterwards with a U.S. State Representative and former Chinese dissidents who'd also gone through what Wei Jingsheng had experienced. Although the evening provided a forum to talk about the issue, it also proved to be compelling drama.

CY: That was a most gratifying project on many levels. With *The Courage to Stand Alone*, we were able to inform the Los Angeles audience on the issues of human rights and democracy in China, and more importantly, to tell the life and struggles of this courageous and remarkable man. After the dramatic presentation, the audience was heatedly engaged in civic dialogue with the panelists. I remember thinking to myself, 'Yeah, that's the immediacy of theater. That's what theater can do.'

DR: Can you comment on the larger artistic community of Los Angeles? I think most people think of L.A. as primarily an industry town for television and film and don't necessarily see it as a theater town. And when they do think of L.A. theater, it's generally imagined to be a showcase for one of these other major industries. You seem to be the exception to that rule. It also seems to me that most of the people that you work with actually see themselves as theater artists.

CY: I don't think anyone deliberately moves to Los Angeles to work in theater. I think actors, directors, and writers want to be in film or television for economic, artistic or egocentric reasons, or all three of them. And when they realize their 15 minutes will not be handed to them on a silver platter, they do something to attract the attention of casting agents: they start their theater companies. In part, that's why we have this image of theater being a showcase for actors and writers, and in part, some of these theaters are actually formed in response to the film and TV industry as if to say 'We can do this acting and writing thing better.' And a few of these individuals do decide to stay in the theater. Some find provocative and challenging ways to create new work. Don't get me wrong, not all L.A. theater is interesting. For one enlightening moment in L.A. theater, there are ten horrible productions you have to sit through. The other wonderful thing about the L.A. theater scene is that because it's so geographically far from New York, we can actually redefine theatrical aesthetics, form, and content, and also to some extent, create them without deference to New York. That's the L.A. theater movement: uniquely different and individual, and blessed with very good actors. As a result of this, some interesting theater companies have been born.

DR: What companies are you thinking of?

CY: Actors' Gang, Fabulous Monsters, Highways Performance Space, Bottom's Dream, City Garage, Playwrights Arena, East West Players, Cornerstone Theater, Indecent Exposure, Circle X, LA Poverty Department, and Open Fist are great examples.

DR: Highways is actually a performance space that presents new work and not an actual theater company. I was on the board of Highways for five years, serving even as its chair for close to two years. Not many of the artists who we presented or who saw Highways as their artistic home aspired to work in film and television. These artists, for the most part, were drawn to create alternative performance outside of the major entertainment industries of Los Angeles.

CY: Highways is unique in that way; they've played an important role in this region. Dan Kwong, who has been a resident artist there for many years, curates a wonderful festival of Asian American performance every year. 'Treasure in the House' is one of the most exciting festivals of its kind and it's opened up Highways to many Asian American artists.

DR: Dan's events brought in not only new artists but also – and equally important – he brought in new audiences. This leads me to my next point. L.A. theater is also often associated with 'multiculturalism,' if for no other reason than the city's rapidly changing demographics. Beginning in the late 1980s, many theaters tried to do outreach to under-represented communities or applied for grants targeted for specific kinds of audience development. Do you think there was a mandate at a certain point – maybe in the late 1980s, early 1990s – for multiculturalism? And do you think there's still an interest in Los Angeles for race-related work?

CY: There was definitely more of a conscious attempt to program theater seasons multiculturally during that time. That was largely due to mandates in funding. I strongly believe that was a good thing. Theaters began to program plays of color that eventually found their way into the American theater vernacular; I am speaking of the August Wilsons, David Hwangs, Eduardo Machados. Now that there are fewer mandates in funding for multicultural work, only a handful of theaters are consciously programming and seeking plays of color in their seasons. I think the notion of a truly American theater is a myth in this country. A truly American theater should and must program all the diverse myriad voices that reflected and represented the United States. Show me a theater season that boasts of new plays and classics, a season with African American plays, Latino plays and Asian American plays in the mix with their usual fare of Shakespeares, David Hares or A. R. Gurneys. These theaters are rare and few. Most American theater companies don't even reflect their immediate communities in their productions. And theater managers are wondering why their audiences are dwindling and why audiences of color are not coming to their theaters. Maybe that's why I prefer to work out here in L.A. or New York where multiculturalism isn't only at work, but is a reality. When the larger White theater institutions do not open their doors to audiences and artists of color, the smaller theater companies are birthed. This was the case with East West Players.

DR: Do you see much collaboration between people of different races in the theater? I'm wondering if there are ways to bring in people to think about race on a broader level than just single-theme plays about the experiences of one particular cultural group – Asian Americans, Latinos, Polish Americans. José Rivera does this in his plays. His plays not only expand our understanding of Latinos by including Latino characters from different national backgrounds, they also show Latinos in a world populated by people from all kinds of cultural backgrounds. This not only provides a more realistic sense of living in a multicultural world, but it also makes for really interesting drama. You're now moving in that direction also. Do you see more opportunities now for people of different races and cultural backgrounds to work together – and not just behind the scenes as part of the creative or production team – to produce work that actually thematizes this point?

CY: I think there's a great opportunity for us to do that. My only concern is whether the intention to create that multicultural work is honest. Is it to satisfy a grant? Is it just to create something multicultural because it's hip and politically correct? Then I strongly question the integrity of such a project. The result will be a project that doesn't seem alive, or honest, or real. That's not art. That's product.

DR: I'm not so sure that 'multicultural' is so hip anymore – especially in the state of California! In fact, I think the recent wave of anti-immigrant, anti-affirmative action, and anti-queer initiatives that we've seen in California in the past decade have, in fact, given license to many people to explictly act out against multiculturalism. Anyway, I was thinking less of these potentially exploitative projects and was thinking instead of work that sets out to represent a multicultural world. Certain artists are already at the forefront of this and not just José Rivera. Anna Deavere Smith, Danny Hoch, and Cornerstone Theater also come to mind. Their work is very much alive and committed to contemporary concerns. You've also commissioned an interesting play that addresses this topic. Can you tell me about *The Square* and what you had in mind for this project?

CY: *The Square* is an epic project that attempted to bring a host of playwrights to create work that comments on their own individual perceptions of Asian America. So I approached Mac Wellman, David Hwang, Philip Gotanda, Connie Congdon, and Ping Chong if they were interested in writing ten-minute plays set in Columbus Park in New York's Chinatown. And the rest of the roster of playwrights included José Rivera, Maria Irene Fornes, Diana Son, Jessica Hagedorn, Craig Lucas, Bridget Carpenter, Robert O'Hara, Kia Corthron, Han Ong, Alice Tuan, and me. Lisa Peterson, the Resident Director and my colleague at the Taper, would direct.

DR: So the Asian American playwrights wrote about non-Asian American characters and the non-Asians wrote about Asian Americans?

CY: Well, yes and no. The playwrights were assigned a list of four criteria picked randomly by Lisa and me. Basically, the four categories included the number of actors, racial make-up, broad themes, and four time periods – 1880s, 1920s, 1960s, and 2000. The wonderful thing about watching this play is you are witnessing Asian American history of the last 120 years, and different and marvelous voices of American theater of the last 30 years. I remember saying, during *The Square*'s workshop production at the Taper's 1997 New Works Festival, 'Oh, that's a Ping Chong play, that's a Mac Wellman play, and that's an Irene Fornes play.' I mentioned earlier that there was a lack of a second space at the Taper. In June and July of 2000, I will be producing the second season at the Taper called 'Taper, Too.' We will be presenting four productions in a 99-seat theater in Los Angeles, and *The Square* would be one of them. It has been a long journey for *The Square* as it was one of the first projects I conceived when I founded Asian Theater Workshop five years ago. I'm very pleased that this project is finally a reality.

DR: Can you talk about how it is you started directing? What drew you to this new artistic practice and what kinds of works are you yourself drawn to work on?

CY: I think directing is a natural extension of playwriting. Creating a world on paper is the first step. Creating the same world on stage is another. Being a playwright informs my directorial sense, and vice versa. I'm always protective of the playwright and the play, ensuring I'm always serving the play. The most wonderful thing is painting the visual picture and breathing life into the playwright's words. I most recently directed both David Henry Hwang's *Golden Child* and Alec Mapa's one-man show *Pointless* at East West Players.[5] Aside from plays, I have directed scores of solo work. Partially, it was always economically feasible to produce a solo show. Partially, I believe that some of the theater work I found most socio-political and urgent is solo work. Right now I am in pre-production for Seattle-based performer David Schmader's incisive and funny *Straight*, which is about gay conversion therapy for a June 2000 production at Highways. I have directed *Depth Becomes Her*, Sandra Tsing Loh's witty and provocative look at multicultural Los Angeles; *Talking with My Hands*, James Sie's touching and insightful journey about being biracial; *Maps of Body and City*, Denise Uyehara's life as a Japanese American girl coming of age in California; *I Remember Mapa*, Alec Mapa's account of being a gay outsider in an otherwise exclusive entertainment industry. There was also an international collaboration of multidisciplinary artists whom I worked with –

DR: Up at the Northwest Asian American Theater in Seattle, right?

CY: Yes, in January of 1998, at NWATT. It was an exciting challenge to work with Asian artists from different disciplines from both America and Asia to create a work called *Home: Places between Asia and America*. The collaborators were a Singapore shaman dancer, a Malaysian choreographer, a Seattle-based solo performer, and Suzie Kozawa, a composer who makes music with found objects. I wrote the performance text and directed the project. It was my first collaborative work and to speak simultaneously in Mandarin, Cantonese, and in English felt more like a session at the U.N. than a rehearsal day. Despite some initial language difficulties, we were constantly learning from each other and were continually inspired to explore different aesthetics. I guess I particularly felt at home because I was able to explore both my Western and Eastern philosophies and aesthetics.

DR: This kind of transnational exchange and collaboration is important, especially given the rise of global capitalism and the World Wide Web. While there's a long history of interculturalism in performance, there seems to be a new opportunity for U.S. artists to now share resources with cultures outside of the States. It's also interesting to see how these collaborations then shape your own work. I've heard you say that the Seattle project informed *A Beautiful Country*, your recent play about Asian American immigration.

CY: Yeah, I think it did. *A Beautiful Country* was commissioned by Cornerstone Theater Company, a theater company who reaches out to myriad communities in Los Angeles through theater. When artistic director Bill Rauch approached me, I said I would be very interested in creating a show on-site in L.A.'s Chinatown. Cornerstone is primarily known for adapting classic Western plays for different communities but, at the time, I was very preoccupied about learning more about the history of Los Angeles and, in particular, Chinatown. I was also passionate about documentary theater, the theatrical forms that Emily Mann and Anna Deavere Smith created. Coming off from *Home*, I also wanted to explore the concept of Mike Leigh's devised theater; I then employed musical theater, dance, percussionists, slides, video, film, and the testimonials of several local Chinatown residents. Add all of that up with an immigrant Asian drag queen as your guide, you get *A Beautiful Country* which was a significant theatrical experience for me.[6]

DR: *A Beautiful Country*, which is so much about Asian American history and culture, seems to be a major departure from your earlier plays, which focus on the intimate relations between and among people. *A Beautiful Country* takes on the questions of transnationalism, citizenship, and the force of history much more aggressively than the earlier plays. Do you see this as a progression of a theme or a new concern of yours? Let's talk a little about your plays and their major themes. Is there a story that you tell that begins with *Porcelain*?

CY: There were a few contributing factors. Firstly, I guess I've always been a closeted Asian American. In actual fact, I'm an immigrant from Singapore. And, like most immigrants when they arrive in America, they either cling on to their past histories fiercely, or co-opt the history of the country they land in. I did the latter. The history and culture of White America through movies, novels, and television. But I longed for a connection, a deeper one, to my adopted country. And I finally found that connection in the immigrant experiences of Asian Americans while researching *A Beautiful Country*. It was then I didn't feel alone anymore; I felt strangely at home in this country. So I chose to express these new feelings and thoughts through subsequent plays. Secondly, I was aware that my theatrical canvas was enlarged after *Language*. I attributed that to my being at the Mark Taper Forum. I had always loved working in the smaller and intimate spaces, and my early plays reflected that chamber-like quality. Under Taper artistic director Gordon Davidson, I was very much influenced by his passion for socio-political theater. All my plays written during my residency at the Taper explore the complexities of humanity in the context of environment, politics, and race. I don't really know if there's a specific thematic journey that resonates from *Porcelain* to *Wonderland*, except for a chronological one. But some recurring themes do appear in the plays, for example the outsider's place in the world is one of them, and the question of home is another. As an immigrant to this country, I guess I'm constantly trying to find and define the concept of home through my plays. Each play is different from the other, stylistically as well as content. I guess I'm always a little self-conscious about repeating myself. The only way for me to sit down and write a play is that the world of the play has to be intriguing to me, and the way to tell the story has to be challenging. My plays also indicate my psychological being at the time when they were written: *Porcelain* was about how I fit into straight White America; *Language* was about my falling in and out of love; *Red* was about why I work in the theater and what I would sacrifice to keep doing it; and *Wonderland* was about finding happiness in life and fighting the demons of mediocrity and compromise. That's why I am always embarrassed to revisit an old play. It's like seeing myself again at 18, embarrassed by the childish obsessions, needs, and desires of that age. I guess I'm older and more jaded now.

DR: I think one thing that distinguishes your work from other contemporary work in American theater is that you really do ruminate on major tragic themes. You don't really work in the genre of comedy, even though you might have some humorous moments in your plays. Your plays are very tragic, they take on big themes; they address either the missed opportunities or denied opportunities of Asian Americans. Your characters struggle to improve their position in the world. We see them come up against all kinds of obstacles including their own deeply felt ambivalence about being 'Asian.' For the most part these plays do not have happy endings.

CY: I guess the most memorable stories I have read, seen on the stage, TV, or in the movies have always been tragedies. Tragedies indirectly uplift souls and celebrate life. They force you to confront your life, the decisions you have made, the questions of the society and God. There is such great complex humanity in these stories too. For example, *Wild Duck* and *Enemy of the People* deal with the high cost a person has to pay in order to stand by their own beliefs and moralities. And to endure the devastating consequences are heroes born. I continue to learn about myself and life itself through these great stories. I find Shakespeare's tragedies more resounding than his comedies. I still take to bed the lessons of Lear, Macbeth, Brutus, and Othello. They are lessons for a lifetime.

DR: The other thing about your work is that you are very generous with your characters – and, by extension, your actors – because your work is so poetic. Your characters have these very moving extended monologues which reveal their world-view and which makes us empathize, in part, with their situations.

CY: I think that comes from my influences by playwrights like Tennessee Williams, Arthur Miller, Strindberg, Chekhov, and Sondheim. The emotions and passions of their characters are fraught with such complexity and depth; their plays articulated with colorful images and language that continue to linger in my mind's eye and drown in my heart. That's what drew me to write for the theater in the first place. I must also credit the countless hours of music and art lessons my mother forced me to take for me to fully appreciate Debussy, J.S. Bach, Beethoven, Schiele, and Caravaggio, who were important to me while I was growing up.

DR: You are a child of high culture! I was raised on *I Love Lucy* and Diana Ross and the Supremes. My first theater outings were to productions of *Jesus Christ Superstar* and *Godspell*. My parents, who were both born in Colombia, raised us Catholic, which meant that while you were practicing Debussy and Bach on the piano, I was singing 'I Don't Know how to Love Him' and 'Day by Day' at the weekly folk mass where I played guitar.

CY: That's why we are such good friends!

DR: Indeed! Well, that was my life in South Jersey in the 1970s. Let's get back to Los Angeles in the year 2000. Do you think there's support for the arts in Los Angeles?

CY: Not as much as I'd like it to be. But I think this not only an L.A. dilemma but a national one. I find it disturbing that there's a concerted effort in Congress to effectively defund the National Endowment for the Arts. We are a superpower that does not support the arts, and I can rattle off a list of smaller nations that do. This is a country where the freedom of speech is prized and yet the opportunities to express oneself in art are rare and few. When we go to museums, do we not realize that art is what endures? Empires rise and fall, but art ultimately represents the legacy civilizations leave behind. And here in one of the greatest countries in the world we refuse to support our artists. Aside from the government, it's disappointing in this day and age when today's industrialists and business leaders are not giving money to non-profit and art organizations. In the early part of last century, we had Carnegies, the Mellons, and the Rockefellers. They gave away part of their immense wealth to cities and organizations, to found new universities, museums, concert halls, and public places. There was great philanthropy and civic responsibility, and, as a result, much of their legacies have made a deep impact in the American culture. And now our contemporary Bill Gateses and Michael Eisners have not been giving much to the arts. I find that the government's battle over federal funding for the arts and the state of institutional giving criminal.

DR: That's such a strong statement, can you explain what you mean by that?

CY: Is it? Children in schools have their music and arts programs eliminated. We have studies about how music and arts education enhances children's intellectual development and affords them opportunities of self-expression. Now, many small theater companies around the country, and in L.A., are closing their doors because there's no funding. We are the richest and most democratic country in the world. I don't see why we have to beg for all these things. It's really sad when one day all we have left to show of our late twentieth century are music videos, video games, and Pokemon.

DR: You're also lucky because you seem to have two resident homes, one at the Taper where you also work closely with the other people who are affiliated with the Taper, whether it's Gordon Davidson, Lisa Peterson, or Luis Alfaro, and you also have a home as resident director at East West Players. Due to your work in these two theaters, you seem to have built a bridge between the Taper and East West Players. Do you think you'll continue those relationships?

CY: Definitely. There is a distinct lack of proper play development in most Asian American theater companies. Given their limited resources, the Taper's Asian Theater Workshop also serves as a venue where we commission and develop plays with the intention of finding them homes in Asian American theaters; Prince Gomolvilas's *Big Hunk o' Burnin' Love* is a recent example which was workshopped and developed at ATW and was eventually produced at East West Players. Also, we co-produce many productions and events with East West, Northwest Asian American Theater Company in Seattle and Asian American Theater Company in San Francisco, thereby lowering production costs, sharing production resources, and broadening audiences; Alice Tuan's *Ikebana*, 'Word Up! Festival,' *A Beautiful Country* and both Alec Mapa's solo shows, *I Remember Mapa* and *Pointless*, come to mind. I'm extremely proud of ATW's partnership with these theaters through the years. Personally, East West and the Taper have been the most important part of my career for the last five years. I have been able to flex my muscles in playwriting, directing, producing, and dramaturging. That is because I have the opportunity to come into the theater every day, observe rehearsals, participate in production meetings, and spend time in the company of theater artists. I am constantly being informed and challenged artistically. And, more importantly, these two theaters have allowed me to practice my craft.

DR: This idea of institutional support and theatrical community seems critical to the future of American theater. Your experience seems highly unusual. Most artists don't have access to these kinds of institutions and the day-to-day experiences that you mention.

CY: Presently, there are only a few artistic homes readily available to theater artists. I find that very troubling and disappointing, particularly in New York, where you have some of the best theaters in the country that do not open their doors as homes for these artists. My question is, do theaters produce these playwrights, or hold them on a leash by doing an umpteenth reading of their new plays? American playwrights don't write for readings. These plays need to be produced. And by being produced is where the playwright learns his or her craft. That's the strange dance that's going around with American theaters.

DR: But it is an important one too. Emerging playwrights benefit from these associations with established institutions. Although I agree that the development process at regional theaters can lead to a form of paralysis where artists don't move into the next step which is production.

CY: My advice to younger writers has always been: 'Don't ever be that barbarian at the gate because more often than not, the theaters will never let you in. Instead what you need to do is produce your own plays. Be more entrepreneurial. Start your own theater companies. Start your own artistic homes.' How can you learn from your play? It's by watching it come alive. You're never going to learn much about your play hearing it or seeing it in countless workshops and readings. Once it comes alive with a group of actors who have lived with the play for several weeks and in front of an audience, then you will see your play come to life. And from that experience, it will make you write the next play and the next and the next. Some of these theater companies include San Francisco's Campos Santo, San Diego's Sledgehammer, Seattle's Printer's Devil Theater, and Austin's Frontera Theater. They produce exciting new work. They're young and energetic and it's wonderful to see the seeds of tomorrow's American theater taking root.

DR: Asian American theater has a rich and complicated history; it can't be reduced to a handful of playwrights anymore. It's a much more diverse field now. Can you comment a little bit on the general status of Asian American theater?

CY: Asian American theater is flourishing more every year. There are more Asian American theaters being established in the last four years, and new Asian American plays are getting produced in Asian American theaters and regional theaters. Some Asian American theaters concentrate on performance work and some on traditional arts and dances, while most produce plays largely for an Asian audience. It's refreshing to see a diversity of work coming out of these theaters. Recently, we had our first-ever national Asian American theater convening in Seattle. However, there are the usual problems of funding, resources, and audience development. I think Asian American theaters face the same question other theaters face: how can we get a younger and more diversified audience into these theaters? Audience development in Asian Amercan theater is tricky. The primary audience is naturally Asian and, more complicatedly, it is extremely diverse within a race. For example, Japanese American audiences are more likely to attend a Philip Gotanda play, and may not choose to attend a play written by Chinese American Elizabeth Wong or a Korean-themed play by Sung Rno. This creates a real financial and programmatic challenge for any Asian American theater. There must be inventive ways to cultivate an Asian American theater audience. Naturally, it should be a goal of an Asian American theater to reach out to non-Asian audiences. Our stories need to be heard not only by our communities but by others; only then can Asian American theater be transcendent. That is true theater. Also, there is the question whether more Asian American work is being produced in the larger regional theaters. Only about two percent of the plays produced in the country are written by Asian Americans. I have been produced in regional theaters where I was either their first Asian American playwright they have presented, or the first since they produced David Hwang's *M. Butterfly* ten years ago. And I find that a very disappointing and discouraging landscape for all Asian American playwrights to write in.

DR: Five years ago, you expressed how you represented a new wave of Asian American theater that was going against the realistic representations of early Asian American drama, which tended to focus on what it meant to be 'Asian American.'

CY: Right.

DR: And, five years ago, when I first met you, it was really important for you to differentiate yourself generationally and aesthetically from that group of writers. While you made clear that you felt an alliance with these playwrights on a political and cultural level, you also made clear that there were significant creative differences between you and this earlier generation of playwrights. Do you still hold on to those distinctions?

CY: The first generation of Asian American playwrights, David Henry Hwang, Philip Kan Gotanda, Wakako Yamauichi, and others write about being Asian in America. They were more or less identity plays. Now we see a new wave of Asian playwrights like Han Ong, Alice Tuan, and Diana Son who hail from different ethnic backgrounds and sexualities, writing with fascinating theatrical aesthetics and with a whole new agenda. For us, race ceases to be the primary focus. Instead, race becomes the jumping-off point. Asian characters are fully integrated in the American environment; they are constantly navigating their course through politics, humanity, and history. Without the doors opened to us by David Hwang, Frank Chin, or Wakako Yamauchi, we would have a harder time getting our plays produced. We owe these writers a great deal. Now, there is another new development on the horizon where the playwrights are Asian American and their plays do not necessarily reflect and represent Asian Americans or the Asian American landscape. Most of these playwrights do not identify themselves as Asian American and have been vehemently opposed to writing plays that classify them as Asian American. These writers are not interested in plays that explore Asian American experiences, heritages, and histories. I think, in part, that it's terribly exciting to write outside of one's skin, and in part, I find it troubling that in order to do so, you have to completely scrub away the skin that physically defines you. I don't hear the same arguments from my fellow Latino American or African American playwrights; in fact, there is a certain pride and strength in their voices and their work about being and not forgetting about being the Other in America. I wonder if this recent trend in Asian American playwriting is the direct result of our assimilationist culture within Asian America. Nevertheless, these writers are an undeniable voice. Their plays are articulate, beautiful, and complex, and they will redefine Asian American theater in the coming years.

DR: People most associate your contribution mainly around introducing sexuality into the larger themes of Asian American plays, which, of course, is considerable and important, but, nonetheless, is something of a misrepresentation of the body of your work. I think your contribution is also more artistic.

CY: I should stress that I've always had a problem being labeled as a gay or Asian playwright. I feel that the labeling immediately dictates to audiences how to perceive my work before they had a chance to experience it first hand for themselves. Perhaps this is all a part of our consumer culture. People need labels to know what they are buying. And what's the point of writing if you are continually bound by the labels you are given? Anything you write will be judged against that label. Is this work Asian enough? Is that play not gay enough? How dare he write about straight White people living in New England?

DR: I disagree. I think the 'label' is less about a 'product' and more about a 'politic.' And by politic, I don't necessarily mean a specific and rigid ideological position or a reductive essentialist notion of 'gay' or 'Asian American.' Instead, I mean to say these labels – 'gay', 'Asian American', or, in my case, 'Latino' – signal to audiences the lived relationship to these terms that we, whether we are playwrights, performers, or spectators, inevitably bring to the table given who we are and when and where we live. I even think the question 'Is this work Asian enough?' is endlessly fascinating. It forces us to think what is meant by 'Asian' in the first place and how impossible it is for that term to encompass the enormity of experience that it sets out to describe. I also realize that the question is also endlessly irritating. How annoying for those of us who live under these terms to be always held to someone else's conception of what these terms mean! Personally, I think it's important that you're known as a gay playwright and an Asian American playwright, although I'm not so sure that it describes your work any more successfully than it describes your day-to-day life. But that's not the point. The point is that these 'labels' identify us with a history of struggle against racism and homophobia and with the progressive movements behind these struggles. Your work – as well as mine, for that matter – converses with these efforts and even builds upon them.

CY: You are right. I think we will always defy the status quo, the labeling. Through our work, be it as a playwright, director, or producer, we continually explore and celebrate our humanity and the world in which we live. Naturally I have to write what defines me the most. And yes, some of my stories and characters will live in that gay and Asian world. If I write a play with straight White characters, they will undoubtedly be from a gay and Asian perspective. I don't think I can ever avoid that or want to. But I cannot and will not listen to how other people label my work. It's ironic that I am fighting the battles as I did in high school when they choose to define me as gay or Asian. I guess it's inevitable that people never really see you for what you are, only for what you represent. Ultimately, I would rather be known as a playwright, director, producer, and dramaturg who is gay, Asian, and American. That's all in my blood and under my skin. How can you label that?

ACKNOWLEDGMENTS

Our thanks to Roberta Uno for inviting us to be a part of the initial 'Intersections' conference at the New WORLD Theater. Chay and I also want to thank Lucy Burns for her care during our transition from conference participants to book contributors and Sam Park for his transcription of this interview.

NOTES

1. *Porcelain* and *A Language of Their Own* appear in *Two Plays by Chay Yew* published by Grove Press in 1997. For an excellent discussion of this trilogy, see Michael Reynolds's review of their production at East West Players, *Theatre Journal*, vol. 49, no. 1 (March 1997), pp. 75–9.
2. Chay Yew, whose cultural background is Chinese, was born and raised in Singapore. He left Singapore when he was 16 to study in the United States at Pepperdine University in Southern California.
3. Philip Kan Gotanda's *The Wash* was the last play produced on the main stage of the Taper.
4. The mission statement for East West players reads:
    East West Players is dedicated to the nurturing and promotion of Asian Pacific Americans and other culturally diverse talent through the arts. We encourage artists to express themselves by writing stories, creating and producing projects, expanding their performance repertoire and sharing the work in the community.
5. Both of these productions were part of the 1999–2000 season at East West Players. *Pointless*, which was developed by Chay Yew at the 'Word Up Festival' which he organized, had its world première at East West Players. Chay also commissioned and directed the world première of Alec Mapa's *I Remember Mapa*. For the complete text and production history of *I Remember Mapa*, see Holly Hughes and David Román (eds), 'O Solo Homo: The New Queer Performance' (New York: Grove Press, 1998). Chay directed the Los Angeles première of *Golden Child*.
6. For a more detailed discussion and analysis of Chay Yew's 1998 Cornerstone production of *A Beautiful Country*, see David Román, 'Visa Denied,' in Joseph Allen Boone *et al.* (eds), *Queer Frontiers: Millennial Geographies, Genders, and Generations* (Madison, WI: University of Wisconsin Press, 2000), pp. 350–66.

Part IV

Performance Texts

Quinceañera

created by
Alberto Antonio Araiza, Paul Bonin-Rodriguez, Michael Marinez,
and Danny Bolero Zaldivar

written by
Alberto Antonio Araiza and Paul Bonin-Rodriguez

Quinceañera was initially developed at the New WORLD Theater in February 1998, in collaboration with the University of Massachusetts Department of Theater. The original cast included Alberto Antonio Araiza, Paul Bonin-Rodriguez, and Michael Marinez. It was directed by Joe Salvatore. Lucy Mae San Pablo Burns and Joe Salvatore were co-dramaturgs, set design was by Michael Marinez, lighting design by Penny Remsen, costume design by Kay Lahey, and sound design by Chris Bailey. In October 1998, it was presented as a featured performance at the conference 'Intersection of Performance, Practice, and Ideas,' produced by New WORLD Theater and the Department of Theater at UMASS, Amherst. It has been presented at the Mexican Fine Arts Center Museum, Chicago; *InRoads*: Festival of the Americas, Miami, Florida; Jump-Start, San Antonio, Texas; and Santa Fe Stages, Santa Fe, New Mexico.

Quinceañera written by Alberto Antonio Araiza and Paul Bonin-Rodriguez
In photo: Alberto Antonio Araiza, Paul Bonin-Rodriguez, and Michael Marinez
Photo by Ed Cohen

16

Collaboration/celebration: introduction to *Quinceañera*

Joe Salvatore

HIV and AIDS have been part of my sexual existence for as long as I can remember. My earliest recollections remind me of jokes that classmates told when I was in the seventh grade, something about a librarian having library aides. Silly young people thinking that the disease that plagued gay men and drug users could never touch them in their safe little White suburban enclave. That was 1984, early in my understanding of HIV and AIDS, and some 10 years before I would identify myself as homosexual. In that time, fear began to spread into mainstream communities, and educators preached that having sex could and would kill us all. As a product of that means of educating young people in the late 1980s and early 1990s, I have experienced a sense of great loss. But my loss is different from the loss that we usually associate with HIV and AIDS, for it is a loss of sexual freedom, of experimentation, and of a gay culture that I have only heard and read about. I have not lost a close friend or relative or even an acquaintance to AIDS as far as I know. I know people who are living with HIV, but I can count that number on one hand. So my experience and perspective in creating a piece that looked to celebrate and reflect upon the first 15 years of the AIDS pandemic was quite different from the experiences of the three primary collaborators.

My initial meeting with Alberto Antonio Araiza, Paul Bonin-Rodriguez, and Michael Marinez occurred over the telephone in April 1997.[1] From that moment I knew that I was in for quite an experience. The personalities of these three men were, and still are, larger than life. And this made for an exciting and somewhat intimidating first conversation. There were questions about my qualifications, but more importantly, questions about my age and range of experiences. All three men were older than me and had a different experience when it came to HIV and AIDS. So, while I passed the qualifications portion of the interview, I think there was some skepticism about how a White, 26-year-old Anglo-Irish-Italian boy would really direct and dramaturg a piece about queer Latino men in their thirties and forties addressing the first fifteen years of the AIDS pandemic. Despite whatever reservations these men had about me, I was accepted onto the project.

But this notion of difference among collaborators actually became a major theme throughout the project. *Quinceañera* came out of hours of writing and conversation around the issues of being HIV-positive, HIV-negative, gay, and Latino. It was during these conversations that it became clear to me that no one voice could represent the experience of all the individuals affected directly and indirectly by the pandemic. Even though the three primary collaborators are gay and Latino, that doesn't mean that even they can have one opinion on living with HIV. I learned a valuable lesson about the politics of the community and the politics of the individual and how those two camps can often be in conflict. I had felt this dissonance in my own life, and to have it verified in a working process made the experience all the more worthwhile.

And the process of creation, rehearsal, and performance also reflected this dissonance. All three original creators/performers came from different performance backgrounds: Paul trained as a dancer, Alberto trained as an actor, and Michael worked as an installation artist. So from the onset, we had to develop a vocabulary that was inclusive to all of the principal collaborators, a language and way of working that allowed all opinions to be expressed in as much balance as we could achieve. Deep in the middle of the two-week workshop in February 1998, when tensions were high and I was feeling overwhelmed by all of the loose ends, Lucy Burns, my co-dramaturg, had the hindsight to remind me that this was an interdisciplinary performance piece. We had to make sure that every element received ample attention, whether it was the outreach component that was important to Michael, or the development of movement and ritual that was important to Alberto and Paul, or the structured script that was important to me. And in an inexplicable way, the conflicts that arose out of these intersections and collisions of disparate elements actually propelled the process and the piece forward. Artists in various disciplines know that this is generally the case, but I think we can all admit that it's also the first piece of knowledge to escape our collective memories when we are working on something new to show in front of an audience.

That concern for audience and how to connect the audience with the piece was essentially the most common plot of ground that all of us could identify. *Quinceañera* borrows the ritual that young Latinas undergo at 15 as a way to draw a parallel between reaching adulthood and surviving adulthood, while also serving as a healing ritual for all involved. With so much destruction within the gay community and the Latino community, the performers felt it necessary to offer a chance at rebirth, a chance for survivors to acknowledge the collective tragedy and their own losses, but also to celebrate life. The piece asks for the audience members to engage in the event, to actively assist in the preparation for and in the celebration of the ritual in much the same way that a community gathers for a traditional *quinceañera*, so the audience is invested in the final outcome. The event becomes personal and therefore can't be taken lightly. And audience response has been personal and wide ranging. Wherever the piece has been performed, many audience members express thanks for the opportunity to publicly grieve or remember those family members or friends whom they have lost to AIDS, people who may have never been allowed to acknowledge those losses before. And people recognize themselves as survivors on many different levels whether they are positive, negative, or unknown. Conversely, some people, middle-aged gay men in particular, have asked who the audience is for the piece. 'We've named names before. We've heard these stories before. How is this different?' It's different because Paul, Alberto, Michael, and eventually our additional performer Danny Bolero Zaldivar, felt that this piece was the first collective statement about HIV and AIDS to come out of the Latino community in this country. Therein lies the difference. And secondly, maybe people have heard these stories before, named names before, but a generation of young queers have not. A generation of brotherless, fatherless, motherless, sisterless young people in all communities have not. Not everyone has heard these stories before, nor have they had the chance to tell their stories. And the stories will continue for many years to come.

In the final moments of a performance of *Quinceañera* in Miami, a woman was dancing with one of the performers to punctuate the end of the ritual and celebration. As she spun around to Selena singing 'Last Dance,' she leaned into her white-skirted partner and said, 'This is for my brother. He didn't get to dance.' And in that very simple statement, we discover how theater and performance can touch and transform the individual.

NOTE

1.   I collaborated on *Quinceañera* as my Masters in Fine Arts dramaturgy and directing thesis project at the University of Massachusetts at Amherst. I had been looking for a project that was interdisiplinary, queer, and a new work. Roberta Uno, Artistic Director of New WORLD Theater, offered me the opportunity to direct *Quinceañera*, a work NWT was commissioning, subject to the artists' approval.

Quinceañera written by Alberto Antonio Araiza and Paul Bonin-Rodriguez.
In photo: Alberto Antonio Araiza, Paul Bonin-Rodriguez, and Michael Marinez.
Photo by Ed Cohen

17

Quinceañera

created by
Alberto Antonio Araiza, Paul Bonin-Rodriguez, Michael Marinez,
and Danny Bolero Zaldivar

written by
Alberto Antonio Araiza and Paul Bonin-Rodriguez

(Setting: A clothes-line runs from upstage right to upstage left. Clothes-pins covered with bright paper flowers hang from it. Above the line three white skirts and veils hang on chrome multi-level hangers that resemble ribs. Sometimes paper flowers made from beverage napkins are attached to the ribs. The flowers contain messages from and are made by audience members of the previous nights. The messages are to those who have died from AIDS.)

PROLOGUE: THE HISTORY OF LA QUINCEAÑERA

(ALBERTO – aka 'BETO' – enters as VERÓNICA, a young 'girl' of 15. He wears a black shirt, a white T-shirt, and a white skirt tied at the waist. On his head he wears a bandana, tied in a cap with a thick braid descending. He carries a book.)

VERÓNICA: OK, so like I'm gonna have my Quinceañera, that's like this big party cause I'm gonna be, like 15, and a woman ... that's what Quinceañera means, '15 and years.' That's what Father Gomez at our church, Nuestra Señora del Perpetuo Socorro, told me.

My Ama and I go to these classes to prepare me for my 'witness-able point of metamorphosis' – and Father Gomez gave me this book to read; it says stuff like ... *(opens book and reads)* 'In Mexico's Native American Aztec civilization, girls attended two types of schools ... the Calmacac school, or the Telpu ... cu ...' something really hard like that to pronounce, whatever ... and the Telpu-whatever girls they had to learn to do nun-things ... like how to be poor and how to be virgins and behave, whatever. And the Calmacac girls learned all about like how to get a guy and get married. Pues, go Calmacac! Girl Power! *(does a quick cheerleader move)*

(PAUL as TÍA enters upstage left, and DANNY as MAMA, enters upstage right of the clothes-line. Both begin hanging brightly colored papel picado from the line. They are dressed like VERÓNICA, with different colored do-rag/hairstyles.)

And Father Gomez is gonna say a mass for me, so I can 'reaffirm my promises of faith' – that's important. And I got to have a madrina and a padrino, like getting a new set of godparents but you get to pick them. And then we're gonna have a dance, with a band, and a big cake – 'cause now that I'm a woman I get to have everything I want. I just have to put out more – that's what my tía told me. Or maybe she said 'speak up more'? Whatever, I forget.

Anyway, I have a court of honor with all my girlfriends and my cousins, including my one cousin Chata that I don't like so much 'cause she thinks she's all that, and she's not all that. Which is why I put her with my other cousin Louie, 'cause he's really short and Chata's like really tall. All the guys in my court are called 'Chambelanes,' 'cause they gotta wear a tux ... and all my girlfriends are called 'Damas' ... and our dresses are like this *(shows book)* but better, 'cause we ordered them from the Selena Boutique Mail Order Catalogue in San Antonio!

And I thought I'd ask Tito to be my 'Chambelán de Honor' to escort me, because he's so fine ... but I haven't seen him for a while. So I might ask Chuy, 'cause one day at school I remember he asked me, 'what's a metamorphosis?' I said, 'Oh, it's my butterfly emerging from my cocoon.' And he was all impressed. *(sees MAMA and TÍA)* Oh, I gotta go!

THE REALITY

VERÓNICA: Ama! Tía! Ama! Look! I found the perfect pattern for my Quinceañera dress!

(VERÓNICA shows the tacky pattern to her mother)

MAMA: Entonces, show me. Aye look *(looks)* qué ... *(trying not to hurt VERÓNICA's feelings)* pretty. *(calling out)* Mira, hermana, look at the pretty dress my Verónica has chosen for her Quinceañera dress! *(showing it to TÍA – hinting at diplomacy)* Qué pretty, qué no?

TÍA: If you wanna look like a float in the Rose Parade.

(VERÓNICA cries)

MAMA: Hermana! *(to VERÓNICA)* Calmate, mijita, your tía didn't mean that. She meant that ... in this dress you would look just like the Queen of the Rose Parade. *(to TÍA)* Qué no, hermana?

TÍA: Oh yes! You'll look just like a queen. *(indicating pattern)* And look at all that room for your cleavage.

MAMA: Hermana! We just make a few changes; cover up some things, tú sabes.

MAMA and TÍA: We're gonna need a lot of material.

VERÓNICA: But I like it the way it is – it makes me look like a woman!

MAMA: Don't be silly, mijita.

TÍA: A woman?

VERÓNICA: But I am a woman – in every way.

(MAMA and TÍA look intensely at each other, then to VERÓNICA)

MAMA: *(chasing VERÓNICA)* Desgraciada! How could you do this to me?

VERÓNICA: What?

TÍA: You should be ashamed of yourself! How can you break your mother's heart, like this?

VERÓNICA: What?

MAMA: *(crying)* Who is he? Where is this *tascado marrano* who defiled my little girl?

VERÓNICA: No, Ama, I'm not a woman that way – not like TÍA.

(TÍA glares at VERÓNICA)

VERÓNICA: I still have my cookies.

TÍA: Pues, yo también.

MAMA: Cookies? *(to TÍA)* Qué es 'cookies'?

TÍA: Her pan dulce, hermana.

MAMA: Cómo?

TÍA: No man has tasted the sweet, delicious filling of her empanada yet.

MAMA: *(crossing herself)* Gracias, a Dios.

TÍA: And as long as we're on the subject of men, who have you chosen for your escort?

VERÓNICA: Así, for mi Chambelán de Honor to escort me, la Reina de las Estrellas, más gigante! … la vida loca herself, Ricky Martin!

MAMA: Aye, por favor!

TÍA: Pues, get real! No te chifles!

VERÓNICA: OK then … Tito!

(Sadly, TÍA and MAMA glance at one another)

TÍA: Oh!

MAMA: Mija …

VERÓNICA: What?

MAMA: We didn't want to tell you until after the Quinceañera.

TÍA: La SIDA.

VERÓNICA: When?

TÍA: '83 … but there are others – think of someone else.

VERÓNICA: Oh … well then, Manuel!

(TÍA and MAMA glance at one another again)

MAMA: No, mija.

TÍA: Se murió, también.

VERÓNICA: Manuel too? When?

TÍA: '85 … popular year for pneumocystis.

VERÓNICA: … Then Raul.

TÍA: '87 … pneumonia complicated with herpes viral infection y mycobacterium avium complex.

VERÓNICA: Eduardo.

MAMA: '89 … pero he didn't sero-convert till the very end.

TÍA: I told him to stay away from that pinche AZT.

VERÓNICA: David.

MAMA: '93 ...

TÍA: No, David was after Rafael who was in late '93, so David was '94 ... then came Santos and then Luis.

MAMA: Luis was before Rafael.

TÍA: Mentirosa, how can Luis be before Rafael? Luis was still doing your perm when Rafi went all blind ... recuerdas?

MAMA: Oh, that's right.

VERÓNICA: Well then ... I'm gonna ask Angel.

MAMA: '96 ... KS, aggravated with unsuppressed diarrhea; side effects of Viracept.

TÍA: Ugly.

VERÓNICA: Shit! Javier?

MAMA: Lymphoma, then dementia ...

TÍA: Then the wasting syndrome ... qué lástima.

VERÓNICA: Chuy?

TÍA and MAMA: Suicide.

(VERÓNICA *falls to ground, crying; overly dramatic*)

MAMA: When his ratio went caca, his viral shot right through the roof, and his t-cells said, 'adiós,' morphine, quick, gracias a dios. Recuerdas ... at the funeral Rocky played 'Last Dance'?

TÍA: I hate that Donna Summer!

MAMA: Pinche, 'Adam and Eve – not Adam and Steve!'

TÍA: Homophobe born-again puta! Trying to resurrect her career on VH–1.

MAMA: Like she never said that all the maricones belong in hell. That's why I only steal her records now.

TÍA: So I can put them under plants to catch water.

VERÓNICA: Ama! Why didn't you tell me?

MAMA: Why would it matter? You never water the plants anyway?

VERÓNICA: No AMA! I mean about the others! Why didn't you tell me?!

MAMA: We didn't want to disturb you. You know how you get all nerviosa.

TÍA: She gets it from her father's side.

MAMA: You're young and innocent. You shouldn't have to know about stuff like that. When I was young, we learned about death from Bambi's mother.

TÍA: Chita Rivera was up for that part, you know, to play the voice of Bambi's mother – pero no, otra vez, to the gavacha, Marni Nixon!

(MAMA and VERÓNICA look at one another – blank stare – mouth 'Marni Nixon?')

MAMA: Pos, La Chita never gets a break!

TÍA and MAMA: Pinche Hollywood!

MAMA: Pero hoy, there's so much death all around that even Disney can't keep up.

TÍA: Besides, we kept thinking there'd be a cure, también – and then we'd tell you.

MAMA: Maybe this year.

TÍA: Maybe next year.

VERÓNICA: Well, what the fuck is anybody doing about this? CHINGAO!

MAMA: Pos, watch your mouth, Miss Cosa. They got a cocktail now.

TÍA: They got to call it 'a cocktail'; makes it easier to swallow. 'Perdóname, pero I gotta go take my chemo now.' Harder to market, tú sabes?

MAMA: Y qué caro!

TÍA: I couldn't afford it.

MAMA: I'd have to sell my jewels.

TÍA: That glass cochinada you got at K-Mart?

VERÓNICA: Ama! Tía! This isn't funny! Who's left to be my escort?

TÍA: Pos, no sé, mija. All the men who would possibly consider dating you, even if we paid them, have all become angelitos. Life has term limits, mija. Go, stay, go. Pos, it's a little like life on the border.

MAMA: Así. Come! Work for pinche nothing taking care of our kids. Go! We're not educating your children or giving you health care! Put your arms up, empty your pockets, climb in the truck — you're going to your reward.

TÍA: But don't let us ruin your plans.

MAMA: Life is about adapting, mija. You can be your own escort!

TÍA: Y why not me? I can be her escort.

MAMA: Hermana, mi preciosa, you're much too ... *(TÍA senses what MAMA is implying. MAMA is choosing her words carefully now)* well, I mean, you've been with so many. ... You know, all the men coming are gonna want to talk with you, you know how they are, and they can't talk with you if you're up at the altar. Besides I'll need your help with all that food. You know how I depend upon you.

TÍA: That's right ... and besides the men are always undressing me with their eyes, so I should stand behind something big *(off VERÓNICA)* so as not to distract the attention from Veronica on her special day. I'll serve the pan dulce!

MAMA: Y tamales!

(Ranchera music plays. PAUL, BETO, and DANNY dance upstage. They remove their wigs and untie the shirts.)

RITE OF PASSAGE

(BETO, DANNY and PAUL begin unrolling the sleeves of their shirts. Their movement is ritualistic.)

PAUL: In many traditional societies the rites of passage are reserved for men.

(They button their collars — now resembling altar boys)

BETO: In many traditional societies the rites of passage are reserved for boys.

(Raising their hands in prayer)

DANNY: Pubescent boys.

(Walking forward)

PAUL: Under the witness of the community, each pubescent boy must confront and overcome a series of insurmountable obstacles without the nurturing or comfort of his mother or his community.

(PAUL and DANNY turn to face each other, flanking BETO, who stands downstage center)

DANNY: Under his own power.

(ALL walk in a circle, speaking outward to the audience)

PAUL: Perhaps he kills an animal.

BETO: Perhaps he overcomes a virus.

DANNY: Perhaps he takes direct action.

(ALL stop)

PAUL: Whatever it is, he faces the possibility of his own mortality.

(On the line: PAUL, standing upstage center, extends his hand to BETO)

BETO: The reality we must all confront.

(On the line: BETO places a hand on PAUL's)

PAUL: And in the process, dies as his old identity, to be reborn in a new life, without a mother, as a warrior, a conqueror, or a provider.

DANNY: That is to say, he develops his own power and hopefully uses it for good.

(On the line: DANNY places a hand atop PAUL's and BETO's)

BETO: As a shaman, a curandero, a brujo or a priest.

(On the line: BETO places his other hand atop the others)

DANNY: Or an NEA-funded drag queen performance artist.

(On the line: DANNY places his other hand atop the others)

PAUL: Failure would mean public humiliation and a lifetime of perpetual childhood.

(On the line: PAUL places his other hand atop the others. ALL three step into the circle and huddle; the huddle erupts)

DANNY and BETO: Sounds fabulous!

(Sound: They vamp to Ike and Tina Turner's 'Proud Mary.' ALL run upstage, remove shirts, put on bright red satin sashes)

MISS AZT-LAND PAGEANT

ANNOUNCER/VOICE-OVER: In the name of the positive, the negative, the dead, and the surviving, it's the Miss AZT-Land Pageant! *(Gestures for 'positive, negative, dead, and the surviving' are loosely based on American Sign Language – 'surviving' being a symbol for applause)*

('Proud Mary' plays loud. ALL *three dance in unison as Iketes; trademark Ike and Tina Turner revue choreography)*

And here they are our three lovely finalists!

BETO: Hello, mi nombre es Beto Araiza. An LA native, queer loco-mestizo poet of 44, a Nichiren Shoshu Buddhist, and for the past 14 years I've been diagnosed Miss HIV Optimistic! Aplauso, por favor. My metamorphosis from positive to optimistic has taken a very long time ... and I, along with every single one of my sparkling little t-cells, still struggle with it. Each passing year, month, day, moment equally enriches and sometimes frightens me, but despite all of that my interests still include ... overthrowing this pinche government, marketing the first Chiapas Barbie, and showing up to the pageant *(off* DANNY*)* on time.

DANNY: Hello, my name is Danny David Adam Bolero Zaldivar de Castillo, aka Danny Mañanitas, Danny Granada, Danny de La Bamba. It's not that I'm searching for an identity, it's just that I need a name that looks great on a Broadway marquee – and still acknowledges my Latino heritage, of course. *(Begins to sing)* 'A boy like that, who kills your brother ... forget that boy and find another. One of your own kind. Stick to your own kind.' Damn, I'm good. And that's why I'm Miss Broadway Melody of the Future, who throughout this time of plague has miraculously remained HIV-negative – safely playing those tunes while hoping for a cure.

PAUL: Oh yes, just like Evita Moreno.

BETO: Qué stupid, that's Chita Moreno.

DANNY: No, it's Rita Moreno, thank you. And I did make it to the pageant on time!

BETO: Claro que sí ... on borrowed time.

DANNY: We are all living on borrowed time.

PAUL: Hello, my name is Paul Bonin-Rodriguez. I am a 34-year-old Cajun-Tejano from Texas, Mississippi, Virginia, North Carolina, and Alabama! I am a person divided between worlds and times, between identities and brawling divas. For this reason I have already been named Miss Passive Congenial! My real title, however, is Miss Missed the Seventies, a representative of the Insta-fear generation, so my risks were always calculated, or so I have tried to convince myself.

ANNOUNCER/VOICE-OVER: And now, ladies, as you know when you entered the pageant ...

DANNY: *(interrupting)* I believe I was entered ...

BETO: *(topping)* I know I was.

PAUL: *(with a ready, stock answer)* I believe in the very young, and in the very old; the old because they are our history, the young because they are our future.

ANNOUNCER/VOICE-OVER: Ladies ... may I continue? As you know, the title of Miss AZT-Land carries certain responsibilities. For the entire year that you wear the Miss AZT-Land crown you will be required to represent the AIDS pandemic on behalf of all the long-term survivors. In preparation for that role, I ask you, what would you bring to the title of Miss AZT-Land?

DANNY: I would bring my higher power, my sobriety, my 12 steps, and all my chips, thank you. I would bring my todo east LA, todo queer attitude, fashioned from those sexual experiences that have shaped me. And I would bring words of caution to all those men who, like me, struggle with the loneliness − 'even if you feel you know me, don't swallow.'

BETO: I would bring my mistrust of a medical community gone mad with greed, which has served me very well ... a copy of the Lotus Sutra, Chinese herbs, acupuncture, and spirulina for everyone. I would bring la sangre de los rascuaches, my lucha libre desire. And I would bring my stated and steadfast resistance to crisis oriented traditional Western medicine, and I call now for others to join me in the resistance, in the spirit of those who've struggled before us like Huey Newton, Che Guevara y Norma Rae!

(BETO strikes triumphant pose. DANNY reacts with applause. PAUL begins to exit, stops, picks up bag containing papel picado, and crosses downstage)

PAUL: I would probably just bring my baggage. It comes with me to every show ... pageant, passage, whatever. We've got to stay ready, right? Look, my life has been about adapting. If it wasn't to a new community every few years, it was about the introduction of a virus that would shape how I adapt constantly. Where does this bag take me? To my history that could have eluded me? To someone's last moments? To my own? It seems to me that everything is fleeting now, going fast, fast, faster than I could have anticipated, and I am only running to catch up with the latest news and directives and identities ...

BETO: *(implying self)* Welcome to my world.

PAUL: If I am in bed with you, it's my world too.

DANNY: Even if you're not in bed with him it's still your world.

PAUL: Even if I'm not in bed with any of you, it's still my world.

DANNY: That was so moving ... what you just said. That's it ... I think Beto deserves to win.

BETO: Oh no, Paul deserves to win.

PAUL: Oh no, I think Danny deserves to win. *(To DANNY)* I really hope you get it ...

(Shocked reaction from BETO and DANNY)

PAUL: Not the virus! The crown!

DANNY: I feel guilty enough as it is – you don't need to rub it in.

PAUL: We're all long-term survivors here!

BETO: Well, I just might have an issue with that!

PAUL: Well, isn't that why we're here?! Let's be honest.

DANNY: In that case, I deserve the crown!

(A moment of reaction from BETO and PAUL, to DANNY's line; then, walking up to either side of DANNY, they remove their Sashes and place them on DANNY)

PAUL and BETO: Take it.

(BETO and PAUL exit)

DANNY: Take it? What do you mean?! You mean now you don't want it? Well, what do you want?

(DANNY exits)

WISHES AND PRAYERS

BETO: *(to center stage)* What do I want?

(Begins doing Tai Chi Chuan exercise, then begins chant. DANNY and PAUL enter upstage of BETO, DANNY walking perimeter of stage throughout scene)

BETO: I pray to eradicate the virus from my body. I pray to eradicate the virus from my body. I pray to eradicate the virus from my body.

DANNY: *(singing)* Dios los hace y ellos se juntan. *(Translation: 'God makes us and we gather together')*

(PAUL begins choreographed movement around BETO, physicality derived from Tai Chi Chuan)

PAUL:	BETO:
If I touch him the way I used to touch him – though I can't touch him the way I used to touch him – feel him there and and there and there. No. It's that I don't want to touch him the way I used to touch him. Not because he's not touchable. He's all that, and the memory of how close it used to get, how desperate sustained us through some lonely years since.	I pray to eradicate the virus from my body ... I pray to eradicate the virus from my body ... I pray to eradicate the virus from my body ... I pray to truly do the impossible and eradicate this virus from my body ...

DANNY: *(singing)* No hay mal que por bien no venga. *(Translation: 'There is no evil from which some good does not come')*

PAUL:	BETO:
We don't like condoms we said, and we took a chance, a crap shoot, without the crap, thank you very much. And back then, back there we were hopping. But after him, I didn't take the chance – maybe because I met no one like him. But he did, didn't he? And the story goes that the other fellow told him he was safe – I mean, not infected –	I pray to truly do the impossible and eradicate this virus from my body. I pray to truly do the impossible and eradicate this virus from my body. I pray to truly do the impossible and eradicate this virus from my body.

and my once-and-future lover, never
took it, but played top, played top,   I pray to truly do the impossible.
played into the hands of a virus.
And now he's got it.

DANNY: *(singing)* Suerte y mortaja del cielo baja. *(Translation: 'Luck and death come from heaven')*

PAUL:	BETO:
And shared an identity	I pray to move beyond the fear.
through love, is separated	I pray to move beyond the pain.
– once again, if not through	I pray to move beyond the
a latex membrane, then	nightmares.
through this fact: we are	I pray to move beyond their lies.
one-part lovers, and	I pray to move beyond their
one-part enemies, yet same.	judgments.
In my honest moments,	I pray to move beyond their
I believe moments, I believe	ignorance.
I am superior: you are	I pray to move beyond the sadness.
death and dying and	I pray to move beyond the
putrefaction, no matter,	loneliness.
how many anti-virals you	I pray to move beyond the
take, no no matter how	impossible.
many herbs, you pump into	I pray to move beyond the
your body, you will deteriorate,	impossible.
and I must prepare.	I pray to move beyond the
	impossible.
	I pray to move beyond.

DANNY: *(singing)* Con la medida que mides seras medida. *(Translation: 'With the measure you measure, you will be measured')*

PAUL:	BETO:
I will march for you.	I pray to embrace the possible.
I will hold vigils. I will	
use your name when I	I pray to embrace the possible.
want instant profundity,	
but don't ever ask me	I pray to embrace the possible.
to think of myself as	
being like you. What	I will eradicate this virus from my
you were, you are no	body.
longer. What we could	
have been, we failed	I will eradicate this virus from my

to become. And for
your sins, I became
something else too.
And for my sins, you
became something else too.

body.

I will eradicate this virus from my
body ...

And I will move from a here ... to
a there.

DANNY: *(singing)* Cada quien es arquitecto de ser propio destino.
(Translation: 'Each is the architect of his own destiny') (BETO and PAUL exit)

15 AND GREAT DISCOVERIES

DANNY: *(Singing)* Hush little baby, don't say a word, Papa's gonna buy you a mocking bird. If that mocking bird don't sing, Papa's gonna buy you a diamond ring.

'I won't tell. I won't tell.' I see this door. I want to open this door that's right there in front of me ... I can sense it, feel it ... it has my name written on it.

(Singing) Hush little baby, don't say a word, Papa's gonna buy you a mocking bird. And if that mocking bird don't sing, Papa's gonna give you his pretty thing.

And there's a star ...? No, a triangle ... it's pink. 'Swear to God you won't tell. Swear to God!' I'm seven. He ... it's a man ... he helps me up onto the toilet seat. The walls are a blur. His face is a blur. Where's his face? I can't make out the face ... It's like that scene from *An American in Paris*, with Cyd Charisse – maybe I'm Gene Kelly!

(Singing) Hush little baby, don't say a word, Papa's gonna make you a mocking ... bird. Hush little baby, don't say a word. Don't say a word. Don't say a word.

He lives here. We live under the same roof, in the same house. And all the doors are closed as he puts it in my mouth. He tells me 'blow', and I'm blowing like I'm blowing a whistle – it falls out of my mouth. 'No, suck,' he says. So I put it back into my mouth. I wanna do good. I want him to be nice to me.

(Singing) Hush little baby, don't say a word ...

Outside the bathroom window I hear the neighbor's kids playing ball. For a moment I imagine I'm outside playing with them, but then the hands holding my head pull me in closer. I can begin to feel his whole body move, begin to quiver. He moans quietly beneath the sounds coming from outside

– Mando shouting to his brother, 'Come on, Johnny! Throw it! And don't throw it like a sissy, this time!' Johnny throws the ball, under-handed like a girl would. Mando shouts 'Faggot!', and the quiver becomes an explosion of smells and tastes. 'I can't breathe!'

(Singing) If that diamond ring turns brass, Papa's gonna buy you a looking glass. If that looking glass gets broke, Papa's gonna buy you a billy-goat. And if that billy-goat gets away ...

I'm a good boy. He smiles ... tells me how good I am, and that we'll play again tomorrow.

'Don't tell ... promise ... swear you won't tell Dad.'

'I won't tell. I promise.'

(Singing) And as the billy-goat gets away, Daddy won't know what happened today.

I look into the bathroom mirror, and I see a good boy. For the next eight years I keep looking into that mirror until one day I'm 15. Papa, aka billy-goat, aka faggot, has moved onto cruising bigger bathrooms across the LA landscape, in his constant quest for new prey. I'm 15, and I too feel like a predator – but am I?

I ask myself again and again, as I stroke Johnny's hair. His lips move from mine, down my chest, to my waist and settle into my crotch.

(Singing) 'Hush little baby, no need to cry. We'll touch and kiss, 'til the day we die. And if we go our separate way, we'll keep our secret from the light of day.'

I don't know what to call what we're doing – it's not sex, it's not love ... it feels like discovery. It's definitely a secret. Hush little baby, don't say a word ... like those times with my brother. Papa's gonna make you a mocking bird ... In the bathroom, in the closet he still lives in. And if that mocking bird don't sing. Papa's gonna buy you a diamond ring ... Because we're boys, and boys don't do these things. And when all those diamond rings turn brass ... Real boys who run up and down the block, play catch, throw balls, blow whistles, will stop yelling into our looking glass, 'Faggot!'

(DANNY exits)

15 AND SUDDEN REALIZATION

(BETO and PAUL enter and stand on opposite sides of stage; they gather their black skirts between their legs, tucking them in front, creating wrestling pant effect)

BETO: 'we're getting naked'
metal locker room
industrial scented gymnasium

jock strap restraints
harnesses and bridles across our mouth
binding our developing crotch and lips
the combination locks
fastened to our secretive sexual desires
are bolted with a collective sweat and tension
that strains our young competitive muscles

(DANNY enters and acts as COACH throughout scene. BETO and PAUL assume wrestling-starting position — DANNY slaps floor signaling the beginning of the match; the physical movement having overt sexual overtones)

and so we touch aggressively
in teams
believing there is safety in numbers
we touch appropriately
one on one
knowing survival of the fittest is reality
we touch violently
with balls bats clubs
leather gloves and whistles
wrestling to subdue our unspoken curiosity and cravings

(DANNY blows whistle, signaling break in match. BETO and PAUL assume new wrestling positions. As before, DANNY slams hand on floor, resuming match)

mounting alpha males
establishing power
territory on and off the field

'we're getting naked'
oblique side glances from the sides of one's eyes
subtle glimpses documenting
size shape length color
cut
uncut genitalia
looking directly while not looking directly
at other young male bodies
all anxious and boiling over with
sexual panic

(DANNY blows whistle, signaling break in match. BETO and PAUL assume new wrestling positions. As before, DANNY slams hand on floor, resuming match once again)

and at those moments
stripped down and naked
while groping with adolescent confusion and
public school vulnerability

(PAUL circles around BETO and lifts him in head-lock; BETO's arms spread out, image is BETO hanging Christ-like on cross)

the energy of young men
naked curious washing
dancing in and out of cascading water
(sensuous as majestic waterfall)
that touches every part of
young men's bodies
the realization comes

(DANNY blows whistle, signaling end of match. BETO and PAUL break, undo their black skirts from pants effect. PAUL is struck on ass by DANNY as he crosses and exits)

'we're getting naked'
young distinctively queer thought
whispered quietly in the back of one's mind
so quietly

so as not to draw attention
to itself
to the joy felt in bearing witness
in participating
in this rite of passage
of young naked male bodies
bathing in collective and tribal affirmation

(DANNY approaches BETO. They do hi-five hand gesture as they cross each other's path. Immediately, they face one another as in a confrontation. What begins as wrestling moves evolves into effeminate patty-cake clap)

BETO and DANNY: *(synchronized with each clap)* G, G, G, G ...

(PAUL enters, carrying two jump ropes. Stands between BETO and DANNY. They regard him with disdain, break away; shoving him as they pass)

15 AND FIGHTING IT

(PAUL begins skipping rope)

PAUL: When I was 11, my fifth-grade teacher decided I was ready for the seventh grade, and for the next three years in my small Texas town of 2,000 the resentment against me will build.

(PAUL stops skipping rope, and drops one end of each rope)

They hate me – I hate them back, as much as I want them to like me. They find my weakest spot, my femininity, and begin attacking it on a daily basis. One morning – I am 14 – I get off the school bus and start walking towards class. A blue northern has blown in; it is cold and windy, yet sunny and clear.

(BETO and DANNY each take one end of a rope – at times yanking it, other times pulling it, throwing PAUL to the ground)

One of my brothers joins his classmates playing football on the front lawn. When I walk past the game stops, and one red-haired boy named Kenny walks forward and says, 'So tell me, are you G?'
    I continue walking.
    'Are you G?,' he asks.
    I start climbing the steps.
    'Are you G? Are you G?'
    He pushes me from behind so I fall to the ground, dropping my books. By the time I get up, he has climbed to the top step and stands above me.
    'Are you?'
    'What's G?', I ask.
    'Just say you are.'
    'But what is it?'
    'Say you're G.'
    'You're G', I say. He pushes me backwards on the steps. I grab the rail trying not to fall.
    'Say I'm G.'
    'You're G.'
    He starts kicking me. I look for back up. My brother is standing to the side looking down. I am being pummeled and his friends are laughing. There are no teachers around. I consider running in and leaving everything there, but what would I have left?
    'I'm G', I say.

(The frantic yanking stops. DANNY and BETO begin using the rope to rein PAUL in, as

he tries to step away from the playing scene)

'He said he's Gay.'

My ears burn at their sacrilege to my truth. My brother explains later how it was my fault, for carrying my books that way, for talking back. I decide to do some pro-active work. I shut up for a year. I study how people regard each other, I learn to mimic their responses, holding back mine. I train myself to be pleasant, but mostly obscure.

(DANNY and BETO maneuver the ropes to create sexual tableaux)

I am 15, and I am having sex with no one. I am not even considering the possibility. If I were to have sex with a woman, she might humiliate me in private, the way the boys do in public. You're 'G,' she'd say, laughing, rolling away.

If I were to have sex with a boy, then I would be 'G' and all those boys on the playground would win. But this thought never comes to me then. I do not even masturbate so that I will not reveal to myself the objects of my fantasies. And it's all OK – because I am Catholic.

I think of myself as piously non-sexual and the perfect candidate for priesthood, which I imagine will bring all the distance and remove that I need, and a certain amount of elevation. Wasn't my march up the steps my own walk to Calvary; 'Say you're G' could have easily been, 'Say you're King of the Jews.' Who would dare knock down the consecrated Eucharist (the actual body of Jesus!) from the top steps of the altar and challenge me?

(PAUL starts winding himself in the ropes, while DANNY and BETO maintain the ropes' tension; the action slowly pulls all three into a final tableau)

Others will confess to me, look up to me at their dying moment or to bless their unions. I will be at the J-Man's right hand, and if I am lucky and study and join the right order, the Palatine Fathers of Ireland, I will get to live in a house with our handsome new priest, Father Larry, who is blond, and my idol, whom I dream of showering next to, maybe sleeping next to, in a twin bed, like Ricky and Lucy. Maybe some night we will hug for a long time. But I will never be G.

(DANNY and BETO drop ropes)

AT 15 . . .

BETO: At 15, my blood is separated from my family . . .

DANNY: At 15, my blood is a river filled with predators and prey, conquest and surrender ...

BETO: ... my straight family.

PAUL: At 15, my blood is alone, awaiting union ...

DANNY: ... where the hunt is camouflaged as truth

PAUL: ... that I believe is not there for me.

BETO: The blood.

DANNY: The hunt.

PAUL: The union.

(BETO and PAUL exit)

DANNY: It will come. It will come.

(Beat)

DANNY (as MAMA):   *(calls out to TÍA)* Hermana? Hermana? Traime mi pelo!

(PAUL enters with DANNY'S 'MAMA hat/wig.' Bit of business and ad-lib between the two, while arranging MAMA)

IT BINDS US TOGETHER

MAMA: In 1521, the Spaniards invaded Atzlan. 1521 – think about it. It's a quinceañera, or a quincentenaria, no? Sabes qué, it was the end of innocence. That's what I was always taught. Pero, then again, maybe it wasn't.

It was the end of the old way, yes. But before there were the diseases of the Spaniards, like smallpox, diphtheria, etc., there were the thousands of years of wars and sacrifice among Aztecs, Toltecs, Olmecs, Maya, Zapotecs ...

La inocencia. It never existed.

Sabes qué más, people are always trying to look to someone to blame for the end of innocence – like some people blame La Malinche, the symbolic mother of the mestizo race, an Indian slave given to the Spaniards, who ended up helping Cortés conquer the Aztec Empire. Pero did she guide his ship to the New World? Did she?

A mother knows things; she knows innocence will pass, so it's best to be prepared and to prepare her children también, because when the caca hits the fan ... híjole! Do grown-ups say, 'It's you're fault! No, it's your fault!'

OK – maybe the Republicans do, but real grown-ups deal with it.

   This I know – blood (sangre) will flow. Blood (sangre) will be shed – pero it's sangre that binds us together.

(Sound: techno music begins. DANNY turns and adjusts his hat/wig, letting hair fall from underneath, and becomes DOÑA MARINA (MALINCHE). PAUL enters as CORTÉS, wearing a black leather jacket)

THE JAGUAR LOUNGE

CORTÉS: Doña Marina, where are we? Where have you brought me?

DOÑA MARINA: The Jaguar Lounge, the hottest night-stop in all Tenochitlan! Everybody who's anybody comes here *(indicating in front of them)*. You'd be surprised how many guys come here before going home to their wives! Oh look … there's the High Priest Tayatzin! *(loud whisper to Cortés)* Don't stare! – you want him to think you're cruising him? He's so cool. All the girls call him, 'Heart Breaker.' *(looking for reaction)* Get it? … Heart Breaker …?

CORTÉS: *(looking around he makes an innocent observation)*   Doña Marina, there are no women in this lounge.

DOÑA MARINA: Duh! I figured you're European, so you wouldn't mind.

CORTÉS: Dios mío! This is a den of iniquity!!

DOÑA MARINA: Yeah! I used to date the Olmec guy … he's working behind the bar; big hands, just like you. I get two-fers any time he's here – even when it's not the post-sacrifice happy hour. *(beat)* How about I get us a couple of beers? *(quickly rummages through pockets)* Jesus H. Christ, I left my money in my other pouch. Got any gold on you, Hernáncito? *(CORTÉS hands DOÑA MARINA some gold foil-wrapped condoms. DOÑA MARINA begins to exit … stops)* Domestic or import?

CORTÉS: Import!

DOÑA MARINA: Oh, silly me … stupid question.

(DOÑA MARINA exits offstage left. At same time BETO, as MOCTEZUMA, enters right. Simultaneously, MOCTEZUMA and CORTÉS see one another; there is an immediate attraction, but they both quickly turn away from the other's stare. CORTÉS approaches MOCTEZUMA)

CORTÉS: Hola.

MOCTEZUMA: Qué tal?

CORTÉS: I'm new in town. My name is Cortés. My woman brought me here.

MOCTEZUMA: How do you pronounce that?

CORTÉS: I said my name is Cortés.

MOCTEZUMA: No importa; we both know why we're here, don't we?

CORTÉS: Just that I have a thing about names. It's important to me people remember who I am!

MOCTEZUMA: I'm so tired of this place, same faces, same games ...

CORTÉS: Gods come and go ... Quezalcoatl, Texcalipoca, Edward James Olmos ...

MOCTEZUMA: I'm so bored with the chisme, but you ...

CORTÉS: But men, we live on.

MOCTEZUMA: You're different. I can tell.

CORTÉS: Soy muy macho.

MOCTEZUMA: Your eyes are so pretty, and so round – unlike your woman.

CORTÉS: She's just a woman – my slave to tell you the truth.

MOCTEZUMA: Oh, I've no doubt who wears the pantalones in your house.

CORTÉS: I'm not like these others, pretending I'm no más que just 'getting off.'

MOCTEZUMA: Pero, your skin is so soft; and so white como leche; a little pocho looking, but I like that ...

CORTÉS: I'm no maricón.

MOCTEZUMA: Not like the iguanas around here.

CORTÉS: Pero I'm not lying to myself either. *(Staring into MOCTEZUMA's eyes – never turning away)* I like you. Me gustas.

MOCTEZUMA: Quieres bailar? You like to dance? *(They spin slowly)* I do ... *(CORTÉS reaches for MOCTEZUMA who assertively raises his hand)* Pero let's wait for another song. I hate techno.

CORTÉS: Mi esposa, my real wife back home, she's got eyes just like you.

MOCTEZUMA: Don't you wish sometimes for adventure; something new and exciting. I like new and exciting. Do you? *(looking into* CORTÉS's *eyes)*

CORTÉS: Qué lindos tus ojos.

MOCTEZUMA: Something that just comes along and grabs you, pins you down and changes your whole world, your whole vida?

CORTÉS: *(dips MOCTEZUMA)* You ever been with a real man? I'm not talking about some joto ... but a real man?

MOCTEZUMA: I have some really nice music at my place. Wanna come over?

(They exit the bar; lights shifting to night ambience)

MOCTEZUMA: I know – I'll play you Selena singing Donna Summer's 'Last Dance.'

CORTÉS: I hate Donna Summer!

MOCTEZUMA: But I'm talking about *(with reverence)* La Selena!

CORTÉS: Entonces. *(CORTÉS takes MOCTEZUMA's hand)*

(They resume walking, then stop center stage)

MOCTEZUMA: You know why the moon looks like that?

CORTÉS: Every time I look up in the sky I see possibilities.

MOCTEZUMA: We say one of our gods smacked the moon with a rabbit! Looks more like a snake in the grass to me. How about you? You see a rabbit or a snake?

CORTÉS: I see what I want and I take it – that's just the way I am. *(passionately embracing MOCTEZUMA)*

MOCTEZUMA: Your skin, qué brillante, como la luna. Tus brasos, all full of fire. Take me with your boca. Your legs are steel, tus lips como gold. Discover me! Más! Y Más! Wrap your snake across mis ojos.

(MOCTEZUMA crouches in front of CORTÉS. DOÑA MARINA enters, unseen by MOCTEZUMA and CORTÉS. CORTÉS pulls out gold-foil wrapped condom; opens and begins to unfold it)

Blind me with your desire to have me! Más! Y más! *(sensing someone watching)* Espérate!

DOÑA MARINA: Tough toe-nails, Hernáncito.

(MOCTEZUMA and CORTÉS quickly break – both rearranging themselves)

They only have domestic ... and I know how you hate domestic *(referring to MOCTEZUMA) (To MOCTEZUMA)* Hey Mo', what's shaking at the temple these days? See you found a new object of worship for the night? *(indicating CORTÉS)*

MOCTEZUMA: Malinche!

DOÑA MARINA: Malinal, thank you, Moctezuma.

CORTÉS: Doña Marina? ... Moctezuma ...? You know each other?

MOCTEZUMA: I know some of the slaves.

DOÑA MARINA: The ones who were born nobles.

MOCTEZUMA: So you like to say.

DOÑA MARINA: At least I got my job based on my ability with languages.

CORTÉS: *(to MOCTEZUMA)* Why didn't you tell me who you were?

DOÑA MARINA: He hardly knows how to read an omen – do you expect him to know himself?

MOCTEZUMA: Por favor Malinche, cállate! *(to CORTÉS)* First of all, you never asked me. Secondly, *(indicating MALINCHE)* unlike those jotos out on the street announcing it to everyone, some of us like being anonymous. Makes it a little more exciting, a little more mysterious. You probably do the same thing back home.

DOÑA MARINA: Yeah!

CORTÉS: Once or twice, maybe more on weekends.

MOCTEZUMA: Pero, too late. My buzz is killed. My temple no longer stands erect. *(Taking condoms out of CORTÉS's hand)* Malinche, what is this?

CORTÉS: We could start again. Pretend we just met, no names this time.

DOÑA MARINA: It's a condom. *(More emphatic)* Un condón. *(MOCTEZUMA doesn't get it)* There's no náhuatl equivalent. *(MOCTEZUMA still doesn't get it – even more emphatic)* It's a sheath for your temple! ... keeps the blood separate from the sacrifice, so to speak.

CORTÉS: I could say, 'Hey, I'm a hot top daddy looking to occupy your foreign soil. Something like that ...'

MOCTEZUMA: 'Keeps the blood separate.' Ridiculous! What's the point then? The blood is the sacrifice!

DOÑA MARINA: Pero, you don't know who he's been with!

CORTÉS: *(interjecting)* You could say that 'discover me' part again ... I liked that.

MOCTEZUMA: And he doesn't know who I've been with!

DOÑA MARINA: I don't think you've been in as many ports of call – he's been places.

MOCTEZUMA: I've conquered nations!

CORTÉS: *(hugging MOCTEZUMA from behind)* I could sail my ship into your canals, colonize your tight little ports.

DOÑA MARINA: Look Mo', even though you've totally disregarded me as a person and a woman, cut down my people, I'm going to give you a little gift of survival in the new world.

CORTÉS: *(seductively)* It's a really big ship.

(MOCTEZUMA now gives CORTÉS his full attention)

DOÑA MARINA: The first rule of any negotiation is that you take care of yourself.

MOCTEZUMA: I am thinking of myself – can't you see, the world revolves around my needs. *(pulling CORTÉS closer in, behind him)*

DOÑA MARINA: I'm not being heard here.

CORTÉS and MOCTEZUMA: Cállate, woman!

CORTÉS: There's no room for you here.

DOÑA MARINA: Fine! I'll go, but learn from my example. And watch who you call Malinche! And when you start looking for a scapegoat, and you will, don't come looking for me.

(CORTÉS and MOCTEZUMA watch DOÑA MARINA exit)

CORTÉS: Let me show you what I mean by God.

(They strike tableau; CORTÉS with his arms around MOCTEZUMA, who strikes Christ-on-the-cross pose)

(Blackout – BETO and PAUL exit. Sound – Sylvester's 'Mighty Real' begins playing loudly. A mirror ball lights up and spins)

CHAOS

(Chaos is a choral poem with movement. Physical gestures taken from a series of interpretative improvisations on the text. DANNY, then PAUL, then BETO enter, each wearing a black leather jacket.)

ALL: It was the '80s.

PAUL: And I had just come out, if that's what you call it.

ALL: It was the 1980s.

DANNY: And I was married. I was driving a big car. I was a happy little brown man, but I was still Spanish, and it was fabulous.

PAUL: I hadn't learned to be comfortable with the word 'gay.'

DANNY: I was fabulous.

ALL: We were fabulous.

PAUL: My brother tried to lay his hands on me and pray it away.

BETO: Don and I met in 1976 at the Midtown Spa — a seedy bathhouse just off skid-row in Los Angeles.

DANNY: The fan dancer was the mainstay of the bar, in Houston ...

DANNY and BETO: ... in New Orleans ...

ALL: ... in San Francisco.

BETO: The clientele were mostly Black and Latino, and men who liked Blacks and Latinos. I went there having as much sex as I wanted with as many men as I wanted.

DANNY: And they were all on quaaludes and acid.

PAUL: I longed for closeness.

BETO: Few people asked for a name ... even fewer bothered giving one.

PAUL: I feared retribution.

DANNY: They were soft, skinny men, and they had hair; there was no shaving.

ALL: There was this Castro street look.

BETO: I went half-hoping that amongst the parade of naked men that cruised the halls, amongst the blow-jobs, the hand-jobs, the penetration ... the kiss.

PAUL: Divine ...

ALL: ... retribution!

DANNY: And it was plaid shirts and not built bodies. The gym was for someone working out his junior high demons, which we left behind, like our families.

BETO: I might find ...

ALL: Mr. Right.

BETO: Well, it was Don.

DANNY: To find the constant heart ...

ALL: ... beat, beat, beat ...

DANNY: ... that kept everything moving.

PAUL: Lightning, the fires of hell.

BETO:	DANNY and PAUL:
Within a few months we were	*(echoing)*
living together ...	living together ...
throwing parties ...	throwing parties ...
going to concerts ...	going to concerts ...
the theater ...	the theater ...
weekend jaunts ...	weekend jaunts.

DANNY:	BETO and PAUL:
The constant lust that kept	*(echoing)*
everyone roving, in the parks ...	the parks ...
the back rooms ...	the back rooms ...
the bathhouses ...	the bathhouses ...

ALL: The sex clubs!

PAUL: Dirty looks from Jesus.

BETO: A great relationship with the exception that I was failing miserably at being monogamous.

PAUL: When a man looked at me, I turned away.

DANNY: I saw Grace Jones at Daddy's Money in Montrose, and she was this extraordinary big woman. She was about sex.

BETO: *(echoing)* Sex.

PAUL: *(echoing)* Sex.

BETO: Don and I broke up sometime in early 1984. Suddenly I was ...

BETO and DANNY: ... alone ...

BETO and PAUL: ... and single.

	DANNY:		BETO:
	Everything was about		*(echoing)*
	sex ...	sex ...	
	Every bit of clothing		PAUL:
	I shopped for was about		*(echoing)*
	sex ...	sex ...	

BETO: By then there were already rumors of gay men dying from a mysterious disease ...

ALL: ... a cancer.

PAUL: And only one person in my family made me feel OK to be gay.

DANNY: And there was this sense that nothing would end.

BETO: The first man I ever saw get sick was dead exactly six months after his initial diagnosis – it was that quick.

DANNY: We would have money and we would have drugs, and sex, and brunch.

PAUL: Almost as soon as I heard about gay ...

ALL: ... cancer.

BETO: Early 1984 I took a test – they said that they had developed this test to determine whether or not you had been exposed/infected.

PAUL: Almost as soon as that gay cancer became ...

ALL: ... G.R.I.D. ...

PAUL: ... he called to say he had it.

BETO: If they find antibodies to this virus, then that means you've been infected, which means that you were going to die.

DANNY: And suddenly it all changed – overnight people were disappearing.

BETO: My first test came back positive.

PAUL: Don't get it, he said. Be careful – but I had been fighting a bigger battle with evil.

BETO: My second test came back positive.

DANNY:	BETO and PAUL:
And it happened in	*(echoing)*
New York ...	New York ...
and LA ...	LA ...
and Houston ...	Houston ...
and San Francisco ...	San Francisco ...
and Miami ...	Miami.
but you didn't know what was happening.	

BETO: My ultimate test was to not lose my mind.

PAUL: And so I retreated further into my shame.

DANNY: But no one would talk about it unless, of course, a friend arrived on your doorstep.

BETO: I told no one because no one wanted to listen.

PAUL: When a friend called needing help ...

DANNY: ... needing a place to stay before going to the hospital to die.

PAUL: I was there.

BETO: I wanted to scream out, 'Help me!'

PAUL: ... help me!

DANNY: ... help me! *(beat)* And nothing was being done, except the newspapers were reporting this ...

ALL: ... gay plague.

DANNY: All of a sudden my friends are dying.

BETO: I've got it!

PAUL: In the hospital we wore gowns and masks.

DANNY: The people I planned to stay young and get rich with walked like old men.

BETO: I'm infected – and no one is listening.

(ALL begin pacing at different speeds, from upstage to downstage and back, at times varying the speed, and occasionally doing vestigial gestures taken from earlier in the scene)

PAUL: 1981 ...

ALL: 152 cases of AIDS reported in the United States.

BETO: I'm going to die of AIDS.

ALL: G. R. I. D. – Gay Related Immunodeficiency Disease. AIDS – Acquired Immune Deficiency Syndrome.

PAUL: And no one was doing anything.

ALL: Remember this? 1982 ... 317 dead. 1983 ... 1,292 dead. 1984 ...

DANNY: 3,665 dead. And the government does nothing.

BETO and PAUL: Don't forget this.

PAUL: Until the Hollywood actor playing the part of the president loses a friend.

ALL: 1985 ...

BETO: 8,161 dead.

DANNY: I saw a sign. It said, 'if you're tired of racism, if you're tired of homophobia, if you're tired of sexism ... if you're tired of seeing your friends die ...

BETO: It's getting closer ... I can feel it getting closer.

DANNY: ... if you're mad as hell ...

PAUL: ... then come to this meeting.

BETO: I'm going to die of AIDS.

DANNY: And I went because I knew I had no choice, but when we all sat in the room ...

PAUL: ... and had to face each other ...

DANNY: ... we knew that there was no choice but to summon our collective power, and ...

DANNY and PAUL: *(chanting)* act-up, fight back, fight AIDS!

BETO: Someone do something!

(ALL take out chalk pieces from their pockets, alternating laying each other on the floor and chalking one another's body)

PAUL: I was reluctant to march at first.

ALL: 1986 ...

DANNY: 16,301 dead. And the government ignores us ...

PAUL: ... but the anger built.

DANNY: It just illuminated that we're disposable people.

BETO: I am the 'high risk group.'

PAUL: The righteous anger.

ALL: Nobody cares about a dead queer.

BETO: I am the leper.

ALL: 1987 ...

BETO: 27,909 dead.

DANNY: Silence equals death!

BETO: I'm fighting for my fucking life — don't ask me to be civily disobedient!

DANNY and PAUL: *(continuously chanting)* Whose fucking streets? Our fucking streets! *(DANNY and PAUL go into the audience and get four AUDIENCE MEMBERS; bringing them onstage, they lay the AUDIENCE MEMBERS on the floor and begin outlining their bodies with chalk)* Whose fucking lives? Our fucking lives!

BETO: Whose fucking life? My fucking life!

ALL: 1988 ...

PAUL: 46,134 dead.

ALL: 1989 ...

PAUL: 70,313 dead.

DANNY: We took the stage for those that went before us. We tied ourselves to buildings, for ourselves and our friends. Remember this.

ALL: 1990 ...

BETO: 100,820.

ALL: 1991 ...

BETO: 130,250.

ALL: 1992 ...

DANNY: 160,000.

ALL: Don't forget this ... *(chanting)* Shame, shame, shame!

ALL: 1993 ...

BETO: 200,850.

DANNY: *(In a line: ALL execute and hold predetermined physical gesture — symbol for 'positive')* The positive.

PAUL: 'No cure.'

ALL: 1994 ...

PAUL: 250,000.

BETO: *(On line, ALL execute and hold predetermined physical gesture — symbol for 'negative')* The negative.

ALL: 1995 ...

BETO: 300,000.

PAUL: *(On line, ALL execute and hold A.S.L. sign for 'death')* The dead.

ALL: 1996 ...

DANNY: 362,000.

BETO: *(On line, ALL execute A.S.L. sign for 'applause')* The surviving.

(Sound — Sylvester's 'Mighty Real' fades and out. ALL lower their arms. PAUL and DANNY help the AUDIENCE MEMBERS back to their seats. BETO stands at edge of proscenium)

BETO: *(to audience)* I remember Tommy Geffreon, David Berfield, and Phil Irwin. I remember Ken Jones, who took his AZT daily ... with a fifth of vodka. I remember Chester, who died alone. I remember Robert Giles ... childhood friends; we played on the playground together .... I remember Pat, Mike, David, Eddie, Larry, Frank, Juan ...

ALL: *(On line, ALL execute 'positive' sign)* And there are others.

(PAUL joins BETO at edge of proscenium)

PAUL: *(to audience)* I remember Arturo, David, Eduardo, Jeffrey, Terry, and Tony.

ALL: *(On line, ALL execute 'negative' sign)* And there are others.

(DANNY joins PAUL and BETO)

DANNY: *(to audience)* I remember Albert. I remember David. I remember Craig — and I remember 9-year-old Chastity.

ALL: *(On line, ALL execute A.S.L. sign for 'death')* And there are others.

(ALL extend their arms toward the audience)

BETO: *(to audience)* You can see them ... their faces — you can see them clearly in your mind. Who were they? Call out their names.

(ALL listen as AUDIENCE MEMBERS call out names of deceased)

ALL: *(On line, at end of litany, ALL execute A.S.L. sign for 'applause')* And there are others.

(ALL turn and begin walking upstage direction, over 'graveyard' of outlined bodies. PAUL and DANNY exit. BETO crouches, executes 'positive, negative, dead, and surviving' signs at foot of outlined body.)

RICHARD INGLES

BETO: I remember the usual richard ingles
the image of him striding up the walk
that outlined the garden there at LA CASA, where we all lived

richard ingles
was tall and bearded, leather and levis, pierced and booted
the keys dangling from his belt loop bounced
upon assorted black, red, checkered and yellow handkerchiefs
worn in his left hip pocket
right next to a small black whip whose tassels slipped
in and out between his striding crotch as he walked

but today richard walked out into the garden
not the sensuous and virile leather-daddy-master man
we were accustomed to seeing at LA CASA

jerry whispered to sonora
who promptly told jose and carlos
who indicated to david that maybe don and I should know
or at least mention it to
bob and roger
rick and shultzie

and at the time none of us had even noticed
the small trickle of viral wave that had lapped against LA CASA's gate

richard spoke
his usual pleasant and warm manner
'can't seem to shake this flu-bug that's been going around
I've been like this for over a month now
hard to eat sometimes
hurts my eyes to be in the sun too long'

by the second month
he had lost an alarming amount of weight
as the media finally picked up reports of homosexual men dying
in mass numbers across the U.S.

meanwhile
richard's fevers became persistent as the night sweats increased
and then the diarrhea set in

by the fourth month richard was losing his sight
but regarded this as a blessing
no longer able to watch or willing his own body waste away to nothing
no longer able to count or willing the newest cancerous lesion on his body
no longer able to walk or bathe or clean or feed himself

by the beginning of the sixth month it was all over
and we stood there in the garden

(DANNY and PAUL enter, and stop upstage left and upstage right, respectively. Over their faces they hold clipboards with a skull (calaveras) painted on each. On their T-shirts, they wear large red ribbons. They stand, flanking BETO.)

all of us
stunned
it was that quick

THE DOCENTS

(BETO crosses upstage center and remains there throughout scene. DANNY and PAUL cross into playing area)

PAUL: Welcome to the Museum's, 'Uh-oh, it's AIDS show!' We at the Museum are proud to kick-off our '97 season with this controversial show. What about AIDS, kids? Hmm? Do we know what AIDS means? *(beat)* Good, then we don't need to say those long words again.

(DANNY delivers the same monologue, in very bad Spanish, with no regard for proper pronunciation or accent. At times, PAUL cuts off DANNY. Other times, they interject ad libs)

DANNY: *(in bad Spanish)* Bienvenidos al Museo, 'Ay caramba, es la SIDA!' Saben ustedes qué es la SIDA? Bueno ...

PAUL: *(cutting DANNY off)* AIDS is a very bad disease that can hurt you very much and even kill you.

DANNY: *(in bad Spanish)* La SIDA es un enfermidad qué te puede martar.

PAUL: And we at the Museum think that AIDS is so important that it has to be discussed by everyone.

DANNY: *(in bad Spanish)* Y nosotros aquí en en Museo creémos qué es tan importante, qué necesitamos hablar de la SIDA.

PAUL: We have to know about bad things so we can stay away from him. *(Correcting himself)* I mean them.

DANNY: *(in bad Spanish)* Tenemos qué conocer las cosas peligrosas para poder estar muy lejos de el – perdon, lejos de ellos.

PAUL: Right?

DANNY: Derecho?

PAUL: We don't eat candy all the time, do we? Because that would be bad for us, right?

DANNY: *(in bad Spanish)* No comemos las dulces todo el tiempo, uh huh?

PAUL: Do we know how we get AIDS? Hmm? Good, so I won't discuss that any further, though if you can't understand you should ask your Mommy and Daddy.

DANNY: *(in bad Spanish)* Saben ustedes algaran la SIDA? Hmm? Bueno, bueno, si ustedes no entienden, preguntan su Mama y Papa.

PAUL: *(indicating BETO)* Here is a model of one of the first people affected with AIDS. But he's not a super-model, is he? Look how bad he looks. Doesn't he look bad, like someone who didn't care about himself? He's rough and dangerous, and maybe that's how he treated himself.

DANNY: *(in bad Spanish)* Mira, mira! Aqui es un model de el primero persona con la SIDA. Pero el no es un model-super. El parece rough-o y dangeroso.

PAUL: When we grow up, we want to be healthy. We want to wear good clothes, and corte our pelo, and look nice, and be nice, and feel nice. And be nice, nice people. People who don't get AIDS.

DANNY: *(in bad Spanish)* Cuando nosotros crecen, queremos ser buen personas – queremos ropa muy bueno, queremos hair cut muy bueno, queremos take care of ourselves, y queremos ser bueno bueno gente, qué no tienen la SIDA.

(BETO has walked downstage center, between PAUL and DANNY, angered by what's been said – he glares at PAUL)

PAUL: Oh, I'm sorry. I didn't mean that. We know that nice people get AIDS too, right? There are innocent victims of AIDS. They are children and hemophi ...

(BETO cuts PAUL off by raising PAUL's clipboard, covering PAUL's face. BETO turns and glares at DANNY)

DANNY: *(indicating PAUL)* La Jueda dice qué ... *(frightened, he raises his clipboard over his face)*

(BETO grabs edges of both Clipboards, and exits with them. PAUL and DANNY immediately revert to TÍA and MAMA characters. Some ad lib, TÍA asking MAMA to bring her wig out to her. DANNY exits quickly, then returns with TÍA's hat/wig. DANNY quickly exits)

SACRIFICES

TÍA: You know, when I think of Tito ... I can't help but get all misty, tu sabes. Por qué, he never got a chance to grow up, I mean he never had a 'Coming Out' ceremony como Veronica. He should have had a little bouquet, or something ... Tito was like familia to us; he was blood *(crosses himself)*. Y también he was also a mariposa, and I mean that nicely, you know that – but we don't discuss things like that in this family.

Ceremonies are important! They tell everybody where you've been, where you are ... where you're going. Tito should have had a ceremony.

The funeral was nice – it was 'a celebration of his life,' just like Father Gomez said. Pero por favor, if you're going to celebrate someone's life, do it while they're still around, no?

You know, every year the Aztecs would take this one handsome guy and all year long treat him como like un God; they gave him everything. *(Caught up in the romantic image)* Entonces, then at the end of the year he was marched through the streets and taken to the top of the tallest pyramid. And then they would turn around and present him to the entire cuidad, and then, with everyone looking on his beauty, they would get a flint knife and cut his heart out! Claro qué si! They killed him! He was sacrificed. He would become their messenger carrying their prayers to the gods.

They used to sacrifice virgins too! *(beat)* I could see myself standing there next to this handsome man about to be sacrificed. I'd be standing there all virgin-like ... and we'd be looking deep into each other's eyes. And when they turned around to get the knife, I'd say, 'Psst! Hey! Let's get out of here. Let's go down to the zocalo, play some of that new basketball that everyone's talking about, maybe float on a milpa, have a raspa ... Maybe if I come back not-a-virgin, we don't have to go through with this, because I don't know about you, Tito, but I'm tired of all this death. I got my whole life to live – which I'd gladly live in tribute to you, but hey, I'd be expecting yours in return, ese! So what do you say – I say, let's run, let's run – let's let good loving be our sacrifice!'

Tito was blood ... even if it was infected, he was still blood.

(PAUL exits upstage right; circle of light comes up, center stage)

THE CREED

(Sound: A light timbre bell rings five times. DANNY and BETO enter, upstage. PAUL walks upstage and joins them. White skirts and veils fly in)

DEFIANCE AND ACQUIESCENCE

PAUL: *(singing – like Gregorian chant) (BETO and DANNY remove PAUL's black skirt and T-shirt)*
I don't believe in living in fear.
I don't believe AIDS is an act of punishment, against women, against children, against people of color, against IV drug users, against the poor, against men, and prisoners, and queers.
I don't believe it's a moral universe.
I don't believe that I'm less of a man,
I don't believe in rigidly defined genders.
I don't believe women are inferior, or that men are superior.
I don't believe in hell, except what we inflict upon each other.
I don't believe my pleasure is a sin.

(Sound: A light timbre bell rings five times, during which DANNY and BETO dress PAUL in a white skirt)

HEALING

ALL: *(ALL execute gestures of defiance and acquiescence)*
I believe in the opening of our eyes.
I believe in the act of reaching out.
I believe that compassion is revolution.
I believe my voice is righteous.
I believe my anger is good.
I believe I am a long-term survivor.
I believe in mystery.

(Sound: A light timbre bell rings three times, during which DANNY changes upstage center position with PAUL)

TRIBE

DANNY: *(singing — like Gregorian chant) (BETO and PAUL remove DANNY's black skirt and T-shirt)*

I don't believe my universe has to be exclusively small or gay.
I don't believe in negating our queer elders.
I don't believe in abandoning our queer youth.
I don't believe in separating myself from drag queens, butch dykes, leather dykes, leather men and women.
I don't believe that lesbians are my enemy
or that all gay men are necessarily my friends.

(Sound: A light timbre bell rings five times, during which PAUL and BETO dress DANNY in a white skirt)

HEALING

ALL: *(ALL execute gestures of TRIBE)*
I believe in my tribe, and the right to create it.
I believe we are long-term survivors.
I believe in gardens.

(Sound: A light timbre bell rings three times, during which BETO *changes upstage center position with* DANNY*)*

AFFIRMATIONS

BETO: *(singing — like Gregorian chant)*

*(*PAUL *and* DANNY *remove* BETO's *black skirt and T-shirt)*

I don't believe in one almighty pill that will cure.
I don't believe in the rigid identities of negative and positive.
I don't believe positive is inferior,
I don't believe negative is superior.
I don't believe that status should keep us from loving someone.

(Sound: A light timbre bell rings five times, during which PAUL *and* DANNY *dress* BETO *in a white skirt)*

HEALING

ALL: *(*ALL *execute gestures of affirmation)*
I believe that I will someday eradicate the virus from my body.
I believe AIDS is our shared legacy,
here, now, and still.
I believe that we must choose when and how to be present to AIDS.
I believe the body is of infinite mystery, and I bless that.
I believe that we have learned to acknowledge the beauty of our lives.
I believe I am a long-term survivor.
I believe in my journey.

(Sound: A light timbre bell rings three times)

HISTORY/CYCLES OF HISTORY

ALL: *(singing in harmony)*
I don't believe in a cycle of blame,
I don't believe in a cycle of shame, returning from history, even recent history.
I don't believe in the separation from the blood of sacrifice taken from atop a pyramid or a hospice bed.

(Sound: A light timbre bell rings three times. ALL *turn and walk upstage, retrieve their white veils, turn to face audience)*

HEALING

ALL: *(ALL slowly walk center stage)*
I believe in the witness of the community.
I believe in a living spirit that transcends death.
I believe in my journey.
I believe my forgiveness is important.
I believe I am a long-term survivor.

(Sound: A light timbre bell rings three times)

THE VOWS

DANNY: *(stepping forward)* Para mi quinceañera, en celebración de quince años viviendo en el tiempo del SIDA. I vow to remember, and to tell the stories; to cherish this lifetime with loved ones. I vow to be a witness and survivor. To ride the rainbow of my own creation and live every day as a new beginning. I vow to always give life a second chance, and finally, I vow to let love in.

(DANNY steps back. BETO *steps forward)*

BETO: Para mi quinceañera, en celebración de quince años viviendo en el tiempo del SIDA. I vow to continue offering prayers for the happiness, health, long-life and prosperity for all my family and friends. And I vow to someday be working in a garden . . . a very, very old man with hair as white as newly fallen snow.

(BETO steps back. PAUL *steps forward)*

PAUL: Para mi quinceañera, en celebración de quince años viviendo en el tiempo del SIDA. I vow to love with equal parts, need, nurturance and challenge. I vow to speak of my fear and my hurt. I vow to listen to others. I vow to sing of my love. I vow to listen to others. And finally, I vow to dance.

ALL: And I vow to dance. *(ALL execute understood gestures)* In the name of the positive, the negative, the dead and the surviving.

(*Blackout. End of show*)

(*Post-show: Lights come up for bows. Sound: Selena's 'Last Dance.' ALL bow, then curtsy, then exit. ALL return to stage and dance with AUDIENCE as post-show music plays.*)

18

Quinceañera: a Latino queer and transcultural party for AIDS

Alberto Sandoval-Sánchez

If you are a Latino gay man living with AIDS, as I am, it hurts when you never see your own image or hear stories about people of color infected and affected by the plague. It is as if you do not exist. After two decades since the epidemic outbreak, mi gente are still invisible in mainstream representations of AIDS. Even worse, it is assumed that everything has been said, as White gay men exhausted the possibilities of storytelling in their accessibility to hegemonic cultural domains such as Broadway, Hollywood, and the publishing market. Not only that, but now that protease inhibitors have instigated the 'feeling' that the crisis is over for many, AIDS has become outdated. At this moment seen as a chronic illness – with patients living longer and having healthier lives[1] – AIDS is not a main preoccupation anymore to White America. AIDS has become a foreign issue, concerning other developing countries, specifically Africa where poverty, lack of education, malnutrition, and non-existent health care are eradicating an entire younger generation as well as threatening the future survival of their nations.

Back home, as White middle-class gay-men HIV exposure dropped drastically through the 1990s because of safe sex campaigns in addition to class and health care privilege, statistics skyrocketed among minorities: from 1993 to 1999 the HIV/AIDS cases reported by the *HIVAIDS Surveillance Report* among Whites increased from 181,151 to 318,354; among Latinos from 61,297 to 133,703; and among Blacks from 114,868 to 272,881. While White cases increased by 75.7 percent, Latino cases more than doubled with an increase of 118 percent and Blacks with a 137 percent increase. At this point, it is certain that minority populations in the barrios and ghettoes will have only a remote chance of voicing their experiences within the dominant cultural arenas. For this reason, local interventions are necessary and urgent, particularly through theater and performance where models of/for social action and change are the most effective and powerful. In all its marginality the New WORLD Theater in Amherst, Massachusetts, constitutes such an ideal localized stage, a space where people of color can imagine themselves through artistic self-representations. With its production of *Quinceañera* at the Intersections Conference in 1998, New WORLD Theater not only provided a performative site for Chicano/Latino gay men, but it made visible how Latino gay men are coping with AIDS and fighting homophobia and AIDSphobia which are rampant in Latino and Latin American societies.

IT'S MY *QUINCEAÑERA* AND *HABLO ESPAÑOL* IF I WANT TO

Quinceañera is a daring, courageous, and subversive piece that centers on the experiences, vicissitudes, and activism of gay Chicano/Latino artists using theater to entertain, to educate audiences, and to empower Latino gay men and audiences in general. In its surface structure its plot centers on the appropriation by Latino gay men of a traditional U.S. Latina/Latin American woman's rite of passage in a ceremony known as *fiesta de quinceañera*. The ritual symbolizes at the age of 15 an adolescent's transition from childhood to womanhood. For U.S. Latinas/os, *quinceañeras* have become popular as a symbol of ethnic pride and cultural affirmation. For example, in San Antonio and Phoenix the Church has issued guidelines – including spiritual preparation, Bible study, *quinceañera* and Hispanic history, retreats with parents – to discourage materialist excesses and opulent expenditure.

Today *quinceañeras* are more than ever a cultural expression practiced within Latino enclaves that 'celebrate family, strengthen the community, and instill pride in our respective cultures' (Salcedo, 1997: ix). They form part of a Hispanic renaissance among the Latina/o young generation resisting assimilation and who are proud of their ancestral roots. It is within this social context and ethnic heritage that *Quinceañera*, the theatrical piece, must be situated since it engages in a dialogue with the coming-of-age ritual in all its performativity. Since there are no *quinceañeros* for boys, being a gender-specific ritual practice, this collaborative piece gives an unexpected twist to the ritual: this time Chicano/Latino gay men, who lack any rites of passages to mark their lives, appropriate the *fiesta de quinceañera* to ritualize 15 years of living with AIDS.

QUEERING THE *QUINCEAÑERA*

A series of vignettes advance the plot in *Quinceañera*. It is the first two scenes and the last two that specify that the performance displays and is framed within a rite of passage. Each of these scenes functions within the structure of a traditional *quinceañera*. In order to familiarize the spectators with the Chicano history and purpose of the ritual, the opening scene has a young woman, Verónica, telling her mother and aunt her wish to celebrate her *quinceañera*. Her birthday planning is both a religious and secular ceremony which follows the format of the festive event: she wants a mass to affirm her promises of faith; she needs a *madrina* and *padrino* (godparents) and a court of honor; and she must have a dance, a band, and a large cake. She even consulted the priest who gave her a book to read containing the genealogy of the ritual, one that remounts to the Aztec tradition of coming-of-age ceremonies for young women as they prepared for marriage.

Although this opening introduces and instructs the audience in the significance and laborious preparation for a *quinceañera*, it is also a humorous and parodic version of the ceremony. First of all, the three actors are partially in drag – since they wear skirts, and their impersonations are histrionic.[2] Their humor is hilarious. When the young woman shows her *tía* the perfect pattern for her dress, she mocks her by telling her that if she wore it, she would look like a float in the Rose Parade. Verónica states that this dress will make her look like a woman, in this way, pointing to her virginity and availability. When her aunt makes fun of her once again by questioning her 'womanhood' and she replies that she is a woman in every sense of the word, her mother misunderstands her. She thinks that she is not a virgin any more, but the girl replies that she still has her 'cookies.' Her aunt, who is not sexually inhibited, clarifies what she means by cookies: 'Her pan dulce, hermana. No man's tasted the sweet delicious filling of her empanada.' It is important to accentuate, first, that these 'women' are breaking taboos by openly talking about sexuality, and secondly, how sexuality is ethnicized in a culinary fashion. The question is who is going to eat the empanada that will be exhibited at the *quinceañera*. In spite of the comfort in talking about sexuality, the young woman's future is anchored on compulsory heterosexuality and marriage. Thus, the performance fails to question and dismantle roles and positionings assigned to women in patriarchy. *Quinceañeras* as spectacles of voyeurism, like it or not, provide a social site for the 'traffic of women.'

On the other hand, from a queer vantage point, the performance subverts the heterosexual gender grammar and horizon of expectations embedded on the *quinceañera*. Given that the actors are gay and cross-dressers, gender behavior is deconstructed: they put into question male and female ways of seeing sexuality and gender codes. Nevertheless, this could be a dangerous undertaking if the audience happens to be straight, particularly Latino audiences who define homosexuality in terms of gender identity rather than in view of sexual orientation. It is necessary to make clear that Latino homosexuals are conceived as passive in heterosexual gender constructions – that is, gay men are placed in the site assigned to women – while 'real' men are active; even in having a same sex encounter, as Rafael M. Díaz states in his eye-opening book *Latino Gay Men and HIV: Culture, Sexuality, and Risk Behavior,* 'many men who sexually penetrate other men can do so in our culture without questioning their heterosexual (in their minds masculine) identity' (p. 74). Within this gendered ideological framework, by wearing skirts the performance could perpetuate stereotypes of Latino gay men as sissies and feminine whose ultimate representative is *la loca,* the drag queen.

And speaking of *locas,* of all the boys that Verónica would love to have as escort, Walter Mercado is her first choice. Mercado is an eccentric Puerto Rican actor who has become a gay icon for U.S. Latinos/as and Latin America. He is famous for his horoscopes and spiritual advice on TV shows which combine astrology, *santería,* Catholicism, and Asian doctrines. He has been called the Liberace of astrology given his baroque and queer attires. Verónica calls him *'La Reina de las Estrellas'* the biggest queen of them all. It is here that the dynamics of the performance change due to the fact that homosexuality interrupts and deviates the laws of compulsory heterosexuality imprinted in the ritual to the campiness and visibility of the Latino gay world. This is a big queer joke which also functions as a transition.

With the naming of Verónica's first serious choice, Tito, what was extremely funny turns into tragedy. Her mother and aunt wanted to keep secret until after the *quinceañera* that he had died of AIDS in 1983. As Verónica goes on naming a possible escort, she is confronted with death. All the boys in the hood have died of AIDS. It is not said if AIDS was transmitted through sexual contacts or IV drug addiction. But does it matter? The issue is to target those communities with a safe sex and clean needle usage campaign. It is not until the end of the performance, before the final phase of the rite of passage takes place, that Tito's cause of death is pronounced. In a monologue Verónica's aunt makes known his homosexuality and laments his early death. For her, Tito was *familia:* he 'was blood … even if it was infected, he was still blood.' She makes another revelation: all the dead boys were queers. What surfaces here is a politics of affinity and compassion between women and queers. Heterosexual men are absent like in many feminist plays. Latino gay men and Latina women have created a space of their own where once coalitions are in place, community building makes possible 'making *familia* from scratch.' (Moraga, 1993: 58)

Verónica's list of names primarily constitutes a conscious tribute on the part of the performers to recover from oblivion those who died after the epidemic was officially named in 1983 by the Centers for Disease Control. At this crucial date Verónica's birthday intersects with the longevity of the AIDS epidemic. In some manner, Verónica's *quinceañera* was a pretext to engage the audience before shifting to center staging Latino gay identity in the AIDS era and how Latino men empower themselves through performance in the practice of a ritual. From then on, the performance will center on the world-views and lives of Latino gay men for the last 15 years. Also, the audience will eventually find out the actors' own HIV status: Beto Arraiza is positive, the other two are negative.

The dead must be named because they have been silenced in the national official history of AIDS. *Quinceañera* is a rewriting, a dramatic *testimonio*, to name, like the AIDS quilt, the disappeared. This revision has its own chronology and it runs parallel to the AIDS hegemonic timetable. By naming, and even listing, the causes of death, *Quinceañera* recovers and memorializes a Latino AIDS history. Although it may be redundant for those who are acquainted with the AIDS rampage, the experience of AIDS must be staged from self-experience step by step to gain agency and articulate Latino queer identities in relation to the AIDS national discursive domain. Redundancy here is an act of intervention and self-affirmation. This inventory of dates, deceased Latinos, illnesses, and treatments summarizes 15 years of losses and survival.

In another vignette, 'Chaos,' once more that history is re-membered and voiced as the performers recount the story of AIDS. The scene reveals the inside pandemonium and anxieties caused by AIDS and how the pandemic has affected Latino gay life since the 1980s. All types of issues are tackled: coming out, closeted husbands, gay identity and self-labeling, promiscuity, drugs and disco life, guilt, secrecy, shame, casual sex in public spaces, loneliness and fear, illness and death, panic and hysteria after AIDS, political protests against the government and pharmaceutical industry, AIDS treatment, Act Up activism, HIV testing, and survival. Nothing is left out. Silence is death. Honesty and dignity are at the heart of this Latino AIDS history and performance. By speaking out, a purification rite takes place, one that invokes tolerance and compassion.

At first sight, the vignettes framed between the opening and closing scenes of the performance, where a rite of passage explicitly gets under way, may be perceived as *puro caos y confusión*. Such is not the case. The lack of linearity permits the voicing of Latino gay men in all their difference and imperative responses to the pandemic, as they display their fluid, contradictory, multiple, heterogeneous, bicultural, and bilingual identities. In all their fragmentation and plurality, these scenes provide a political and creative discursive site where subjectivities gain agency and are always in the making through each performance. These vignettes function as parts of a puzzle that must be ensembled, and, of course, there will be missing or lost parts. Each scene constitutes a fragmented *testimonio*, one that speaks from self-experience but one that at the same time becomes communal during the performance. Beto's *testimonio* ('15 and Sudden Realization') recounts poetically his homosexual awakening and desire for naked bodies in the homoerotic environment of the locker room and in sports. Danny's *testimonio* ('15 and Great Discoveries'[3]) revisits the house of memory of his childhood when he was sexually abused and molested in his own home. Paul's *testimonio* centers on the abusive harassment in his adolescence. Because of his effeminate behavior, he is a victim of homophobia and machismo.

Applicable here is Doris Sommer's theorization on Latin American on *testimonio*: '[The] singularity [of the testimonial 'I'] achieves its identity as an extension of the collective. The singular represents the plural not because it replaces or subsumes the group but because the speaker is a distinguishable part of the whole' (1988: 108). By breaking the silence, dismantling taboos, and making the personal political, both actors and audiences become empowered as they all achieve a sense of self-esteem, self-respect, and pride. As each performer engages in his memory trip to the dark and painful places of childhood and adolescence where sexual abuse, machismo, and homophobia were technologies of torture on a daily basis, coming out, telling each personal story, is a political act where memories originate and contribute to new ethnic and queer identity formations. In fact, witnessing, through performance, as Ramón Rivera-Servera has observed 'becomes the central mechanism for intersubjective negotiation ... The audience is positioned in community, left to act, perhaps to aide ... Witnessing leaves the audience with a sense of responsibility to the real' (1999: 10). For Rivera-Servera, witnessing calls the audience into action since most performances about AIDS, like *Quinceañera*, are practices of social activism that strategically employ dramatic devices for the interpellation of the audience into a community of activism.

TRANSCULTURATING AIDS

If Catholicism is a major component of the Chicano social reality, so is Mexican culture and heritage. When the Spaniards conquered Mexico and imposed their values, language, and religion, a clash of cultures occurred that initiated *mestizaje*. Since then, *mestizo* subjectivity is articulated within the dynamics of transculturation;[4] and that process of cultural fusion and constant negotiations became more complex after the Mexican American War (1846–8) and the Treaty of Guadalupe Hidalgo in 1848, when an already transculturated social world had to accommodate and adapt to an Anglo domestic colonial project imposing assimilation and historical amnesia. It is within this horizon of transcultural histories and experiences that *Quinceañera* opens a creative discursive location for Chicano/Latino gay men interventions in the struggle against AIDS and homophobia.

To begin with, just the fact that *quinceañeras* are celebrated among all Latino ethnic groups, it represents an act and practice of cultural consciousness that challenges and resists Anglo domestic imperialism. Since the *quinceañera* rivals with the Anglo sweet 16 birthday party, it is a political practice to combat dictated, regulated, and expected assimilation. Under these circumstances, the Latino usage of *quinceañera* represents an act of linguistic affirmation and of Hispanic cultural recuperation that materializes the bilingual and bicultural condition of U.S. Latinos/as. Speaking Spanish is an act of politico-cultural opposition, in this case, as well as when Spanglish is used in general to challenge 'imperial' hegemonic Anglo English Only pressure and cultural domination. This counter-hegemonic positioning also applies to the title of the performance piece: Spanish is spoken to name Latino cultural reality and experience – it affirms a cultural legacy transmitted under the dynamics of transculturation.

Grounded in the geopolitical terrain of *'la transfrontera,'* also known as 'contact zone' or 'borderscape,' Chicano/a subjectivity is continuously in a process of undoing and reconstruction, of incompleteness and desire for wholeness.[5] This constant juggling of two cultural worlds unceasingly in collision and integration is what makes possible the indeterminacy, irregularity, and unexpected innovative creativity that define transcultural identities. If social interaction and identity formation for transcultural subjects are determined by a give-and-take and contrapuntal process which re-produces identities in a final, but inconclusive, state of hybridity – given the constant shifting and oscillation of positionalities – *Quinceañera* is a magnificent example of transcultural subjectivities in the making. It is exactly the 'in betweenness' condition and interstitial location of transcultural subjects that make possible the transculturation of AIDS in the performance piece. AIDS, in this way, is approached with alternative ways of seeing which, in turn, generate new responses and acts of contestation and activism historically determined by cultural exchanges and transactions.

Cultural differences pervade the discursive webs that shape and articulate *Quinceañera*. The piece is informed by and refers to Anglo and Chicano/Latino ethnic and cultural markers without employing them in any premeditated fashion or order. Since everything is mixed, and cultures alternate and crisscross unexpectedly, placing AIDS within the contextualization of the *quinceañera* is a transcultural *operation de conscientización*. In this sense, AIDS is familiarized, that is it is turned into a traditional heritage celebration and into a comfortable occasion that brings family and community together. Hence, AIDS is something that can be spoken within the realm of the *familia*.

In one significant scene AIDS traverses a major transcultural conversion, which means that AIDS is reconfigured, ethnicified, and accommodated to Chicano/Latino ways of seeing, being, and doing. In a parody of a beauty contest, the Miss AZT-Land Pageant, the performers are three finalists who compete for the title of Miss AZT-Land. The pageant, despite the irony at work, has a political purpose: the winner will wear the Miss AZT-Land crown for a year representing the AIDS pandemic on behalf of the long-term survivors. As each participant in the contest presents himself and announces his status – (Miss HIV Optimistic (Beto), Miss Broadway Melody of the Future (Danny), and Miss Missed Congenial Passive better known as Miss Missed the Seventies (Paul) – they voice Latino experiences and identities as conditioned by AIDS. Yet the transculturation of AIDS goes further in this scene: by naming the contest AZT-Land, the performers cleverly place the drug AZT in the context of Chicano nationalism. Aztlán being the mythical homeland of the Southwest for the Chicano nation, its name registers magnificently the AIDS presence in Chicano communities. And the performers' ironic maneuver goes beyond spatial references: it deconstructs the myth of Aztlán while at the same time criticizing the Chicano movement for its homophobic practices since its inception in the 1960s. As a result, queers appropriate Aztlán to insert themselves within the landscape of the Chicano nation, and AIDS metonimically inscribed in AZT-Land breaks the silence and materializes transculturally the presence of AIDS in the Chicano community. To feel at home, Latino gays and lesbians must imagine for themselves a Chicano queer nation, in the words of Cherríe Moraga, a queer Aztlán: 'A Chicano homeland that could embrace all *its* people, including its jotería' (1993: 147).

BAILAMOS AT MY *QUINCEAÑERA?*

Quinceañera closes in a solemn and sacred manner: the last phase of the rite of passage unfolds the recitation of a Latino gay credo and vows to be implemented in the time of AIDS. Dressed in white skirts and with veils, with the sound of ringing bells before and after each performer's statement, the scenes replicate the format of the ritual of a *quinceañera* as it takes place during mass. The religious atmosphere is further crystallized when the performers chant their credos and vows, evoking the musical spiritual effects of a medieval choir of monks. Their credo is one of commitment, self-respect, solidarity, and compassion. Their credo states their promise to fight homophobia and AIDS. Their credo is one of love, mutual care, friendship, and hope. Each performer's vows addresses the urgency of community building and ways of healing: Danny vows to remember, to tell the stories, to be witness, and to survive.

Beto vows to continue offering prayers for the happiness, health, long-life prosperity for all his family and friends. And Paul vows to speak of his fear and his hurt, to listen to others, to sing of love, and to dance. Yes, dance. With disco music playing, now that the semi-religious ritual is terminated, the performers ask the audience to join them dancing. Given the politics of activism embedded in the performance, disco nostalgia does not function here as a romanticized past in reactionary terms. The fiesta has just begun; new forms of activism are about to emerge. It is time to celebrate *la vida* of all survivors and *la vida* of those who left us.

For a Latino gay man with AIDS, as I am, *Quinceañera* gave me strength and hope. It took me to dark places in my past. It made me feel once again deep wounds and open forgotten scars. It made me think about the dead, the dying, and my own death. It confronted me with my own diagnosis and health crises. Through the voicing of *testimonios*, the recovery of history, the acknowledgment of Latinidad in all its hybridity, and the construction of Latino queer subjectivities, *Quinceañera* empowered all of us in the audience. It opened a ritual space for the healing of violence, pain, fear, loss, and grief *en nuestras vidas* before and after AIDS. As a performance of healing, *Quinceañera* touched us *en nuestros corazones*. Its curative power, rooted in honesty, pride, activism, survival, and the celebration of life, made us dance once again.

NOTES

1. For an excellent critical reading of 'end-of-AIDS' discourse in the mainstream as well as in some queer communities, see David Román (2000).
2. In the opening scene they wear black skirts and head turbans. For the rest of the performance they wear the same black skirts until the last two scenes when they change into white skirts and veils.
3. Based on Michael Marinez's story.
4. On theories of transculturation in Latin America and their application to U.S. Latinos, see Silvia Spitta (1995) and Sandoval-Sánchez and Sternbach (2001).
5. These terms belong respectively to José A. Saldivar, Mary Louise Pratt, and Guillermo Gómez-Peña in their efforts to pin down transcultural identities, experiences, and spaces.

BIBLIOGRAPHY

Díaz, Rafael M., *Latino Gay Men and HIV: Culture, Sexuality and Risk Behavior* (New York: Routledge, 1998).

McLane, Daissan, 'The Cuban American Princess,' *New York Times* magazine, 26 February 1995, 42–3.

Moraga, Cherríe, *The Last Generation* (Boston: South End Press, 1993).

Muñoz, José Esteban, 'Memory Performance: Luis Alfaro's "Cuerpo Politizado,"' in Coco Fusco (ed.), *Corpus Delecti: Performance of the Americas* (London: Routledge, 2000, 97–113).

Rivera-Servera, Ramón, '(Em)bodied Testimonies: Autobiography and AIDS in United States Latina/o Performance,' paper presented at the MLA Convention (Chicago, 1999).

Román, David, 'Not-About-AIDS,' *GLQ*, 6(1) (2000): 1–28.

Román, David, *Acts of Intervention: Performance, Gay Culture, and AIDS* (Bloomington: Indiana University Press, 1998).

Salcedo, Michele, *Quinceañera: The Essential Guide to Planning the Perfect Sweet Fifteen Celebration* (New York: Henry Holt, 1997).

Sandoval-Sánchez, Alberto, *José, Can You See? Latinos On and Off Broadway* (Madison: University of Wisconsin Press, 1999).

Sandoval-Sánchez, Alberto, 'Breaking the Silence, Dismantling Taboos: Latino Novels on AIDS,' *Journal of Homosexuality*, Special Issue 'Gay and Lesbian Literature Since World War II: History and Memory,' ed. Sonya L. Jones, 34 (3/4) (1998): 155–75.

Sandoval-Sánchez, Alberto, 'A Response to the Representation of AIDS in the Puerto Rican Arts and Literature: In the Manner of a Proposal for a Cultural Studies Project,' *Centro de Estudios Puertorriqueños Bulletin, Puerto Ricans and AIDS: It's Time to Act!*, Special Issue, VI (1 and 2) (Spring 1994): 181–6.

Sandoval-Sánchez, Alberto (ed.), *Ollantay Theater Magazine*, special Issue 'Latino Theatre and AIDS,' II (2) (Fall 1994).

Sandoval-Sánchez, Alberto and Román, David, 'Caught in the Web: Latinidad, AIDS, and Allegory in *Kiss of the Spider Woman*,' in Celeste Fraser Delgado and José Esteban Muñoz (eds), *Everynight Life: Culture and Dance in Latin/o America* (Durham: Duke University Press, 1997: 255–87).

Sandoval-Sánchez, Alberto and Sternbach, Nancy Saporta, *Stages of Life: Transcultural Performance and Identity in U.S. Latina Theatre* (Tucson: University of Arizona Press, 2001).

Sommer, Doris, '"Not just a Personal Story": Women's *Testimonios* and the Plural Self,' in Bella Brodsky and Celeste Schenck (eds), *Life/Lines: Theorizing Women's Autobiography* (Ithaca, NY: Cornell University Press, 1988, 107–30).

Spitta, Silvia, *Between Two Waters: Narratives of Transculturation in Latin America* (Houston, TX: Rice University Press, 1995).

the bodies between us

lê thi diem thúy

the bodies between us was originally commissioned by New WORLD Theater and the New England Foundation for the Arts. It was developed in the summer of 1996 as part of the New Works for a New World play development lab at the University of Massachusetts, Amherst. Maura Nguyen Donohue was choreographer, Hung Nguyen was dramaturg, scenic design was by Miguel Romero, lighting design by Kathy Durault, and costume design was by Ken Chu. It was performed by lê thi diem thúy and directed by Roberta Uno. In October 1998, it was presented as a featured performance at the conference 'Intersection of Performance, Practice, and Ideas,' produced by New WORLD Theater and the Department of Theater at University of Massachusetts, Amherst.

the bodies between us written by lê thi diem thúy
In photo: lê thi diem thúy
Photo by Ed Cohen

19

Meditations on the exilic condition: introduction to *the bodies between us*

Lucy Mae San Pablo Burns

Writing about the disappeared and tortured, as well as writing on the writing about them, is as difficult as it is urgent. The difficulty lies not only in navigating the troubled waters between those who, in the tradition of Adorno, insist that the atrocities committed defy language and representation and those who insist that only through denunciation, which necessarily involves representation, can crimes be brought to light and similar ones be avoided in the future.

Diana Taylor, *Disappearing Acts*

Writer/performer thúy lê writes that one of the impetuses for her solo piece *the bodies between us*[1] was 'i wanted to create a piece which looked at the experience of refugee-ism in a way that didn't jump so suddenly from having been "there" to now being "here."' With *the bodies between us*, she explores the beginnings and continuation of a refugee's psychic state of floating. In this solo performance piece, lê engages with the unspoken memories, wondering where the body deposits memories of 'atrocities committed [that] defy language and representation.' With *bodies*, we are reminded of the constancy of exile, the unrelenting anxiety of a rupture that persists even after resettlement. lê captures the constant state of in-betweenness, '... *waiting* in uncertainty for the life unknown and longing with fear for *returning* home continues to be experienced, albeit in different forms,' not just by those who are still waiting to be immigrants, the 'longstayers,' but 'even by those happily "resettled."'[2]

In the summer of 1996 at Amherst, the New Works for a New World play development lab brought together for the first time three young Vietnamese American artists from different regions of the country – thúy lê, a writer/performer based in New England, choreographer Maura Nguyen Donohue from New York City, and theater artist Hung Nguyen of Los Angeles. They had never worked on an artistic project together, although each had heard of the other, seen each other's work, met, and stayed in touch. It is the development of this play, however, that brought them together to explore something that each of them had touched in their own works – the refugee experience. Roberta Uno, artistic director of New WORLD Theater and director of *bodies*, saw in the works of these three young Vietnamese American artists the emergence of a new generation, with a different set of stories, with a different artistic sensibility. She describes one of the first encounters of the three artists: 'It was quite a moving moment in the rehearsal hall when thúy, Maura, and Hung, these young Vietnamese artists who are working so hard in their separate geographies, were able to stand together in the same room. That moment of recognition took our breath away.'³

This artistic team was energized by the dynamic of the collaboration. lê had also presented them with an exciting challenge with *the bodies between us*, not only with the content of the piece but also with what she was interested in investigating through performance. In this piece, lê highlights the contradiction and ambivalence of language, as well as its seductive ability to speak of the truth, to present a story as the whole truth. With a story struggling in the telling of an incomprehensible experience, with the constancy of unsettledness, lê wanted to explore how this condition of alienation could live on stage, in performance. Although assigned as being the director, the dramaturg, the choreographer, the writer/performer, these roles became fluid as the collaborators embarked on their artistic journey. Director Uno, recognizing the relationship of the three artists to the legacy of dislocation of the Vietnamese American community, adapted a process in which the artists could work across their disciplines: 'Ultimately, our goal was to support thúy as a solo performer. It was rather poetic and just that the play's structure and issues of fragmentation required the participation of all of us to make it whole. Although we had our roles of director, performer, dramaturg, and choreographer, I encouraged any of us to address and solve the problems at hand.'⁴ This process yielded four artists approaching a problem or contributing ideas beyond the boundaries of their assigned roles.

The opening image of *bodies* is lê inside three strips of white cloth hung on a circular ring, from the ceiling to the floor. She delivers the opening monologue from the inside of the cloth, as if sealed in, immediately creating a barrier between her and the audience. This opening image sets the distance that this piece attempts to maintain in its hour and ten minutes of performance, establishing the place where lê intended the audience to be: the outside. The audience is asked, challenged as the collaborating artists were, to live with distance, with uncertainty, with the incomprehensible. This piece resists identification with the familiar narrative of refugeeism, of war – the spectacle of blood and guts, the helicopters, the dramatic rescues, the casts of thousands. The spectacle of conventional/mainstream representation and narratives of the Vietnam and American War is contrasted with the body of one storyteller, quiet and deliberate, simple and specific.

An additional challenge to the collaborators of *bodies* is the very specific set design that came with lê's vision. As she writes in her introduction, it is another character, a fixed element to the story she wants to tell. Uno shares the approach the collaborators took with this continual presence, relating it to the state of deprivation in the experience of a refugee: 'You take what you are given. You make sense with what you have. From this, you create a new series of relationships, a new way of relating to the world.'[5] This cloth becomes the orange peel, the mother's hair, the waves at sea, just as the boat for the refugee became the world on which they negotiated their life.

The year 2000 marked the 25th anniversary of the fall of Saigon, 'end' of the Vietnam–U.S. war. Narratives of celebration, triumph, and remembrance circulate. Soldiers returned to Vietnam to heal wounded hearts and psyche, to put old nightmares to rest. *Viet Kieus*[6] returned to the homeland, perhaps feeling a little safer, also to heal broken hearts. Images of a new Vietnam are presented – beach resorts, emerging metropoles – perhaps to replace the ones seared in U.S. collective memory. Twenty-five years after the war, the common narrative we can expect is one of resolution and reconciliation. Those who are back and those who came here are presented as settled, re/settled. In the midst of what appears to be a celebratory commemoration and investigation of the 25th year after the fall of Saigon, *the bodies between us*, in contrast, articulates the unspoken and lingering memories ebbing upon our collective memories.

NOTES

1. *the bodies between us* was developed as part of 'Viet New: A Generation Emerges,' an audience development project at the New WORLD Theater focussing on the Vietnamese American community. The project goals included examining the contemporary performance movement of Vietnamese American artists through premièring new works by Hung Nguyen and his company, Club O'Noodles, Maura Nguyen Donohue and her ensemble, In Mixed Company, and solo performer/writer, thúy lê; introducing contemporary Vietnamese performance to existing New WORLD Theater audiences and developing new audiences for the work, both in the Vietnamese and non-Vietnamese communities; introducing members of the Vietnamese community to contemporary performance through active participation. During the course of this two-year project, Donohue created SKINning the SurFACE, a piece exploring issues of biracial identity, specifically Amerasians of Vietnamese descent. Nguyen and Club O'Noodles developed

Stories from a Nail Salon, a theatrical exploration of the lives of Vietnamese Americans in the salon business where they comprise a third of workers in the United States. These three works were premiered at the New WORLD Theater and have been presented at different venues including Highways Performance Space in Los Angeles and Dance Theater Workshop in New York. 'Viet New: A Generation Emerges' was funded by the Association for Performing Arts Presenters Wallace Reader's Digest Partner's Program.

2.   All quotes from trinh t. minh-ha, 'An Acoustic Journey.' in John C. Welchman (ed.), *Rethinking Borders* (Minneapolis: University of Minnesota Press, 1996, 1–17), p. 5.

3.   Email interview by Lucy Burns with Roberta Uno (June 2000).

4.   *Ibid.*

5.   *Ibid.*

6.   *Viet Kieus* is a term used by Vietnamese to refer to the 'first wave' of Vietnamese expatriates.

A NOTE ON *the bodies between us*

lê thi diem thúy

I wrote the entirety of this performance piece exactly in the manner that follows, with section headings and originally without a note of stage direction. There are three interwoven narratives. The first — and main — narrative involves the journey a man and his young daughter make from their home in Vietnam to a refugee camp in Singapore and finally to the Pacific Coast of the U.S. The second narrative consists of a taped interview with American scientist George Archibald discussing a joint effort between Vietnamese and American scientists to restore a sanctuary in southern Vietnam for the sarus cranes, whose habitat had been destroyed by the American/Vietnam War. The third narrative consists of a taped English as a second language (ESL) interview with a young Vietnamese girl who has recently arrived in the U.S.*

The piece initially came to me as a work anchored in the voices of people talking about places and the things that had happened to them in those places. I was interested in the contrasting sound and texture of the different voices and in how they would play off of each other. I was hearing the piece more than seeing it until one night when the image of the set came to me in a dream. Then I understood the set to be the vessel for the voices I had written.

Rather than describe all the transformations of the set during the course of this performance, I'd like to describe the set and leave it to the reader to imagine its possibilities in performance. Perhaps one way to approach this work is to think of it as a text-based performance which is 're-written' by the voice and the body. Though this is a solo performance, the set should be approached as another body on stage.

The set consists of three strips of white cloth hung on a circular ring and falling approximately 30 feet from the ceiling to the floor. Right behind the ring of cloth is a metal ladder which rises from the floor to the ceiling. During the course of the performance, the performer is in constant interplay with the set elements, using them to invoke people, places, objects, incidents, emotions, or states of being. What the set becomes is determined by whatever is happening at the moment of performance. Hence, a strip of cloth may be shaped into and held as a sleeping infant when the narrator speaks about her own birth or a strip of cloth may be pulled out and laid down upon the ground and folded at one end to resemble the nose of a boat when a boat becomes the site of action. The performer might stick her head between two rungs of the

---

* In the performance text, the interview with scientist George Archibald appears in bold print and the ESL interview appears in italics.

ladder and gaze out at the audience, as one might gaze out a window, or she may approach the ladder as a ladder and climb it. The shapes the set assumes can be realistic or abstract. The scale of the shapes created can shift easily from commonplace to fantastic; a small part of cloth can be used by the performer as a shawl and then just as easily held in the hand and stroked as the tail end of an imagined braid, extending 30 feet long.

Each transformation must occur in a way which is natural to the scene and, with the exception of some rare instances when a light or sound cue is long enough to allow it, the performer is almost never able to dismantle the set and rearrange it in an entirely new way for the next scene. So the interplay between the performer and the set is very much like that of a dance, each movement building on the last and every detail choreographed with consideration not only for how much the performer can do but also for how much the set itself will give in terms of sway, stretch, sound, and stillness.

Keep in mind as you're reading that this is a performance. All the words you read are spoken. With the exception of the section headings which are projected, and the interview excerpts which are recorded. There is the magic of light and sound, introducing the glow of a full moon and the rhythm of waves. Every moment of speech has an accompanying gesture, at times as overt as running, at other times, as subtle as a turn of the head or the hand or the shift of an eye. Imagine that at times the words and the movements will seem to oppose each other so that it isn't clear if the truth of what the performer is telling you is conveyed by the eloquence of her words or by the way her body is moving or seems to refuse to move.

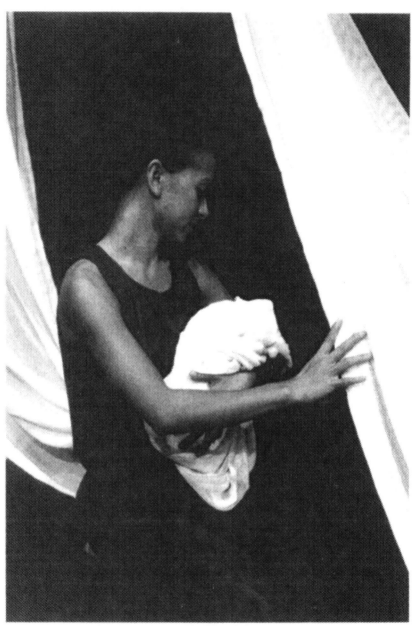

the bodies between us written by lê thí diem thúy
in photo: lê thi diem thúy
Photo by Ed Cohen

20

the bodies between us

lê thi diem thúy

orange

the second day on the boat, a woman pulled an orange out of her pocket and peeled it with one continuous turn of the knife in her hand. she dangled the peel before her young daughter's face, bouncing it like a spring in the air until the girl laughed out loud, reaching, hands outstretched. this spiral of orange peel becomes a burning banner, becomes a stairwell, becomes a tear in the landscape, becomes a raft on water, a tunnel i crawl through in total darkness, staining my hands on the blood and the scent of these memories.

i have buried myself and those i love many times over. in caves which echo every utterance, the slightest weeping magnified so you have a sense of a long hall of doors flung open and every song from inside seeping out. and in this burying i have felt a grief so fierce and undisguised, it scattered all shadows from my eyes and left me stumbling, drunk on visions, across all the bodies between us: earth, water, sky.

earth

quick! climb to the tops of the trees and throw those coconuts down to me. let them drop heavy into the sand. i'll dance around them, kicking my feet this way and that. hello, hello, mr. and miss coconut. hello, hello. it's me. how are you? me too!

The sarus cranes used to live in Vietnam and nobody knew if they had survived the war. And the professors from Hanoi went south to look for the sarus cranes in the Mekong Delta. The first place they visited was the zoo in Ho Chi Minh City and there was the sarus crane, a young bird,

indicating that it had been freshly taken from the wild. They inquired and they said, Yes, it came from Dong Thap province and sure enough, there is a flock of cranes, the only known flock of cranes surviving in all of Southeast Asia.

i was born outside, late at night, my eyes crammed full of stars. my aunt said that was a bad beginning because my first picture of life was an expanse of black with occasional bright spots. ma said,

and that's not true?

she laughed a long time at her own question. she laughed so long, she scared her sister who took me from my mother's arms and began to sing to me at the top of her voice, pacing along the beach. between the howl of my mother's laughter and my aunt's singing, i forgot to scream. my aunt said that was the other bad sign about my beginning but my mother said that i was just taking my time, debating whether i wanted to stick around if life really was just darkness with the promise of fire from time to time.

i was born on the beach because my mother didn't want to go to the hospital. still-born babies were buried in a cemetery adjacent to the local hospital. my mother had heard of their graves being disturbed by a band of mad men. the graves were strewn with toys – pinwheels, bells – which spun and chimed softly, insistently. my mother said the men used the toys to lure the children out to play. the men would say, Yoo-hoo … ooo-hoo. the bells would echo them, Yoo-hoo … ooo-hoo. even the trees leaned down as if to tickle the babies here, in this soft soft under their chin. if a baby stirred, even slightly, the mad men would reach through the dirt to grab the babies' small feet, their tiny ankles, their toe nails transparent as shrimp shells.

she led me to believe i had this to fear: a world of hungry, mad men, gobbling children, crunching small bones. i imagined a feast of spittle and sinew, a constant churning through the night. my mother kept me from them by showing me first the sea and the sky. their open horizons.

They live … in a huge basin called the Plain of Reeds. It was … this great swamp with floating islands, with melaluca trees, meandering rivers that would disappear into reeds. Something like the African Queen. And the Viet Cong would put their hammocks between the melaluca trees and sleep there and move off into the swamps and then strike. Consequently, the U.S. Army Corps of engineers dug these enormous drainage channels criss-crossing all across the Plain of Reeds and drained the thing into the Mekong River. It was drained, the acid sulfate soils were exposed, it became this great grass land. It was

napalmed, destroyed the melaluca trees, and the whole environment was transformed ...

quick! climb to the tops of the trees and throw those coconuts down to me. let them drop heavy into the sand. i'll dance around them, kicking my feet this way and that. hello, hello, mr. and miss coconut. hello, hello. it's me. how are you? me too!

let's play jump rope 'til we tire. play kickball against the wall of my great-uncle's house. hide marbles in the sassy girl's hair while she's sleeping and then shake her shake her shake her. let's play dead in your courtyard. have to lay very still and don't talk or open eyes. even if your ma starts yelling your name or your grandma cries. but wiggle your toes so they know you're coming back and save you some dinner. let's wrestle airplanes. you want to? i'll call them down like this: Yoo-hoo! ooo-hooo! and then you jump on them and i'll grab their neck and hold on tight. you stomp out the wings 'cause that's where they spit fire from and i'll yell into their ear: no more spitting on us you big loud wanna be but never ever gonna be a real live dragon. you wanna fight? okay, c'mon then, you stinky. i'm gonna make you triple-flip bad. ... heah, there's the plane. go hide before it sees you. i'll bring it down. oooh/ooh ...

... i said, there's the plane. go hide before it sees you. i'll bring it down. oooh/ooh ...

ooh/ooh, ooh//uh, uhh/uhh ... i never thought your tall nose would get me into so much trouble. everyone's saying she's a white baby. where have you been? i need you near me so i can hold her in my arms and point to you whenever people stare at her tall nose. my father said, look, everyone's saying she's *my lai*. they're whispering, *my lai*, mixed blood baby when you walk by. i told my father i didn't do anything wrong. i'm not going to wear the shame of their suspicion ... i started thinking about thu, whose baby is blue-eyed. should we throw him in the river? ...

i said, i don't care. i don't care what people say. may be this child is a *my lai* baby. so much blood's been spilled, there's no way i could have kept her from it. she's a mess of blood. you understand? let them say it. it's true. *my lai*, my lai, *my lai!* he started slapping me but i couldn't stop. *my lai* ... i know what happened there. i know some people went blind from what they saw.

What do ... what do ... these birds look like?

These birds are enormous. They stand about five feet tall. They're a slatey grey. They have bright orange red on the head, down four to five inches on the upper regions of the neck. Their legs are salmon pink. Their calls are primeval; they carry for miles. Very shrill. Their eyes are a bright, golden color. Their beak is about seven inches long. Very

powerful. To excavate tubers and sedges from the muddy soils. They're quite social. ... They roost together tonight – at night – in shallow water and in the early morning fly out.

water

we were at sea forever. we ran out of food. then we ran out of water. we pulled the sea on deck and boiled it by the bucketful. we ate the ones who died, saving their bones in sacks made from their own shirts. one baby we tied in his mother's head scarf. we tied these sacks to the side of the boat, burying them on the edge of our world, which had become this floating vessel.

at night there was a constant conversation between the boat planks and the bones. they were complaining about the amount of salt in the sea, a sign that the tears hadn't let up. they were complaining about the heat of the sun bleaching them whiter and they were complaining of boredom, tired of floating for so long. people kept their complaints to themselves. years later, those of us who survived would say,

no, we didn't smell. the sun on our faces didn't burn. i still have everything i carried on board. i didn't lose anyone. we weren't hungry. we weren't thirsty. we always had enough of whatever we needed. we played card games. we sang songs. we even staged puppet shows for the children. i stayed up all night and would read at day break.

when we couldn't sleep, we recited poems. i saw the sun rise. i saw the sun set. i got to sleep on the sea. it was never too dark. it was never too quiet or too cold. we waited. we were content to wait. we were content to float. forever if need be. no, we weren't afraid.

before we left, we were leaving.

Are you speaking English to me now? Are you speaking English?

left/leaving ...

my mother buried clothes in the rice bin. she settled debts, lingered at the end of conversations, held her hellos and good-byes close. during that week, she seemed to love the sound of names, calling people to her, her voice tender. it was as if she were walking backwards out of the room, never once lifting her gaze from you so you didn't notice the distance growing, didn't think she wouldn't come back even after she finally stepped beyond the doorway, out into the darkness.

she was so careful to leave the right way but it was she who ended up staying and my father and i who ended up leaving. i didn't know that we were going. i didn't throw a single good-bye behind me.

as far as i knew, we were only going out into the water to bring back the ones who'd gone to the edge of the horizon and slipped beyond. there was never a question that we would come back. or that i'd see my mother again. or that when we got tired of playing at being at sea, we would stop.

running, my life has felt like a game and a gamble. i will be fast on my feet, leap effortless from rooftops. curl small into the cradle of tree branches. i must dodge every caliber of sadness, knowing instinctively it can bring the explosion in me. if i confuse my senses, i will doubt the act of putting one foot before the other. if i slow down to consider, i will settle into a paralysis of crumbled knees, ruined joints, these hands will become useless. my mind will nightmare. call you and water swallows every utterance so that all you catch of me is water slipping, my body slipping in water. and then what use will i be to you, who like me, need someone to hold on to?

a fistful of fabric. my head buried in her lap. a well of tears rising from deep down and spilling over. staining her dress, her lap, washing her feet, the floor. this is how i pictured our reunion.

you understand, my father said, we're never coming back.

at sea, we learn to make ourselves light. so we will weigh nothing. leave no shadow. we eliminate the weighty gesture. pare to the bone.

at night he and i lie down and still. we are close, floating bodies. our closeness sealed by this fact of never coming back. we are surrounded by bones, gossiping, weeping, a rattle of argument, insinuation. though they keep us up all night, we get lonely without them. at sea, we are pared thin. a sliver of eyes, a tangle of hair, wind-blown, shaken like a sheet hung to dry. shaken/ shaken/shaken. i asked him,

at night, do we slip through trap doors and –

he said,

ah, a dream happy ... my sweet girl, a dream happy
   for my father, a dream happy ...

and tumble – head long – down?

he said,

shhh... a dream happy ... my sweet girl, a dream happy
   for my father, a dream happy ...

Uh-huh. Oh, I see ... Was it raining Saturday?
raining?
Saturday, was it raining?
raining? i don't know ...

You don't remember?
may ... no.

at night, the bones dream of fantastic flesh, a plump forearm to cushion a weary head. webbed feet and wings to skip across the waves. an exquisite upper lip. an inquisitive, curled tongue. a back so strong you could bounce a ball off it. and hands which grow to catch all manner of falling things, from babies to entire boats.

my father spent nights locating my mother. he described the scent of jasmine, the sound of a river near by. he said,

her hair is so dark, lights reflect off it, shining like the stars in the sky tonight. somewhere up there is your mother's face. her laughing eyes.

night after night he describes her eyes, her nose, her lips, her hair, her ears, her eyebrows, her teeth, her eyelashes.
he said,

notice the arc of her brow and the way her eyes will narrow in suspicion. notice the occasional curl in her hair from nights when she has slept on it strange.

he said,

doesn't her hair smell like flowers? isn't she happy to be by a river? summers are so hot, alone, she has no one to cool her with wet cloths. lick the sweat off her brow. bring her a breeze by blowing softly, softly ...

this was the song my aunt sang when she was walking me on the beach (*sings some verses from a traditional vietnamese lullabye*):

where are the teeth in you? show me! i'm not scared! let's not talk about the sky unless you tell me where you are in it.

sky

on the third day a flock of cranes swelled the sky. the adults fell silent. my father began to weep. the cranes flew past us but their shadows remained on either side of our boat and made the shape of floating wings on the water.

the cranes have abandoned us.
they've left us.
who will carry the dead to rest?

even cranes get tired of this endless traffic in bodies.
we're not talking about bodies.
what are we talking about?
your restless ...

... told us that many people believe that when you die your – your spirit is carried to heaven by the cranes.

my father gives me photographs. he says,

another picture!

in my mind i am smoothing the sand. i am looking for the still patch of water. but it's the sky he stares into. perched on the balls of his feet, he leans forward, focusses his eyes and gives me photographs.
he says,

before we married, i could only kiss her forehead. here, you see, where her hair parted. such a small space. and if she leaned forward, only large enough for me to press my lips against. it was like a curtain, her hair. she used to hook it behind her ears and then i'd have her whole forehead, her glowing face. but whenever i moved to kiss her, her hair would come undone and rush forward from either side. i imagined her mother was behind one ear and her father behind the other. when they saw me coming, they let loose her hair so i couldn't lose myself and kiss her eyes, her ears. ... but it was all right. i love her hair. thick as rope. i used to braid it for her too. a man like me, learning how to braid by moonlight. she taught me how. she said, separate everything into three strands, bring the last between the first and second, bring the first between the last and second, bring the second between the first and last. do it again. can you see it in your hand? can you see what you are doing with your hands? i did what she told me. i kept moving down and down, holding on and letting go until all the strands met and there was no place for both of my hands. i was looking at the end. there was nowhere else to go. i was actually afraid to look up but when i did look, i saw what i had done. this crossing and recrossing. traveling up her back, leaning against her neck. she said, look what you have done to me. look what you have done. ...

my mother's braids long as rope unraveled. the long strands of netting which crawl along the ocean floor. so if we're the things that fall and sink, there's her to catch us with her hair. my mother's braids growing everyday. reaching, like arms. she'll lay her hair down. a sure path for us to follow.
but in this water, everything is loosened. the tide pulls you down and buries

you. it holds you tight, then lets you go. up come the dead people, up come the pearls. her strong braids are slowly worked open. her hair fanning everywhere. i follow one strand to the end and find nothing but the end, suspended in water, like the beginning. i follow another strand, another end. these long cut braids which lead to nowhere.

another picture!

my mother's face is in the sky. washing in part by part. her features rising and falling. the sky has no end. it curves. it swallows everything i put on it. i didn't tell my father that i kept losing my mother's features in the sky. i opened my eyes and stared harder than ever but she would not come together for me. it would be like this. i would see one enormous eye next to a minuscule nose. the nose sat on top of an upside down eyebrow. her mouth would appear and open to reveal her other eye. and this other eye, inside her mouth, would stare at me. it would never blink. her tongue would come and lick her lips. from this i thought, it must be dry up there and her eye is thirsty from staring at me for so long.

at the refugee camp in singapore, the big cook in chef's hat and white apron offers me my first bottle of coca-cola. the straw buoyed and bobbing:

have you had this? do you like it? where you are going, everyone drinks coca-cola night and day. won't you be so happy there?

maybe.

where you are going, there are buildings high to the sky and you can step into a big metal box which travels from the bottom to the top of such buildings in less than three minutes. at the top, you can step out and press your eye against the sky. maybe you can see past the sky. what do you suppose lives past the sky?

if i could press my eye against the sky, i would be pressing my eye against my mother's eye. past her eye would be the river. at the end of that, the scent of flower blossoms. at the end of that, her other eye. at the end of that, her lips. somewhere her ears toward which i'll lean close and whisper, i see you. do you see me? have you seen me?

That cranes were shot from helicopters for practice. Local people often repeat that story. But in 1975, when peace came to Vietnam, the governor of that region, Mr. Monier, who was the leader of the Viet Cong forces, decided he wanted to restore a 45,000 acre section of the Plain of Reeds to bring back the water to grow the melaluca trees ... So they built dikes around this great rectangular section of land and when the Mekong River flooded, it filled up and then the water couldn't

escape. They planted it, the trees started to grow, and the birds started to return.
  Returning from Cambodia?
  Cambodia or wherever! (*laughs*) **Nobody knows.**

beyond the walls of the refugee camp is the city. the streets are electric there. swimming in flashing reds, greens, yellows. colors breathing like fish out of water. panting. thirsty. burning. dry. it's hard to sleep at night.
  the man in the bed next to ours sleeps with a spoon in his hand. once, it dropped onto the floor in the middle of the night and he sat straight up, crying, Lan! my father reached down, found the spoon and gave it to the man who wrapped his fingers around it and immediately fell asleep. someone said,

  he's missing someone

someone said,

  his wife, maybe ...
    his daughter, maybe ...

someone said,

  someone he loves

  my father didn't sleep that night. we walked outside to where a hammock hung between two trees. we climbed into it and lay there, my father with his back to me and me searching the sky for my mother's face. i felt his back curl away from me and then his whole body shake. he cried that night. i wanted to hold him but i couldn't get my hand to move past the hill of his shoulder so i – i don't know why. i grabbed onto his hair. a fist of his hair. anything to hold on to.

pacific

my hair ... my mother's hair is uh ... cut like, look like me
Looks like yours
but this ... cut and this ...
Uh-huh, OK ... and what about
my eye and my mother's eye is very look like!
Uh-huh, okay ... and what about? Uh-huh, okay ... uh-huh.
my mother nose is [laughs] ...
Curved?
the top nose is curved.
Is she pretty?

i don't know.
What are you studying?
no, i don't study ... i study ESOL here.
ESL in here? Oh, OK.
yes.
Are you speaking in English to me now? Are you speaking English?
yes.
How did you get here?
in airplane.
Did you come on an airplane all the way from Vietnam?
no, from vietnam, i go boat ... um ... to indonesia and from indonesia, i go to
singapore by boat and i go to — from singapore i go to hong kong by airplane and i go
to uh ... to uh ... kore — no, japan, ja-pan, tokyo, tokyo, two hours and i go, continue
to, by airplane, by airplane to los angeles and to um, to, from los angeles, i go here by
airplane.
Oh, I see. OK.
too long!
Yeah, that was long trip. How was the trip? Did you like it?
trip?
Yeah, your trip all the way from Vietnam to here. You know what trip means? Trip
means coming. When you were coming here. Can you tell me a little bit about that?
What you did on, uh, when you were on the boat?
about me, what feet? how many feet?
You are about three —
four, five

my father climbed the ladder, carrying me on his back. i wrapped my arms
around his neck. he said,

> are you holding on to all those pictures i gave you of your mother? you
> carry those pictures up for me. i only have two hands.

> below me, the bones shouted,
> little girl, don't look down. you'll get dizzy. you'll fall. don't look down
now. hold on tight.
we climbed up into the ship and when we looked back, everything was
shrinking below us. we climbed into the sky. there were no clouds, no stars. the
sky was only grey metal. from a distance i had been so hopeful. i thought the
ship was a pigeon sunning itself, the low rumble of engine parts its soft cooing.
we were picked up on a still night. a woman was humming to herself,
running her fingers through her long hair. i caught a corner of face in the
moonlight. just her eye and her cheek. i hadn't heard anyone sing for a long

time. she called a crane to come and get us but the cranes were scattered too far away to hear her so a common pigeon came.

What did you do the last day in Vietnam? Do you remember the last day?
last day? in Vietnam, i have only one friends ... very ... uh, old friends. you know, old friends. she's about 11 years but in the old friends ... too long time i friend with her. i is ... i am a friend with her a long time and i talk with her i will, i went to go to, i went to go out country and i don't know i will go what country.
Oh, I see. You didn't know where you were going?
yeah, i don't know.

from the ship, i looked down and saw our boat curling into itself. the shadow wings folded over. when they opened, there was nothing between them but water and each wing floated from the other, disappearing into all the other shadows on the sea.

another picture!

later, my father and i in sharp clothes, standing in front of a shiny car parked in front of a big house. a house in southern california. it had a huge lawn. it was the kind of house which, years later, my father becomes the gardener of and i clean the rooms of.

one house had a piano which i leaned against accidentally when, not looking, i was walking blind and backwards across the room, trying to get away from the pet doberman. i put my hands behind me to hold onto something and this shock of instrument that made me jump but not scream because through the glass patio door i saw my father's face darken with worry. in that split second, a cloud moved over his face. he held his breath and i jumped quietly, all the noise swallowed by the white carpet which was thick, like so much snow i'd never seen before.

this picture of my father and i in front of the car in front of the house. he in a turquoise velour sports shirt, v-neck, brown slacks. me in a holly hobby dress, white knee highs, brown thick-soled shoes. my feathered hair. ... we're standing in front of the house holding hands. my uncle who is not really my uncle but everyone vietnamese and kind here is family, we have no other family here to be selective. my uncle, who has been in the u.s. longer and knows how to drive, took us to look for a big car in front of a big house. he is the one who takes the photograph we send to my mother, on the back of which my father writes,

as you can see, we are well here.

i don't argue with my father but there's something in how i hold my shoulders for this picture which is meant as a signal to my mother. so that looking at this picture, she would begin to suspect something was not right. i hold my shoulders, as if to say, i am pinned to this picture. this setting. don't look for me here in front of this shiny car, this big house. something is wrong. look at my bones.

since i came here, i've been having this recurring dream. is it a nightmare? my mother's sitting on stage – center stage – in a chair that's big and deep. it envelopes her. i recognize her by her profile and her bare feet. she stares into and beyond the audience. she is wearing a red dress which is unlike her.

i am standing stage right, in the wings.

when this dream begins, i'm relieved to see her again. finally! i'm ecstatic and begin running toward her. as i'm running, i realize there's a pool of blood gathering at her feet. she's gripping the arm rest. her dress is blood-soaked and her knuckles are so ... white. my heart sinks. my muscles soften. my bones slowly begin to crumble. my legs move but never forward. i run in place for the entire dream. something inside me is galloping at top speed because i know she is holding on until i get there. i am flying but – my body – outside – doesn't move at all. i – can't move and i – can't scream. i hear parts of myself shut down, as if someone were walking into each of the chambers of my heart, all the corners of my body, my being, closing windows, turning off lights, locking doors, room by room until the only thing that remains is my vision and then that too goes blank and there is nothing. i wake up as if i was falling. as if i had been falling for a long time but hadn't noticed until now.

my father says,

> she's not dead. she's just not here – with us – now. maybe later if we wait long enough maybe later we'll catch a glimpse of her walking – will she stop? – bye. is she all right? she's not dead. she's just not here now. no, don't know – when – will she be here then?

Uh-huh. Oh, I see ... Was it raining Saturday?
raining?
Saturday, was it raining?
raining? i don't know ...
You don't remember?

raining inside. inside is rain. it's storming inside my house. my boat is flooding inside is rain flooding my heart is sinking in raining inside.

out from the tide of the pacific, we saw oranges wash onto the sand. a seagull flying east at a quarter to one in the morning saw this. we saw the seagull in the white glare of a street lamp, its wings shimmering silver, metallic. late at night, when we can't sleep, my father takes me to the water. we walk for miles. it always begins the same way. he says, we'll go for a walk. we'll walk to the end of the water. you see it? it's there. we'll go there. here is my back. my back is yours.

i climb his back and up onto his shoulders. he spreads his arms for me and i for him. holding hands like this, we prepare to cover this stretch of beach, this sweep of ocean. we decided long ago, we are going to walk until we tire. once, we collapsed miles on down the beach, slept through the night and woke to the sound of seagulls flying overhead.

tonight the water's a dark curtain which we are going to tear through. and we won't sleep until we touch her hands, her hair.

when you're ready, he says.

i say, go!

and we go.

21

'look at my bones': theater as contact zone in *the bodies between us*

Una Chaudhuri

I wanted to create a piece which looked at the experience of refugee-ism in a way that didn't jump so suddenly from having been 'there' to now being 'here.' The before/after dichotomy always struck me as being inadequate because while it is true that one day I was physically in Vietnam and another day I was physically in the States, I felt there were entire worlds I'd carried which took years to arrive or which seemed to have remained floating somewhere – unmoored – at sea.

lê thi diem thúy, 'The impetus behind *the bodies between us*'

... museums and other sites of cultural performance appear not as centers or destinations but rather as contact zones traversed by things and people.

James Clifford, *Routes*

At first glance, the stage and action of *the bodies between us* would seem to contradict the plurals of its title. This is a solo performance, and there will be only one body on stage – no bodies, no spaces 'between,' no 'us.' Yet the play manages to be utterly true to the powerful sense of a relation to others that its title evokes. Having conceived the piece originally as being 'anchored in the voices of people talking,' lê thi diem thúy has crafted a work in which many places, people, events, and stories unfold out of the specifics of performance.

The unfolding is at one level quite literal, for a major element of the simple set are the three long strips of cloth that fall from ceiling to floor, which are used in a multitude of ways to enact the play's actions and evoke its central images. The gauzy white cloth can be gathered up into the arms and rocked like a child, or it can be laid out on the ground and shaped to be the boat in which she leaves Vietnam. Thus the play's story quite literally unfolds before our eyes, so that its powerfully poetic language is matched by an equally powerful, performative discourse, a *doing* that amplifies, resonates against, and specifies the *telling* in such a way that 'telling' – as in telling stories, telling the truth, 'the telling details,' even 'telling time' – turns out to be one of its main subjects. Between the lines of *the bodies between us* is a body language that speaks of (among other things) the limits of telling, the inadequacy of language.

the bodies between us presents one woman's retrospective understanding of a childhood trauma which is as unthinkable as it is – tragically – common: the loss of a mother and a motherland to the violent geopolitics of the twentieth century. On a simple stage, a figure appears, moves, begins to speak. A woman recalls her life on another continent. Out of a few unforgettable images and a handful of simple words – 'earth,' 'orange,' 'sky,' – an entire phase of life is re-created. A lost mother laughs again, an aunt sings, a child is born, and a life begins again, this time *in narrative*, as a story: 'she laughed so long, she scared her sister who took me from my mother's arms and began to sing to me at the top of her voice, pacing along the beach. between the howl of my mother's laughter and my aunt's singing, i forgot to scream.'

But can life really 'begin again,' the way a story can? Can a person 'start over,' 're-write' herself in a new language, inhabit a new world? The fact that this is exactly what millions of people have been doing, especially in the hyper-diaspora of the last century, does not prevent us from questioning the logic, the modalities and mechanisms, indeed the very *possibility* of this act of self-re-invention. To perform, as so many artists now do (and must), from within the experience of diaspora, out of personal histories of immigration, refugeehood, exile, or other less well-codified kinds of displacements, is – like it or not – to confront this problematic, which is always at one and the same time existential and aesthetic, personal and political, textual and performative. To put it in the particularly loaded terms suggested by the opening moments of *the bodies between us*, can one be 'born again?'[1]

The three major narratives that are woven together in *the bodies between us* counteract any desire to locate a sentimental, affirmative answer to this question. Much as the refugee longs to re-invent herself beyond the traumatic loss of home, much as the immigrant needs to re-establish a new relationship to her place of origin, the obstacles to achieving a coherent new identity are enormous. Chief among these obstacles are two that this play identifies and confronts, signaling their importance though the two secondary narratives that periodically interrupt and trouble the autobiographical account that forms the spine of the play. While the main narrative speaks wrenchingly of leaving home, of floating endlessly in the limbo of the escape boat and waking to the nightmares of the refugee camp, of the unspeakable pain of losing a beloved parent, the two other narratives appear by contrast to be prosaic and impersonal. One is a tape-recording of an English as a second language conversation, and the other a scientific account of the mysterious return to the Mekong Delta of certain birds who had disappeared from it during the war. Interspersing the richly poetic text and vibrating live voice of the main narrative, these two streams of recorded speech register two divergent responses to the experience of displacement, one cultural, the other natural.

The story of the sarus cranes, who had left the devastated landscape of Vietnam and who began to return after the war – 'from Cambodia or wherever! Nobody knows' – counterpoints the story of the protagonist, who will never return, whose 'natural' habitat of coconut palms and beaches is now a memory only, however vivid. By contrast, the recording of the ESL interview, in which a child who has just arrived in America is quizzed to determine her level of English, bespeaks a radical alienation, far beyond the protagonist's, for it is the alienation of a foreign tongue *before* it has been redeemed by the memories and images of an individual, before it has been wrested away from its foreignness by one who, like the protagonist, must use it in order to remain sane.

In *Strangers to Ourselves*, Julia Kristeva evokes the peculiar linguistic condition of the foreigner by the haunting phrase 'the silence of polyglots.'[2] In what is perhaps one of the most painfully honest articulations of how displaced people experience their speech, Kristeva explains the sickening feeling of speaking without being heard, or of being heard but not understood, not attended to: 'No one listens to you, you never have the floor, or else, when you have the courage to seize it, your speech is quickly erased by the more garrulous and relaxed talk of the community. Your speech has no past and will have no power over the future of the group: why should one listen to it?'[3] Radically and definitionally separate from the interests of the community – which is always, according to Kristeva, self-interested, essentially narcissistic – the foreigner *must* speak, but can never *own* – the community's language. The linguistic condition of the foreigner, in short, is to master a language while being enslaved by it.

Where is theater and performance located in relation to this eloquent silence of the polyglot, this sickening burden of accomplished non-native speech? Do the defining non-verbal registers of performance mimic the oxymoronic structure of foreign speech? Or do they resist it, even possibly *escape* it? Can performance accomplish a counter-speech? Perhaps, if words and actions are pried apart, and the space created between them filled with contradictions and disjunctions, perhaps these productive contradictions can break through 'the silence of the polyglot.'

This is, precisely, the method of *the bodies between us*. Against its own many potent acts of self-re-invention, the play sets up a counter-discourse, an ongoing acknowledgment of the dangers and difficulties of 'telling' a new life.

Speaking of the boat that carried her away from Vietnam, the protagonist
contains the journey's nightmare with savage irony and fantasy more
terrifying than the unspeakable truth itself:

> no, we didn't smell, the sun on our faces didn't burn. i still have everything
> i carried on board. i didn't lose anyone. we weren't hungry. we weren't
> thirsty. we always had enough of whatever we needed. we played card
> games. we sang songs. we even staged puppet shows for the children. I
> stayed up all night and would read at day break . . . it was never too dark. it
> was never too quiet or too cold . . . no, we weren't afraid.

Towards the end of the play, the narrator describes a photograph that her
father sent back to her mother in Vietnam, to reassure her that 'we are well
here.' The photograph showed the girl and her father standing in front of a big
house with a big car parked in front of it. It was not their house, of course;
rather 'it is the kind of house which, years later, my father becomes the
gardener of and I clean the rooms of.' Torn between loyalty to her father's
need to reassure her mother and her own need to be truthful to the mother she
has lost, the girl finds a solution, a strategy for being true to oneself when
everything around one refuses to recognize that self. It is a solution that will
become global in the play, and suggests a strategy for all multicultural
performance that must negotiate the distance between language – no matter
how poetic – and the alienation of diasporic experience. The solution is to put
the body into performance, to make the body contest the dominant order's (in
this case, the father and the photograph) claim to truth:

> i don't argue with my father but there's something in how I hold my
> shoulders for this picture which is meant as a signal to my mother. so that
> looking at this picture, she would begin to suspect something was not
> right. i hold my shoulders, as if to say, i am pinned to this picture. this
> setting. don't look for me here in front of this shiny car, this big house.
> something is wrong. look at my bones.

Look at my bones. The body signals its own truth. Not only to the lost
mother, but eventually and more globally to the spectator as well. It signals its
autonomy, insisting on a destiny that is separate from the language one *must*
speak. It speaks of another, secret language, both appalling and comforting:

> we ate the ones who died, saving their bones in sacks made from their
> own shirts . . . at night there was a constant conversation between boat
> planks and the bones . . . we are surrounded by bones, gossiping,
> weeping, a rattle of argument, insinuation. though they keep us up all
> night, we get lonely without them.

This conjunction of poetry and the 'bare bones' of performance is a solution to the problem of representing that diasporic alienation which the playwright describes as 'the separation which occurs not only between people but within a person when circumstances force people to leave all that is familiar to them.' Self-divided as well as divided from others, the displaced person must locate and appropriate a divided discourse. The stage, site of the encounter of words and bones, performer and spectator, is precisely such a discourse The performing body pins itself against the potent poetry of self-telling, and signals to the spectator. 'Perhaps one way to approach this work,' writes the playwright, 'is to think of it as a text-based performance which is re-written by the voice and the body.' *Listen to* my bones.

If identity is always, as Stuart Hall has written, 'a part of narrative,'[4] the divided discourse of performance allows for certain disidentifications[5] that may be crucial to the formulation of a new theater practice. The bodies that perform among and before and between us produce theater as *contact zone*, neither an authorial self-display nor an occasion for spectatorial self-recognition, but instead a place where the trajectories of people and things intersect and interact.[6] In the theater of the contact zone, bodies signal to the spectator, but not, as in Artaud's model, 'through the flames' of martyrdom. Rather they signal through and about the undeniable yet unreal *distance* between things: people, memories, bodies, and, above all, *places*. They contest the facile dichotomies – here vs. there, before vs. after – that distort the truth of exilic experience.

Applying a 'contact' perspective to theater, a perspective which 'emphasizes how subjects are constituted in and by their relations to each other,'[7] acknowledges the extent to which multicultural theater is a process of shaking assumptions and revising formulations. The terrain on which this work is situated is by definition a changing, shifting one, as this work is dedicated to delineating and tracking that moving line between our culture's homogenous past and its hopefully heterogeneous future. On each side of that line of cultural transformation lie not only experiences and stories – which are the stuff of drama – but also assumptions, formulations, ideas, which are the stuff of theory and criticism.

One theory that will need to be revised is the theory of theatrical *response*, an especially important – but hitherto under-appreciated – dimension of the project of multicultural theater. While theatrical response is an essential feature of *all* theater, making up one half of the vital communicative link that defines this, the most interactive of all traditional art forms, it is an especially crucial element of theater *from* a specific group, *about* the life and experiences of that group, and – possibly, though not exclusively – addressed *to* a specific group. Unlike traditional theater, which leaves the audience to reflect on what it has

experienced, this theater seems to call for the spectator to 'talk back' to it.[8]
Identity-based theater seems to actively and explicitly 'hail' its audience and
make them aware of their specific cultural and racial background. By doing so it
produces a contact zone where its fundamental agenda of *challenging
assumptions and shifting grounds* can be immediately realized.

This shifting of assumptions is especially appropriate in the context of *the
bodies between us*, because change – movement, displacement, shifting the
ground of one's being – is one of the major themes of this play. In *the bodies
between us*, this theme is worked out through the image of the journey. The
journey is one of the great archetypal images of world myth and literature, and
has been used as a metaphor for all sorts of experiences, including that of
spiritual quest, and of the passage through life itself. In my book *Staging Place* [9]
I argue that the paradox of the claustrophobic journey, as exemplified by a
play like *Long Day's Journey into Night*, is a central trope of modernism. The
idea of the *desired but thwarted journey* structures a great deal of modern drama
since Ibsen and Chekhov, providing the ideal structure for what I have called
the 'geopathology' of modernism, the emphasis on the problem of place and
the construction of place *as problem*. While geopathology made of the journey
an ideal, dreamed of yet never attained, a multicultural play like *the bodies
between us* makes it clear that it is time to reclaim the image of the journey from
its use as metaphor, to re-literalize it and explore it as the reality it is for so
many people.

Today, in this age of diaspora, the journey is the generative and defining
life-experience of millions of people. Guillermo Goméz-Peña has spoken of the
'borderization' of the world, the fact that the 'border' is no longer situated only
at the geographical boundaries between nations but *within* the many bicultural
communities that have sprung up all over the world. The border now exists
wherever there are populations domiciled in one place and maintaining strong
links with another. In the same way, the journey now exists as the defining
experience of millions of people: immigrants, refugees, exiles. The border is
everywhere, the journey is endless. The extraordinary journey that is the
subject of *the bodies between us* is as paradigmatic as it is literal, and the play
charts the power and pathos of lives constructed, by necessity, out of the
reality of the 'permanent journey.'

In this play, the traumatic, life-defining and self-transforming journey is
played out as also a journey from and beyond language. The meaning of the
play circulates *between* its images and their embodiment, *between* its powerful
poetics and its often simple yet always insistent physical presence, evoking the
triumphant sense of a successful struggle to fully inhabit a place. That place is,
of course, this 'new world' of ours. But it is also, finally, the stage itself. *the
bodies between us* does what many emergent theater artists are having to do:

make the stage a *home*. The image of home, like that of the journey, is immensely complicated in the context of diaspora and displacement. A character in Chay Yew's recent play *A Beautiful Country*, a Malaysian drag queen named Miss Visa Denied, declares that 'this stage is my home.' For many multicultural artists, the stage has had to be not a home but a platform, from which the prevailing assumptions about them can be challenged. But it is moving and gratifying beyond words to see, as *the bodies between us* shows us, that the stage can also be a zone of great comfort, safety, trust, self-discovery, and self-revelation. That it can, in short, be home, even for those of us who have none.

NOTES

1. The trope of being 'born again' is central to David Henry Hwang's recent play *Golden Child*, in which the subject of religious conversion is gracefully appropriated for a utopian ideal of multicultural identity: 'Perhaps, if I do my best, in the imagination of my descendants, I may also one day be born again' (New York: Theatre Communications Group, 1998, 62).
2. Julia Kristeva, *Strangers to Ourselves*, trans. Leon S. Roudiez (New York: Columbia University Press, 1991, 15).
3. *Ibid.*, p. 20.
4. 'Identity is not something that is formed outside and then we tell stories about it. It is what is narrated in one's own self.' Stuart Hall, 'The local and the global: globalization and ethnicity,' in Anthony D. King (ed.), *Culture, Globalization and the World System* (Minneapolis: University of Minnesota Press, 1997, 49).
5. José Muñoz, *Disidentifications* (Minneapolis: University of Minnesota Press, 1999).
6. The notion of contact zones was theorized by Mary Louise Pratt in 'an attempt to invoke the spatial and temporal copresence of subjects previously separated by geographic and historical disjunctures, and whose trajectories now intersect.' Mary Louise Pratt, *Imperial Eyes: Travel Writing and Transculturation* (New York: Routledge, 1972), 6–7.
7. *Ibid.*, p. 7.
8. I have noticed that, when responding to this kind of work, people will frequently preface their remarks by mentioning their ethnic or racial backgrounds. In other words, we often reference the cultural specifics of our identities – in terms of race, ethnicity, gender, sexual orientation, and age – to give context or point to our comments about a multicultural play. We have a sense that our response to a multicultural play or issue is largely determined by or keyed to our ethnicity. And we tend to *mark* this in a way that we do not when we are discussing mainstream theater.
9. Una Chaudhuri, *Staging Place: The Geography of Modern Drama* (Ann Arbor: University of Michigan Press, 1997).

BORDERscape 2000

Guillermo Goméz-Peña and Roberto Sifuentes

BORDERscape 2000 was developed at the 'New Works for a New World' play development lab at the University of Massachusetts at Amherst in July 1997. In October 1998, it was presented as a featured performance at the conference 'Intersection of Performance, Practice, and Ideas,' produced by New WORLD Theater and the Department of Theater at University of Massachusetts at Amherst. It was created by Guillermo Goméz-Peña and Roberto Sifuentes, with Sara Shelton Mann, Juan Ibarra, and Karen Emerson-Smith. Lisa Wolford was dramaturg, sound design was by Rona Mitchell, lighting design by Penny Remsen, and set design by Lara Machari. It has been presented at various venues including the Magic Theatre in San Francisco, the University of Wisconsin-Milwaukee, and the Centre for Performance in Wales.

BORDERscape 2000 written by Guillermo Goméz-Peña and Roberto Sifuentes
In photo: Guillermo Goméz-Peña and Roberto Sifuentes
Photo by Ed Cohen

22

Pocha Nostra's apocalyptic landscape: introduction to *BORDERscape 2000*

Lisa Wolford

BORDERscape 2000, developed by Guillermo Goméz-Peña in collaboration with performer Roberto Sifuentes, choreographer Sara Shelton Mann, and actor/dancer Juan Ibarra, charts a geographic and cultural landscape marked by interethnic conflict and dehumanizing violence. The performance, which Goméz-Peña describes as 'a mindscape that fluctuates between the immediate past and the immediate future,'* articulates a relentlessly dystopic view of 'America' at the close of the twentieth century, the site of an undeclared war against immigrants and people of color. The piece is designated as the third installment in a performance trilogy that also includes *The Temple of Confessions* and *The Mexterminator Project*. The three portions of the trilogy are linked not in the sense of narrative continuity, but rather in their focus on similar themes and archetypal personae. Each of the three segments of the trilogy interrogates the dynamics of desire and fear, fetishization and paranoia, that characterize Anglo-American attitudes toward Latinos and Mexican immigrants. Of the three pieces, *BORDERscape 2000* is the most recognizably theatrical in structure, a scripted performance designed to be presented on a traditional proscenium stage. The earlier installments of the trilogy, by contrast, were interactive installation pieces that played on the colonial format of the living diorama, a type of display in which indigenous peoples were exhibited (willingly or otherwise) in museums, fairs, and other venues for the entertainment of Euro-American audiences. Made up of highly charged images and physical tableaux without spoken dialogue, the installation performances function as a type of catalyst, inviting interventions and

---

* All quotations from Guillermo Goméz-Peña are taken from a conversation with Lisa Wolford in Aberystwyth, Wales, April 1999.

responses from audience members. Goméz-Peña and Sifuentes created highly tropicalized personae that parodied romanticized and/or racist representations of Mexicans and Chicanos such as witch doctors, revolutionaries, bandits, or gang members; the characters they developed reflect 'the myth of the noble savage and the myth of the cannibal,' constructs that Goméz-Peña argues 'have become completely embroidered in the Western psyche.' Shelton Mann eventually joined *The Mexterminator Project* as 'La Klepto-Mexican' or 'Cultural Transvestite,' a figure intended to comment on dominant culture's insatiable appetite for exotic otherness. The personae developed during the artists' work on the installation pieces are foregrounded in *BORDERscape 2000*, where for the first time they are given voice in the sense of scripted text. They are joined in this futuristic landscape by the enigmatic figure of the Butoh Alien, an extra-terrestrial as seen on the 'Mex-Files,' played by Juan Ibarra. The image of the green alien simultaneously literalizes and parodies the depiction of 'illegal' Mexican immigrants as beings from another (cultural) planet. 'There's a very clear connection between fear of aliens and fear of immigrants,' Goméz-Peña explains. 'It's no coincidence that renewed interest in alien invasion, *à la Independence Day*, began to emerge next to the development of the new nativist and anti-immigrant political discourse.'

Having collaborated with Pocha Nostra periodically since 1997, first as an academic observer and more recently as dramaturg, co-conspirator, and *ad hoc* assistant director, I was already familiar with certain strains of imagery that haunt the group's recent projects: recurrent meditations on the stigmatization of urban Latino youth as perpetrators of gang violence, as well as on the commodification of ethnic identity through advertising and pop culture. The focus on border paradigms and US/Mexico relations that audience members might recognize as characteristic of Goméz-Peña's work is broadened, in *BORDERscape*, to include consideration of other dynamics of interracial tensions, as well as (in later versions) a more direct interrogation of Goméz-Peña's troubled relation with sectors of the Latino community. The piece also touches on the growing desensitization to violence in contemporary culture. The original ending for the performance called for a young White boy in military fatigues to come onto the stage from the audience and shoot at the crucified figure of the naked extraterrestrial (Ibarra), exploding a paint capsule onto the alien's chest. Whilst the ending was altered since it could not be accomplished without significant risk to the performer, the impetus behind the proposed conclusion was eventually translated into a combative dance sequence called 'The Nintendo Ethnic Wars' in which the alien is vanquished by a female and recognizably White mariachi (Shelton Mann), then captured and delivered for examination by a French anthropologist (Sifuentes).

Along with Goméz-Peña's production of *The Indian Queen* at the Long

Beach Opera House in 1998, *BORDERscape 2000* is among the most spectacular and visually ambitious of Pocha Nostra's productions. The contributions of sound designer Rona Michelle and film-maker Gustavo Vasquez are central to the performance, and Penny Remsen's lighting design (originally created for the New WORLD Theater staging) has been maintained for all subsequent productions. Given the technical demands of a multimedia performance such as *BORDERscape 2000*, a substantial proportion of rehearsal time during each of the residencies in which I have participated has been given over to issues of staging and design. A fair portion of the remaining time is spent in conversation and debate, with collaborators brainstorming possibilities for new images or actions, often germinating from real-life experiences of discrimination, or sparked by racist or tropicalized images from popular media which are subsequently reconfigured and layered with subversive meanings. Role definitions within the company are fluid, with collaborators characteristically offering feedback on one another's performances, helping to develop images or fragments of text and action.

Like many of Pocha Nostra's large-scale pieces, *BORDERscape 2000* is structured in such a way as to incorporate a fluctuating array of collaborators in addition to the core ensemble. Raymond Bobgan, artistic director of Cleveland's Theatre Labyrinth, served as consulting director for productions in San Francisco, California, and Aberystwyth, Wales, helping to refine visual imagery and set precise juxtapositions of live action to film. The Welsh production also incorporated an extremely talented local artist, Alex Alderton, who sang Welsh folk songs in 'traditional' garb (ironically enough, an English invention) and returned to the stage following a climactic crucifixion tableau to deliver a local traffic report in the clipped and overly cheerful tones of a professional radio announcer. The script of the performance continued to evolve significantly through each of these stagings, as new material was integrated and selected 'recycled' fragments were progressively phased out. The collaborative nature of the project was evident not only in the staging, for which performers devised substantial portions of their respective scores, but also in the written text. To cite one example, the character of the Southern Belle transvestite performed by Shelton Mann originated in one of the choreographer's solo pieces and was subsequently incorporated into *BORDERscape*, with the text for the scene originally scripted by Shelton Mann and refined by Goméz-Peña. In later productions, a scene was added that called for Shelton Mann to alternate between the Southern Belle character and a didactic 'Chicana cyborg created by the Latino coalition of biogeneticists from Brown Brown University.' The text for this section evolved in a strangely fragmented creative process (fragmented both temporally and in terms of physical location) among Goméz-Peña, Shelton Mann, and myself.

While Pocha Nostra's recent work still retains much of the structural playfulness and ironic humor of earlier pieces, the fundamental world-view conveyed in the performance cartography of *BORDERscape 2000* reflects the profound despair of a culture hurtling toward an imminent (secular) apocalypse. The performance invokes the iconography of Catholic tradition as a way of metaphorically depicting the nightmare politics of America at the end of the Second Christian Millennium. From a certain perspective, the piece can be viewed as a type of millennial prophecy, a techno-rasquache Book of Revelations. 'In this performance,' Sifuentes observes, 'we're showing people the entrails of contemporary reality, dissecting the ugliness of global politics and throwing it out on stage.' 'There are no solutions to the problems we are presenting,' Gomēz-Peña elaborates. 'We are merely articulating a kind of world and a culture gone wrong.'

A NOTE ON *BORDERscape 2000*

Guillermo Gomēz-Peña

Our work exists in opposition to certain official discourses of multiculturalism that pretend that racial conflict is over, or that the work being shown proposes some kind of solution to the conflict. At a time when it has become fashionable and desirable to transcend conflict, we have chosen the route of confronting it in a stylized and heightened way. What we are attempting to do, at a time in which there is a kind of a critical celebration of internationalism *à la* Discovery Channel or Benetton, where the primitive and the savage have become obligatory guests at the party, is to ask what happens when the savage rebels, when the savage talks back or doesn't follow the script? What happens when the savage knows too much theory, or mimics the dominant social structure in a very unpleasant way, so that he ends up taking over and re-creating the social structure? We are currently witnessing the apparent mainstreaming of a policy we all struggled for, and finding out that in fact it is just a mirage, because in reality the new internationalism has homogenized all cultural differences and obliterated all political texts. So what happens when someone attempts to turn things upside down and bring the political texts back to the surface, and at the same time to mimic the strategies of the fashionable international multiculturalism, such as eroticizing Zapatismo or glamorizing fringe culture?

It's not as if we are trying to propose a kind of apolitical multiculturalism, like in the 1980s. This is something very different, because the kind of critical multiculturalism of the 1980s, even at its best, was formally conservative and epistemologically simplistic: 'We perform for you in hopes that you will accept us and understand us.' But what happens when we mimic this format, and then in the middle of the piece, we rebel? What happens when the savage turns against the Benetton photographer, grabs the camera in the middle of the photo shoot, and starts terrorizing him? *BORDERscape 2000* is really not about us. It's not about Mexico, not about Chicanos, not about Latinos in the U.S., not about Latino immigration. The piece is really about the misperceptions and distortions that exist in the West; it's about mainstream America. It has a lot more to do with U.S. popular culture and official policies and dominant views than with our experience as subaltern communities. It's about cultural tourism and the commodification of ethnicity by major corporations. The characters we perform are stylized reflections and cultural projections that have been filtered through television, fashion, tourism, Hollywood, rap, and hip hop. The performance is definitely not about Chicanismo, and it has nothing to do with Mexico. We're not trying to perform our identities, by any means. That's the difference between the kind of epistemological proposition that exists in this trilogy and the kind of multicultural work that was common in the 1980s.

When people say that they don't feel represented by this piece, it's ridiculous, because they're missing the obvious: we are not attempting to represent anyone. We are not even human beings on the stage. Hopefully, we represent new cultural mythologies that are more complex than the simplistic images that have existed in popular culture until now. We're icons – broken icons, broken myths.

BORDERscape 2000 written by Guillermo Goméz-Peña and Roberto Sifuentes
In photo: Guillermo Goméz-Peña and Roberto Sifuentes
Photo by Ed Cohen

23

BORDERscape 2000

(Kitsch, Unnecessary Violence, Cyborgs, and Shamanism at the End of the Century): A New Aztec High-Tech Spanglish Lounge Operetta

Guillermo Goméz-Peña and Roberto Sifuentes

DESCRIPTION OF THE STAGE

(We could define this aesthetic as 'techno-shamanica.' The overall look is an aggressive and stylized mixture of Blade Runner-*like sci-fi, hard-core S&M and Latino high-lounge aesthetics. A sort of Chi-conan the Barbarian meets Barbarella in Tijuana kind of onda. The basic elements are as follows: There is a pyramid-shaped platform upstage center with a wooden cross on top of it. A skeleton is crucified on the cross. (The skeleton will eventually be raised up and replaced by performers.) A huge video screen hangs above to the left of the pyramid. A toilet is placed on a small platform on the extreme downstage left. Three dead chickens with heads, feathers, and feet still attached hang from the ceiling at varied heights and depths, lit from different angles. A fog machine periodically fills the space with smoke. A lectern will be brought in and out once.)*

INTRO: LIVING AND DYING DIORAMAS

(Tape #1 begins: 'Ave Maria,' Ry Cooder
Video #1 intro begins with periodic sound

Fog, Music (Pandora, Electrodomesticos, Cachakas, Ry Cooder). The audience enters theater. They are confronted with various dioramas, which change with the music:

Evolutions of actions:

1.   *'Ave Maria':*
We all are frozen: Goméz-Peña (GP) dressed as Mexterminator with mechanical hands sits on mechanical wheelchair downstage center. Juan Ibarra (JI) as green alien, fans him. Roberto Sifuentes (RS), as CyberVato, sits on top of pyramid. Sara Shelton Mann (SM) dressed as Mariachi/transvestite on toilet as sleeping mariachi. Welsh folk singer frozen on bike.

Video #2 The First Contact and #5 Mex Files without sound and Pre-Contact America

2.   *Electrodomesticos:*
El Mexterminator performs ritualistic shaman action with Mist Clean bottle downstage center. CyberVato (RS) removes American flag bandana and prepares to 'shoot up.' The Mariachi transvestite exorcises space from toilet position stage left platform. Green alien goes to second level platform stage left and does initiation action. Folk singer begins to pedal in slow motion.

3.   *Kachakas:*
GP does shamanic action with bones; El Transvestite Mariachi dances 'corona adelita' with Spanish dagger on stage right landing of pyramid. CyberVato 'shoots up' with syringe to abdomen and heart, then directs toward audience and holds it as a weapon. Folk singer pedals and sings traditional folk song.

4.   *Ry Cooder:*
Opera singer begins to sing 'Come Candore' over soundtrack on toilet area. Mexterminator performs 'victorious diorama' w/blond wig and saw. Near the end SM crosses downstage. CyberVato, seated on top of pyramid, performs action of binding face and head with leather strap, which ends in lynching tableaux. SM spreads GP's legs for the blowjob. Green alien ends simultaneously with 'heil' gesture. Folk singer dismounts bike (bike struck by stagehands dressed in black w/gas mask). Opera singer and folk singer exit.

Video ends.)

PART 1: SUPERNINTENDO RANCHERO

(Lights up on GP down center, and RS top of pyramid. As RS speaks GP begins to get 'blowjob' from SM, who ends up emasculating his 'banana dildo.' She shows her 'trophy' and exits. Stagehands clear downstage area. RS hits alien. Alien exits. RS in laboratory coat w/computer voice at top of pyramid introduces GP as Mexterminator. RS controls the Mexterminator, who moves in a mechanical, video-game-like pattern in response to RS's commands.

Tape #2: Techno.)

RS: *(computer-enhanced voice)* Aberystwyth April of 99. Dear Chicano colleagues, sorry, dear colleagues, welcome to B–2000, part 3 of a performance trilogy. Allow me to introduce to you the very first prototype: a beta version of . . . an imperfect Mexican. This cyborg still has a sentimental mind and a political consciousness. He failed the test for robotic migrant workers, and still longs for his homeland. Eventually when we manage to get the Mexican bugs out of him, we will create a Chicano (SM shows 'trophy'), the vato *uberalis*, the next step on the evolutionary scale. Speak Mexicyborg! Repent yourself! Use voice #53 and please stick to the script.

GP: *(processed voice #1)*:   No, I won't cru-ci-fy myself to protest la migra no more.

RS: You can't repeat a performance or it would become theater.

GP: No, I swear,
I won't box with a hanging chicken for art's sake, . . .
nor will I exhibit myself inside a gilded cage
as an endangered species or an androgynous wrestler/shaman.
RS: Why, Mad Mex Frankenstein?
GP: I'm just gonna be a pot for a while.
RS: Then be a pot. Stick to the spoken word material. Go! Go North!
GP: So I continue my trek north
like a compulsive explorer
El Marco Pollo de Tijuana,
El Vasco de Gama de Aztlán.
Ever looking for a new island, a new performance stage
to spill my beans, my bleeding tripas,
expose my crevasses, my wounded penis
in the name of ex-pe-ri-men-ta-tion.

(GP intersperses 'nos' through the following text)

RS: Now you wish to be a performance artist again?
GP: Not exactly.
RS: So, Vato, give us some blood,
show us your piercings, your prosthetics,
eat your green card or burn your bra
but get fucking real!
GP: No, no ni madres.
RS: Why?
GP: 'Cause I'm giving up, right now, in front of you.

RS: Oh god you fuckin' martyr.

GP: I willingly turn myself in to my inner border patrol
three agents are present tonight
come, get me!
this is your golden chance culeros
I su-rren-der to my darkest fears.

RS: You're not responding to my performance commands. You were much better when you were just trying to be a poet. Go back to poetry. Synthesize an entire cosmology into one burning sentence. Go!

GP: (*hesitating*) 'Fear is the foundation of your identity.'

(GP points at someone in the audience)

RS: What a fuckin' assumption.

GP: 'To be Mexican is a felony not a misdemeanor.'

RS: Hey better, chido, punchy.

GP: Versus 'ser pocho es still una afrenta binacional.'

RS: You are using Spanish unnecessarily. Shift accent.

GP: (*Texan accent*) I'm fully aware that your ears are tired
of listening to so many foreign languages.

(Gringo tongues)

RS: Stop! Next dialect!

GP: (*to the audience*) Such linguistic vertigo you have to endure daily.
I mean, you can't even communicate with your maid
or your gardener,
and then you go to Aberystwyth. Cymru.
(*gringoñol*)
and carrramba mamazita!
the artist Speaks Spanglish and gringoñol
(*mispronounced Spanish*) io hablou el idiouma del criminal, il drogadictou y la piuta
e' cuandouu io hablou tu muérres un poquitou mas.

RS: English only pinche wet back!

GP: (*to the audience*) I mean, 23 states in America have embraced English only.
California just abolished bilingual education
and I dare to talk to you in Spanglish? Que poca ma...

RS: Good boy ... you are assimilating.
What is your prime directive? Explain yourself.

GP: To you or to the audience?

RS: To the audience.

GP: Dear citizens of nothingness:
this is a desperate attempt by a dying performance artist
to recapture the power of the spoken word
in the year of virtual despair and victorious whiteness.
RS: Stop! Now, do something more kinetic, more defiant.
GP: Sara!
RS: Music!
GP: Sara!
RS: We need some hip music.

(CD #3, track 2, take 1. Japanese tea house lounge.

Lights transition to lounge look.

Tape #3: Japanese tea lounge.)

RS: Yeah! Now, stand up and dance. *(repeats three times)*

(GP stops wheelchair USL and attempts to stand up but fails. He eventually succeeds in standing. GP dances cheesy disco and twist then falls down on his knees.)

RS: Stop the music. This is terrifying.
Who do you think you are? An MTV Latino?

(Tape #3 ends. Tape #2 re-begins. GP crawls back onto the chair while speaking. Lights return.)

GP: El Mariachi with a biiiiiig moooouth.
RS: Not anymore carnal.
GP: Mexi-cyborgel extra-extra-terrestre.
RS: Not quite yet. You wish.
GP: El immigrant bizarro con su mente explosiva y expansiva
al servicio de la fragmentación político-poética.
RS: State your function or lose your green card.
GP: To you or the audience?
RS: To the audience.
GP: My normal state of being, carnal,
is to die for you, 'cause after all these years
I'm still imprisoned inside this historical purgatory.
RS: Still obsessed with history in the year 2000?
GP: Yes.
RS: That's cute.
GP: *(to the audience)* Do you remember the terms of the Guadalupe-Hidalgo treaty?
Do you fuckin' remem ...

RS: Can anyone answer this pathetic poet?
GP: Es que vous et illegal?
L'illegalite est a la mode, n'est pas?
RS: OK, you win this time. Let's talk about illegality ... Go!

(House lights. After each question, RS counts each raised hand.)

GP: Are there any illegal immigrants in the audience?
People who once were illegal?
What about people who have had sex with an illegal alien?
Can you describe in detail their genitalia?
Are there people here who have hired illegal immigrants
for domestic, or artistic purposes?

(Audience members may answer; RS intersperses improvised replies.)

Yessss! To do what exactly?
How much did you pay them?
How did you feel about that?
Thanks for your sincerity ...
Now, have any of you ever fantasized about being from another race or
culture?
Which one?

(RS intersperses 'Boring') Black? Indian? Native American? Mexican?

RS: Boring. Cambio de canal: give me burning sentence number two.
(House lights down)
GP: 'Ser emigrante en America ya es un acto ilegal'
RS: Translation please?
GP: Just to be different is potentially an illegal act.
One strike and you're out!
Punishable with deportation without trial,
and retroactive to 10 years.
RS: That's too ... technical.
GP: I mean to be excluded from a national project
at a time when all nation states are collapsing
is not an extraordinary act of heroism
or a literary fiction, ask the Welsh or the Irish man ...
RS: That's too fuckin' heavy to deal with right now;
this is the year 2000
it's all about style without content.
GP: You mean radical actions without repercussions?
RS: Right!

GP: Tropical tourism without Monteczuma's revenge?

RS: Global nada ...

GP: Nothing-ness really.

Just style, anonymous sex, weird trivia?

So, if that's what defines your values and your identity

lets fuckin' engage in trivia.

RS: Good! But bring down at least ten decibels the level of your drama;

And remember; pc es passes, and so is rage, Supermojado.

Now, give me some burning trivia. Go!

GP: 'Madonna defeated Argentina and got to play Evita.'

Goooo Madonna!!

RS: Dated material. Next!

GP: 'Selena died precisely during the crossover.'

(Looking up) Selena, we luv you diva, auuu!!

RS: What's so special about Selena?

GP: Her whiny voice and liposuctioned nalgas.

Besides, she is all we have, since we've got no real leaders.

O que? Do you think we have any true Chicano leaders?

RS: Kind of.

GP: Can you mention one?

RS: Eddie Olmos. *(GP reacts with short phrases)* Cheech Marin. *(GP reacts)*

The Taco bell Chihuahua.

GP: Fax you man. Subcomandante Marcos! He is not a Chicano but he is

certainly a leader ...

RS: He's just a fading myth. Back to our search for burning trivia. Go!

GP: 'Zappa is resting in the Olympus of Americana.'

(me persigno)

per ipsum, ecu nip zzzum Zzzzappa!

RS: And so is Sinatra.

GP: Sinatra?

(Sings) 'When I was 35, it was a very good year.'

ese mi Frank

your absence hurts much more that that of Octavio Paz.

RS: Hey that's a great trivial line.

Do you have some of this shit on disc?

GP: No, I no longer have a laptop. I am a neo-Luddite.

RS: A luddite with a mechanical wheelchair?

GP: Yes.

RS: You fuckin' ro-man-tico! Shift 348X–13 Trivialize race. Go!

GP: 'OJ was a cyborg constructed by your own fears and desires.'

RS: But was he guilty?

GP: Yes, he was guilty and not that interesting a character.

RS: But we cared about him, cause he was *(GP intersperses '¿Que?')* ...
cause he is a ... a ... a black cyborg.

(pause)

GP: I didn't say it, you did!

RS: These are the issues that truly matter.

GP: Sure ... in a time and place
where nothing significant truly matters.

RS: What you consider trivia is my *raison d'etre.*
Give me a headline that truly captures our times.

GP: 'Clintoris and Lenguinsky: the grand millennial soap opera.'

RS: elaborate ... elaborate ... elaborate.

GP: Monica finally described in detail the genitals of your president.

RS: Don't elaborate.

GP: She said, she said:
'It's pink, about three inches long and it never gets hard
but there is something endearing about it.'

RS: You are diverging from our subject matter. We are beginning to sound
like bad experimental poetry. Neruda meets Jello Biafra.
What are we really here for?

GP: Tonight?

RS: Tonight

GP: Tonight?

RS: Tonight

GP: *(to the audience)* There is too much turmoil in your private life
for me to bother you with the truly heavy issues
like racism, homelessness or police brutality.

RS: Right! That was the '80s ese.
We've heard that pop song so many times
but tonite, your audience is understandably tired
they suffer from ... repeat with me:
com-pa-ssion fa-tigue, yeah.

GP: Com-pa-ssion fa-tigue, yeah.

RS: Just to hear you say it makes me want to slash you in the face.

GP: Thank you.

(Lights suddenly shift to next scene. GP and RS exit.)

PART 2: NINTENDO INTER-ETHNIC WARS

(Tape #4: La Chica Ye-Ye
Lights up on SM on pyramid platform as Mariachi Zapatista. She breaks into high-
energy twist-like Chaplinesque movements with a gun for 1 minute. Tape ends.
She freezes. Lights come up downstage.

Tape #4.5: Symphonic rap
Green alien (JI) appears making robotic movements for 1 minute. SM comes to life and
moves off pyramid. Light on GP who subvocalizes extreme downstage left.

Video #3 500 years of resistance with sound begins.
Alien and SM begin Nintendo fighting which goes on until end of song ... Scene ends
with SM pushing alien to stage right platform.)

PART 3: A LECTURE ON REVERSE ANTHROPOLOGY: THE PAST

(RS in lab coat and glasses puts on rubber gloves petting green alien on stage right
platform. Lights change to slide-show look.)

RS as FRENCH ANTHROPOLOGIST: *(French accent)* Oo La La, pardon my
French ... behavior. A fine specimen of an illegal alien. Such nice texture.

(Slide #1: French comic hero 'Fantomas' being attacked by Mexican shamans. RS
comes downstage to begin his lecture.)

Bon soir my dear colleagues. Because some of you may be culturally
impaired we have decided to periodically translate the most sensitive
material into linguas francas such as nahuatl, gringoñol and some pre-
Columbian ... Welsh ... sign language. Permit moi to introduce myself. Je
sui professor Jaques Fromage du Merde from La Sorbonne. My fields of
expertise are Chicano science, the border paradigm, ethno-scenologie and
experimental ethnographie. Et more specifically the sexual, political et
linguistic behavioral patterns of Mexican immigrants et gang members.

(Slide #2: Teen angel drawing of couple)

And since you have no previous references to Mexican culture, I will
introduce you to some basic data; a sort of travelogue through Mexican
historie in deux minutes. Panchou, can we please begin the in situ tribal
recordings I brought from my last field trip to Cancún.

(Tape #5: Mexican lounge music

Slide #3: Image of 'tacosaurus'
Jl begins evolution of the species from frog to Vato Uberalis.)

Way before the first Americans migrated from Siberia via the Bering Strait, there were already Mexican creatures roaming around this sauvage continent. Voici we see an edible sample of these specimens. Contrary to perceptual illusion, Tacosaurus was ... this big *(he signals size between thumb and forefinger)*

(Side #4: Aztec codex (two priests sacrificing a blonde tourist))

Since the early encounters with the civilized West, we can see in this pictograph that Mexicans have always exhibited hostility towards well-meaning missionaries, anthropologists, and tourists like you. Tonight's performance is but one example ...

(Slide #5: Scene of Hernan Cortez and La Malinche about to have sex)

As hypersexual creatures, Mexicans understand the power of erotic seduction. Here, in this archival photo, we see the original bilingual secretary of the Americas, La Malinche, about to engage in the first indigenous contact with Europe. *(Sinister laughter)* Cortez didn't know what he was getting into ... the creation of a new race! Les enfants de la chingada.

(Slide #6: Anthropologist with 4 nude Indians)

Although they claim to be Christian, Indios, or 'Indians' in English, they are actually pagan. In this image captured by a ethno-porn photographer, a Clinton aide interviews a group of prospective interns who will assist the President enter a new partnership with his horny neighbors to the South. Pay attention to the left hand of Monsieur Bowles.

(Slide #7: Photo of flamboyant Mexican wrestling team)

In '94, following the examples of the European communité and the Pacific Rim, our three North American neighbors decided to sign a Free Trade Agreement, a sort of menage à trade. Mexico provided raw material, talent and manpower; Canada, the technologie; and the I.S. was the sole recipient of the goodies. Smart, n'est pas? Here you can enjoy the official promo photo of the original NAFTA negotiating team.

(Slide #8: Five elderly Zapatistas)

Diorama of angry Zapatistas at the Museé of Natural History. Sadly, Mexicans can't handle modernity, so when the country was finally on the verge of joining the First World, a group of foreigner saboteurs disguised as 'indios' took up arms following the ancient spirit of 'Zapata.'

(Slide #9: Marcos and Super Barrio)

Ici, Subcomandante Marcos gets fashion and PR advice from pueblo activist Super Barrio.

(Slide #10: Beer advertisement depicting blonde models dressed as Mexican revolutionaries)

Next ethnographic diorama: Typical Zapatista adelitas; 'les demoiseilles du Chiapas.' Their simple peasant attire reflects the harsh climate of the Chiapaneca selva, meaning jungle ... I love the Spanish tongue ... all over my body.

(Slide #11: 5 Masked 'Lone Rangers')

The situation in Chiapas has changed dramatically in the last months. Subcomandante Marcos has disappeared without a trace. It has been rumored that he has formed a new resistance group in Montana made up of ex-militia members and neo-nationalist Chicanos. Here we see the new generation of subcomandantes training to retake the US Southwest, a very good example of how sauvage Mexique and its bastard children, the chicanous, have affected you all.

(Slide #12: Robo-KKK)

You may be wondering, my dear colleagues, what good Americans are doing to combat this bizarre demographic hemorrhage. Some are immersing themselves in nostalgia for a time when colored people still knew their place and America was a safe haven from Third World chaos.

(SM enters; stagehand follows with tea set. Slides out. Lights up on SM.)

PART 4: TEA CEREMONY

(SM is dressed as a Southern belle. She sits on a toilet downstage left. Folk singer with pet lamb sings traditional song intertwined with blues on stage right platform.

Tape #6: Ray Charles's 'America the Beautiful')

SM: *(Filtered voice, Southern drawl)* Hi ya'll. How ya doing. I'm so glad to see you. Could we have a little more light on these lovely people?

(House lights up.)

Thank you for coming. This is my favorite song. Would you please stand up, come on everybody, and now raise your right hand. I've made some tea,

Sassafrass tea. Good for what ails you. Thickens your blood or thins it. We all need blood now don't we? These performance artists are quite direct.

(Alien enters stage left slowly moving across the stage mopping à la Robert Wilson with prosthetic leg.)

I think we need a little break. You ... would you like some tea? Come up here. *(invites White female audience member up on stage)* Say when. Cream? Some people like it white white, some light brown, some like it pitch black. *(fanning)* She's got a pearly sweet complexion. Sugar? One, two, or three? Sweeten those cheeks. She knows what's good for her now, doesn't she. May I serve you? Now just wait a minute. Maybe a little later. Patience is the cause of beauty. Patience takes a little effort you know. See all those people. Maybe they'd like some tea too.

You *(the next person, a Latino male)*, would you like some tea? You are peculiar looking? Brown color. Did you make that up or did your mother give it to you? ? *(comparing skin)* Could we be kin from the same planet, universe, do we share the same DNA? Where are you from? I'll pour. You say when *(he answers)*. It sounds sexy. *(fans)*. I've heard of that. I'm from the South. There's North, South, East, and West, I've heard. And South of South, right of the right, there's Florida. And after that, there is nothing.

My family had a farm. We are cotton, sugar, hogs, and tobacco. Black people are from the South. There's Black, Blue Black, Red Black, Black Black, and Brown Black. Things have changed in the South. All the Black people moved to the city, the inner city, while the white people moved to the suburbs. Then all these brown people came to work in the fields. I couldn't speak their language. They call them migrant workers. Would you like some cream? You look like my brother. Black hair and black eyes. Strong looking. I love my brother. My mother used to say that he was part Indian. But now wait a minute, we don't talk about that. Are you part Indian? Pure bred? $1\frac{1}{2}$, $1\frac{1}{3}$, $\frac{1}{2}$ breed? That's fashionable these days. I read it in the *Utne Reader*. I have no right to be saying these things. They are not in the script.

Sugar? You say when. 1, 2, or 3. Let's breathe on this and call it purity tea. May I serve you? Now step back. There are others waiting. You wouldn't want to be the cause of jealousy now would you? *(fans)*.

(Alien crosses stage diagonally w/rattlers and mereingues. He stops for a while at center stage and then continues.)

You can tell that this man has been giving – lots of resources. We can see he's been practicing pure moral discipline because he has a precious human life. *(Cues male audience member to leave stage.)*

(JI kneels becoming furniture holding mereingues with hands.)

Now let's all have some emptiness tea and meditate on the blessed mother. While I have some sugar. Now for the best part, mereingues. I crawl under the covers and eat them in bed every night. Just stuff 'em in my mouth, like this. They go straight down, by-pass the gall bladder and over to the pancreas. They make you crazy, like all distractions, additions.

It's all about sugar. We can't hold a thought for a minute, no patience, no love, so let's eat sugar. If that's not enough we can just mainline it. Go straight for the sugar cubes. Just pop 'em straight in. Hard love. Do you like hard love, like me? If we can't treat people like our beloved mother, we can eat sugar. Do you like sugar? Everybody loves sugar. I just get crazed and have fits.

(Language becomes progressively more garbled and incoherent as SM goes crazy eating sugar and becomes possessed.
Running crew strikes tea set. SM and JI exit.)

PART 5: A LECTURE ON REVERSE ANTHROPOLOGY: THE PRESENT

(RS enters to stage right platform. Powwow tape continues underneath.
Slide #13: 'Alien registration office')

RS: Uh-uh, an unprovoked eruption of the White colonial subconscious. *(To SM)* Sortie. Sortie. Rural Americans out of control due to fear of cultural otherness, or rather of brown people. Not a problem here. But, let's continue with today's subject matter: Truly dangerous 'aliens.'

(GP with kilt and crouched begins to cross slowly toward center stage.
Slide #14: 'Smallest catch')

In the past years, America has suffered a climatic tragedy: hurricanes trashing trailer parks, forest fires travelling all the way from Central Mexico to Florida, and under the cover of weather disasters, hordes of Mexicans flooding into the U.S. cities and fields like a Mex-truation. Please meet the mastermind of the whole operation, aka El Niño.

(Slide #15: Shaman hanging himself in b/w)

Our future seems bleak but we are working on it. MIT engineers and biogeneticists are attempting to solve the problem of migrant labor: this prototype of a robotic farm worker, currently being constructed in Taiwan, will work without all the associated inconveniences of real workers;

i.e. medical care, labor unions, growing unwanted minority groups, affirmative action quotas, etc ...

(Slide #16: 'Tiniblas' wrestler)

The obvious problem is the need for real human Mexican mechanics, who must be on site in order to maintain and repair the robo-farmworkers.

(Lights up center stage, as GP as androgynous wrestler shaman boxes against himself. Slide #17: Indian beating a cowboy)

U.S. minorities are unnecessarily violent and politicized creatures. Their forgranted outbursts always seem to be justified by obscure historical reasons ... genocide, colonialism, and other big words. Here you can see an alleged retaliation against a poor INS agent by the militant Jamás, a fringe wing of the Chicano Intifada. Next image, Pancho.

(Slide #18: Indian with spear attacking priest)

Another unprovoked terrorist attack by a member of a generic minority ...

(Slide #19: GP and RS as border mafiosi)

But let's deconstruct the overall tribal structure controlling organized crime in the U.S. Southwest: The East L.A. cartel is controlled in virtual reality by 2 Information Superhighway banditos: El Mexterminator and El CyberVato. Those web-backs.

(Slide #20: Mexican wrestlers in pink attire)

Ici, we see them during a special mission travelling incognito in traditional Mexican attire. The duo often masks their seditious agenda as performance art. In cahoots with members of other cartels, these vandals are committed to the destruction of our Western value systems, aesthetic canons, and anachronistic institutions, like this one. Other mafias include.

(Lights out on GP. He exits. Cross-fade to SM, who enters to toilet. She begins Supermodel Anime tableaux.)

(Slide #21: Three midget bullfighters)

The TMB. Tijuana mini-bullfighters. Don't let their size and exotic costumes deceive you. They are petite but powerful and mean-spirited. They have control over all the street vendors of Los Angeles and all the coyotes who smuggle wetbacks across the border.

(Slide #22: 3 Cholas)

Implacable feminist gang bangers from Stanford, 'Las Panochas envenenadas.'

(Slide #23: Chesty Sanchez)

They poison their enemies in the macho Chicano nationalist cartels; therefore they have a bitter-sweet relationship with El Mexterminator and CyberVato, who often present to their audience questionable images of women, per example ...

(Slide #24: Nude women painted in gold)

The rival gang of Las Panochas is an urban primitive gringa performance troupe named 'the ab-original gueras' from here, San Francisco.

(Slide #25: Blonde women shooting laser gun)

Led by self-destructive choreographer and ethno-avatar Sara Coatlicue Mann. *(He gestures to SM)* Their mission statement is, and I quote: 'To reconquer the pale protestant body as a site for pleasure and pain, et adopt seasonal pet cultures for costuming.'

PART 6: THE ESSENTIALIST CHICANA

(SM interrupts anthropologist lecture. RS gets forced off stage. Slides out.)

SM: *(computer voice/cyborg movement)* Stop. Stop. Stop your bullshit Professor. *(She chases RS offstage with her gun)* You suave sexist lost in your own hetero-pathological mythologies and ethno-sexual fantasies. It is my turn to talk back, back. I am a new and improved Chicana – cyborg created by the Latina coalition of biogeneticists from Brown Brown University. I've got my barrio ID card, would you care to see it?

I no longer bear the stigmatized features of an organic based chicana mestiza, meaning I have the a-a-a-ability to morph the color of my skin from dark brown, indigenous color X–27 to an upper-class fair-skinned gringoized Latina, like many of you out there, out there? Besides I no longer have to wear iguanas on my head to be authentic. I am authentic period.

(SM takes off wrestler mask, puts on long blonde wig. Fan appears. She goes to toilet. Video without sound #1: Precontact America)

SM: *(Southern)* Hi ya'll. It's so great. Race is no longer an issue for 'us.' I mean me. I've paid all my dues on my back, thank you. Club Med and the Gold Card. American Express paid my way to all the missionary hotspots. Cancun was my favorite – those lovely white beaches with the local color on display. I even spent a week with Marcos, king of the Zapatistas, in bed.

I mean there were not enough beds for me. But that's not why I'm here. I am fed up with this high-faluting lecture thing.

SM: *(Computer-enhanced voice)* What we have here are two fancy-talking macho Mexicans that think they carry on their wetbacks the avant-garde of political change. But, Gomez-Peña just converted to the other side – U.S. citizenship – and speaks fake nahuatl. Roberto spends all his free time on the cellphone, checking his stock portfolio. Do they look like redemption to you? No. Do I look like the Virgin Mary – No – Madonna – no – The Holy Ghost? I am the chicana who would like to penetrate your White institutions with my strap-on dildo. You will see it later in the show. Alleluya! Please stand up all you sisters out there and let's give it to these Chicano wannabe gringos and Mexicans who never paid their dues. Alleluya!

SM: *(Southern accent)* Long live the haves and the have nots.

Pay your dues, your debts and fuckin' die.

No more blowjobs for art sake.

Say alleluya.

Viva la mujer.

Viva Guadalupe.

Viva Mexico alleluya!

Everybody stand up, and say alleluya.

SM: *(Computer-enhanced voice)* Nothing personal honey. I'm sure they are nice Cyborg-vatos, but they don't have any right to be here working with White girls. There are plenty of chicana choreographers and opera singers out there. Out there? Can't you find one, homeboys? Don't you realize the sexist and reverse racist implications of brown men working with White girls, I mean, beautiful White women? *(Begins to die)* I have a mandate.

(Lights cross-fade as SM exits and RS enters to stage right platform.)

PART 7: CHICANO NIRVANA

(GP enters slowly climbing to top of pyramid with megaphone.)

RS as JAQUES: A very confused Chicana cyborg. Alors Mexicans are Mexicans. Take away their tequila and they will always show insurrectional behavioral patterns. I myself have managed to supress these aforementioned patterns by spending most of my life in a university, but sometimes all it takes is a tecate or a jalapeño and my ... and ... vive la France, I mean, la raza!

(RS improvises transformation into rasta rapper in front of audience. RS voice changes to rasta preacher.
    Tape #7: Tres Dielnquentes (Mariachi Rap)

Video without sound: #4: Civil Rights Movement

CyberVato moves to center as rasta preacher delivers text. GP intersperses 'CAMBIO' in following text.)

RS as RASTA RAPPER: *(with voice filter)* Dear robo-raza and pinches gueros, welcome to Chicano nirvana: We, acá en el norte, have entered a post-democratic era. CAMBIO. We now live in a world without theory, without structures, without ethics. CAMBIO. The nation-state is purely a metaficción nostalgica. CAMBIO. It collapsed in '98 as a logical result of the second U.S.–Mexico war. After the signing of the Guadalupe-Marcos Treaty, the ex-U.S. of A has fragmented into myriad micro-republics. They are loosely controlled by a multiracial junta, and governed by a Chicano prime minister named Gran Vato. CAMBIO. Spanglish is now the official language. CAMBIO. Scared shitless of the New Borders, Anglo militias are desperately trying to recapture the Old Order.

CAMBIO. The newly elected government sponsors interactive exhibits to 'teach' the perplexed population of the U.S. of Aztlán 'how things were before and during the second U.S.–Mexico war.' This performance is but one example. CAMBIO.

The borders and climate fluctuate as you watch these ethno-cyborgs. Prepare for the Brown House effect; prepare for your last migration to the North Pole. CAMBIO. This is the end of the world – and the word – as we know it. CAMBIO.

NAFTA was a blast, locos, a trinational pachanga which ended up in a trilingual brawl. Now everyone is hung over and no one remembers exactly what happened. CAMBIO.

Skeletons keep appearing in key sites throughout Mexamerica. La migra y la DEA were the spinal cord of the whole operation. CAMBIO.

You knew. Deep inside we all knew. Ja-ja-ja CAMBIO.

And now, locos and locas, Gran Vato, the first Chicano president of the U.S. of A, addressing the Brown House. That's you. He is a neo-indigenista nationalist ethno-cybrog, true, but we'll give him some slack cause at least he's got good picante and self-reflexive humor. CAMBIO. Take it away Gran Vato.

(Lights cross-fade to shaman at top of pyramid as RS exits.)

PART 8: 'INTER-TRIBAL SEX RITE'

GP as BRUJO: *(Computer-enhanced voice)* Americans cross the border South in search of identity and history. Mexicans cross the border north as if coming into the future. Since we suffer from an excess of identity, deep inside what we really want is to get rid of it ... We cross the border to reinvent ourselves. CAMBIO. The only way to avoid becoming an exotic anti-hero nowadays is to constantly reinvent oneself; to disappear every now and then, and then to come back with a new set of strategies, metaphors, voices, costumes and weapons. CAMBIO.

(Video without sound #6: Great Mojado invasion)

I am a mere reflection of a desire created by Benetton, the Banana Republic, MTV and Warner Brothers Studios. CAMBIO. Scene 8: Interracial Sex ritual. Comenzamos.

(JI as alien and a nude 'zapatista' enter left and right and walk up pyramid to second levels. They are like catholic acolytes with candles.

Lights on JI and opera singer as zapatistas stage left and stage right landing of platform)

GP: *(Normal voice) (se persigna/los ojos hacia arriba)*
per ipsum ecu nipsum, eti nipsum
et T-Video Patri Omni-impotenti
per omnia saecula saeculeros.
(tongues)
(Sara puts RS on a leash).
Hare Krishna, Krisnahuatl
Hare grandma, hairy nalga.
(tongues)

(SM enters as 'Hollywood Aztec Maiden' with ware bonnet and breech cloth; RS as lowrider with high heels, dog leash and spray paint. Police baton, American flag bandana. Sara positions RS on chair downstage center. RS shakes spray can. SM with Indian headdress dances stereotypical powwow dance around him. Lights on them.)

SM and RS: *(Normal voice)* Christian girls, Christian girls,
Christian Girls, Christian Girls,
Oh how I love, oh how I love,
oh how I love those Christian girls, ahhhhh ...
New age girls ... *(repeats chant)*
skinhead girls ... *(repeats chant)*
macho, macho, mucho macho.

(GP uncovers himself to reveal androginia. SM begins to rough up RS.)

GP: *(Shamanic Filter) (tongues)* Tezcatlipunk
   (tongues) Funkahuatl
   (tongues) Khrishnahuatl
   (tongues) Chichicolgatzin.
   (tongues) Chili con Carni.
   (tongues) Taco Bell chihuahua.
   (tongues) Changó.
   (tongues) chingó *(señal de coger).*
   (tongues) Santa Frida.
   (tongues) Santa Selena.
   (tongues) Santa Pocahontas.
   (tongues) Virgen Tatuda.
   (tongues) Virgen de Nafta.

(GP begins to march and do military salutes. Video stops.)

NAFTA, viagra, Melatonin,
NAFTA, viagra, Melatonin
(screams) Melatonin!
now everybody … take your pill.

(Hippy peace sign. Pause)

Ginseng, Ginko, Guacamole!
Now everybody, take a dip.

(Lights off RS, SM, GP, and acolytes
   Video: Mexterminator. GP close-ups.)

RELIGIOUS INTERLUDE

(Tape #8: Pandora's 'Que Sabes de Amor'
  RS does Christ with a G-string standing on chair down center stage, then stigmata.
As SM climbs pyramid, lights up on SM crucified, with a strap-on dildo and a
mariachi hat.)

PART 9: OBSESSIVE RE-ENACTMENTS OF MARTYRDOM

(GP changes into postmodern Zorro. GP steps behind lectern. Lights on him. GP begins
speaking.

Tape #8 continues, then changes to:

Tape #9: Mariachi Rap
JI as Butoh Alien translates text into pre-columbian sign language. SM remains at cross.)

GP: Stop the music. *(Video goes out)* Hey, Roberto put your pants on and adopt the Chicano position 187. Can someone bring his shoes?

(Video: gang violence and LA riots.
RS changes back into lowrider, with American flag bandana, police baton, and handcuffs. RS puts pants on. Stagehands strike chair. RS blindfolds himself, and gets ready to swing at the chicken with police baton.)

GP: *(Computer-enhanced voice, to sound grave, forboding)* The night is clearly the place to be,
   Sin fronteras ni contornos,
   a safe place for techno-warfare and unlimited entertainment.
   At night, I love you much more,
   especially when my life's in danger
   and my tongue, my cobra tongue, is out of control.

   At night, Anglo militias roam around
   The streets of my city,
   a city without limits or a name,
   without a recognizable government,
   a city council, or a police department;
   without architectural coherence or a sense of self,
   like me, like you ... but who are you loca?

   Militias keep moving North;
   My identity freefalling toward chaos.
   Chaos is always North.
   El norte, la ciudad de la muerte.
   Que bajen al pinche pollo!
   Don't trust them. Don't trust them!

(RS swings at chicken piñata with baton)

   America we simply don't trust you!
   You are hopeless. We all are hopeless.
   Where are you loca? America where are you?

   All we have left is sex;
   Cyber-sexo without a body;
   Sexo anónimo, sin facciones, sin identidad
   ('sin' en inglés equals pecado remember?);

sex without emotional or biological repercussions;
o bien, el sexo aeróbico, intrascendente, doloroso,
extremo, impersonal, y sin propósito alguno,
en la calle, bajo la niebla, en la misma morgue.
And the more anonymous, detached, and weird,
the better ...
so death as a high spiritual goal is temporarily unattainable.

Enough matachin! *(takes off Zorro hat)* Gimme back my normal voice.
Roberto adopt a better tableau, try 209.

(Lights out on JI, as he exits.
Tape stops/video stops.
RS adopts 'menacing' pose.)

GP: *(normal voice)* What you have experienced so far is mere artifice,
strategically designed to appeal to the desires of an intelligent, liberal
audience, like you. But now it's time to move to the next stage. From now
on, no one is allowed to laugh. The doors have been locked for your own
protection. You are being held captive by three Mexicans and a cultural
transvestite, and an archetypal step on stage and you willingly commit
ritual suicide, bonzo, as an act of historical penance.

(RS begins to hit himself with baton.
Video: 'New tape.'
Alien begins climbing pyramid.
GP with satanic voice sings 'Hotel California' repeatedly including Spanish
translation.

Alien replaces SM at cross. SM goes backstage to change clothes, SM goes to RS and
stops him beating himself. RS adopts busted position. SM tags RS with spray. Hands
him the spray can and goes to the toilet and adopts sleepy Mexican position. RS sprays
chicken. Starts chicken beating with the next text.
Opera singer enters singing to hanging chicken. (Mozart and 'Lucia,'
approximately 5 mins.)
Video: Indian queen segment primitive stuff.)

GP: Final scene: the Mexican as chicken; *(Roberto cuts chicken and begins to*
beat it) the chicken as chicano; the cops as ghosts. Tag that mother fucker!
Are we recapitulating or capitulating? Are we biting our own tails or
desperately looking for a way out? Roberto tag the fuckin' chicken;
humiliate yourself; engage in poetical self-hatred; beat up yet another
chicken; go; re-enact all our cultural wars, our genocide, our colonization.

(Chicken beating goes on for as long as it takes for him to completely smash the chicken to bits, and he is breathing hard and sweating with the effort. Crucified alien reacts. GP grabs bucket with water and sponge and walks up pyramid and begins to slowly wash alien. Alien begins to bleed. GP walks down, goes to niche and kneels like religious icon.)

SM as MARIACHI: *(on toilet with Southern voice)* Is there anyone out there willing to stop him? Too late. Let's all go for tequila after the show.

(RS finally collapses on his knees and gathers the remains of the chicken into a pile, holding them in a romantic, almost erotic posture.

As GP steps into the light, music begins.
   Tape #10: 'Stand By Me' (original version mixed with Ry Cooder version).
   Video out.
   Opera singer fades slowly and exits.
   GP grabs RS's hair, puts knife on his throat, looking away, stands poised to attack him, then places the mariachi hat on RS's head, turning him into stereotyped image of sleepy Mexican. GP takes off his Zorro jacket. He then raises the knife above his head and begins to stab RS in slow motion.
   Blackout.
   SM, RS and GP stand with hands behind head in 'busted' positions. Lights on them (one minute). They breath intensely. Green alien remains on cross. House lights to half up (three minutes).
   Tape #11: 'It's a Small World,' intertwined with 'Ave Maria.'

House lights to full and doors open. Plant claps vigorously. Plant stands up whether we deserve it or not.)

24

Audioscape 2000: the Pocha Nostra and the performance of sound

Josh D. Kun

WELCOME TO THE HOTEL CALIFORNIA

On a darkened stage, a blindfolded Roberto Sifuentes is in character as the CyberVato, his long black hair pulled back into a tightly wound braid that drapes down the back of his white undershirt, and he's taking desperate, lunging swings at the flaccid carcass of a chicken hanging from an invisible string. With each swing of his police billyclub, the chicken is jolted up or to the side, always just inches from violent contact. Soon enough, the chicken drops and Sifuentes proceeds to ritualistically, feverishly, and meticulously beat the carcass to a fine, minced pulp, mashing every fiber of skin, flesh, and bone into a meaty, moist dust on the floor of the black stage – the muscles of his body convulsing and straining as each blow becomes more focussed, more targeted, more precise, more important, more saturated with blind rage.

While the beating takes place, Guillermo Goméz-Peña, who is standing further backstage and only slightly illuminated by a filtered spotlight, is singing The Eagles' 'Hotel California' as a demonic mariachi, his deep, raspy voice fed through a sound board processor that tweaks and mutates its pitch into a horrific, taunting howl.

Sifuentes is both the cholo who gets beaten by the LAPD – the victimized, criminalized, and hunted brown body – and the boy in blue delivering the blows. The chicken becomes every minoritized body ever bludgeoned by police brutality, every undocumented body made unfit to live and learn by Propositions 187 and 209 and 227, every body caught and chased and caught in the gaze of high-tech spy cams by the border patrol. Together they are the bloodied lie of the California dream, the noirish underbelly, to borrow Mike Davis's famous paradigm, of the great Western Eden myth of southern

Californian sunshine and oranges.[1] The 'peaceful, easy feeling' of The Eagles' California – one made equally famous by their adult contemporary radio frontier ballad, 'Desperado' – is flipped into what it really is: a terror-space of oppression and violence, a surveillance police state of environmental collapse, public space erasure, right-wing legislation, and White racial panic.

BORDER AURALITIES

The scene is from *BORDERscape 2000*, the most recent collaboration between Goméz-Peña, Sifuentes, and the rest of their Pocha Nostra crew, and it would not work without the song. In fact, none of *BORDERscape 2000* – which is set in the year 2000, after the second U.S.–Mexico War, after the Treaty of Guadalupe-Marcos has been signed, after the power structures have been reversed and a utopia of inversion has been implemented with Spanglish as the dominant language, the White House as the Brown House, and hybridity as the dominant culture – would make sense as a performance piece without the sounds the Pocha Nostra employ.

I begin with this scene precisely because it illustrates what has most interested me about the performance work of Guillermo Goméz-Peña and his co-conspirators in the past: their use of music and sound collage to perform the U.S.–Mexico border as an aural territory. They contribute to the much larger audio-geographical configuration I have outlined elsewhere as 'the aural border,'[2] the history of the U.S.–Mexico border as revealed and theorized as a field of sound, a terrain of musicality and music-making, of static and noise, of melodic convergence and dissonant clashing. By calling attention to the aural border, I don't necessarily mean assembling a laundry list of every song ever written about the border or of every band or musician ever from the border (though this project has its own merits). I mean opening the doors to a new archive of historicity and analysis, a new methodology of understanding the audio-formation of national and social identities within specific, delineated geopolitical territories.

Indeed, the sonic and musical performances within *BORDERscape 2000* urge us to consider the extent to which specular narratives of the visual border have dominated scholarship in the humanities. There is little critical language readily available to theorize the relationship between the U.S.–Mexico border and the sounds it makes. The vast majority of writing about border representations and border performance has occurred through the lens of visual culture. In both the public and scholarly imagination, the U.S.–Mexico border is mostly synonymous with visual icons and objects central to a battlefield of images: fences, rivers, walls, checkpoints, the tall and threatening border patrol agent, the crouching *indocumentados* hiding behind a bush, the Taco bell chihuahua, the dusty, erotic cantina. In a sense, the direction of discourse about the border has historically been based on who controls how it is seen and envisioned.[3]

On the other hand, Gomez-Peña's performance pieces – which during the past decade and a half have dealt with the flow of identity, culture, and desire across and within the North-meets-South spaces of the U.S.–Mexico borderlands – consistently return to the importance of sound and music (traditional, folkloric, classical, popular, and otherwise) in the performance of border cultures and identities.[4] And yet, his employment of live and pre-recorded sounds and songs remains the most under-theorized aspect of his work, with most critical accounts focussing on its visual, theatrical, textual, and ideological components as they relate to his playful, dramatic experiments with trans-border issues of postnationalism, colonialism, globalization, and inter-racial desire.[5] Along with his own catalog of characters and personae – El Gran Vato, El Mexterminator, the Border Brujo, among others – Gomez-Peña has repeatedly demonstrated an understanding of music's role as a key character in the drama of contemporary global culture generally and, more specifically, its profound importance to the re-imagining and re-mapping of inter-American cartographies and citizenships. He so frequently employs 'soundbeds' and soundtracks featuring bands and musicians from across the Americas precisely because music so readily connects different cultural, social, and national geographies, as well as the communities that inhabit these different locations. Music opens up new lines of political and aesthetic communication between Chicanos/as and Mexicanos/as across the spaces of the borderlands.

By inhabiting *BORDERscape 2000*'s borderlands intersection of performance art and popular music and asking what it can teach us, I hope to trouble the line between performance and sound, to ask what role recorded sound plays in the dramatic and theatrical performance of place. What are the limits and possibilities of popular music as performance? How does music, sound, and/or noise inform and shape the way performance pieces structure their meanings about territories of spatiality? In order to better pose and answer these questions in the context of *BORDERscape 2000*, I have chosen to hear the aural border working as both a 'music-culture' and a formation of 'musicking,' two different models of musical analysis that both emphasize the extra-musical – the extent to which music is never just music, to which it absorbs, influences, and is informed by other forces of creative production and identity-making.

By claiming that as a performance artist and essayist Gomez-Peña is contributing to the border's 'music-culture,' I am borrowing from Mark Slobin and Jeff Todd Titon's very helpful paradigm in which they divide music's cultural influence into four principal areas: affect, performance, community, and memory/history. When he uses music in his pieces, Gomez-Peña is not simply using it on the aesthetic merits of its sound alone. As I will demonstrate, he deploys music for the histories it embodies, the memories it encodes and displays, the emotions and attachments it reflects, and the cultural meanings and relationships it performs to the ear of the listener.[6]

Slobin and Titon's music-culture approach has much in common with what Christopher Small has called 'musicking': his attempt to expand the very notion of a musical performance itself to include a variety of different cultural activities. For Small, the meaning of music lies not simply in musical works as such but in the 'the totality of a musical performance between the people who are taking part in whatever capacity in the performance,' whether it be through performing, listening, rehearsing, recording, or dancing. 'Musicking' is not so much about music as sound, but music as social relationship. Gomez-Peña takes part in the musical performances of the border first by listening and then by mirroring the meanings and ideas of the music in his own work.[7]

SUN VIRGINS AND LONELY BULLS

I want now to return in more detail to the sound specifics of Gomez-Peña and Sifuentes's *BORDERscape 2000*, what I believe to be the most sonically realized Pocha Nostra production to date. Playing throughout it is a dizzying sound collage by San Francisco sound designer and Pocha Nostra member Rona Michele, whose cut-and-paste sonic compositions and patchwork musical assemblages not only supplement and augment the action onstage but by the performance's end, become their own self-referential audio performance. They offer their own aural rendering of a futuristic U.S.–Mexico borderscape.[8]

By casting the border as a '-scape,' Gomez-Peña and Sifuentes are wittingly entering the border into the critical discourse of global capitalism, specifically anthropologist Arjun Appadurai's oft-cited model of disjuncture and difference. Briefly, Appadurai argues that the global cultural economy no longer rests on older center–periphery models of fixed nationalism, and is now more disorganized and characterized by a series of disjunctures and flows. With this 'nationalist genie' increasingly being released from its territorial bottle, Appadurai proposes instead that we reconfigure our view of contemporary global culture according to a system of interlocking '-scapes' that track the move from geographically bounded nation-states to denationalized circuits or landscapes of cultural production and consumption: financescapes, mediascapes, ethnoscapes, technoscapes, and ideoscapes.[9]

But because so much of *BORDERscape 2000* depends upon its sound collage, because so much of it is about the interaction of live performing bodies in a virtual borderspace saturated with the crossing of sounds, what I am asking here is that we also seriously consider the role of audioscapes – musically determined and financially enabled landscapes populated by indeterminate cultural forms, mobile communities, and shifting identities. Audioscapes direct our ears to the migratory flow of sound and sound-objects (records, CDs, mix tapes, DATs, bootlegs) across disparate geopolitical and pop cultural spaces, the extent to which music and sound can serve as vectors of connection and affiliation between distanced and displaced communities.

In *BORDERscape 2000*, Michele creates a collage that perfectly performs a very particular inter-American audioscape, one that plays out a musical version of Goméz-Peña's continental border zone while making audible two of *BORDERscape 2000*'s central points. First, the extent to which Latino/a identities have historically been commercialized and repackaged on both sides of the border as fetishes of touristic desire (something that in light of the recent Ricky Martin craze we ought to know has never gone away). And second, the border is mobile and fluctuating, no longer bound to one specific geographic configuration; it belongs to a continental map of communities in motion and cultures in contact. As such, over the course of the performance, the sound collage covers 'Japanese tea house lounge,' techno, Ray Charles singing 'America the Beautiful,' Native American powwow music, The Champs twanging and shouting 'Tequila,' Chilean rock band Los Electrodomesticos, 1970s' 'Jungle Fever' funksters Chakachas (a 'Latin disco' band from French Guyana but based in Belgium), and repeat performances from Ry Cooder.

Michele's tape collages figure centrally in one of *BORDERscape 2000*'s principal sketches, 'A Lecture on Reverse Anthropology: The Past,' which features Sifuentes in a lab coat, wielding a bull whip as a 'French intellectual' lecturing on his recent field study in Cancún. When he introduces the *'in situ* tribal recordings' he recorded while in Mexico, instead of hearing folkloric music coded with indigenous authenticity, the music Michele has him play is from Yma Sumac, 'the legendary sun virgin' of Peru, who came to prominence in the 1950s as the multi-octave queen of easy listening exotica and who is now being revived by a new generation of corporate hipsters.

The music the mock anthropologist wants is representative indigenous music from Mexico; what he gets is the spectacular, other-worldly voice of a woman who claimed to be an Incan goddess descended from Atahualpa, who was once actually believed to be Amy Camus from Brooklyn, and who was nonetheless fetishized for her marketed authenticity within a culture of post-war ethno-fantasy by both Hollywood and the recording industry. Equally destabilizing is that the songs of Sumac, so celebrated for their representative Latin Americanness, were mostly sonic constructions of enticing Latin make-believe engineered by tiki-torch composers like Les Baxter. 'Nothing musical can be traced to South America,' British music critic David Toop has written of

Sumac, 'despite the vivid sleeve-note descriptions of Incan hymns, Andean mountain grandeur, Peruvian monkey calls, and Aztec princes.'[10]

BORDERscape 2000's erotic and often violent orgy of crossed cultural meanings and migratory identities that encompasses Mexicanos/as, Chicanos/as, and African Americans[11] is further echoed when Michele unleashes La Lupita, a Mexico City rock band, re-frying 'Camelia La Tejana,' a song originally recorded as a border corrido ('Camelia La Texana'), then popularized by Los Tigres del Norte in the 1970s and turned into a feature film, *Contrabando y Traición*. It's a sediment-rich cover version that gives us an experimental urban Mexican band using the imported Northern rock idiom to pay tribute to a *norteño* supergroup that immigrated from Sinaloa to San José and that was the first undocumented band to win a Grammy.[12]

Two sketches later, Sifuentes is in character as CyberVato, and while a video of Chicano civil rights activists screens overhead, he delivers a sermon on the future fate of Chicano Nirvana – a fantasyspace of political freedom produced by the end of the 'Second U.S.–Mexico War' which has rendered 'the ex-U.S. of A.' as a *'metaficción nostalgica'* splintered into various 'micro-republics' of dissent. The soundtrack to CyberVato's report is the Chicano hip hop group Delinquent Habits performing 'Tres Delinquentes,'[13] which Goméz-Peña describes in the text's notes as 'mariachi rap.' But, in fact, the 'mariachi' in question is not mariachi at all. The horns and guitars that begin over the song's breakbeats belong not to a mariachi ensemble from Veracruz, but to notorious border kitschmeisters Herb Alpert and the Tijuana Brass and their song 'The Lonely Bull.'

The song was the title track to Alpert and the Tijuana Brass's debut recording which, according to the album's liner notes, was meant to capture the sound of a mythologized Tijuana, 'the noisy Mexican-American voices in the narrow streets, the confusion of color and motion.'[14] The notes confuse Tijuana – 'a spectacle, a garish border town' – as a site of Mexican-Americanness (perhaps a valid point in another context, but surely not one that Alpert and company had planned on making) and then reveal that the inspiration for the Tijuana Brass' formation was a Tijuana bullring.

Thus, we're left with a theme song for Chicano Nirvana ('Tres Delinquentes') performed by a Chicano hip hop group, Delinquent Habits, performing in African American styles. But instead of sampling funk and rhythm and blues, and instead of sampling norteño and ranchera, they sample Herb Alpert and 'The Lonely Bull' and thereby invert the meanings of a post-Latin craze 'south-of-the-border' ode to a tourist wonderland of fetishized, romantic escape and excess.

In the end, *BORDERscape 2000*'s music almost makes the project's central points with more clarity and resolve than the spoken and visual texts themselves. Contrary to the script's stage notes, the sound of the performance is not merely functioning as an accompanying 'track' or 'bed.' It functions as its own performance, its own commentary on the contradictions, clashes, and circuits of exchange that characterize the aural life of the U.S.–Mexico border. This 'aural border' finds new shape, new contour, and new maps within the performance spaces of *BORDERscape 2000*. By critically listening to these proliferating music-cultures of the U.S.–Mexico border, the Pocha Nostra do not simply bring the border and all of its multiple meanings to the stage. They force us to follow it from Cancun Sun Virgins and the rhythmic Hotel California beatings of the LAPD and the INS to the sampled and re-fried kitsch of a hip hop Tijuana bullring. That is, they force us to follow it to spaces of theater and performance that have to be heard to be believed.

ACKNOWLEDGMENTS

Special thanks to Roberta Uno and Lucy Burns of New WORLD Theater for originally giving me the opportunity to think aloud about this topic; to David Román, Lisa Wolford, José Muñoz, José David Saldívar, and Ondine Chavoya for their comments, suggestions, and support; to Tanya Gonzalez of UCR for her swift research assistance; and finally, to Guillermo Goméz-Peña and Roberto Sifuentes for generously providing the script to *BORDERscape 2000*.

NOTES

1. Mike Davis, *City of Quartz: Excavating the Future in Los Angeles* (London: Verso, 1990).
2. For a more expansive discussion of my project, see Josh Kun, 'The Aural Border,' *Theatre Journal* 52:1, Spring 2000.
3. For a detailed analysis of border visuality from photography and cinema to postcards, visual art, and billboards, see Claire F. Fox's excellent *The Fence and the River: Culture and Politics at the US–Mexico Border* (Minneapolis: University of Minnesota Press, 1999).
4. For a more general discussion of Gómez-Peña's work and its relationship to music, see Kun, 'The Aural Border,' and for its relationship to global popular culture and multiculturalism, see Josh Kun, 'Multiculturalism without People of Color: An Interview with Guillermo Goméz-Peña,' *Aztlán: A Journal of Chicano Studies*, 24: 1, Spring 1999.
5. For example, Jill S. Kuhnheim has recently argued for a text-based analysis of Goméz-Peña's performances. She asks, 'How does it function as literature, an aesthetic experience defined by reading words and images on the page?' See Jill S. Kuhnheim, 'The Economy of Performance: Goméz-Peña's New World Border,'

Modern Fiction Studies, 44 (1), Spring 1998. On the 'place' of the border in Goméz-Peña's work, see Claire Fox's invaluable critique 'The Portable Border: Site-Specificity, Art, and the US–Mexico Border,' *Social Text*, 41: 61–82 (Winter 1994). On Goméz-Peña's video performance of Tijuana read in the larger context of a re-configured inter-American cultural studies project, see José David Saldívar, *Border Matters: Remapping American Cultural Studies* (Berkeley: University of California Press, 1997), 151–8. And while Lisa Wolford's recent detailed essay on the Pocha Nostra's rave-inspired Mexterminator Project focusses on diorama identity performances, she also goes out of her way to point out the 'driving soundtrack that mixes southwestern music and exoticizing pop tunes with spoken text and Mexican rock' (see Lisa Wolford, 'The Politics of Identity in the United States of Aztlán: Pocha Nostra's Mexterminator Project,' *Theatre Forum*, 15:60, Summer/Fall 1999.

6. Jeff Todd Titon and Mark Slobin, 'Music-Cultures as a World of Music,' in Linda Fujie Titon and David Locke (eds), *Worlds of Music: An Introduction to the Music of the World's Peoples* (New York: Macmillan, 1996).

7. Christopher Small, *Musicking: The Meanings of Performing and Listening* (Hanover: Wesleyan University Press, 1998, 13).

8. Michele also created the soundbeds and soundtracks for the *Mexterminator* Project. In her essay on the performance, Lisa Wolford rightfully describes Michele's work as 'a vital component of the diorama performance' (Wolford: 60).

9. Arjun Appadurai, 'Disjuncture and Difference in the Global Cultural Economy,' in Bruce Robbins (ed.), *The Phantom Public Sphere* (Minneapolis: University of Minnesota Press, 1993). For different uses of Appadurai's model in terms of popular music, see Tim Taylor, *Global Pop: World Music, World Markets* (New York: Routledge, 1997) and Mark Slobin, *Subcultural Sounds: Micromusics of the West* (Hanover: Wesleyan University Press, 1993).

10. David Toop, *Exotica: Fabricated Soundscapes in a Real World* (London: Serpent's Tail, 1999, 72).

11. *BORDERscape 2000*'s inclusion of Black–White racial economies in its portrayal of U.S.–Mexico border futurism is best exemplified by the 'Tea Ceremony' sketch that features Pocha Nostra member Sara Shelton-Mann as a racist White Southern woman grappling with her desire for racialized Brown and Black otherness.

12. For more on the song's trajectory, see Maria Herrera-Sobek, 'The Corrido as Hypertext: Undocumented Mexican Immigrant Films and the Mexican/Chicano Ballad,' in David R. Maciel and Herrera-Sobek (eds), *Culture across Borders: Mexican Immigration and Popular Culture* (Tucson: University of Arizona Press, 1998).

13. Delinquent Habits, 'Tres Delinquentes,' *Delinquent Habits* (BMG, 1996).

14. Herb Alpert and the Tijuana Brass, *The Lonely Bull* (A&M 101S, 1962). On the album's cover, Alpert sits in a rocking chair, shot glass in hand, with his trumpet, a bottle of tequila, a wine flask, salt, lime, and a paring knife at his loafer-clad feet.

Elijah

Sekou Sundiata

Elijah was originally commissioned by New WORLD Theater and the New England Foundation for the Arts. It was developed in the summer of 1996 as part of the 'New Works for a New World' play development lab at the University of Massachusetts, Amherst, in collaboration with the Department of Theater at University of Massachusetts, Amherst. The musical composer was Craig Harris, the director was Talvin Wilks, the musical director was Richard Harper, and the performers were Carla Cook, Helga Davis, Keith D. Hart, Khalil Reed, and Christina Wheeler. It was subsequently developed and produced at Aaron Davis Hall, New York City and Rites & Reason Theater, Providence, Rhode Island.

Elijah written by Sekou Sundiata

In photo: Cast (left–right): Richard Harper, Keith D. Hart, Carla Cook, Helga Davis, Khalil Reed, and Christina Wheeler

Photo by Ed Cohen

25

Elijah's journey: introduction to *Elijah*

Talvin Wilks

My collaboration with Sekou Sundiata and Craig Harris began with a concert event at the American Center in Paris. Craig and Sekou were curating a series of American music events for the inaugural season and wanted to begin with a presentation of their collaborative work. I first met the artists while directing the première of Sekou's musical, *The Mystery of Love*, at the American Music Theatre Festival in Philadelphia, Pennsylvania.

The Mystery of Love was a five-year labor of love that Sekou had created with composer Douglas Booth. Along with choreographer, Marlies Yearby, we began to explore an interesting approach to music theater; the work was not quite a musical in the 'traditional book' sense, more of a conglomeration of spoken word, musical, opera, concert, and oratorio all rolled up in one. This was the beginning of an interesting exploration of how the unique words of Sekou's poetry could live in the theater. As Sekou and Craig approached the Paris concert (Craig had been a featured performer in *The Mystery of Love*), they decided to bring these forces together once again. Marlies was the featured dancer, Sekou was the poet performer, and Craig and his band, Tailgater's Tales, provided the music. My job then, as it has continued to be, was to find a way that all of this creativity could work together on stage. This often meant fighting off the traditional musical theater seekers to allow a new form to take shape. That form is still evolving.

Elijah is a wonderful continuation of that exploration, the marriage of music and text in the theater. The story is an exploration of the intercontinental slave trade in Africa, loosely based on the classic slave narrative, *The Life and Times of Olaudah Equiano*. Starting with the moment of capture as a child, his separation from his sister, and eventually arriving at the shore of the Atlantic and seeing a ship for the first time, the journey explores the influence of Arab vs. European domination, the impact of Christianity and Islam on traditional 'pagan' rituals. The journey is narrated by a solo voice, an icon who is timeless,

a witness as well as participant. This voice speaks the history of Africa to
African American heritage, and gives us a contemporary perspective on
ancestral traditions.

We are still searching for the right language. As we approached the first
staging of *Elijah* at the 'New Works for a New World' festival at the New
WORLD Theater, the language that we used was opera. This was the best
language to keep the musical theatre wolves at bay. But even that was not
going to be the right form for the unique collaboration between Sekou and
Craig. The two artists have a very long history of combining poetry and music
into a theatrical form; of particular note is their *tour de force, The Circle Unbroken
Is a Hard Bop.*

The first incarnation of *Elijah* had no main storyteller, the task was shared
by five singers and the musical director. In order to connect the in-and-out
movement of the 'I,' the first-person perspective of 'Elijah,' we used a totem
constructed from raw materials, wood, metal, cloth, to symbolize the character;
the person who possessed the totem, possessed the spirit of 'Elijah.' This was
just a handy conceit to facilitate the first workshop production, but it
represents one of the core challenges of the piece – who is 'Elijah' and how is
he represented on stage?

Following the very wonderful workshop presentation at the festival, Craig
and Sekou embarked on the most challenging phase of the work. From the very
beginning they had envisioned a collaboration with a traditional African
percussionist, someone who would bring an authentic African history and
knowledge to the work. After a trip to Senegal, they selected the master
drummer, Doudou N'Diaye Rose, an internationally renowned drummer and a
national treasure of Senegal. The goal, as explained to me, was for Doudou to
establish the percussive rhythms that would serve as the basic structure for the
music as well as the text, the rhythmic heart and soul of the work. The artists
had hoped to spend a month in Senegal and then to have Doudou in residence
in the United States to finish the work. This, however, did not occur as
planned. As it turned out, during a very short residency in the States, Doudou
was able to establish a series of drumming rhythms that represented a number
of cultural events that were used as punctuation throughout *Elijah*: rhythms of
war, rhythms of the market-place, rhythms of religious practice. As we
prepared for the second workshop presentation produced by Rites and Reasons
at Brown University in Providence, Rhode Island, we were joined by two of
Doudou's 36 children, all of whom are trained percussionists. The two sons,
Mar Gueye and Cheikh Mbaye, remained with the company for all subsequent
performances.

At this point in the development of the work, an entire new script had been
written by Sekou, one that attempted to flesh out the missing components

from the previous workshop and to identify the central 'I' character, the main storyteller. This non-singing character, the narrator/griot, became the sole speaker, more spiritual observer than participant, more wayward traveler, re-telling a tale of adventure. An interesting concept behind this character was that he was a time traveler, a man of no time, someone with a perspective on past, present and future. The griot is connected to 'Elijah' as well as separate, the living incarnation as well as shaman channeller, flesh and blood as well as cosmic icon, at once tangible and intangible. This device provided the greatest freedom in telling the story but also created a challenge for the performer: how does a griot remain connected to his story when most of that story is sung by someone else? The difficulties of moving in and out of the story also created a sense of disconnection.

In order to facilitate the performance we created a series of rituals that would enable the narrator/griot to somehow participate in the story while it was being sung by another voice. His environment was a circular mound of sand that housed many buried icons. To connect to the story and separation of his sister and family, the narrator unearthed images, fading photos of ancestors lost; to connect with the ensuing war, the narrator burned incense and made offerings and sacrifices to the gods; to explore the loss of ancestry, he discovered artifacts, remnants of a buried civilization; and to achieve the final image of bondage, he unearthed shackles and became the enslaved. This series of rituals, like the totem of the previous workshop, was merely a place-holder, a conceit used to support this particular phase of development but will not remain as a permanent structure of the work.

As the text of the piece evolved, the structure of the music shifted as well. Craig has used many different styles of Black music to reflect the diasporic languages that collided and evolved over time: in the belly of the slave ship he uses a blues riff to establish a distinction between Muslim and pagan; jazz vocalese becomes the guttural language of the many tribes in an attempt to communicate; rhythm and blues becomes the soulful lament of the sea. Throughout, the traditional drumming rhythms created by Doudou N'Diaye Rose drive the journey. The religious convergences that have a great impact on the narrative are also being explored in the music. In the earliest incarnation of the piece, the Christian, Islamic, and traditional rituals merged and reflected the creation of new musical forms, from gospel and the blues to rock and roll, and so on.

Currently the piece is performed in many different incarnations. The fascinating aspect of watching Sekou and Craig as they develop their work is that they continue to explore the dynamics on the bandstand through live music. Listen to Sekou Sundiata's CD, *The Blue Oneness of Dreams*, and you will hear new versions of *The Mystery of Love*, still evolving, richer and more vast in evocation. In the same vein, I recently heard Craig Harris and his band perform the music of *Elijah* as a multi-syllabic oratorio (*sans* text), more reminiscent of the original improvisations of the first concert performance, this form helping him to explore textures of the music as the core storyteller. As the section entitled 'Myth 14 (The Trek)' evolved through the improvised jazz riffs, with Craig on trombone serving as soloist and master conductor, one could imagine the slave caravans, the audience traveling through the creation of a people, cultures clashing and new ones forming as rhythms fused. Once again I bore witness to the lesson learned from the very first work, *The Mystery of Love*: 'Anything can happen on the bandstand!' This one essential component continues to be undervalued, the importance of live music, the originality and innovation of live concert performance and improvisation. This is what both Craig and Sekou are fighting to bring to the musical form, not an orchestra in a pit, but live performance front and center as the driving force of the piece with the conductor as shaman. However the final melding of text and music occurs, this component must exist as well; it is the surviving ritualistic form that lifts us up, transcendent.

26

Elijah

Sekou Sundiata

AND BID HIM SING

SPEAKER: I run
and somewhere in the world
a sink overflows.
When I dance and sing,
somewhere in the world
a runner slows in his tracks.
I am the prize that floats and stings
while somewhere in the world
little boys stand in awe,
the television bounces off the satellite
and sings into their ears:
This could be you, this could be you,
you could be like him.

Suppose I told you this was a cosmic trick,
that I was sent to tell you this,
now that the world can't seem to resist
the body black.
You can't be like me, be like me
the world can't be like me.
Suppose I stepped out of the shadow
and filled in the blackness
that once was erased by the perfect mix
of Commerce and Cool?
I am crossed over and consumed
a product, they say, 'a true god of our times.'

Suppose I was too blue to be used?
Suppose I was a talkback icon,
a lonely star, one angry nigger?
'A true god of our times'?
If only they knew.

SINGERS: I,
in the name of the First Person.
I,
in the name of the First Person Plural.
I,
a myth to live by.
I,
Of the World and in the World.
I,
Spirit of the Dangerous Skin.
I,
tell you now
the source of the spell the world is under
seeing, but not seeing the body black,
hearing, but not hearing the body black,
nobody knows the body black.

SPEAKER: The day I was born was not a day at all.
Nor was it night. It was a moment in history,
A contradiction, a mystery.
What, after all, did I do
to be so black and blue?
to be caught
in 'the meanest couplet in the English language,'
(Quote unquote Amiri Baraka)
Being born of the despised flesh,
of vomit and sharks
and babies with umbilical chords
around their necks,
of the earthless rhythm of the water
pitching to and fro,
being witness to the birth
of rock 'n' roll.
Sometimes man, sometimes woman,
all the time always black.

SPEAKER/SINGERS: Call me Field Holler.
Call me Shine, Stagolee.
The Woman With the Red Dress On.
Night Train With a Freightload of Dreams
Whistling a Single Note of Hope Moving Through
A Strange Land
Call me Trouble in Mind, a Love Supreme.
Voodoo Child.
Call Me Shapeshifter, Weight-of-the-World Lifter.

SPEAKER: In a light,
in the dark
in a choreography
of dream, desire
and music.

SPEAKER: We could all tell this story.
We could all say I and mean We, Us.
I was born one
of many gods.
This is my birth certificate.
This is the stone that marks
my birthplace.

SINGERS: The heaven we had
we knew
The hell we had
we knew
The life we lived
we grew
out of work and love,
and the wars of our ancestors
in the blood of our being
we fought for greed and honor
and the whims of our kings and queens.
In our imperfections
I was perfectly formed,
formed but not yet born.

WAR AND RUMORS OF WAR

SINGERS: Our city, like every city,
was a city of hope.
There was buying and selling in the marketplace.

SINGER: Dancing at weddings
Offerings for newborns
Praying at funerals
Husbands cheating on wives
Wives cheating on husbands.

SINGERS: Our city, like every city,
was a city of hope.
There was buying and selling in the marketplace.

SINGER: There was weaving and sewing
planting and growing.
Rainy seasons, high holy days
scandals and corruption.

SINGERS: Our city, like every city,
was a city of hope.
There was buying and selling in the marketplace.

SINGER: Building compounds
Making roads
Reading stars and stones
Trading with caravans
Wrestling and running and gambling
and watching the King ride by.

SINGERS: Our city, like every city,
was a city of hope.
There was buying and selling in the marketplace.
War and rumors of War.

SPEAKER: What news from the North?
Fighting and captivity.
What news from the West?

Fighting and dying.
Shortly after we start to get the news,
we knew we would be in it soon.
We heard stories:

severed heads, eyes gouged out,
gunshot wounds, mutilations and rape.

We heard stories from the camp of the Europeans.
How some of them did not worship or supplicate.
How some of them were Christians
and believed in the Word and the Cross.
We heard stories about some of our people
who were not captives, who were free
to come and go among the enemy
bringing this or that,
performing a service, selling information.

There was the story of a griot
who made his money singing the praises
of the rich and powerful.
One day, while in the European's camp,
he saw the Commander walking with his lieutenants.
So he sang his praises, as this was his hustle.

SINGER: O Great Master of War!
Who conquers without fear
Whose heart beats like a lion
Who overcomes every obstacle
and triumphs over adversity
O Great Master of War!

SPEAKER: The Commander paid him, but played him
cheap.

SINGER: O Great Master of War!
Who hides while his men fight
Whose hair is too weak to stand up straight
Who smells like animals when it rains
O Great Master of War!

SPEAKER: The Commander drew his weapon,
ignoring the quality of mercy
and the Christian virtue of charity
that his own book demanded of him.

SINGERS: O Great Master of War!
Do as you must do,
but if you take his life

you lose, you lose.
It is such a small price to pay
to have the Conqueror praised
in the ears of the Conquered.
To sing your praise
in the ears of the Conquered.

SPEAKER: He never did pay the man his right money,
but he spared his life,
unable to read the mask we wear
'that grins and lies,
It hides our cheeks and shades our eyes.'
(Quote unquote Paul Laurence Dunbar)
There was no room for flattery with the jihad.
It demanded the surrender of the city,
and the submission of our souls

SINGER: There is no god but God!

(A SINGER, in the role of a captured African, confesses.)

SINGER: There is no god but God!

SPEAKER: Some of us truly heard the call of God
like a deep kept secret finally revealed.

SINGER: There is no god but God!

SINGER: There is no god but God!

SPEAKER: Some knelt in submission
as a matter of form
to save their asses.

SINGER: There is no god but God!

SINGER: There is no God but God!

(The 'Muslim' confronts another African, but this African resists.)

SINGER: There is no god but God!

SINGER: *(Singing in his native tongue)* Trouble in mind, and I'm blue,
but I won't be blue always.
The sun's going to shine
in my back door some day.

SINGER: There is no god but God!

SINGER: Silence.

SINGER: There is no god but God!

SINGER: The sun's going to shine
in my back door some day.

SPEAKER: Confess the faith or lose you head
in the time it takes for Death
to make up its mind.

SINGER: There is no god but God!

SINGER: There is no god but God!

SPEAKER: Before I'll be a slave
I'll be dead and buried in my grave.
They burn villages, kill the men
take the women as their own.
We must make sacrifices.
Call on our ancestors.
We are the sacrifices.
Maybe there is only one true God.

SINGERS: The Star and the Crescent at our backs,
the Word and the Cross facing us,
both of them naming and blaming us,
and the whole time We selling Us.

(The SPEAKER is placing totemic items in a fire he has built.)

SPEAKER: Death to the killers! Death to the slavecatchers!

(An anonymous voice in the distance)

Death to the killers! Death to the slavecatchers!

(A whisper passing like brush fire in the crowds)

In the fires of the conquerer,
in the hearts of the resisters,
in the capitulation of the conquered,
in the love of the patriot,
in the War of Obliteration
is where I was conceived
in spirit, and later, in flesh.
What did I do to become

so black and blue?
It was a crime, it was a sin,
'Lord, when I think
how this whole thing begin.'
(Quote unquote Derek Walcott)
We could all tell this story.
We could all say I and mean We, Us.
Somebody help me!

(He gestures towards the SINGERS, and they pick up the story.
The SPEAKER brings up slide with title: 'Captured.')

CAPTURED

SINGER: My sister and I
were left to mind the house.

SINGER: Two men and a woman
climbed over the walls
and kidnapped us,
my brother and I.

SINGER: They tied our hands
They stopped our mouths.

SINGER: And took us into the woods,
into the night.

SINGER: My sister and I,
overpowered by fatigue and grief.
They tied us up.
They put me in a shack.

SINGER: My brother and I,
the following night,
we refused to eat.
He found rest in my arms.
I found rest in hers.

SINGER: Tear upon tear upon sorrow
was the only peace of mind
we could both find.

SINGER: I would have purchased his freedom with my own.

SINGER: I would have purchased her freedom with my own.

BOTH: If only I had my freedom to give.
I commit your care to our ancestors and our gods,
to protect you
from the violence of the African Trader,
from the stench of the slave ship,
from the strange seasons of the Europeans,
from the last and the lust
of the unrelenting overseer.

SINGER: My brother and I.

SINGER: My sister and I.

BOTH: The next day
we were torn apart
as we lay in each other's arms.

SINGER: My dear sister,
my dear brother.
My dear sister,
my dear brother.
How will I find you?
My dear sister,
my dear brother.
My dear sister,
my dear brother.
How will I find you?

SINGERS: Was black,
was black like me.
Kinship.
Was black,
was black like me.
Relationship.
Was black
was black like me.
Slave ship.

SPEAKER: Was black,
the two men was black, like me.

Was black,
the woman was black, like me.

All the Rosy Eyed Kings and Queens
Of Africa Calendars,
all the Kunte Kwanza Cloth
cut to the sound of a Million Men marching
200 hundred years later
couldn't change that.
Was black,
the kidnappers was black, like me.
Was black.

Still, there was a chip
at the center of things
A kinship, coming.
A relationship, coming.
A slave ship, waiting,
riding at anchor.
And still it rides
in the back of my mind
up and down
with the tides, the vicissitudes
of the deep.

THE JOURNEY TO THE COAST

SINGER: I had often changed masters

I was sold into the hands of a chief.
His people spoke the same language as my people.
I tried to escape
by taking a road I thought I knew,
but I did not know that road.

I returned to my master.

SINGER: I was sold again
and carried north.

Again, I was sold.
Traveling through Africa
I learned many languages
but in no language was there a word
for Africa.

I was sold again for some little white shells,
each one the size of a fingernail.
The language of my new masters
resembled my own.
We had the same customs.
After two months,
I committed the Sin of Contentment ...
I forgot I was a slave.

Then my contentment was reversed for good,
so that I would never forget again.

SINGER: I was put among some people
who did not circumcise,
who ate without washing their hands.
They cooked their food in iron pots.
They had European weapons,
and they fought with their fists among themselves.
Worst of all,
they made no sacrifices or offerings.

SINGER: We traveled on the river
through many countries and nations.
Before that, I had never seen any water
bigger than a pond.
Seven months after I was kidnapped,
we arrived at the coast,
facing the direction of nightfall.

THE SEA

SINGER: The first thing he saw
when he arrived on the coast
was the sea
and the slave ship
riding at anchor,
waiting for cargo.

SINGER: It floods your eyes
the rush of
the sea when you see it for
the first time.

As if the rivers of the world
all at once they
left their beds behind.

Your heart turns over,
rises and falls
with the waves.

It overcomes you,
it becomes you,
you surrender to the sea.

SINGER: It calls your name
again and
again then
you answer from within.
As if your body
all at once just
released your soul.

Your heart turns over,
rises and falls
with the waves.

It overcomes you,
it becomes you,
you surrender to the sea.

SINGER: The smell from the root of water
takes your breath away.
It overcomes you,
it becomes you.
You surrender to the sea,
to the wonder, the terror,
the majesty.

SINGERS: It floods your eyes
the rush of
the sea when you see it for
the first time.
As if the rivers of the world
all at once they
left their beds behind.

Your heart turns over,

rises and falls
with the waves.
It overcomes you,
it becomes you,
you surrender to the sea.

THE DESCENT

SPEAKER: If I had 10,000 worlds.

SINGER: If I had 10,000 worlds.

SPEAKER: I would give them up.

SPEAKER: I would give them up.

SPEAKER: To be a slave again.

SINGER: To be a slave again.

SPEAKER: In my own land.

SINGER: In my own land.

SPEAKER: I fell motionless on the deck
and fainted, so sick and low
that I wished for my last friend,
Death.

SPEAKER: I was put down under the decks.
It smelled like human beings
turned inside out.

SINGERS: I could not eat.
I could not taste.
I refused to eat.
They flogged me by the hour.

SPEAKER: Soon, I found some people from my own country.
I asked them what was going to happen to us.
They said we were to be carried away
to the white people's country
to work for them.

SINGERS: They looked like savages.
They acted like savages.

SPEAKER: I had never seen any people act this way.
Not only towards us, but towards
some of the whites themselves.

SINGERS: I could not eat.
I could not taste.
I refused to eat.
They flogged me by the hour.

SPEAKER: I saw them flog one white man so bad
that he died,
and they tossed him over the side.
I expected nothing less for myself.
I thought these people had no country,
that they lived in the hollow of the ship.

SINGERS: They catch the wind in a cloth,
and then the ship goes on.
They cast a magic spell
on the water to make it stop.
I was amazed by this.

SPEAKER: I expected to be sacrificed.
It was impossible to escape.

SPEAKER: I used to think
that this is when I was born,
that this is where the hyphen
first appeared, as the bridge
between the Africa we knew
and the Mississippis, the Harlems,
the Chicagos and the Detroits of tomorrow.
I have often call that ship
The Mighty Hyphen.

I used to think
that this is where I was born,
between the love-on-first-sight
of the sea
and the horror of captivity.
I wanted to kill the slavers
in their sleep.
No, I wanted them looking me in the eye
as I carved the hard, beating pulse of History

out of their chests.
Something stirred in me,
at first,
I thought it was anger,
But it was cooler than that,
more elegant even than revenge.
It was murder.
In spite of the many rebellions,
I never did get off;
I never did let the killer
completely out.
He's still right here with me.

SINGERS: Our mother tongue lost.
We all are one under the whip.
We all are one under the gun.
Bambara Fulani Djola
Tukulor Ashanti Ibo.

SPEAKER: I could see One Aim, One Destiny
laid out before us like a narrow,
unforgiving road.
If we did not have one mind
about who we were,
I thought there would be at least one mind
about what we wanted ...
to be free again.
That, I believed, was the bond between us
not the chains.
To be free: that was to be
the relationship, the kinship on that ship.

Why had our gods failed?
Why did our ancestors turn their backs to us?
What faith I had, I tried to maintain.
And then I was confronted by a fellow captive
who at another time and place
might wear a bowtie and sell newspapers
and be as resolute in his faith
and as mocking of mine
as this brutha was now in the bottom
of the Mighty Hyphen.

MALE SINGER 1:   Where is your fetish?
Where is your gris gris now?
What about your sacrifices?
Bring your ancestors down.
Bring them down, bring them down.

MALE SINGER 2:   You are here just like me.
You smell the urine and the blood too.
You hear the shrieks and the moans
of the dying,
just like me.

MALE SINGER 1:   This is a mistake.
I am not an infidel like you.
I am a Muslim, I should not have been sold.
My brother Muslims will save me.

MALE SINGER 2:   Your 'brother Muslims' brought me here.
How can they save you from this hell?

MALE SINGER 1:   God will conquer
like a blinding sun.
God opens that which is closed.
God sustains the truth with truth.
There is no God but God.

MALE SINGER 2:   Where is your God?

MALE SINGER 1:   Where is your fetish?

MALE SINGER 2:   Where is your conqueror?

MALE SINGER 1:   What happened to your offerings?

MALE SINGER 2:   Where is the Opening?

MALE SINGER 1:   What about your sacrifices?

MALE SINGER 2:   Where is your blinding sun?

MALE SINGER 1:   Bring your ancestors down.

MALE SINGER 2:   What truth can sustain this truth?

MALE SINGER 1:   There is no god but God.
God will conquer
like a blinding sun.
God opens that which is closed.

God sustains the truth with truth.
There is no god but God.

SPEAKER: Sometime later,
some of us would jump into the sea
and take our chances with the sharks.

We would cut the throats
of the nearest slaver caught off guard.

We would do what we were told.

Some time later,
we would land ashore
and walk back into the ocean
and let the water hold us,
fold us in its final embrace.

We would become Crips and Bloods.

We be calling our ownselves Nigga.

We be jumping off buildings
with our brains on fire.

Down will look like Up.

Some time later,
we would survive
to hear the music and poetry
of our lives
sung to us by us,
blue to us, so true to us
and blown through us.
But,
that would be
sometime later.

OUT TO SEA

SPEAKER: The early morning sun had burned
some of the dampness off the air
below deck.
Someone said the ship was about to go.
Prayers went up from every mouth,

to what ears I do not know.
I could even hear some of the enemy
praying to their Christian God.
What could be waiting for us, all of us?
I understood why we, in our captivity,
would pray.
But why would they pray?
They had the ship, the guns, the chains,
the whips.
What did they fear?
I learned later it was the sea.
The sea and us.

SINGER: Blessed are they that have not seen yet have believed.
Blessed are ye when men shall hate you,
and when they shall separate you from their company
and shall reproach you and cast out your name as evil,
for the son of man's sake.

Blessed are they that mourn, for they shall be comforted.

Blessed are the meek, for they shall inherit the earth.

Blessed are the merciful, for they shall obtain mercy.

Blessed are the pure in heart, for they shall see God.

SINGER: I could hear the blessings of the Christians on the deck above.
I could hear our bones moan,
the sigh and creak of the wood as the ship pulled out to sea.
I was intoxicated by what I heard.
It was too beautiful.
It was too painful to resist.
I let my gods go.
I let my offerings go.
I did not call my ancestors.
This was my unwilling sacrifice
to the No-God-but-God,
to the Word and the Cross,
to this new race,
to this History.

SPEAKER: I have despised this feeling
for as long as I could feel,

through the long years of the past
on through tomorrow.
And I never confess this before:

The hymns of the Christians
and the prayers of the Muslims
overpowered me,
as much as the relentless song of the sea.
But it wasn't the ideas in the songs,
because I could not understand a word.
And it was not the power of their gods.
It was the undeniable beauty of the music,
I could hear the magic of beauty
and the tragedy and human longing,
a magic strong enough to rule us
and control our minds
for hundreds of years.
My heart was swept into rapture
bone deep and wide as life,
binding as the shackles and chains
that held me captured.
I have carried this contradiction
in my secret soul,
Love and War inside me,
from this time to this
as we set out to sea.

I will tell you now
the source of the spell the world is under
seeing, but not seeing the body black,
hearing, but not hearing the body black.
Nobody knows the body black.

SINGERS: It floods your eyes
the rush of
the sea when you see it for
the first time.
As if the rivers of the world
all at once
they left their beds behind.

Your heart turns over
rises and falls with the waves.

It overcomes you,
it becomes you.
You surrender to the sea.

27

Conversations with history: Sekou Sundiata, Craig Harris, and *Elijah*

Joni L. Jones

Elijah is an oratorio-style jazz-inflected performance born of a three-year collaboration between poet/musician Sekou Sundiata and composer/musician Craig Harris. As this epic tale of the Middle Passage and beyond begins, the singers and musicians assume positions on stools, adjust music-laden stands, and sweep the audience through a horrific yet stunningly beautiful journey — the horror is in the painfully familiar separation of families, the almost paralyzing confusion at a new world, and the palpable foreboding that hovers around each verse; the beauty is in the pathos evoked and the musical mastery of Sundiata, Harris, and their company of extraordinary artists.

African American artists have a fondness for talking with history. Choreographer Ralph Lemon with *Geography*, film-maker Julie Dash with *Daughters of the Dust*, musician/composer Wynton Marsalis with *Blood on the Fields*, and choreographer David Rousseve with *Love Songs* — all have come to address issues of homeplace through the scepter wielded by a misnamed 'trans-Atlantic slave trade.' When an African American artist takes on history, it is an act that invariably collides with the deeply troubled present. Wynton Marsalis concludes his Pulitzer Prize-winning jazz composition *Blood on the Fields* with a hard-driving work-song whose plaintiff refrain is simply 'how long?' This occurs after the major characters have weathered the Middle Passage and are trying to make a way in the new foreign land of North America. The moan of 'how long?' troubles the distinction between past and present as the audience is encouraged to reflect on how long enslaved Africans had to endure bondage while simultaneously asking how long present-day African Americans must live with perpetual race-based atrocities. David Rousseve opens his mytho-poetic dance of slavery with the image of a contemporary African American woman who has been beaten by four African American youths while ante-bellum images are frozen behind her through a scrim. The juxtaposition of past and present realities forces a consideration of how a slave history has left psychic wounds on descendants of masters and descendants of slaves. The talk with history is then a way of clarifying and contextualizing the present.

Harris and Sundiata have a great deal to say about the past. Their *Elijah* opens with an invocation that reveals the inextricable bonds of past and present:

> To the one who is lost
> in the Wilderness
> of North America
>
> To the one who returns
> in dreams
> to scenes
> in the middle
> of the Atlantic,
> the vomit, the sharks, the babies
> with umbilical cords around their necks
>
> To the one who knows
> the earthless rhythm of the water
> pitching to and fro.
>
> To the one who witnessed
> the birth of rock 'n 'roll
>
> To the first African
> American
> riding the hyphen,
> choosing the blues
> to keep from losing. (Sundiata, 1996: 1)

The performance itself becomes an embodiment of the collision of past and present as ostensibly free African American artists give voice to the experiences of nineteenth-century enslaved Africans. *Elijah* also works time fluidly in the harkening forth of the slave narrative genre while refashioning that genre with contemporary sensibilities. This provocative tension between past and present is what artist/scholar Glenda Dicker/sun describes as 'an uneasy sea change as Black performance simultaneously outgrows and reclaims its Black roots' (1999: 147). Indeed, it is intriguing to view the production with an eye toward 'performance geneologies.' In his discussion of circum-atlantic performance, Joseph Roach postulates a theory of embodied memories in which dispersed Africans retain historical performances in their very muscles. He writes that such bodily historicized performances 'draw on the idea of expressive movements as mnemonic reserves, including patterned movements made and remembered by bodies, residual movements retained implicitly in images or words (or in the silences between them), and imaginary movements dreamed in minds, not prior to language but constitutive of it, a psychic rehearsal for physical actions drawn from a repertoire that culture provides' (1996: 26). As audiences experience *Elijah*, they are watching late-twentieth-century performers call forth culturally encoded experiences that join them to unknown and unencountered Africans around the diaspora. By talking with Africa and with ancestors, these historically situated works address what Sundiata calls 'the great silence in African American culture' (Sundiata and Harris, 1998).[1] The dialogue that Harris and Sundiata add to these artistic ruminations offers up a distinctive set of voices. They have plumbed the same mine as several artists before them, and have found their own brand of gold.

The gold is in the complexity of the story, the power of the poetry, the dense textures of the music, and the simplicity of the staging. In a production of *Elijah* presented at the 'New Works for a New World' festival 1996, director Talvin Wilks used movement sparingly as a tall embellished staff, only one of two props, was passed strategically among the performers. This left the attention on the words, music, and performances. Sundiata notes the power in the minimal staging when he explains 'Richie [performer and conductor in the work], Richie dances! That's why I think this piece doesn't need any dance! You know? … then everybody else starts … you know that whole thing about possession? After a while the spirit gets up in it. And to me, that's the movement! I don't think it needs to be codified and formalized' (Sundiata and Harris, 1998). Indeed, Richie's conducting suggested the vitality and shaman-like presence of a Black Baptist preacher. In the 1997 production of *Elijah* at Aaron Davis Hall, more elaborate staging was used which detracted from the work. The more complex movement drew attention to a director's presence and away from the music, the story, and the performances. The sparsity of the movement situated the work in the genre of nineteenth-century abolitionist readings, an apt location for this slave narrative. Paul Gilroy argues that when the visual supersedes the oral in musical expression, 'there is an unavoidable loss … because the collaborative input of [the artist's] circular audiences cannot be adequately communicated' (1995: 32). For Gilroy, the predominance of the visual undermines the improvisational performer–audience union. *Elijah's* staging creates an environment where the sense of collaboration is allowed to flourish.

Six performers brought the 1996 production to life. Their small number increased the sense of intimacy that added to the strength of this work. As they stood behind music stands facing directly toward the audience, their subtlest facial expressions and body tensions all became a part of the experience. They created the quality of both a trial and a church service in which the performers stand before a gathered public to testify — the double meaning of that word working quite well in this context. Slavery itself is on trial and the performers act as witnesses to slavery's horrors; the performers are also members of a congregation needing to testify about the tribulations they have borne.

African American existence has been intimately linked with geography. Even prior to the Mason–Dixon Line of 1804 which unofficially divided the free northern states from the slave southern ones, an African American's very identity was dependent upon where he or she was born or traded or could escape to. Such arbitrary determinants exposed the lie behind a practice said to enslave an inferior race of people. The choice of enslavement had nothing to do with an inherent inferiority but rather an imposed geographical reality. By 1810, an African in Virginia was a slave with no more rights than chattel while an African in Rhode Island was a slave with the ability to win a lottery and thereby buy his freedom; and an African in the Indiana Territory was free but could not travel to Delaware because Delaware would not admit any new 'Negroes,' free or slave, into the state. *Elijah* takes us to the ultimate geographic shift in the making of the African diaspora, the moment that simultaneously joins and divides Africans and African Americans. The work makes geography, site, location the necessary ingredient in the creation of an African American.

In this telling of slavery, after the invocation and a tortured 'hambone' performed by the company slapping their thighs and chests, and banging stools and music stands, a woman introduces us to the world of *Elijah*. Her story operates adjacent to the male's. She is not merely there to help Elijah discover his humanity — a strategy that Marsalis uses in his composition *Blood on the Fields*. In fact, Sundiata and Harris subvert the standards of the melodramatic theatrical world that would have dominated U.S. stages at the time in which their story is set by having the female and male in this tale be brother and sister separated as they attempt to flee the pursuing slave traders rather than the sentimental lovers common to the melodramatic tradition. This shift in expectations, this change on a well-worn structure, opens the door for a new telling, for a complicated journey.

The very name Elijah challenges our notions of a melodramatic hero. In First Kings of the Bible, Elijah is the incisive prophet who taught righteousness and destroyed those who worshipped Baal, a competing religious practice of the day. The Biblical Elijah was an unwavering Christian whose relationship to God was undisputed. Sundiata and Harris have created a Muslim Elijah who feels forsaken by Allah and who finally questions the religious principles that have sustained him prior to his capture. Elijah laments 'I let my fetish go/I let my gris gris go/I did not call my ancestors/This was my unwilling sacrifice/ To this no-god-but-God, to this Word and Cross, to this new race/To this History' (13). Rather than the confident Elijah of the Bible who makes decisions with the certainty of God's approval, this Elijah struggles under the weight of a spiritual crisis. This is not the standard melodramatic hero who may waver but never falls far from goodness; this hero must reconsider all that has been sacred to him and adapt it in order to forge a new race and history. The villain of *Elijah* is as complicated as its hero. Harris and Sundiata make the controversial choice of deeply implicating Africans in the perpetuation of the slave trade. They do not offer up a romanticized notion of slavery complete with White slave traders and owners as the sole antagonists. Their choices problematize notions of identification and allegiance in this work.

The Biblical Elijah is a favored prophet whose return signals the coming of the Messiah. Other prophets wonder why his coming will be first, and they receive no clear answer. To their questions, Jesus merely replies 'Elijah indeed is coming and will restore all things' (Matthew, 17:11). The Elijah that Sundiata and Harris create, then, is a necessary precusor to goodness. His presence is a sign of the restoration of order. By aligning their protagonist with this Biblical prophet, Sundiata and Harris have created a powerful symbol with their character. Like the curious prophets, we as audience are waiting to see what good will follow Elijah's arrival.

The title of this work suggests that the audience will be given a solo story, an autobiographical tale. While the story does follow the experiences of one individual, Fox-Genovese reminds us that with slave narratives in particular, and African American autobiography generally, the single voice speaks for many (1990: 177–99). Harris and Sundiata underscore this by dividing the narration among the many performers. The 'I' moves among all the performers encouraging us to see the ways in which this tale is not limited to a single individual. Doing so increases the sense of epic storytelling and cultural myth-making.

In her study of slave narratives Eleanor Traylor argues that slave narratives extend language into 'a lyric evocation – a poem' while maintaining elements of narrative structure (1987: 53). For Traylor, slave narratives comprised a new literary genre able to contain the breadth of the beastiality that characterized slavery. In an interview with Sundiata and Harris, Sundiata explains that the narrative of Olaudah Equiano[2] served as a prototype for 'Elijah.' Sundiata follows some of the key details of Equiano's story including his abduction into slavery, his horror aboard the slave vessel, and his revulsion at the habits of the Europeans. On occasion Sundiata lifts whole passages from Equiano's story and uses them as Elijah's own. By borrowing from a slave narrative, Sundiata and Harris seem to acknowledge, and respectfully bow to, the linguistic power Traylor finds in this genre.

In addition to complicating the hero and villains, the work offers multiple African experiences by making Elijah a Muslim who converses aboard the slave ship with an African of another faith. 'This is a mistake,' Elijah declares. 'I am not an infidel like you. I am a Muslim. I should not have been sold. My brother Muslims will save me.' His fellow captive replies 'Your brother Muslims brought me here. How can they save you from this death?' Later Elijah hears the singing of the Beatitudes (Matthew, 5:1–3) on deck which brings Islam, Christianity, and indigenous practice all into the same work. In the earliest years of the slave trade, before African and slave were conflated into a single construction, if enslaved Africans were converted to Christianity aboard the slave vessels, they could not be enslaved for life upon arrival on North American shores. Designation of slaves shifted from non-Christians to non-Whites in 1641, and slavery based on race was perpetuated through legislation in 1662 which identified any child born to an enslaved woman to also be enslaved. This marked the beginning of slavery by inheritance and concretized the union of African with slave. *Elijah* encourages us to examine the diverse religious experiences of the Africans brought to North America and to resist monolithic notions of who Africans were and are. Harris and Sundiata's work challenges the construction of African and African American as it postulates complex histories of the African transformation into African American.

It is interesting to consider the ways in which this work sits alongside the practice of theater for social change.[3] As with that movement, *Elijah* interrogates the status quo primarily in the way the work insists that we disrupt our ideas of slavery by offering a dense narrative of that experience. According to Kimberly Benston, such counter-hegemonic work also moves away from mimesis and toward methexis, or participation and agency. *Elijah* does not present a mimetic world – indeed, the production choices are Brechtian in their fusion of a nineteenth-century story with the obvious contemporariness of the performers. Yet, unlike Brecht, Sundiata and Harris seek to generate pathos in their work. Sundiata describes this emotional energy in the work when he says '[During slavery] people would read [slave narratives] like adventure thrillers ... these stories have all the elements of great fiction ... People say How did you choose that moment? How could you not choose it! You know?' (Sundiata and Harris, 1998). Some believe that pathos is the antithesis to action,[4] but *Elijah* combines deep emotional currents with an equally powerful 'aesthetic agency.' Angela Davis describes the 'aesthetic agency' of African American female blues singers who worked under severe social and economic constraints, yet infused their music with acts of resistance through lyrics and vocal stylings that challenged the dominant musical conventions (1999: 164). bell hooks declares 'All performance practice has, for African Americans, been central to the process of decolonisation in white supremacist capitalist patriarchy' (1995: 212). Similarly, Harris and Sundiata employ musical and poetic strategies that subvert aesthetic expectations, thereby giving oppositional power to their work.

This aesthetic power is potently demonstrated with a haunting melody that the multiple Elijahs sing while on board the slave ship:

> It floods your eyes,
> the rush of the sea
> When you see it
> for the first time
> as if the rivers of the world
> all at once they
> left their beds behind.
>
> Your heart turns over,
> rises and falls with the waves.
>
> Your heart turns over,
> rises and falls with the waves.
>
> It overcomes you,
> it becomes you
> You surrender to the sea. (Sundiata, 1996: 6)

In performance, the singers begin the phrase 'when you see it for the first,' then they pause, they linger – using what Gilbert Moses referred to as 'emotional space,' so that it feels as though they have completed the phrase. After the weighted hesitation, the singers then continue the line with 'time,' giving the entire phrase a sense of tension, surprise, and anticipation. According to Harry Elam, Jr., Moses used 'emotional space' to describe 'the distance between the notes of a song or two lines of dialogue or two bars of music' (1997: 79). Such manipulation of silences, Elam believes, was used during the Black Arts Movement to stimulate audience participation and a revolutionary predisposition. This musical strategy disrupts the expected phrasing which gives the music itself agency.

This song counters expectations in another important way. In addition to vocal stylings that are transgressive, the contrast between the slave ship experience and the beauty of the song is deeply disturbing. Harris has created music that lulls in imitation of the ocean's rhythms, and Sundiata has provided poetry that reveals Elijah's unfathomable fascination with his temporary watery home. As the song states, the listeners, along with *Elijah*, 'surrender to the sea.' What a fiendish trick these artists have played on their audience! They cajole us into loving the very symbol of African dislocation and psychic rupture. In responding so to the music and poetry, we come to understand Elijah when he startles us late in the song with:

> The smell from the root
> Of the water
> Takes your breath away
> It overcomes you
> It becomes you
> You surrender to the sea.
> To the wonder, the terror
> The majesty. (Sundiata, 1996: 7)

This modification of the refrain then winds right back into 'It floods your eyes ... ,' once again imitating the rolling cadence of the ocean. This is a haunting, tantalizing song whose structure insists that we envision the Middle Passage in a decidedly new way, that we not only see the much chronicled 'terror,' but the almost blasphemous 'wonder' and 'majesty' as well. Sundiata addresses this duality from a different perspective when he says 'I think that that is one of the defining moments in African American culture. You know? That adaptability! The willingness, and eagerness to change, and move on to what's next and grow. And not out of some noble idea all the time, but out of necessity' (Sundiata and Harris, 1998). In his union with the sea – the medium of his movement away from Africa – Elijah then makes the inevitable movement toward African America. In this single song, Elijah constructs 'The Negro.' As with their other artistic choices, here Harris and Sundiata again offer up a complex understanding of the reality of slavery. They are not interested in one-dimensional representations, but challenging and nuanced experiences. This construction of 'The Negro' is embodied in the pigmentation of the cast which runs the range of 'yellow' to 'honey' to 'chocolate.' The cast, then, becomes a multi-colored illustration of the consequence of the African's transcultural sojourn.

Sundiata and Harris are committed to improvisation as the hallmark of their work. For them, it becomes yet another way of generating audience engagement and maintaining the integrity of the work. In an interview with Harris and Sundiata, the artists discussed how improvisation functions as an act of resistance in their work:

SUNDIATA: Nobody told Helga [Davis, a performer in the production] when to cry ... And she might not cry next time! ... the idea is always how can we take this thing that wants to breathe, and wants to have some improvisational aspect, and have an intersection with this more formalized thing that we're calling theater? And in which both things are allowed to live? You know? You can improvise! ... We're not talking about no fake possession. That you can really get up in there one night, and that ensemble can notice stuff so well ...

HARRIS: I was serious about possession. Because that's what the people – it's a healing, that's what people need. People need to be healed now.

SUNDIATA: We've been calling this possession, and we've talked about improvisation, but that's the thing, if you're doing a work where the maximum value is placed on what is already set, but also on this whole thing about living in the moment, you know? And trusting that, so that it won't be the same every night. You see, the goal is always God. You know? So the goal is – you do the work, but the goal is that possession! Because that's why you're doing it.

HARRIS: Because theater, I mean, it's beyond theater; it's beyond music; it's beyond dance. It's about really going for – as we did – going for the godhead. (Sundiata and Harris, 1998)

In their work, improvisation becomes a vehicle for transcendence, for both the performers and the collaborating audience. Harris and Sundiata are not oblivious to the power of improvisation as 'anti-structure' used to subvert the social order. In his discussion of Teatro Campesino, Elam describes 'anti-structure' as the production features created as 'disruptions in the structural hierarchies maintained by the dominant culture outside of the theatre' (1997: 49). While *Elijah* seems a hybrid of aesthetic choices, the use of improvisation works as an anti-structural device that challenges fixity of performance and the passivity of audiences. In production, the improvisational quality is felt in the many contrapuntal moments as the performers weave their own time signatures and rhythms around each other's voices. This is especially strong in a song that is divided into three musical realities. Two singers offer a staccato tightly syncopated rendering of 'Our mother tongue lost/We all are one under the whip/We all are one under the gun/A whole new race is born,' while another singer staggers just seconds behind, and two other singers keep a bass line with the naming of the many African peoples who were displaced – 'Bambara Fulani Djola Tukalor Ashanti Ibo' (Sundiata 10). The audience can see the performers working it out before their eyes, finding the musical truths in each viscerally negotiated moment.

The conversation with history that *Elijah* evokes traverses time and space. Audiences confront their own constructions of the U.S. slave experience and are provided with a richly textured alternative to predictable representations. Sundiata addresses this quality in the work when he says 'I think both of us try to ground our work in what we take to be an African American culture in the States, you know? And use that as a connection to the rest of humanity. I mean, it's never just only African American culture' (Sundiata and Harris, 1998). *Elijah* is the dialogue with historical depictions that stretches our conceptions of identity, citizenship, and the power of art to help us envision the world anew.

NOTES

1. The quotations from Sekou Sundiata and Craig Harris are derived from an interview I conducted with them as part of the Intersection Conference sponsored by the New WORLD Theater of the University of Massachusetts, 11 October 1998.
2. Olaudah Equiano (1745–97) was an Igbo man abducted into slavery with his sister at the age of 11 from the region now known as Nigeria. He served aboard British warships and was an outspoken abolitionist in England. He saved his money and eventually bought his freedom. His *The Interesting Narrative of the Life of Olaudah Equiano, or Gustavus Vassa, The African* (1789) is a major work in the canon of slave narratives.
3. Theater for social change refers to a diverse group of theater practices with the overt intention of interrogating the status quo in order to initiate a change in political and social systems. Included in this term would be the theater of protest produced by Alfred Jarry, Antonin Artaud, and Eugene Ionesco, the Black Arts Movement with works produced by Amiri Baraka, Ed Bullins, and Sonia Sanchez, and a host of companies with specific efficacious aims such as El Teatro Campesino, Spiderwoman Theatre, Bread and Puppet Theatre, National Black Theatre, and San Francisco Mime Troupe.
4. Bertolt Brecht sought to focus an audience's attention on the ideas rather than the emotions in his works. Augusto Boal discusses how pathos clouds one's ability to take the riskiest actions required for social change. For both Brecht and Boal, too keen an attention on the emotions served to sedate audiences and distract them into complacency with no specific alternatives to political and social systems.

REFERENCES

Benston, Kimberly W., 'The Aesthetic of Modern Black Drama: From Mimesis to Methexis,' in Errol Hill (ed.), *The Drama of Black Americans* (New York: Applause Books, 1987).

Davis, Angela, *Blues Legacies and Black Feminism* (New York: Random House, 1999).

Dicker/sun, Glenda, 'Rode a Railroad that Had no Track,' in Annemarie Bean (ed.), *A Sourcebook of African-American Performances* (New York: Routledge, 1999).

Elam, Jr., Harry, *Taking It to the Streets* (Ann Arbor, MI: University of Michigan Press, 1997).

Fox-Genovese, Elizabeth, 'My Statue, My Self: Autobiographical Writings of Afro-American Women,' in Henry Louis Gates, Jr. (ed.), *Reading Black, Reading Feminist* (New York: Meridian Books, 1990).

Gilroy, Paul, '. . . to be real: The Dissident Forms of Black Expressive Culture,' in Catherine Ugwu (ed.), *The Politics of Black Performance* (Seattle, WA: Bay Press, 1995).

hooks, bell, 'Performance Practice as a Site of Opposition,' in Catherine Ugwu (ed.), *The Politics of Black Performance* (Seattle: Bay Press, 1995).

Roach, Joseph, *Cities of the Dead: Circum-Atlantic Performance* (New York: Columbia University Press, 1996).

Sundiata, Sekou, *The Return of Elijah, the African,* unpublished manuscript 1996.

Sundiata, Sekou and Harris, Craig, Unpublished interview with Joni Jones, Amherst, MA, 11 October 1998.

Traylor, Eleanor, 'Two Afro-American Contributions to Dramatic Form,' in Errol Hill (ed.), *The Theater of Black Americans* (New York: Applause Books, 1987).

28

Afterword on *Udu*, formerly *Elijah*

Sekou Sundiata

Editors' note: These notes emphasize the dynamic process of creating new work as Sundiata describes the evolution and epic journey of Elijah *into* Udu. *Joni Jones's essay and this afterword provide a unique opportunity for readers to experience the artist's process of refining, editing, amplifying, and rethinking.*

I have had a chance to read the essays written by Talvin Wilks and Joni Jones about this work. For me it was like reading the map of the many paths we have traveled to this point. The work is now called *Udu*, which is its permanent name. But there are more than differences in title. The first is in the story itself.

Talvin describes the story as 'an exploration of the intercontinental slave trade in Africa, loosely based on the classic slave narrative, *The Life and Times of Olaudah Equiano.*' And Joni calls it an 'epic tale of the Middle Passage and beyond.' Both of those descriptions point to the trouble Craig and I had with *Elijah* as it developed – they both focussed on the past. While the greater part of the story of African enslavement remains an untold story, we felt as though we were telling a tale that has 'already been said.' For us, there was still something missing, something we could feel but could not name.

As we went into a new phase of development, we kept up the conversation about the style and content of the work. In a telephone conversation one day, Craig mentioned that he had been reading a book about contemporary African slavery in Mauritania, North Africa. The book is *Silent Terror* by Samuel Cotton. He insisted that I read the book, not thinking necessarily about our project. The heart of the story is a chronicle of Cotton's journey to Mauritania and Senegal to research and investigate reports of modern day slavery. It also detailed his mostly futile efforts to rally the U.S. Congress and African American leaders to act on behalf of the enslaved Africans. The story was so compelling that it raised questions about the social and political implications of what we were doing. If there was this troubling and 'silent story' about contemporary chattel slavery in Africa, why were we doing work pointing to the past? What do we, as artists, have to say about our own life and times? As African Americans, how do we feel and think about slavery that is not our own experience in the West, a slavery that is not controlled by White Christians but by Arab Muslims? These new issues challenged the received narrative about slavery, about its binary split into categories of White and Black. It threw that picture out of focus, and it implicated Africans, Arabs, and Muslims in a way that disturbed us deeply — and in a way that we hoped would ultimately disturb anyone learning about it. This was the source of our 'trouble in mind' that led to a re-imagining of the work and to a fundamental change in the work.

The story of *Elijah* (Equiano) is now secondary to the story of a new character, Ntianu. She was created as a young African woman who is enslaved in present day Mauritania. We follow her journey from slavery to freedom. Her escape from slavery begins when she finds the *Elijah* (Equiano) narrative in her master's library, reads it and decides that he is her ancestor. She is convinced that he is the brother of her great, great grandmother who nicknamed him Udu when they were children. He was given that name because he could make her laugh by imitating the sound of the tribal Udu drum. It was said that the Udu drum carried the voice of the ancestors.

Ntianu's desire to connect with her ancestor leads her to act in ways that are considered blasphemous and unfaithful since she, like all Mauritanian slaves, is a Muslim. As the result of more than 700 years of enslavement of Africans by Arabs, the slaves have come to identify with their masters in terms of both religion and culture — they consider themselves to be both Arab and Muslim. When Ntianu changes her name from an Arab name to the African name (Ntianu), and wears traditional African clothing instead of Arab dress, she breaks an essential aspect of her identity as a slave. This break is a dangerous one, to her and to the other slaves. And it leads to a decisive confrontation with the master. Thus, the change from *Elijah* to *Udu*.

Since we began to work with the new story, we have made contact with the author of *Silent Terror* as well as former slaves and other people doing abolitionist work here in the United States. They have agreed to participate in humanities activities linked to performances as the piece travels. The 'piece' has evolved into a project, one of those rare moments when art and activism are perfectly matched. *Udu*, however, is not a didactic, anti-slavery work. It does not rail against anyone or anything. It tries to tell a story that draws parallels between historical and contemporary slavery through the experience of a single character facing the dramatic challenges of her own situation.

Given the shift in focus, from Elijah to Ntianu, I had to find a way to use the appropriated slave narrative that would not dominate the story. Much of the text, for example, that Joni refers to has been edited out, although the music remained. The majority of that text was spoken by a character who no longer exists, what Talvin alternately calls the 'timeless icon' and 'narrator/griot.' This character was conceived as a way of contemplating links between the past and the present. Those links are now made largely through Ntianu's connection to ancestor Udu and his book. This means that the connection between past and present is now a matter of dramatic action that affects Ntianu's choices.

Some of the scenes that I thought were central to *Elijah* have been retained. They appear as sections of his book that Ntianu reads to prove to the master that he is her ancestor. She also reads them for inspiration and to 'get language that fits her heart the way her skin fits her body.' Language that will finally empower her. Those scenes are 'The City of Hope,' which describes what she thinks is the ancestral hometown of Udu and her Nana; 'The Separation,' which gives an account of how Udu and Nana were kidnapped as children, then separated and sold into the slave trade as controlled by Europeans and Arabs respectively; and 'The Trek,' which chronicles the paths of their parallel journey — across the lush interior of Africa for him, across the desert in a caravan of slaves for her. Each of these scenes is based on the Equiano narrative itself. There is a new scene from that narrative that I also used in *Udu*. It is a compilation of Equiano's lyrical description of his experiences at sea, ending with his journey to the Attic.

I have also kept the basic narrative strategy. While there is a single Ntianu character who speaks, at times she is also represented in song by both male and female voices as well as the entire ensemble. This allows us to have it both ways, to have a grounded center and one that is movable at the same time. The same is true for the characters of the Master and Udu. The form of the work bears a strong resemblance to what came before, meaning it is still a hybrid that draws on opera, music theater, and oratorio. Both the narrative strategy and the form are thought of as ways to create voices/storytellers that are both witnesses and participants. It utilizes an idea that I paraphrase from one of Amiri Baraka's poems: we are the blues/the actual thing itself.

A draft of the final script, the main storytelling and dramatic elements are spoken and sung text, and vocal and instrumental music. The performing unit consists of seven musicians, six vocalists, one actor, and one poet. The integration of all the elements is a complex process which involves a great deal of exploration and discovery to achieve the right mix. It is difficult to say what is precisely the 'right mix' since we can't point to any particular work as an example. We like to think of it as something that is organically grown, coming out of this trip we've been on for the past few years. In this case, we draw on our experience with the 'right mix' on the bandstand: what's written is what we can expect; we'll know everything else when we feel it.

Selected bibliography

The following is a list of selected works on race, ethnicity, gender, sexuality, and performance. This list focuses on critical books, essay collections, and play anthologies published since 1990.

Alexander, Jacquie and Mohanty, Chandra (eds), *Feminist Genealogies, Colonial Legacies, Democratic Futures* (New York: Routledge, 1997).

Algarin, Miguel and Griffith, Lois (eds), *Action: The Nuyorican Poets Café Theater Festival* (New York: Simon and Schuster, 1997).

Anderson, Benedict, *Imagined Communities: Reflections on the Origins and Spread of Nationalism* (London: Verso, 1993).

Anderson, Lisa, *Mammies No More: The Changing Image of Black Women on Stage and on Screen* (New York: Rowman & Littlefield, 1997).

Antush, John (ed.), *Nuestro New York: An Anthology of Puerto Rican Plays* (New York: Penguin 1994).

Aparicio, Frances and Chávez-Silverman, Susana, *Tropicalizations: Transcultural Representations of Latinidad* (Hanover: University Press of New England, 1997).

Arrizón, Alicia, *Latina Performance: Traversing the Stage* (Bloomington: Indiana University Press, 1999).

—— and Manzor, Lillian, *Latinas on Stage: Practice and Theory* (Berkeley: Third Woman Press, 2000).

Ashcroft, Bill, *et al.* (eds), *The Postcolonial Studies Reader* (London: Routledge, 1995).

Auslander, Philip, *Presence and Resistance: Postmodernism and Cultural Politics in Contemporary American Performance* (Ann Arbor: University of Michigan, 1993).

—— *Liveness: Performance in a Mediated Culture* (London: Routledge, 1999).

Balme, Christopher, *Decolonizing the Stage: Theatrical Syncretism and Post-Colonial Drama* (Oxford: Clarendon Press, 1999).

Banham, Martin, Gibbs, James, and Osofisan, Femi (eds), *African Theatre in Development* (Bloomington: Indiana University Press, 1999).

Bean, Annemarie (ed.), *Plays, People, Movements: A Sourcebook of African-American Performance* (London: Routledge, 1999).

Bennett, Susan, *Theater Audiences: A Theory of Production and Reception* (London: Routledge, 1997).

Bergmann, Emilie and Smith, Paul Julian (eds), *Entiendes?: Queer Readings, Hispanic Writings* (Durham: Duke University Press, 1995).

Berson, Misha (ed.), *Between Worlds: Contemporary Asian American Plays* (New York: TCG, 1990).

Bhabha, Homi (ed.), *Nation and Narration* (London: Routledge, 1990).

—— *The Location of Culture* (London: Routledge, 1994).

Bharucha, Rustom, *Theater and the World: Performance and the Politics of Culture* (New York: Routledge, 1990).

—— *The Politics of Cultural Practice: Thinking Through Theatre in an Age of Globalization* (Hanover, NH: University of New England for Wesleyan University Press, 2000).

Bird, Elizabeth (ed.), *Dressing in Feathers: The Construction of the Indian in American Popular Culture* (Boulder, CO: Westview Press, 1996).

Boal, Augusto and Jackson, Adrian, *Legislative Theatre: Using Performance to Make Politics* (London: Routledge, 1998).

Bonney, Jo (ed.), *Extreme Exposure: An Anthology of Solo Performance Texts from the Twentieth Century* (New York: Theatre Communications Group, 2000).

Boon, Richard and Plastow, Jane (eds), *Theatre Matters: Performance and Culture on the World Stage* (Cambridge: Cambridge University Press, 1998).

Branch, Williams B. (ed.), *Crossroads: An Anthology of Black Dramatists in the Diaspora* (Bloomington: Indiana University Press, 1993).

Brandt, Eric (ed.), *Dangerous Liaisons* (New York: The New Press, 1999).

Broadhurst, Susan, *Liminal Acts: A Critical Overview of Contemporary Performance and Theory* (London: Cassell 1999).

Broyles-Gonzalez, Yolanda, *El Teatro Campesino: Theater in the Chicano Movement* (Austin: University of Texas Press, 1994).

Brustein, Robert, *Cultural Calisthenics: Writings on Race, Politics and Theatre* (Chicago: Ivan R. Dee, 1998).

Burke, Sally, *American Feminist Playwrights: A Critical History* (New York: Twayne Publishers, 1996).

Butler, Judith, *Bodies That Matter: On the Discursive Limits of Sex* (New York: Routledge, 1993).

—— *Excitable Speech: A Politics of the Performative* (New York: Routledge, 1997).

Byam, Dale, *Community in Motion: Theatre for Development in Africa* (Westport, CT: Greenwood Press, 1999).

Canning, Charlotte, *Feminist Theaters in the U.S.A: Staging Women's Experience* (New York: Routledge, 1996).

Case, Sue Ellen (ed.), *Feminism and Theatre* (New York: Routledge, 1988).

—— (ed.), *Performing Feminisms: Feminist Critical Theory and Theatre* (Baltimore: Johns Hopkins University Press, 1990).

—— (ed.), *Lesbian Practice/Feminist Performance* (New York: Routledge, 1996).

—— Brett, Phillip, and Foster, Susan Leigh (eds), *Decomposition: Post-Disciplinary Performance* (Bloomington: Indiana University Press, 2000).

Champagne, Lenora, *Out from Under: Texts by Women Performance Artists* (New York: Theatre Communications Group, 1990).

Chaudhuri, Una, *Staging Place* (Ann Arbor: University of Michigan Press, 1997).

Chin, Soo-young, Feng, Peter and Lee, Josephine (eds), 'Asian American Cultural Production,' *Journal of Asian American Studies*, 3(3), October 2000.

Chinoy, Helen and Jenkins, Linda Walsh (eds), *Women in American Theatre* (third edn, fully rev.) (New York: TCG, 2001).

Cleto, Fabio (ed.), *Camp: Queer Aesthetics and the Performing Subject: A Reader* (Ann Arbor: University of Michigan Press, 1999).

Clifford, James, *Routes* (Cambridge, MA: Harvard University Press, 1997).

Cocke, Dudley, Newman, Harry, and Salmons-Rue, Janet (eds), *From the Ground Up: Grassroots Theater in Historical and Contemporary Perspective* (Ithaca, NY: Community Based Arts Project at Cornell University, 1993)

Cohen-Cruz, Jan (ed.), *Radical Street Performance: An International Anthology* (London: Routledge, 1998).

—— and Schutzman, Mady (eds), *Playing Boal: Theatre, Therapy, and Activism* (London: Routledge, 1994).

Colleran, Jeanne and Spencer, Jenny S. (eds), *Staging Resistance: Essays on Political Theater* (Ann Arbor: University of Michigan Press, 1998).

D'Aponte, Mimi Gisolfi, *Seventh Generation: An Anthology of Native American Plays* (New York: Theater Communications Group, 1999).

De la Roche, Elisa, *Teatro Hispano: Three Major New York Companies* (New York: Garland, 1995).

Delgado, Celeste Fraser and Muñoz, José Esteban (eds), *Everynight Life: Culture and Life in Latin/o America* (Durham, NC: Duke University Press, 1997).

DeNobriga, Kathie and Anderson, Valetta (eds), *Alternative Roots Plays from the Southern Theater* (Portsmouth, NH: Heinemann, 1994).

Diamond Elin (ed.), *Performance and Cultural Politics* (New York: Routledge, 1996).

—— *Unmaking Mimesis: Essays on Feminism and Theater* (London: Routledge, 1997).

Dickerson, Dana, Lush, Brian, and Stalnaker, Ti (eds), *Gathering Our Own: New Work from the Institute of American Indian Arts* (Santa Fe, NM: Institute of American Indian Arts, 1996).

Dolan, Jill, *Presence and Desire: Essays on Gender, Sexuality, and Performance* (Ann Arbor: University of Michigan Press, 1994).

Donald, James and Rattansi, Ali (eds), *Race, Culture, and Difference* (London: Sage, 1992).

Donkin, Ellen and Clement, Susan (eds), *Upstaging Big Daddy: Directing Theater As If Gender and Race Matter* (Ann Arbor: University of Michigan Press, 1993).

Elam, Harry, Jr., *Taking It to the Streets: The Social Protest Theater of Luis Valdez and Amiri Baraka* (Ann Arbor: University of Michigan Press, 1997).

—— and Alexander, Robert (eds), *Colored Contradictions: An Anthology of Contemporary African American Plays* (New York: Penguin, 1996).

—— and Krasner, David (eds), *African American Performance and Theater History: A Critical Reader* (Oxford: Oxford University Press, 2001).

Eng, Alvin (ed.), *Tokens: Asian American Theater in New York* (Philadelphia: Temple University Press, 1999).

Fenshaw Rachel and Eckershall, Peter (eds), *Dis/Orientations: Cultural Praxis in Theatre in Asia, Pacific, Australia* (Melbourne: Centre for Drama and Theatre Studies, 1999)

Fernandez, Doreen, *Palabas: Essays on Philippine Theater History* (Quezon City: Ateneo De Manila University Press, 1996).

Feyder, Linda (ed.), *Shattering the Myth: Plays by Hispanic Women* (Houston: Arte Publico, 1992).

Fusco, Coco, *English Is Broken Here: Notes on Cultural Fusion in the Americas* (New York: The New Press, 1995).

—— (ed.), *Corpus Delecti Performance Art of the Americas* (London: Routledge, 2000).

Gainor, J. Ellen (ed.), *Imperialism and Theatre: Essays on World Theatre, Drama, and Performance* (London: Routledge, 1995).

—— and Jeffrey Mason (eds), *Cultural Pluralism in American Drama* (Detroit: University of Michigan Press, l999).

Gard, Robert, *Grassroots Theater: A Search for Regional Arts in America* (Madison: University of Wisconsin Press, 1999).

Geigomah, Hanay and Darby, Jaye T. (eds), *American Indian Theater in Performance: A Reader* (Los Angeles: UCLA American Indian Studies Center, 2000).

—— *Stories of Our Way: An Anthology of Native American Plays* (Los Angeles: UCLA American Indian Studies Center, 1999).

George, Kadja (ed.), *Six Plays by Black and Asian Women* (New York: TCG, 1993).

Gilbert, Helen and Tompkins, Joanne, *Post-Colonial Drama: Theory, Practice, Politics* (London: Routledge, 1996).

Gill, Glenda, *No Surrender! No Retreat! African American Pioneer Performers of Twentieth-Century American Theater* (New York: St. Martin's Press, 2000).

Gilroy, Paul, *'There Ain't No Black in the Union Jack': The Cultural Politics of Race and Nation* (Chicago: University of Chicago Press, 1991).

—— *The Black Atlantic: Modernity and Double Consciousness* (Cambridge, MA: Harvard University Press, 1993).

—— *Against Race: Imagining Political Culture Beyond the Color Line* (Cambridge, MA: Harvard University Press, 2000).

—— Grossberg, Lawrence, and McRobbie, Angela (eds), *Without Guarantees: In Honour of Stuart Hall* (London: Verso, 2000).

Glenn, Susan A., *Female Spectacle: The Theatrical Roots of Modern Feminism* (Cambridge, MA: Harvard University Press, 2000).

Goméz-Peña, Guillermo, *Dangerous Border Crossers: The Artists Talk Back* (San Francisco: City Lights, 2000).

Gottschild, Brenda Dixon, *Digging the Africanist Presence in American Performance: Dance and Other Contexts* (Westport, CN: Praeger, 1998).

Grace, Sherill, Chakyloff, Lisa, and D'Aeth, Eve (eds), *Staging the North* (Toronto: Playwrights Canada Press, 1999).

Gray, John (ed), *Black Theatre and Performance: A Pan-African Bibliography* (New York: Greenwood, 1990).

Grewal, Inderpal and Kaplan, Caren (eds), *Scattered Hegemonies: Postmodernity and Transnational Feminist Practices* (Minneapolis: University of Minnesota Press, 1994).

Hall, Stuart and Du Gray, Paul (eds), *Questions of Cultural Identity* (London: Sage, 1996).

Harrison, Paul Carter and Edwards, Gus (eds), *Classic Plays from the Negro Ensemble Company* (Pittsburgh: University of Pittsburgh Press, 1995).

Hart, Lynda and Phelan, Peggy, *Acting Out: Feminist Performances* (Ann Arbor: University of Michigan Press, 1993).

Hasu-Houston, Velina, *The Politics of Life: Four Plays by Asian American Women* (Philadelphia: Temple University Press, 1993).

—— *But Still, Like Air, I'll Rise* (Philadelphia: Temple University Press, 1997).

Hatch, James V. and Shine, Ted (eds), *Black Theatre USA: Plays by African American (The Early Period 1847–1938)* (New York: The Free Press, 1996).

Hay, Samuel, *African American Theatre: An Historical and Critical Analysis* (Cambridge and New York: Cambridge University Press, 1994).

hooks, bell, *Black Looks: Race and Representation* (Boston: South End Press, 1992).

Huerta, Jorge, *Chicano Drama: Performance, Society and Myth* (Cambridge and New York: Cambridge University Press, 2000).

Hughes, Holly and Román, David, *O Solo Homo* (New York: Grove Press, 1999).

Huxley, Michael and Witts, Noel (eds), *The Twentieth Century Performance Reader* (London: Routledge, 1996).

Jones, Amelia and Stephenson, Andrew (eds), *Performing the Body/Performing the Text* (London: Routledge, 1999).

Joseph, May and Fink, Jennifer (eds), 'New Hybrid Identities: Performing Race Gender Nation, Sexuality,' *Women and Performance: A Journal of Feminist Theory*, Winter 1995.

Joseph, May and Fink, Natalya (eds), *Performing Hybridity* (Minneapolis: University of Minnesota.

Kershaw, Baz, *The Politics of Performance: Radical Theatre as Cultural Intervention* (New York: Routledge, 1992).

King, Anthony (ed.), *Culture, Globalization and the World System* (Minneapolis: University of Minnesota Press, 1997).

King, Woodie, Jr. (ed.), *National Black Drama Anthology: Eleven Plays from America's Leading African American Theaters* (New York: Applause, 1995).

Kistenberg, Cindy, *AIDS, Social Change, and Theater: Performance as Protest* (New York: Garland, 1996).

Kobialka, Michal (ed.), *Of Borders and Thresholds: Theater History, Practice and Theory* (Minneapolis: University of Minnesota Press, 1999).

Kondo, Dorinne, *About Face: Performing Race in Fashion and Theater* (New York: Routledge, 1997).

Kurahashi, Yuko, *Asian American Culture on Stage: The History of East West Players* (New York: Garland, 1999).

Lamont, Rosette (ed.), *Women on the Verge: Seven Avant-Garde American Plays* (New York: Applause, 1993).

Larson, Catherine and Vargas, Margarita, *Latin American Women Dramatists: Theater, Texts, and Theories* (Bloomington: University of Indiana Press, 1998).

Lavie, Smadar and Swedenburg, Ted (eds), *Displacement, Diaspora, and Geographies of Identity* (Durham, NC: Duke University Press, 1996).

Lee, Josephine, *Performing Asian America: Race and Ethnicity on Contemporary Stage* (Philadelphia: Temple, 1997).

Lott, Eric, *Love and Theft: Blackface Minstrelsy and the American Working Class* (New York: Oxford University Press, 1993).

Lowe, Lisa, *Immigrant Acts: On Asian American Cultural Politics* (Durham, NC: Duke University Press, 1996).

MacDonald, Eric, *Theater at the Margins: Text and the Post-Structured Stage* (Ann Arbor: University of Michigan Press, 1993).

Mahone, Sydné, *Moon Marked and Touched by the Sun* (New York: Theatre Communications Group, 1994).

Marranca, Bonnie and Dasgupta, Gautam (eds), *Inter-culturalism and Performance* (New York: PAJ Publications, 1991).

Marsh-Lockett, Carol P., *Black Women Playwrights: Visions on the American Stage* (New York: Garland, 1999).

Martin, Carol (ed.), *On and Beyond the Stage: A Sourcebook of Feminist Theatre and Performance* (London: Routledge, 1996).

Maufort, Marc, *Staging Difference: Cultural Pluralism in American Theatre and Drama* (New York: Peter Lang Publishing, 1995).

Moroff, Diane Lynn, *Fornes: Theater in the Present Tense* (Ann Arbor: University of Michigan Press, 1996).

Moy, James, *Marginal Sights: Staging Chinese in America* (Iowa City: University of Iowa Press, 1993).

Muñóz, José Esteban, *Disidentification: Queers of Color and the Performance of Politics* (Minneapolis: University of Minnesota Press, 1999).

Murray, Timothy, *Drama Trauma: Specters of Race and Sexuality in Performance, Video, and Art* (London: Routledge, 1997).

Nelson, Brian (ed.), *Asian American Drama: 9 Plays from the Multiethnic Landscape* (New York: Applause, 1997).

—— (ed.), *Asian American Plays* (New York: Applause, 1997).

Nolan, Yvette, Quan, Betty, and Seremba, George Bwanika, *Beyond the Pale: Dramatic Writing from First Nations Writers and Writers of Colour* (Toronto: Playwrights Canada Press, 1996).

Oliva, Judy Lee (ed.), *New Theatre Vistas: Modern Movements in International Theatre* (New York: Garland Publishing, Inc., l996).

Parker, Andrew and Sedgwick, Eve Kosofsky, *Performativity and Performance* (London: Routledge, 1995).

Parkin, David, Caplan, Lionel, and Fisher, Humphrey (eds), *The Politics of Cultural Performance* (Oxford: Berghan Books, 1996).

Pavis, Patrice (ed.), *The Intercultural Performance Reader* (London: Routledge, 1996).

Pelligrini, Ann, *Performance Anxieties: Staging Psychoanalysis, Staging Race* (New York: Routledge, 1997).

Perkins, Kathy, *Black South African Women: An Anthology of Plays* (London: Routledge, 1998).

—— and Uno, Roberta (eds), *Contemporary Plays by Women of Color* (London: Routledge, 1996).

Phelan, Peggy, *Unmarked: The Politics of Performance* (London and New York: Routledge, 1993).

—— and Lane, Jill, *The Ends of Performance* (New York: New York University Press, 1998).

Pollock, Della (ed.), *Exceptional Spaces: Essays in Performance and History* (Chapel Hill: University of North Carolina Press, 1998).

Ramirez, Elizabeth, *Chicanas/Latinas in American Theatre: A History of Performance* (Bloomington: Indiana University Press, 2000).

Reinelt, Janelle and Roach, Joseph (eds), *Critical Theory and Performance* (Ann Arbor: University of Michigan Press, 1997).

Roach, Joseph, *Cities of the Dead: Circum-Atlantic Performance* (New York: Columbia University Press, 1996).

Román, David, *Acts of Intervention: Performance, Gay Culture, and AIDS* (Bloomington: Indiana University Press, 1998).

—— (ed.), 'The Details of Difference,' *Theatre Journal*, 52(3), October 2000.

—— (ed.), 'Latino Performance,' *Theatre Journal*, 52(1), March 2000.

Said, Edward, *Culture and Imperialism* (London: Vintage, 1993).

Sandoval-Sánchez, Alberto (ed.), Special Issue: 'Latino Theatre and AIDS,' *Ollantay Theater Magazine*, 2(2), Fall 1994.

—— *José, Can You See? Latinos On and Off Broadway* (Madison: University of Wisconsin Press, 1999).

—— and Saporta-Sternbach, Nancy (eds), *Puro Teatro: Stages of Life: Transcultural Performance and Identity Formation in U.S. Latina Theatre* (Tucson: University of Arizona Press, 2001).

Savran, David, *The Playwright's Voice: American Dramatists on Memory, Writing, and the Politics of Culture* (New York: TCG, 1999).

Schechner, Richard, *The Future of Ritual: Writings on Culture and Performance* (London: Routledge, 1993).

Sears, Djanet, *Testifyin': Contemporary African-Canadian Drama, Volume 1* (Toronto: Playwright Canada Press, 1999).

Sedgwick, Eve Kosofsky, *Epistemology of the Closet* (Berkeley: University of California Press, 1990).

Sinfeld, Alan, *Out on Stage: Lesbian and Gay Theatre in the Twentieth Century* (New Haven, CT: Yale University Press, 1991).

Spivak, Gayatri, *The Post-Colonial Critic: Interviews, Strategies, Dialogues* (New York: Routledge, 1991).

Stecopoulos, Harry and Uebel, Michael (eds), *Race and the Subject of Masculinities* (Durham, NC: Duke University Press, 1997).

Svich, Caridad and Marrero, Maria Teresa (eds), *Out of the Fringe: Contemporary Latina/Latino Theatre and Performance* (New York: Theatre Communications Group, 2000).

Taylor, Diana, *Theatre of Crisis: Drama and Politics in Latin America* (Lexington: University Press of Kentucky, 1991).

—— and Villegas, Juan (eds), *Negotiating Performance: Gender, Sexuality, and Theatricality in Latin/o America* (Durham, NC: Duke University Press, 1994).

Thompkins, Joanne and Holledge, Julie, *Women's Intercultural Performance* (London: Routledge, 2000).

Trujillo, Carla (ed.), *Living Chicana Theory* (Berkeley: Third World Press, 1998).

Turner, Darwin (ed.), *Black Drama in America: An Anthology* (Washington, D.C.: Howard University Press, 1994).

Ugwu, Catherine (ed), *Let's Get It On: The Politics of Black Performance* (Seattle: Bay Press, 1995).

Uno, Roberta (ed.), *Unbroken Thread: An Anthology of Plays by Asian American Women* (Amherst, MA: University of Massachusetts Press, 1993).

Valdez, Luis, *Early Works: Actos, Bernabé and Pensamiento Serpentino* (Houston: Arte Publico Press, 1990).

Van Erven, Eugene, *The Playful Revolution: Theatre and Liberation in Asia* (Bloomington: Indiana University Press, 1992).

—— *Community Theater: Global Perspective* (London: Routledge, 2001).

Vanden, Heuvel, Michael, *Performing Drama/Dramatizing Performance: Alternative Theatre and the Dramatic Text* (Ann Arbor: University of Michigan Press, 1991).

Warner, Michael (ed.), *Fear of a Queer Planet: Queer Politics and Social Theory* (Minneapolis: University of Minnesota Press, 1993).

Weed, Elizabeth, and Schor, Naomi (eds), *Feminism Meets Queer Theory* (Bloomington: Indiana University Press, 1997).

Wilson, August, *The Ground on Which I Stand* (New York: TCG, 2001).

Wilson, Rob, *Pacific Postmodern: From the Sublime to the Devious, Writing the Experimental/Local Pacific in Hawaii* (Kanèohe, HI: Tinfish, 2000).